WINN 〰 W9-BLN-319
Gordon College
Wenham, Mass. 01984

DISCARDED
JENKS LRC
GORDON COLLEGE

Interaction, Conversation, and the Development of Language

The Origins of Behavior

Michael Lewis and
Leonard A. Rosenblum, Editors

Volume 1
The Effect of the Infant on Its Caregiver

Michael Lewis and
Leonard A. Rosenblum, Editors

Volume 2
The Origins of Fear

Michael Lewis and
Leonard A. Rosenblum, Editors

Volume 3
Structure and Transformation:
Developmental Aspects

Klaus F. Riegel and
George C. Rosenwald, Editors

Volume 4
Friendship and Peer Relations

Michael Lewis and
Leonard A. Rosenblum, Editors

Volume 5
Interaction, Conversation, and
the Development of Language

Michael Lewis and
Leonard A. Rosenblum, Editors

Interaction, Conversation, and the Development of Language

Edited by

Michael Lewis
 Educational Testing Service

and

Leonard A. Rosenblum
 State University of New York
 Downstate Medical Center

A Wiley-Interscience Publication

JOHN WILEY & SONS
New York • London • Sydney • Toronto

Copyright © 1977 by John Wiley & Sons, Inc.

All rights reserved. Published simultaneously in Canada.

No part of this book may be reproduced by any means, nor transmitted, nor translated into a machine language without the written permission of the publisher.

Library of Congress Cataloging in Publication Data:

Main entry under title:
Interaction, conversation, and the development of
  language.

  (The Origins of Behavior; v. 5)
  "A Wiley-Interscience publication."
  Based on papers presented and discussed at a
conference held under the auspices of the Educational
Testing Service in Princeton, N. J.
  1. Children—Language. 2. Language and language
—Origin. I. Lewis, Michael, Jan. 10, 1937–
II. Rosenblum, Leonard A. III. Educational
Testing Service. IV. Series. [DNLM: 1.
1. Language development. 2. Interpersonal rela-
tions—In infancy and childhood. 3. Psycholinguistics
—In infancy and childhood. W1 OR687 v. 5 /
LB1139.L3 I61]
LB1139.L3I53   155.4′18   76–49037
ISBN 0–471–02526–7

Printed in the United States of America

10 9 8 7 6 5 4 3 2 1

Contributors

Elizabeth Bates*
Department of Psychology
University of Colorado
Boulder, Colorado   80302

Laura Benigni
Consiglio Nazionale delle Ricerche
Via dei Monti
Rome, Italy

Inge Bretherton
Department of Psychology
University of Colorado
Boulder, Colorado   80302

Luigia Camaioni
Consiglio Nazionale delle Ricerche
Via dei Monti
Rome, Italy

Courtney B. Cazden*
Laboratory of Human Development
Harvard University
Larsen Hall
Cambridge, Massachusetts   02138

Louise Cherry*
Division of Psychological Studies
Educational Testing Service
Princeton, New Jersey   08540

Rodney R. Cocking
Institute for Research in Human
Development

Educational Testing Service
Princeton, New Jersey   08540

Susan Ervin-Tripp*
Department of Psychology
University of California
Berkeley, California   94720

Roy Freedle*
Division of Psychological Studies
Educational Testing Service
Princeton, New Jersey   08540

Catherine Garvey*
Department of Psychology
The Johns Hopkins University
Baltimore, Maryland   21218

Rochel Gelman*
Department of Psychology
University of Pennsylvania
Philadelphia, Pennsylvania   19174

Timothy V. Gill*
Department of Psychology
Georgia State University
Atlanta, Georgia   30303

Joseph Jaffe*
Department of Communication
Sciences
New York State Psychiatric
Institute
722 West 168th Street
New York, New York   10032

*Michael Lewis**
Institute for Research in Human
Development
Educational Testing Service
Princeton, New Jersey   08540

*Peter Marler**
The Rockefeller University
66th Street and York Avenue
New York, New York   10021

Wick Miller
Department of Anthropology
University of Utah
Salt Lake City, Utah   84112

*M. P. M. Richards**
Unit for Research on the Medical
Applications of Psychology
Cambridge University
Cambridge, England

*Leonard A. Rosenblum**
State University of New York
Downstate Medical Center
450 Clarkson Avenue
Brooklyn, New York   11203

*Duane M. Rumbaugh**
Department of Psychology
Georgia State University
Atlanta, Georgia   30303

*Louis W. Sander**
Division of Psychiatry
Boston University School of
Medicine
80 East Concord Street
Boston, Massachusetts   02118

Marilyn Shatz
Graduate Center
City University of New York
33 West 42nd Street
New York, New York   10036

*Irving E. Sigel**
Institute for Research in Human
Development
Educational Testing Service
Princeton, New Jersey   08540

Virginia Volterra
University of Rome
Rome, Italy

* Conference Participants

Series Preface

"The childhood shows the man,
as morning shows the day."

Milton, Paradise Regained

None can doubt that the study of man begins in the study of childhood. Few would contend that the newborn lacks the challenge of his evolutionary heritage. This series addresses itself to the task of bringing together, on a continuing basis, that confluence of theory and data on ontogeny and phylogeny which will serve to illustrate *The Origins of Behavior*.

Whether our social, human, and professional concerns lie in the psychological disorders of childhood or adulthood or merely in the presumptively normal range of expression in development in different cultures, varied environments, or diverse family constellations, we can never hope to discern order and regularity from the mass of uncertain observation and groundless speculation if we fail to nurture the scientific study of development. Fortunately, the last two decades have seen an enormous burgeoning of effort toward this end, both at the human and nonhuman level. However, despite this growth of effort and interest, no single means of pooling our growing knowledge on development in children and animals and communicating that fusion of material to the broad scientific community now exists. This series seeks to fill the gap. It is our intention to have each volume deal with a specific theme that is either of social or of theoretical relevance to developmental issues. In keeping with the integrated perspective that we consider to be vital, and to provide a meaningful context within which these issues may be considered, each volume in the series will contain a broad range of material and will seek to encompass theoretical and sound empirical studies of the behavior of human infants as well as pertinent aspects of animal behavior with a particular emphasis on the primates. It is our view, furthermore, that not only is it necessary to focus our interest on both human infants and animals, but that the levels of analysis which will explicate the processes of development that are our concern must ultimately involve the study of behavior at all levels of discourse. Thus studies of developmental significance may be found in genetic, physiological, morphological, dyadic, and societal levels and an increased interdigitation of these separate disciplines is among the major goals of this series.

   In light of the diversity of topics to be considered, the breadth of material to be covered, and the variety of orientations that will be included in these discourses on the origins of human behavior, we expect this series to serve the needs of the broad social science community, not merely of those interested in behavioral development alone. Just as the series itself will draw upon the knowledge and research of psychologists, ethologists, sociologists, psychiatrists, pediatricians, obstetricians, and devoted scientists and clinicians in a number of related disciplines, it is our hope that the material in this series will provide both stimulation and guidance to all among us who are concerned with man, his past, his present, and his future.

Michael Lewis
Leonard A. Rosenblum
Editors

June 1973

Preface

This volume, the fifth in the series *The Origins of Behavior*, represents the first comprehensive effort to consider the early development of language from the viewpoint of its social genesis. The role of early conversational interaction, in both its verbal and its nonverbal aspects, in initiating and structuring the emerging language potential of the infant must be considered if we are to appreciate the complexity of language acquisition. The structure of this volume reflects the early language capacity of infants and the ontogenetic and phylogenetic precursors of the complex elements of the communication process. Finally, the volume presents a series of theoretical models which provide a basis for relating the elaboration of early communicative acts into subsequent formal language skills.

The chapters in this volume derive from papers presented and discussed at a conference on communication and language held under the auspices and with the support of the Educational Testing Service in Princeton, New Jersey. The chapters reflect a broad range of interests, linked together by their underlying theme—the social genesis of language and its relationship to social acts. The volume represents an effort toward the integration of speech and social acts into a theory of communication.

The participants in the conference were Drs. Elizabeth Bates, Lois Bloom, Courtney Cazden, Louise Cherry, Susan Ervin-Tripp, Roy Freedle, Catherine Garvey, Rochel Gelman, Timothy Gill, Joseph Jaffe, Michael Lewis, Peter Marler, Martin Richards, Leonard Rosenblum, Duane Rumbaugh, Louis Sander, Irving Sigel, and Daniel Stern.

Michael Lewis
Leonard A. Rosenblum

Princeton, New Jersey
Brooklyn, New York
November 1976

Contents

Interaction, Conversation, and the Development of Language

Introduction

MICHAEL LEWIS

Educational Testing Service

and

LEONARD A. ROSENBLUM

Primate Behavior Laboratory
Downstate Medical Center

The studies reported in this volume are concerned with the social and biological origins of language. Our primary focus is on the development of one aspect of language—conversation. Conversation is one of many early-acquired skills whose development is mediated largely through early social experience, particularly that between mother and infant. Considering conversational language as a skill enables us both to measure current capacities and performance and, more importantly, to focus attention on the shifting array of other skills within which language is embedded.

A CASE STUDY—CONVERSATIONAL DYSFUNCTION

The brief description of a child's interaction with its teacher that follows will be considered within the general framework of the child's attainment of conversational skill. The dysfunctional aspects of the child's speech behavior will be seen as one part of a series of social interaction difficulties. As such, this example provides a concrete setting within which to demonstrate many of the general themes developed in this volume.

C., a physically normal 5-year-old girl, sits quietly at a table waiting for her nursery school teacher to begin her lesson. She watches as the teacher moves toward her but says nothing when her teacher greets her. "What would you like to do this morning?" the teacher asks. No reply. "Would you like to look at this picture book?" C. no longer is looking at either the teacher or the picture book the teacher has in her hand. In response to a second request for directed attention (looking at the book), the child turns toward the teacher—still not toward the picture book itself. Asked the question a second time, C. finally says, "Yes" (still not looking at the book before her). The teacher opens the book and turns to a picture of an autumn scene, leaves of many colors. The request "Show me the red leaves" is finally responded to correctly as the child points to the object in the book.

Trying to engage the child still further, the teacher asks, "Do I have any red on my blouse?" Without looking at the blouse C. answers, "Yes." (In fact, there is red on the blouse.) "Touch the red part" requires that the child turn toward the teacher and look at her blouse. After some hesitation C. finally complies with the request. To the final question, "Do you have red on your shirt?" the child answers (without looking), "Marvin's birthday." (Today is her 4-year-old brother's birthday.)

It appears that the lack of language ability in this child, in terms of both comprehension and production, is embedded in an array of social-interactive dysfunctions. In fact, C. was placed in this nursery school setting because she was found to be seriously neglected by her mother. Inquiries, comments, and replies are curtailed and for the most part absent. Perhaps the architectural support for verbal exchange that lies in more general forms of social focus and attention has failed to develop because of her background of neglect. The child asks little of the teacher, neither information nor affective support, and shows signs of not comprehending the format of question–answer interaction. She fails to show signs of knowing either (1) that questions require answers or (2) how her behavior should be organized to answer correctly (i.e., to direct her attention toward the relevant aspects of her environment which can supply the answer). When forcefully directed and shaped to produce a response, as in the final question above, she produces an answer but it is irrelevant to the question.

It would seem that for this child something of the essential nature and structure of language as a social instrument, one of exchange and interaction, has failed to develop. In view of her particular history of neglect, it is no wonder why speech, particularly speech having exchange function, remains underdeveloped. Why use interactive speech if its historical function in social interaction is obscure?

Experimental research on early social development in nonhuman primates provides further support for the view that the ontogeny of communication requires consideration of the social history of the individual. If infant monkeys, for example, are removed from their mothers shortly after birth, and then raised for most of the first year without interactive experience, a breakdown in the entire constellation of social and communicative abilities emerges. When the socially deprived infants are rather young, their response to the playful overtures of a peer is usually one of fear and withdrawal. Apparently these "paracommunications" that precede play initiations and signal that the initiator's rapid approach is not aggressive or threatening are either unattended to or misinterpreted by the deprived infant. Indeed, work by Alpert and Rosenblum (1974) suggests that isolation rearing retards the development of the infant's capacity to differentiate the specific members of the species group, and thus the infant may lack another communicative element, that is, the ability to respond to a given communication in relation to the identity of the communicator. It is important to note further that monkey infants raised, early in life, under deprivation conditions may continue to show bizarre and often destructive distortions of the communicative process even after long subsequent periods of nominally normal social experience. When they are mature, early isolate subjects are often hyperaggressive. It is clear that at least a major component of this aggressive behavior is the product of the isolate's inability to interpret signals of affiliative behavior when another approaches, or even to respond "correctly" to communicative gestures of submission, which normally serve to terminate overt aggression on the part of the subject receiving this communication. Even when appropriate motivational systems are aroused by the communications of a social partner, the lack of interactive experience of the isolate results in a disordered breakdown in the normal interactive flow. Thus, when a socially sophisticated female monkey sexually presents her hindquarters to a isolate-reared mature male, the latter may become aroused by the "signal" but respond, after some delay, by beginning to masturbate. Similarly, some isolate subjects respond to overt threatening gestures of others, not by flight or with attack on those making the gestures, but by becoming "aggressive" towards themselves, that is, they pull at their own fur and bite their own limbs, often to the point of drawing blood.

Thus, even for a more primitive primate form than man, in whom we might expect less reliance of the communicative system on an individual subject's early life experience, we have evidence to the contrary. Marler (in Chapter 4 of this volume) discusses in some detail the analogous processes through which early exposure to varying song patterns at specific developmental periods may alter fundamental dimensions of the subsequent vocal repertoire of his avian subjects. As with song development in birds, the developing primate's capacity to produce and interpret the communicative repertoire of its group is critically enmeshed with its development of more general social, interactive capacities or skills which require appropriate experience for their attainment.

We return now to a consideration of the functional use and disuse of communication as part of a more general socialization process in children. We can see that language cannot be considered *in vitro* but rather must be viewed *in vivo*, that is, within the total functioning of the individual of which it is a part. Thus we can see the validity of current considerations that intelligence cannot be assessed meaningfully through its reflection in the one-dimensional and culturally distorted mirror of language facility or dysfunction, especially if the particular language involved lacks an integral connection to the social experiences and abilities of the individual in question. In light of our discussion of the experimental production of deficits in monkeys, it is worth noting here that the socially and communicatively dysfunctional isolate, given appropriate time for adaptation (an affective problem), when confronted with a complex cognitive task, such as learning set, devoid of social or species typical communicative demands, performs at perfectly normal levels. Thus specific cognitive capacities of the child or animal may remain unimpaired by deficiencies or distortions in normal early social experience. When exposure to such deficiencies occurs early in development, the requisite skills necessary to utilize and express these capacities in everyday life may fail to develop.

A UNIFIED THEORY AND THE NOTION OF DIFFERENTIATION

These examples of dysfunction raise the more general issue of language development and the context in which it is to be studied. Lewis and Cherry (Chapter 10 of this volume), as well as Bates et al. (Chapter 11), have argued for a model of language acquisition based on the assumption that language, social, and cognitive knowledge are interrelated and interdependent since they all are aspects of the same developing individual. Each of these domains —usually considered separately—can be considered to be highly interactive with each other one. Lewis and Cherry have referred to this interaction as a *Unified Model* since any individual develops social language and cognitive knowledge in interaction with others.

This type of speculation has important developmental considerations. We would strongly support a model of development in which change from a unified, highly interactive system to one that is differentiated and specialized occurs as a function of age. We envision such a system as a tree, the trunk being the unified and integrated system of knowledge and the branches being the separate areas of knowledge, some of which are totally independent of each other while others are still somewhat dependent. This specific model allows for the integration of knowledge from a developmental perspective, as well as a statement of functional independence as an end product of this development. Moreover, it allows for a consideration of what behaviors (or skills) remain consistent and which undergo transformations and change. Consider linguistic knowledge as an example. At first children understand the meaning of a linguistic act only by attending to the occurrence of that act within a specific social context; that is, cognition in general and language in particular are embedded in a unified frame of knowledge. Only with development is knowledge separable into its component parts. Thus, for example, it is only later that the child is capable of understanding or producing language without its embeddedness in a social context. This movement from a unified and interlocking set of knowledge to a large set of specific, single, and separate capacities is the hallmark of early development.

We have assumed the unified framework to be embedded in a social context. This assumption is based largely on our belief that the task and context of the infant's adaptation are to its social world (Lewis & Weinraub, 1977). Without the skills and ability to prosper within its framework, the newborn infant cannot survive (Bowlby, 1969). Moreover, much of its structure, such as hemispheric differentiation for processing speech and nonspeech sounds (Molfese, 1972), as well as its organization principles (Sander, Chapter 6 of this volume; Stern, 1974), may be constructed around its social world. Finally, much evidence is accumulating that the child's earliest knowledge is organized around social information (McGurk & Lewis, 1974). It is our belief that man is a social animal, and it is within and from this social world that the skills uniquely human emerge.

THE NOTION OF SKILL

For the reader to appreciate our position on language acquisition, it is necessary that we enter into a discussion of skill. We suspect that language skill is itself divided into subskills which have developmental histories and etymologies quite separate from one another—some biological, others social. When we attempt to consider language as some whole entity, we run the risk of generating general principles when, in fact, a series of separate rules governing the development of separate skills may be called for.

In the history of psychology the notion of skill has received relatively little attention (Elliott & Connolly, 1974). This is particularly true in the psychology of language, where the domains of study have consisted of phonology, grammar, and semantics. We can consider language as a set of skills, and for the study of skill development we can delineate the various dimensions along which skills may be assessed. This is an important first step toward a reconceptualization of the development of these skills within the general domain of language.

It must be recognized at the outset that no skill exists, or develops, in a behavioral vacuum. An enormous panoply of skills is at various stages of development or attainment at any given time, and there is a complex interplay between them. In short, each skill, including language, is embedded in a network of skills. Some skills may ultimately be incorporated within a complex skill; some depend on the coexistence of others, whereas some may be relatively independent of one another. Each, however, shares with its cohorts a number of identifiable dimensions along which it may be assessed.

The most salient features of skills will be enumerated in order to show that any skill, including language, may be differentiated in roughly similar fashion. We suggest that a skill can be characterized in terms of its quantity, quality, speed of acquisition, utilization, affective tone, generalizability, organizational properties, and intention. "Quantity" refers to the gross frequency and/or duration with which the skill is expressed in any given unit of time. In the case of language it could refer to how much the child speaks. "Quality" refers to the degree to which the act is effective, efficient, or elaborately differentiated. In the case of language a measure might refer to syntactical correctness. "Speed of acquisition" for any skill can refer to the first time the skill is used, or the period of time when specific levels of attainment emerge. The "utilization" of a skill refers to the circumstances or context in which the skill is displayed. For language one might ask when and under what conditions the child uses language as opposed to other forms of communication or a complete lack of either. "Affective tone" refers to the degree of pleasure or displeasure involved in skill utilization. Does talking provide the child with the enjoyment often seen in the playful reiteration of the skill itself? "Generalizability" refers to the use of the target skill in place of other skills, such as speech acts instead of whining. "Organizational properties" of a skill refers to the relationship of the particular skill to other skills in the child's repertoire; thus we might consider the relationship of language use and cognitive skills such as object permanence. "Intention" as a dimension of a skill is rather difficult to define carefully, but generally refers to the child's control of the skill, and possibly even to his awareness of that control, that is, the degree to which there is intentional shaping or altering of the behavior to meet specific objectives. It is the difference between speaking and conversation and preparing a refined set of questions or statements about a particular topic.

Given this type of "skills" perspective, it becomes possible to dimensionalize language in such a fashion as will allow focused study on any particular aspect and its concomitants within quite diverse circumstances. Thus particular aspects of complex communicative behavior skills can be studied in children at different ages, within interactions occurring under different conditions, and even in animals as well as man. Other aspects of the same language acts or, most certainly, monolithic consideration of the behavior may not allow such ready cross-comparisons. Thus we may assess quantity of production or even perhaps the generalizability of a skill in both chimpanzees and children, but would find it difficult to do so with regard to affective tone or to "the meaning of the act" or some similar unitary assessment. Similarly, not all types of language skill are amenable to diverse analyses.

In this volume we direct our collective attention to conversation, a skill that does lend itself to such considerations along a number of skill dimensions. The chapters by Gelman and Shatz, Garvey, and Ervin-Tripp and

Miller examine aspects of conversation among language users—adult and young children. These chapters demonstrate quite clearly that by relatively young ages children's conversational skills have already matured into the structures of formal language. Marler, as well as Rumbaugh and Gill, approaches conversation from a comparative perspective, demonstrating in both birds and chimpanzees principles of conversation which may have merit for the study of human communication. Moreover, these authors' chapters reflect our belief that certain aspects of language skill—conversational skills —may have wide generalizability, extending across diverse species.

Richards, Sander, and Freedle and Lewis discuss conversation in terms of the mother–infant relationship. They provide support for our belief that early prelinguistic forms of exchange, synchrony, and reciprocity—found in the social exchange of this dyad—form the prototype of similar functional relationships once the emergence of language has occurred. Freedle and Lewis specifically provide some empirical support relating these functionally similar yet divergent behaviors.

It is in the three chapters by Sigel and Cocking, Lewis and Cherry, and Bates et al. that theories relating behaviorally different but functionally similar phenomena are examined. Here the synthesis between studies of divergent and ontogenetically different species reaches its full potential.

We started this discussion with an example of a single child. We would like to conclude with this example in mind. Although we cannot reconstruct the developmental history of the child discussed at the beginning of these comments, for indeed too few longitudinal data studying these problems are available on children, we might speculate that the neglect of this child involved a whole spectrum of social experiences which impoverished a number of social skills—of which conversation is merely one. Viewed in this light, the acquisition of conversational skills becomes clearer. Only through synthesis of the studies of conversation in the early years and studies of the form and content of mother–infant conversation and general social interaction can we hope to understand "normal" and "dysfunctional" language acquisition. The material presented in this volume is directed toward that goal.

References

Alpert., S., & Rosenblum, L. A. The influence of gender and rearing conditions on attachment and response to strangers. In S. Kondo, M. Kawai, & S. Kawbmura (Eds.), *Proceedings from the Symposia of the Fifth Congress of the International Primatological Society.* Tokyo, Japan: Science Press Company, 1974.

Bowlby, J. *Attachment and loss.* Vol. I: *Attachment.* New York: Basic Books, 1969.

Elliott, J. M., & Connolly, K. J. Hierarchical structure in skill development. In K. J. Connolly & J. S. Bruner (Eds.), *The growth of competence.* New York: Academic Press, 1974.

Lewis, M., & Weinraub, M. The father's role in the infant's social network. In M. Lamb (Ed.), *Role of the father in child development.* New York: Wiley (in press).

McGurk, H., & Lewis, M. Space perception in early infancy: Perception within a common auditory-visual space? *Science,* 1974, **186**(4164), 649–650.

Molfese, D. L. *Cerebral asymmetry in infants, children and adults: Auditory evoked responses to speech and noise stimuli.* Unpublished doctoral dissertation, Pennsylvania State University, 1972.

Stern, D. N. Mother and infant at play: The dyadic interaction involving facial, vocal, and gaze behaviors. In M. Lewis & L. Rosenblum (Eds.), *The origins of behavior.* Vol. I: *The effect of the infant on its caregiver.* New York: Wiley, 1974.

CHAPTER 1

Early Discourse:
Some Questions about Questions[1]

SUSAN ERVIN-TRIPP

University of California, Berkeley

and

WICK MILLER

University of Utah

Recent work on the early stages of children's language development has been concerned with both discourse features and pragmatics. In this chapter we shall primarily be concerned with discourse properties, that is with the relation of speech to the preceding and following verbal context. Our reason for this focus is practical; the texts we have are not completely specified with respect to the nonverbal context.

The texts that we will examine were longitudinal weekly samples of adult–child discourse of three children during the period from 21 to 42 months of age. The adult for most of the sessions was a linguist, Wick Miller. Table 1 gives the details of the samples used, which included texts at Stages I to V for each child, as defined by Brown (1973, p. 56) in terms of mean length of utterance. Bloom's work on discourse (Bloom, Rocissano & Hood manuscript) employed a similar scale, so despite some problems with this measure we have used it to allow comparison of the various findings of different studies. Since we shall be examining the relation of discourse to syntax, this calibration is especially relevant.

UNIT SIZE

What should be the scope or size of unit in the analysis of discourse? When

[1] The research reported here was originally funded by Grant M3813 of the National Institutes of Mental Health. The data reanalysis has been supported by Grant MH26063 of the National Institutes of Mental Health, and by the Center for Advanced Studies in the Behavioral Sciences and the Guggenheim Foundation. We are grateful for the aid in the most recent data analysis of Thomas Kluwin, Ruth Miller, Jarrett Rosenberg, and Pamela Tiedt.

adults work on research projects or come to conferences, they define goals with respect to very large units of time. These purposes in turn define some constraints on what will be considered relevant in discourse. The location and the amount of other kinds of talk are controlled, and some nontask talk is marked off by channel cues or other indicators. But the relation of the higher to the component units of such discourse still remains to be specified.

TABLE 1.   Mean Length of Utterance (MLU), Age, and Sample Size

		Carol			Sally			Laura		
Stage	Brown's Mean[a]	Age (Years; Months)	MLU Range[b]	Question Sample Size	Age (Years; Months)	MLU Range[b]	Question Sample Size	Age (Years; Months)	MLU Range[b]	Question Sample Size
I	1.75	1; 11– 2; 1 2; 2–	1.26– 1.95 2.00–	90	1; 9 1; 10–	1.50– 1.79 1.61–	77	2; 3– 2; 4 2; 4–	1.50– 2.06 2.00–	85
II	2.25	2; 3	2.52 2.18–	118	2; 0	2.45 2.76–	104	2; 5 2; 5–	2.33 2.44–	53
III	2.75	2; 6	3.07 2.64–	123	2; 1	3.32 2.64–	74	2; 6 2; 8–	3.32 3.20–	99
IV	3.50	3; 0	3.96 3.46–	221	2; 2	3.54 3.92–	135	2; 9 2; 11–	4.02 3.90–	108
V	4.00	3; 6	4.64	464	2; 9	4.16	299	3; 0	4.02	211

[a] From Brown (1973), p. 56.
[b] The MLU range is the highest and lowest mean length of utterance for the weekly texts in the time period.

At age 2 there was no evidence at all of larger discourse frames or scopes. After age 3, we found instances of pretend play which were verbally defined, rather than dependent on object-tied actions. It seemed evident in the early samples that the children were sensitive to larger units of play activity before they could project goals for larger units of talk activity. They did not carry on conversation in an adult sense.[2] Making a puzzle, building a castle, and filling a box are activities that seem to be goal directed. It is true that the activity itself, rather than the end, may be what is wanted, so that a child knocks down and reconstructs or cycles an activity. In the youngest children in the sample, there was frequent verbal marking of the termination of activity ("there!"), the departure of people ("bye-bye"), or the disappearance of substances or things ("all-gone"). These appeared at boundaries after which

[2] Keenan (1974) has provided vivid examples of what seem to be early conversations, in a situation with minimal object cues (a dark bedroom). Such settings (also long car trips) may be the places to find the first appearance of conversation that is activity free, and to look for scope and relevance evidence.

new activities occurred or old ones were recycled. But many activities shifted gradually, some were overlapped as interest waned, or the boundaries were left verbally unmarked.

In the early texts, around age 2, activities and objects were so important to the talk that participants might roughly anticipate the acts that might occur and even some of the formulae. This predictability depended on the particular activity, of course, since some objects allow a greater range of alternatives than others. The pattern of talk may be peculiar to the interaction form called by Shugar (1975) the "discursive workshop," in which an older participant undertakes to keep a child engaged in conversation. Corsaro (1975) has considered some properties of adult–child speech in these conditions, as has Blount (1972; in press).

A strong instance in our texts was the picture book dialogue. As both examined a book, the adult either named the pictures ("That's a duck, isn't it?" "There's a duck"), pointed and elicited names ("What's this?"), or tested comprehension of names ("Where's the duck?"). Viewed from the standpoint of syntax or referential semantics, *where* and *what* questions seem very different, as do identifying and locating. Viewed as a classifying game, What + (pointing) = Name equals Where + Name = (point), though the latter may be easier. On these occasions the adult's questions were turns in an exchange (Blount, in press; Keenan, 1977). The child often was already engaged in naming ("Duck." "A duck." "Here's a duck." "That's a duck."). It is not clear how necessary to the child's activity of naming the adult's intervention might be. By entering the exchange at times when his offering was redundant, since the answer was already the frame the child was using, the adult made the relation of questions to answers obvious; how else could a child learn to answer?[3]

Bloom's texts in *One word at a time* provide some excellent examples of activity cycles. Allison would climb up and say, "Up," get down and say, "Down." The up–down cycle occurred 16 times in the text. Bubbles were produced and disappeared, punctuated with "more" and "gone."[4]

How can we know when the adult's utterances are becoming interpretable by a child away from the activity context? One clue to the dominance of activity is continuation of the cycle despite other adult interventions not in keeping with the cycle. Bloom provided a number of such instances in which she tried to disrupt a cycle. On one occasion she produced a new bag of toys, asking "What's in the bag?" The child then refocused her attention and began object naming. Bloom then interposed, "What do you see?" redundantly entering the naming cycle to make a dialogue.

But another purely verbal interruption was less successful. Allison was

---

[3] Malcolm Coulthard pointed this out to us.
[4] Beth Ann O'Connell found these cycles in a close analysis of the Bloom texts.

engaged in dropping a doll and picking it up again, saying, "Oh-oh," "Up," and "Down." Her mother made dialogue by a gloss, asking for confirmation: "Want the baby to sit up? Is that what you want?" Allison continued, "Up." But when her mother changed the subject, Allison did not follow: "Is the baby happy?" Allison replied, "Down," continuing the cycle as she pushed the doll to the floor again.

In these scenes the ongoing activity and speech cycle is a resource which the adult uses to create discourse. The ongoing activity, especially in the early texts, is a strong determinant of what the child talks about, but the child moves increasingly to using the dialogue form itself as an activity of independent interest, for instance, in pretend roles. During this period the child's knowledge of the local discourse obligations of dialogue increases in ways we will examine below. By the end of the period under analysis dialogue looks highly coherent.

In the rest of this chapter four problems will be explored which are facets of the evolution of dialogue: the development of pronouns tying back to earlier discourse, the development of replies to questions, the relation of replies to other grammatical skills, and the control of dialogue by the older partner to maintain the child's success.

PRONOMINAL TYING

Among the requirements of local discourse between a turn and its sequel are a series of obligatory and optional tying relations. The tying relations help the listener recognize the relation of what is new to what was said be-before. They include markers of logical relations like parallelism and contrast in *and, but, too, also*; ellipsis, which isolates the focal information; anaphora, which identifies which is already known; and deictic transformations in first and second person pronouns. There is a steep increase during the time period investigated in the use of ellipsis and lexical tying markers, the details of which will be reported elsewhere.

In adult discourse, pronoun tying is obligatory. We do not say, "John stopped suddenly. John leaned down to tie John's shoe." A brief place and function marker occurs rather than full specification. An analogy in American Sign Language is the spatial location of referent characters, which allows all reference later to occur by signing from or to those locations. Such reference is simpler than signing a name. During the time period between ages 2 and 3, we saw all the basic pronominal system emerge, as well as its extension from initial spontaneous referential usage into a discourse-tying or text function. These are called anaphoric pronouns.

Third person pronouns differ from first and second person pronouns in several ways. First and second person pronouns shift in reference, depending on who is speaking. Third person pronouns remain invariant for different

speakers, but they are complex in requiring gender as well as number specification. Our data on first and second person pronouns came from a set of
detailed texts from the three girls mentioned earlier, which spanned Brown's
Stages I through V. Our data on the third person pronouns came from
monthly tests of 24 children. The onset of testing ranged from 2.3 to 2.10
years, and this test was given until 3.3 to 4.0 years, since available ages of
onset and termination vary for different children. The source of the data
included in the following summary is a series of answers to questions about
picture cards that formed a story. The pictured characters were a girl, a boy,
and a wagon, and in alternate months the girl and the boy were traded off as
main character. For example, we asked, "What's happening?" "What's
happening to Tom?" "What's happening to Kate?"

The earliest replies usually lacked a subject or agent. The pictures included tooth- and hairbrushing, and many children specified the "inalienable
possessor" of the hair and teeth even before they specified the actors.
"What's happening?" "Brushing his teeth." Eight children in the sample
specified the possessor earlier; two, the agent earlier. Most brought agent
and possessor in at the same time.

Typically, nouns occurred earlier than pronouns in these positions. On the
average, by 34 months the possessor was specified by a pronoun, *his*. The
masculine pronoun, being far more frequent, was learned before the feminine
by most children and frequently occurred for female referents, regardless of
grammatical case (Kluwin, Ervin-Tripp, & Miller, manuscript).

In adult speech, pronominal tying would be probable in reply to "What's
happening to Kate?" We might expect, if children are sensitive to this feature
of discourse rules, that there would be more pronoun subjects in replies to
this question than in replies to "What's happening?" The problem with this
comparison is that replies to the latter question are widely variable in
semantic content. The children did not always talk about an event with Kate
as agent. Fifteen of the tested children began their sequence of agent specifications to both of these questions with nouns. At a median age of 38
months, the last noun agent occurred and pronominal subjects had taken
over for "What's happening to Kate (Tom)?" Yet "What's happening?"
still received sporadic replies with noun subjects. Although the evidence for
the learning of obligatory pronoun tying is not overwhelming in quantity, it
is consistent. These pronouns are among the features which make the children's discourse after age 3 sound like normal dialogue.

A richer and more detailed picture of developmental changes, including
first and second person pronouns, was obtained from the three cases with
weekly texts. The children were less verbose in the early sessions; there is
ambiguity in the text evidence since absence of pronouns from the texts may
be a sampling error.

The typical order of development which we found was from a stage of no lexicalization of the semantic unit to noun specification, then pronoun–noun alternation, and finally pronoun usage. If we look merely at subject pronouns (Table 2), we find a developmental order with *I* first and *they* last, *you, he,* and *she* being intermediate. Most relevant to the question of discourse tying. though, is that in each case there is a delay between the appearance of a pronoun in spontaneous speech and in discourse tying in responding to questions.

TABLE 2. Subject Pronoun Occurrence in Spontaneous Speech and in Replies to Questions[a]

	Spontaneous Speech					Replies				
						Q: *You*	*I*	Masc. Noun *He*	Fem. Noun *She*	Plural Noun *They*
Stage	*I*	*You*	*He*	*She*	*They*	R: *I*	*You*			
I	2[b]	1[b]	0	0	0	0	0	0	0	0
II	2[b]	2[b]	2	1	1	1[b]	0	0	0	0
III	3[b]	2[b]	2	3	1	3[b]	0	1	2	0
IV	3	2	3	2	1	3	2	3[b]	1[b]	0
V	3	3	3	3	3	3	3	3	3[b]	0

[a] Values in cells show how many of the three children used the form at least once in the period under study in texts and tests.
[b] At least one child alternated the pronoun and noun.

Why should there be such a lag? The pronoun differs from the stimulus, in the case of discourse-tying anaphora, and the child must semantically process the partner's words and convert the partner's noun to a pronoun, or change the person of deictic pronouns like *you* and *I*. This task is evidently more difficult than finding a referential pronoun. Bloom et al. have suggested that in general it is easier for a child to frame a new utterance than to attend to the speech of the partner, interpret it, and create an appropriate reply. It is likely that the additional transformations make this task even more difficult in the case of pronominal anaphora.

ANSWERING QUESTIONS

In this study of discourse we have focused on questions since answering questions is among the first clearly discourse-bound obligations to which children are sensitive. In fact, so strong is their responsiveness to questions that adults often frame questions, as Blount (in press) has noted, simply to occupy a turn or keep conversation going, when nobody cares about the information offered or received. One can argue that the neatly arranged semantic structure of questions in the informational sphere is peculiarly important to human language. If it is the case that the structural organization of language centers on its unique evolutionary function for information exchange, it would not be surprising if many other functions piggybacked on the obligatory replies to information questions. In these cases the façade of information exchange is used for other purposes.

This diversity of function was especially apparent in the polar ("yes"/ "no") questions asked by Miller in the conversational exchanges. In the following analysis we have removed the questions which were clearly requests for confirmation or directives, leaving instances which could have been either information questions or discourse-maintaining interchanges disguised as information questions.

TABLE 3. Responses (in Percentages) to Polar Information Questions[a]

Stage	Total Questions	No Response	"Yes"	Affirmative Comment	Imitate Only	"No"	Negative Comment	Correction	Related Remark[b]	Unrelated Remark	Other
Sally											
I–III	39	3	10	20	3	15	0	0	31	10	15
IV	25	0	36	12	0	12	8	8	28	12	8
V	109	1	49	5	0	34	6	9	12	4	6
Carol											
I–III	78	1	5	50	3	17	1	9	12	15	1
IV	76	0	61	1	1	13	3	8	16	4	3
V	117	0	48	4	0	39	3	8	7	1	6
Laura											
I–III	43	7	2	35	19	0	2	5	7	23	9
IV	29	7	17	31	3	7	3	3	21	14	3
V	22	0	18	59	0	18	14	9	18	0	4

[a] Because of double coding percentages may add to more than 100.
[b] Ambiguous whether child meant "Yes" or "No"

In the case of polar questions, it is notoriously difficult to decide when a reply has occurred, given the adult informational ellipsis in replying, as in the following exchange: "Can you come Thursday?" "We give orals that day." This difficulty is apparent in Table 3 in the large number of related and unrelated remarks which occurred in the early stages. These additional comments decreased with age. Thus we did not see, at this stage, the systematic semantic ellipsis of adult speech, where the gap is easily constructed by both partners.[5] Instead, we see an increase in focus on the polarity.

[5] The gap may lie in the adult's inability to reconstruct the child's inferential link that makes it apparent whether the reply is affirmative or negative, rather than in the child's inability to make that link.

For each of the three children studied on a weekly basis, there was an increase in "yes," "no," or affirmative or negative comments with the stage
of development, though the rate of change varied between the children. A
typical response at first for affirmation was to make an affirmative statement
rather than to say, "yes." "No," on the other hand was more frequent than
negative comments, for the most part. Negatives are the "marked" alternative, requiring a negative element. In addition, one child at Stage I answered
a third of the polar questions by imitation: "Is this a bird?" "Bird." "Does
Johnny drink coffee?" "Coffee? Johnny?"

It appears that, as the child's language matured, replies were minimized in
length, being focused on the critical element in question, the affirmative or
negative feature. The addition of syntactic ellipsis to the child's skills facilitated this abbreviation. By Stage V replies were relatively unambiguous, con-
stituting at least 83, 87 and 77% of the replies in the three children if we
consider "yes," "no," and affirmative or negative comments to constitute
unambiguous replies (e.g., "I don't," or "I have three").

Wh Questions

Our first analysis of answers to *wh* questions was reported by Ervin-Tripp
(1970). In this study 24 children were repeatedly given the same test about
the same picture book, at starting ages from 1.11 to 2.5 years. These were the
same children who were involved in the pronoun study mentioned earlier.
There were alternate forms of the questions on alternative months.

How difficult are the standard English question words to answer correctly?
The results depend, of course, on the rigor of standards in scoring. In this
analysis we did not score truth value, but, merely the categorical appropriateness of the answer. "Three o'clock" was a correct answer to any
when question, since our interest was in the acquisition of temporal meaning for *when*. The details of the questions asked were given in the article
cited.

There were several distinct stages in the development of the skills studied
in that project, which included some inflectional, pronominal, and question-
answering tests. By 36 months children could typically give categorically
appropriate replies to *why* questions and could answer with an animate agent
to *who* ("Who is feeding him?"). Significantly more difficult (.001 by sign
test) were instrumental answers to *how*, temporal answers to *when*, locative
source answers to *where from*, and patient answers to *who*-object ("Who is
he feeding?"), which did not reach a median criterion of sustained mastery
until 38 to 40 months (Table 4).

Tyack (1974), using the more difficult task of repeated questions about the
same picture, but a more structurally complete set of items, got similar results on a cross-sectional study. Error percentages increased from nuclear

TABLE 4. Kendall Rank Correlation Matrix (Tau) for Age of Mastery of Language Tests ($N = 24$)

	Inflections		Auxiliary Matching			Category Matching					Stanford-Binet
	Nonsense Plural	Masc. Possessive	Gonna	Will	Past	Who-S	Who-O	Why	How	When	
Nonsense Plural	1.00	.58	.31	.42	.36	.15	.35	.37	.45	.55	-.37
Masc. Possessive	.58[a]	1.00	.39	.52	.56	.41	.25	.44	.32	.57	-.28
Gonna	.31	.39	1.00	.34	.46	.55	.45	.34	.29	.60	-.40
Will	.42	.52	.34	1.00	.49	.51	.37	.35	.40	.52	-.38
Past	.36	.56	.46	.49	1.00	.41	.24	.18	.22	.34	-.12
Who-S	.15	.41	.55	.51	.41	1.00	.27	.36	.23	.56	-.32
Who-O	.35	.25	.45	.37	.24	.27	1.00	.17	.35	.43	-.35
Why	.37	.44	.34	.35	.18	.36	.17	1.00	.38	.52	-.37
How	.45	.32	.29	.40	.22	.23	.35	.38	1.00	.50	-.45
When	.55	.57	.60	.52	.34	.56	.43	.52	.50	1.00	-.57
Stanford-Binet	-.37	-.28	-.40	-.38	-.12	-.32	-.35	-.37	-.45	-.57	1.00
Median months at criterion	34	34	34	36	38	34	40	34	39	39	

[a] When tau > .34, $p < .01$; when tau > .45, $p < .001$.

17

where to *who*-subject, *what*-subject, *why*, *what*-object, *who*-object, *when*, and *how*. Adverbial *where* with transitive verb was in the difficult group.

In this study we also examined tense agreement between *what-do* questions and replies. Tense agreement in the case of future forms could be obtained by repeating the *will* or *going to* form, but for the past required an affix, or appropriate change in a strong verb. It is not surprising therefore that the future forms were significantly easier. However, the progressive was very easy, so affixation alone cannot be the problem. It is more likely that duration is cognitively more apparent than present versus past time.

With respect to *wh*-question categories and tense agreement, there was an earlier and a later (past 36 months) set of mastery ages, dividing the easier and significantly more difficult tasks. In Table 4 the only tasks omitted are those so easy or so difficult that the majority of children did not reach the mastery age or had already passed it.

Another issue, quite separate, is how these skills are related to each other. We found numerous cases in which skills might be distinct in age of mastery, but highly correlated. For instance, the age of generalization to nonsense plurals like *biks* is correlated with the age of mastery of syllabic plurals like *oranges* months later. The mastery of *he's* precedes by 3 months the mastery of *she's* with male and female characters, but they are highly related (tau = .69). A child who has mastered one can be expected to accomplish the other sooner than the child who has not yet reached the easier milestone.

Skill in giving temporal answers to *when* questions was a general correlate of rate of mastery of most of the other questions, and of inflections in speech as well. It was also related to IQ (tau=.57 with the Stanford–Binet.) The test used for measuring IQ, of course, contains many questions, so a child who can give relevant answers to questions should be able to get a better score. If we consider that answering questions appropriately as to category and tense is an important discourse skill, it is clear that common talents or training conditions underlie these facets of discourse agreement and certain other features of syntax and morphology.

ADULT QUESTIONS

When we examine replies by the three intensively studied children to *wh* questions in the texts at various stages of development, we find that the three children were nearly as successful at Stage I as they were at Stage V in matching the question category with a response. This seems puzzling, since the tests had shown that knowledge increases over this period, and in some cases ability to reply correctly to *wh* questions such as *how* and *when* is not achieved until after Stage V. The proportion of responses in the wrong category remains about the same at various ages (Table 5).

TABLE 5.   Responses (in Percentages) to *Wh* Questions for Three Children

	Stage I	Stage II	Stage III	Stage IV	Stage V
Category agreement	70.8	69.4	58.9	84.5	77.8
Wrong category	6.6	7.4	8.5	3.6	6.3
Avoids reply	15.1	10.7	17.0	6.2	8.2
Other	7.6	12.4	15.6	5.7	7.6
Total	106	121	141	194	379

To explain this paradox, we need to explore how adults question. Table 6 omits a few categories in cases where we knew the investigator had special purposes, such as eliciting plurals (*how many*) or possessives (*whose*) and was willing to risk frequent failures—that is, he was testing. In Table 6 it appears that there is a change toward greater use at later stages of questions that the child might be more successful at answering later. The dominant question forms at Stage I were *what-is*, *what*-object, *where*, and *what-doing*. On the other hand some questions do not appear at all, or appear only once until the later sessions, particularly *who*-object, *when*, *why not*, and *which*. Only one child was asked *how* questions. There were increases in frequency with the age of the child in asking *why* and *who*-subject questions. On the whole, the investigator adapted questioning to the difficulty level of the child. In addition, there was some increase in past tense questioning with age. At

TABLE 6.   Adult *Wh*-Question Types. Figures given are percentages of total *Wh* questions. Subtotals do not add to 100 because certain categories were omitted.

	Stage I	Stage II	Stage III	Stage IV	Stage V
Total *Wh* Questions	126	153	174	250	466
Where	9.5	14.4	9.8	9.6	13.3
What-Is	39.7	24.8	10.9	16.0	8.2
Who-Is	1.6	4.6	1.7	4.4	1.7
What-S	1.6	2.0	0.0	0.4	3.9
Who-S	2.4	4.6	15.5	11.6	8.6
What-O	18.2	14.4	19.0	17.2	13.7
Who-O	0.0	0.0	0.6	0.8	0.9
What-Do	9.5	13.7	21.3	8.0	15.4
Which	0.8	0.0	0.0	1.2	2.2
Why	0.8	0.6	2.3	4.8	8.2
Why-Not	0.0	0.0	0.0	1.2	3.9
When	0.0	0.0	0.0	2.4	2.2

Stages I to III only 2%, at Stage IV 5%, and at Stage V 13% of the verbs were past tense verbs in adult questions. If the investigator aimed at an equilibrium state in which a certain level of error was tolerable in replies, we would expect this result. In the case of question categories with enough cases to make percentage comparison reasonable, success ranged from 40% to close to 90%. This is a large range. Hence it is not the case that a successful equilibruim is reached.

TABLE 7.   Category Agreement in Responses to *Wh* Questions by Type for Three Children

Types of *Wh* Questions	Stage I		Stage II		Stage III		Stage IV		Stage V	
	%	N	%	N	%	N	%	N	%	N
Where	43	(12)	50	(22)	71	(17)	87	(24)	79	(61)
What-Is	88	(50)	89	(38)	84	(19)	83	(40)	82	(38)
Who-Is	100	(2)	43	(7)	67	(3)	73	(11)	83	(6)
What-S	0	(2)	33	(3)		...	100	(1)	67	(18)
Who-S	33	(3)	43	(7)	22	(27)	93	(29)	77	(40)
What-O	65	(23)	68	(22)	55	(33)	88	(43)	78	(64)
Who-O		...		...	100	(1)	50	(2)	100	(4)
What-Do	58	(12)	81	(21)	70	(37)	85	(20)	75	(72)
Which	100	(1)		...		...	100	(3)	91	(11)
Why	0	(1)	0	(1)	50	(4)	67	(12)	74	(38)
Why-Not		...		...		...	100	(3)	89	(18)
When		...		...		...	67	(6)	67	(9)
How		...	100	(1)	50	(2)	0	(2)	67	(3)

Another way to examine Table 7 is to ask whether the proportion of questions in each category is related to the relative success rate at that age. For example, at Stage I the rank order of success rates is *what-is*, *what*-object, *what-doing*, and *where*, counting only types with more than ten occurrences. This corresponds perfectly to the rank order of frequency of those questions. At Stage II naming questions are still first in success and in frequency, but the next three categories are tied in frequency. The relationship breaks down at Stage III, for reasons examined below. At Stage IV, five categories are high in success with over 80% correct, and they are also highest in frequency. By Stage V skill seems to be ignored as a selector.

Another approach is to examine differences in the question distributions for each child. If the adult is calibrating question frequency to success frequency, the bursts of questioning to one child rather than another in a particular category should differentiate between children by success rate.

Another view is that the questioner cannot tolerate asking a question if failure passes a certain ratio. *What-do* questions varied between children in the early months. When the success rate fell below 50%, the frequency was low as well.

There is, however, one interesting exception. At Stage III one of the children replied "Hm?" fifteen times, compelling the adult to repeat the question. This was the one session in which this response occurred more than a few times, and in this case the child's request for a repetition threw off the relation between question frequency and response success. The categories of questions that had the lowest success rate for this child, *who*-subject and *what-doing*, had the highest rate of requested repetition.

But could it not be that it is the frequency of the question which leads it to be understood? This can be the case only if the adult times the question to occur just when children know the answer. Something of that sort must happen for questions to be understood in the first place. Macnamara and Baker (1975) and Shatz (1974) have both observed such instruction taking place, in that adults use gestural cues to provide answers to questions while they are being asked, or to indicate the desired directive act.

ADULT INTERACTION STRATEGIES

A number of researchers (Drach, 1969; Holtzman, 1972; Blount, in press; Corsaro, 1975) have pointed out that adults use a high frequency of questions to children for varied functions. Corsaro found that, of eight types of topic-relevant acts by adults interacting with children, six employed interrogative form. For the adult who wants to generate talk, questions have the merit of sustaining interaction. We found questions used as obvious directives with modal auxiliaries, second person pronouns, and a desired act, that is, "embedded imperatives" (Ervin-Tripp, 1976, 1977). We also found requests for repetition, statements with tags asking the child to confirm an obvious fact ("That's a dog, isn't it?"), and permission requests (See Table 8).

Permission requests were not mentioned in Corsaro's analysis, and they may be evident in our text only because of some social features peculiar to this eliciting situation. The investigator was in the children's homes. He was at first a stranger to several of them. He wished to sustain speech participation, but he was also interested in particular items of syntax and had designed materials to elicit them. In trying to persuade the children to use the materials, he asked permission to shift to new toys.

If we compare the first three stages with the last two, we find a decrease in the ratio of directives among the interrogative utterances, and generally an increase in the residual interrogatives which could be information questions. There was also a decrease in tagged comments like, "That's a cat, isn't it?" These appeared to be acts used to elicit speech by offering simple information, and such tactics may have been judged less necessary or appropriate with older children who actively engaged in dialogue. Indeed, as we have seen, any kind of polar question becomes *decreasingly* productive of speech with the child's age, since the child starts giving more "yes" or "no" answers relative to other comments (see Table 3).

TABLE 8.   Adult "Yes"/"No" — Question Types
Figures given are percentages of total YN questions

Stage	Total Yes/No Questions	Confirmation with Tag	Confirmation without Tag	Permission	Directive	*Wh-* Embedded Information	Non-*Wh-* Embedded Information
I–III	432	15.0	23.6	2.6	21.8	14.4	22.7
IV	221	5.9	15.8	7.7	10.0	3.2	55.7
V	527	6.1	34.9	6.6	4.2	3.6	50.7

When we look in detail at the interchanges, it becomes evident that the adult's adaptation to the child's level of knowledge is modified by some other factors. Consider the following dialogue:

(a) D'ya wanna ask Sarah if she wants orange juice?   Uh-huh.
(b) Ask Sarah if she wants orange juice, OK?   (Silence)
(c) Ask Sarah if she wants orange juice.   (Silence)
(d) Ya wanna say Sarah?   Sarah.
(e) Do you want orange juice?   Uh-huh.

The investigator's purpose here is to discover the child's competence in constructing questions. He continues to attempt the route of "Ask Sarah..." at later sessions until the method is successful in eliciting questions. In (a) a "yes"/"no" question ("Does Sarah...") was embedded in a directive act ("Ask Sarah..."), which in turn was embedded in a "yes"/"no" question ("Do you want to..."). The child responded either to the first or last polar question and did not interpret the directive. In directives (b) and (c), the former tagged with "OK" and the latter unembellished, she did not comply. Probably she could not understand a directive with an embedded polar question. In (d) and (e), she made no connection between the two simplified parts, when the questioner split them into an embedded imperative and a polar question, both forms the child understood alone.

But why did the investigator start out in such a complicated way with a double embedding? A single embedding as in (c) was necessary to his eliciting method; and when he did not use it, he could not get the information he wanted. But the embellishments like "D'ya wanna," "Ya wanna," and "OK?" are there because of the social relationship between the investigator and the child. These are forms which normally are used between adults when compliance is assumed but the addressee is unfamiliar, there is a difference in rank or age, or the task is a nuisance or outside the normal role of the addressee (Ervin-Tripp, 1976). What this example suggests is that the investigator's formulations are affected by his social role, which can supersede simplicity considerations. Another evidence is the decrease with time (confounded with the child's age) in the embedding of *wh* questions within polar questions. In the early texts a higher proportion of polar questions contained *wh* questions, such as "Do you know what this is?" or "Where do you suppose this goes?" These longer and more complex sentences were used when the children were younger (Table 8) and the investigator was less experienced.

Examination of the adult's accommodation suggests some hypotheses about what adults believe, which casts light on the way they talk to children. A general statement might be that speakers to children try to aim speech at a difficulty level that balances off the frequency of lost information (i.e., material not understood by the child) against the cost to the speaker of increasing redundancy and reducing semantic compression. How much feedback there is may affect the sensitivity of assessment of the first factor, which may motivate the large amount of feedback-eliciting speech to children.

HYPOTHESIS 1. Speakers may be successful in moderating *semantic* difficulty as indicated by changes in reference to the past with age. The restraint in asking *why*, *how*, and *when* questions may be semantic. The adult may anticipate that young children do not have information about means, time, and causality.

HYPOTHESIS 2. Speakers believe that the youngest children can *name* and *locate*. This is a plausible conclusion from the high frequency of ostensive and locative utterances in early speech of children. Yet the naming of actions is seen as a kind of identifying act, though it is somewhat more difficult than the naming of things, persons, and places in, for example, "Who is this?" "What is this?" and "Where is the dog?" In turn, naming or identifying is regarded as easy for children to understand even if there is a relative clause limiting the noun: "That's the man we saw yesterday," "Where's the man who rides the car?" (Bloom, 1973, p. 163). In these cases the structural complexity of the relative clause was evidently not recognized by the linguist-speaker, as requiring simplification. Just how speakers to children succeed in shortening complex utterances, as they have been found to do in many studies, is not clear. The routes may involve lowering semantic density per utterance or avoiding information outside the nucleus. We have proposed here that identifying is not regarded as significantly difficult and as increasing the difficulty level of the sentence even when it involves a relative clause.

HYPOTHESIS 3.   Embeddings that differ in social distribution are not regarded by speakers as differing in intelligibility. The difference between "Do you think you can put this away?" "Can you put this away?" and "Put this away" is a social one. This difference is not, to the speaker, one of adding semantic complexity. In fact, the processing of some routine requests is so easy ("Can you sit down?" "Why don't you sit down?") that speakers can regard them as idiomatic and as preformulated as the addition of "please" or "OK?" to imperatives (Ervin-Tripp, 1976).

The syntactic analysis of the adults' speech to children yields complexity estimates which do not always match the child's age or linguistic level. On the other hand, an analysis in terms of the speech act involved, the semantic difficulty as assessed by the speaker, or the social appropriateness of the form in maintaining conversational engagement may yield a better prediction of register shifts in which speakers try to maintain a certain level of comprehensibility and participation by a child partner.

In this chapter we have addressed two questions: What is the timing in the development of tying features which are obligatory in local discourse, and how in the "discursive workshop" does the older partner adjust features of interaction to accommodate to the child and to create some success for the child in interaction?

Our evidence here is limited to one adult speaker, whose purpose included systematic testing of knowledge. We can assume that some range of interactional styles will be found for other adults whose purposes are not the same.

The evidence suggests that there is considerably greater difficulty for children in anaphora and tying than in referential deixis for pronouns, that many of the discourse features are correlated and may have some common underlying skill components in their acquisition, and that the older partner adjusts questions on the basis of beliefs about semantic difficulty, the difficulty of speech acts, and social appropriateness, and calibrates only in part from feedback from the child's success in replying.

References

Bloom, L. *One word at a time.* The Hague: Mouton, 1973.

Bloom, L., Rocissano, L. & Hood, L. *Adult–child discourse: Developmental interaction between information processing and linguistic knowledge.* Unpublished manuscript.

Blount, B. G. Aspects of socialization among the Luo of Kenya. *Language in Society*, 1972,1, 235–248.

Blount, B. G. Prosodic and interactional features in parent–child speech: English and Spanish. In C. Snow & C. Ferguson (Eds.), *Talking to children: language input and acquisition.* London: Cambridge University Press (in press).

Brown, R. *A first language.* Cambridge, Mass.: Harvard University Press, 1973.

Corsaro, W. A. *Sociolinguistic patterns in adult–child interaction.* Paper presented at the American Sociological Association, 1975.

Drach, K. The language of parent: A pilot study. *Language, Society and the Child* (Working Paper No. 14), Language–Behavior Research Laboratory, University of California, Berkeley, 1969.

Ervin-Tripp, S. Discourse agreement: How children answer questions. In R. Hayes (Ed.), *Cognition and language learning.* New York: Wiley, 1970. Pp. 79–107.

Ervin-Tripp, S. Is Sybil there: The structure of some American–English directives. *Language in Society*, 1976, **5,** 25–66.

Ervin-Tripp, S. Wait for me, roller-skate. In C. Mitchell-Kernan & S. Ervin-Tripp (Eds.), *Child discourse.* New York: Academic Press, 1977.

Holtzman, M. The use of interrogative forms in the verbal interaction of three mothers and their children. *Journal of Psycholinguistic Research*, 1972, **1,** 311–336.

Keenan, E. O. Conversational competence in children. *Journal of Child Language*, 1974, **1,** 163–184.

Keenan, E. O. Making it last: Repetition in children's discourse. In C. Mitchell-Kernan & S. Ervin-Tripp (Eds.), *Child discourse.* New York: Academic Press, 1977.

Kluwin, T. N., Ervin-Tripp, S. M., & Miller, W. *The acquisition of English pronouns by children.* Unpublished manuscript.

Macnamara, J., & Baker, E. From sign to language. Unpublished manuscript, Montreal, Quebec, 1975.

Shatz, M. *The comprehension of indirect directives: Can two-year olds shut the door?* Paper presented at the meeting of the Linguistic Society of America, summer, 1974.

Shugar, G. *Text analysis as an approach to the study of early linguistic operations.* Paper presented at the Third International Child Language Symposium, September 1975.

Tyack, D. *Children's production and comprehension of questions.* Paper presented at the American Speech and Hearing Association, 1974.

CHAPTER 2

Appropriate Speech Adjustments: The Operation of Conversational Constraints on Talk to Two-Year-Olds[1]

ROCHEL GELMAN

University of Pennsylvania

and

MARILYN SHATZ

Graduate Centre
City University of New York

INTRODUCTION

Speakers talking to different listeners in different situations alter the quality of their speech from one situation to another. When we talk about our work in conference settings, we do so differently from when we address our undergraduate classes. Although the content may remain roughly the same in both situations, the lexicon, the focus, the number of repetitions, the level of jargon, will differ in the two settings. Many investigators have documented this tendency of adult speakers to modify various qualities of their speech (e.g., Ervin-Tripp, 1968; Labov, 1972). In this chapter we will focus on what we take to be a particular case of this general phenomenon, namely, the tendency to "talk down" to beginning language learners.

[1] We thank Marjorie Horton for her assistance with data analysis and Mary Hope Lee for transcribing videotapes. Drs. Louise Cherry, C. R. Gallistel, Lila R. Gleitman, Erving Goffman, and Elissa Newport all read earlier versions of this manuscript and provided helpful suggestions. Preparation of the paper was supported by a Guggenheim Foundation fellowship and National Institute of Child Health and Human Development Grant HD–04598 to R. Gelman and an NICHHD traineeship, 1 TO1 HD–00337, to M. Shatz. Portions of the data reported here were presented at the Conference on Language Input and Acquisition, Boston, September 1974. An earlier working paper entitled "Rule-Governed Variations in Children's Speech" served as a basis for much of what is presented here. Reprints may be requested from R. Gelman, Department of Psychology, University of Pennsylvania, 3813 Walnut Street, Philadelphia, Pa. 19174, or M. Shatz, Developmental Psychology, Graduate Center, City University of New York, 33 West 42nd Street, New York, N.Y. 10036.

A number of students of language acquisition have documented the fact that the speech heard by beginning language learners is notably different from that heard by adults. From a number of studies on the nature of mothers' speech to very young children, we arrive at the following description of what Newport, Gleitman, and Gleitman (1975) term "Motherese." Grammatically, it consists mainly of well-formed utterances (e.g., Brown & Bellugi, 1964) that are short and syntactically simple (e.g., Baldwin & Frank, 1969; Newport, 1975; Snow, 1972; Phillips, 1973). Insofar as it is slower and higher in pitch, it is more intelligible than adult-directed speech (Phillips, 1973; Broen, 1972; Remick, 1971). The lexical terms are more concrete and are taken from a restricted range of those used in adult–adult conversations (Phillips, 1973). It is not just mothers who adjust their speech for beginning language learners; 4-year-olds do too. Whether they have younger siblings or not, children of this age tend to produce shorter and syntactically simpler utterances when talking to very young children than to peers or adults (Shatz & Gelman, 1973). In fact, a 4-year-old will use such altered speech when talking to a doll that has been assigned the role of a 2-year-old (Sachs & Devin, 1973).

Why do 4-year-olds and adults "talk down" to 2-year-olds? Elsewhere (Shatz & Gelman, 1977) we have argued that 4-year-olds do so because their selection of speech for 2-year-olds is regulated by their understanding of the requirements and obligations of conversational interactions, the understanding of which guides the selection of lexical and syntactic forms. In short, we took the view that 4-year-olds "talk down" to 2-year-olds because they are governed by conversational constraints that operate to define such speech as appropriate for the listener who is a beginning language learner. In this chapter we take up the question of what it means to say that speech adjustments are appropriate. We also consider the extent to which conversational constraints govern all speakers of "Motherese," be they 4-year-olds, adults, or any other competent speakers of the language.

In this section we begin by reviewing our reasons for introducing the notion of conversational constraints. Then we address the problem of defining appropriateness. The second section describes the method of speech analysis that we use to marshall evidence for our positions. The third and fourth sections present our evidence for 4-year-olds and adults, respectively. In the final section we examine the general issues that arise from our view of the function and source of "Motherese."

Why Conversational Constraints?

Why appeal to a notion like conversational constraints to explain the observations about language spoken to 2-year-olds? Much of the work on

"Motherese" has focused on the role it might play in providing an environment from which the child could learn the deep structure of his language. The fact that the surface structure of adult language does not necessarily map directly to the deep structure of the language has dominated thinking about both the cause and the function of "Motherese." Much of the initial work on "Motherese" centered around the implicit hypothesis that the relation between surface structure and deep structure is more transparent in "Motherese" than in adult speech. The function of "Motherese" would then be to make it easier for children to find or identify simple grammatical relationships in their early stages of language acquisition. Implicit in this position is the additional hypothesis that "Motherese" is motivated by the attempt to select syntactically simple utterances.

One difficulty with this thesis is that it is not clear that "Motherese" does in fact facilitate the child's acquisition of syntactic constructions (Newport, 1975, 1976). This casts some doubt on the assumed functional significance of "Motherese." A second difficulty, one that motivated our inquiry, is the occurrence of complex grammatical constructions in utterances directed to 2-year-olds (Shatz & Gelman, 1976). Speech to 2-year-olds does tend to be short and syntactically simple, but this is not to say that it always is. Witness such utterances as [1], [2], and [3]:

[1] *And the animals, when they get on, they get on like that and they peek through the window and see everything they wanna see.*
(Said by a 4-year-old to a 2-year-old who was not his sibling.)

[2] *Well, let's see if we can find something to put inside.*
(Said by a mother to her 2-year-old.)

[3] *Stephen, I have to show you how to get gas.*
(Said by a 4-year-old to his 2-year-old brother.)

Whatever the choice of tree diagrams for such utterances, one thing is certain: they will be derivationally complex, representing several sentence nodes and a variety of transformations.

We introduce the notion of conversational constraints into the discussion of "Motherese" because, to put it simply, some aspects of the data cannot be explained by models that recognize only syntactic considerations. The syntactically complex utterances that do occur require explanation. And we can find no way of accounting for the occurrence or nonoccurrence of particular complex constructions to 2-year-olds in strictly syntactic terms. For example, in our initial work (Shatz & Gelman, 1973) we found that 4-year-olds seldom used predicate complement constructions introduced by *that*[2] complementizers, as in

[4] *I think that it is a cat.*

when told to talk to a 2-year-old about the workings of a toy. However, such constructions were used with adults in the same setting. One might suggest that there is a rule, "Don't use predicate complements with *that* complimentizers when talking to 2-year-olds." This is an example of a rule that selects utterances on the basis of syntactic considerations. But such a rule does not account for speech to 2-year-olds in all settings. When 4-year-olds are paired with 2-year-olds and left to their own devices (i.e., not given the task of explaining something), they do use predicate complements with *that* complementizers, for example,

[5] *Now, I think we'll get washed.*
    (Said by a 4-year-old to a 2-year-old during an informal play session.)

A similar problem occurs with the use of predicate complements introduced by *wh* complementizers,[2] as in

[6] *I'll show you how it moves.*

Utterances like [6] occurred relatively often to both adults and 2-year-olds when the topic involved the working of a toy. But when the same-aged speakers talked to adults and 2-year-olds in an unstructured setting, they used *wh* predicate complement constructions more commonly to adults. Not only does the speech to 2-year-olds contain syntactically complex constructions; but also there appear to be no rules as to what syntactically complex

---

[2] In Shatz and Gelman (1973) we described the 4-year-olds' long utterances (those containing five or more words) with reference to a variety of syntactic categories. In this chapter we consider the long utterances which contained one of two syntactic categories: predicate complements with *that* complementizers and predicate complements with *wh* complementizers. Both are instances of sentential complements. A detailed description of these syntactic categories can be found in Shatz and Gelman (1973). For this chapter it suffices to note that the main criterion for assigning a long utterance with a sentential complement to one of the two categories was the form of complementizer that followed the main verb and introduced the sentential complement. Thus predicate complements introduced, either implicitly or explicitly, by the interrogatives *what, how, when, why, who,* and *where* were classified in the *wh* category. Those introduced, either implicitly or explicitly, by *that* were classified in the *that* category.

The same criteria described in Shatz and Gelman (1973) were used to identify instances of *that* and *wh* predicate complements in the transcripts of mothers' speech.

contructions are generally permissible. At least for *that* and *wh* predicate complement constructions, the tendency to use a given syntactic construction with a given listener fluctuates with changes in setting (see Table 1 for a summary of how 4-year-olds use these constructions in different settings with different listeners).

TABLE 1. Relative Frequencies of *That* and *Wh* Predicate Complement Constructions in Long Utterances Produced by 4-Year-Olds to Two Different-Aged Listeners in Two Situations (Based on data from Shatz & Gelman, 1973)

Type of Complement and Listener Class	Situation	
	Toy Explanation Task	Unstructured
That constructions		
Adults	Common[a, b]	Uncommon
Two-year-olds	Rare	Common
Wh constructions		
Adults	Common[b]	Very common
Two-year-olds	Common	Common

[a] Very common = 1 occurrence in every 10 or fewer utterances, common = 1 occurrence in every 11–30 utterances, uncommon = 1 occurrence in every 31–50 utterances, rare = 1 occurrence in every 51 or more utterances.
[b] Read the scale as "1 occurrence in every *x long* utterances."

Although, at one level, the speech to 2-year-olds, whether produced by a 4-year-old or by an adult, in a task-oriented situation (explaining a toy) or an unstructured one, can be given a common description in terms of syntactic simplification, just how, and how much, adjustment will be effected seems to vary with setting and speaker. In all cases, the speech *tends* to be short and syntactically simple, but variations within complexity level do not lend themselves to an account that is confined to syntactic grounds.

The task, then, is to find an explanation that allows for the following facts. There *is* much regularity in the syntactic features of utterances directed to 2-year-olds; speech for 2-year-olds tends to be syntactically simple. But speech to 2-year-olds does contain some syntactically complex constructions, and at least some syntactically complex constructions are used variably, depending on the setting.

Although the function of speech adjustment to 2-year-olds is not readily (or exclusively) described by appeal to syntactic rules, a clue as to how to explain it lies in the observation of a variable tendency to use utterances containing *that* and *wh* complement constructions with 2-year-olds. Work in sociolinguistics shows that the variable use of variety of linguistic devices is governed by speakers' tendencies to formulate their messages in ways that will index their efforts to acknowledge the constraints of a given communication setting. The capacities of a listener, the relative status of a listener, the purpose of the conversation, and so on, are all seen as variables that can influence the speaker's selection of messages and the linguistic form these messages will take. For example, formality of setting, as well as status of participants, determines the appropriateness of using honorifics. Personal friends of the President of the United States use a different style when they talk to him in a casual setting than when they address him in a public forum. Speech adjustments are made in response to a network of situational variables. The variable use of linguistic forms and consequent speech adjustments are often the data for deciding whether the speaker has recognized such conventions about talk exchanges. And the account of speech adjustments is formulated in terms of communication constraints.

It is such considerations that lead us to examine the possibility that predicate complement constructions occur in speech to 2-year-olds because they index the speaker's effort to take into account certain conversational constraints. A demonstration that different constraints operate in different settings would support the use of such constructions as appropriate in one situation but not in another. The sorts of constraints we have in mind include the speaker's assumptions about the kinds of things a 2-year-old can do and understand, and the way he can be treated in order to assure his attention and cooperation. Different settings will require differential amounts of work on the part of the speaker to maintain a very young listener's participation in an interaction.

If complex constructions mark the speaker's recognition of context-specific considerations, they will occur in some settings but not in others, even if the age of the listener is held constant. The occurrence of syntactically complex utterances to 2-year-olds may be appropriate in terms of the meanings the utterances convey in the communicative context. If these complex utterances express messages that are appropriate for 2-year-olds, there is no reason to exclude them from the speech repertoire. Emerging from this position is the view that the primary function of "Motherese" is a communicative one. Speakers of "Motherese" are guided by an intent to communicate, that is, to produce utterances that a 2-year-old might understand or respond to.

A Definition of Appropriate Speech

Before turning to the data, we outline a general view of appropriateness, a view that is influenced by work in sociolinguistics (e.g., Ervin-Tripp, 1968; R. Lakoff, 1972; Labov, 1972) and pragmatics (e.g., Grice, 1957; Gordon & Lakoff, 1971; Searle, 1970; 1975; in press-a). We shall say that speech is appropriate if (*a*) it shows evidence that the speaker is selecting content that a listener is likely to understand and/or respond to; and (b) it honors conventions about politeness, status, flexibility, and the like that may be relevant for listeners in particular settings. With regard to the latter criterion, there are a variety of linguistic devices that index these social conventions. For example, the speaker who knows his listener to be more knowledgeable than he is well advised to hedge the claims he makes. One linguistic device serving this purpose is the use of "I think" (R. Lakoff, 1972) in utterances like

[7] *I think these are dogs and these are lambs.*
       (Serving to indicate a change of mind in a 4-year-old who initially said, "Maybe these are lambs and these are dogs.")

Here the speaker offers his listener the chance to alter, comment on, or accept the utterance. Such devices, then, mark the speaker's confidence in his ability to defend his statements and his willingness to entertain further comments from his listener.

Those who are familiar with Piaget's work on egocentrism (Piaget, 1926) will recognise a difference between our definition of appropriateness and that offered by Piaget. For Piaget, it is necessary to show that the listener actually does understand the intended message of the speaker. In other words, Piaget requires that there be a *successful* meeting of the minds of speaker and listener. We are satisfied with evidence that suggests the speaker has attempted to meet the mind of his listener. We take this position because of the obvious fact that a speaker may have the best of intentions but still fail to meet the mind of his listener simply because the latter is recalcitrant, chooses to feign ignorance, or what have you.

Furthermore, Piaget does not treat the use of conversational devices to mark status differences, hedging, deference, and the like. There are two reasons to consider these features which contribute to speech style. First, a given culture employs such linguistic devices to mark social conventions. To the extent that one follows the conventions pertaining to different contexts, one's speech can be considered suitably adjusted to the setting.

Second, the use of a content criterion alone for judging appropriateness fails to capture the fact that the extent to which social conventions are marked (in speech) can influence the formulation of content. An individual who uses an appropriate conversational device in a given setting may, by virtue of having used that device, obscure the content of his message. For example, the need to express doubt by means of a hedge (G. Lakoff, 1972) may result in a less direct or simple expression of content. But if the context of the conversation dictates that the speaker exercise caution about his assertions, he may be forced to select a complex syntactic form to encode both the content and the hedge. A speaker who increases syntactic complexity by using a conventional means of communicating uncertainty may be producing an utterance which is difficult to understand and may not be "appropriate" for a language-deficient listener. In this sense the two criteria of content and convention may conflict; yet, given that both criteria are relevant to the selection of messages, such utterances are more appropriate than those not governed by a concern for either content or convention. Thus, by considering the extent to which either or both criteria of appropriateness influence speech adjustments, we are in a position to determine just how appropriate a given speech sample may be.

GENERAL METHOD OF DATA ANALYSIS

To determine whether the complex utterances containing *that* and *wh* predicate complements conveyed appropriate messages, it was necessary to determine the function such utterances served in the context of the conversational setting. Our method of assigning a *functional meaning-in-conversation* to the target utterances[3] involved several considerations. We assigned a functional meaning to each of the utterances containing a *that* or *wh* predicate complement construction by asking what purpose the speaker intended the utterance to serve in the conversation. To do this we found it necessary to analyze the speech with respect to the way it was used in the *context* of the conversation. Thus the functional meaning-in-conversation encompassed both the pragmatic and propositional elements of language, where *pragmatic* refers to the linguistic marking of such speaker intentions as assertion, request, uncertainty, and attitude, and *propositional* refers to reference and prediction (cf. Austin, 1962; Katz, 1972; Searle, 1970; Weinreich, 1963). Katz (1972) has noted that pragmatic determinations of, say, propositional type (whether, e.g., an utterance is an assertion or a request) often involve simultaneous considerations of many aspects of a sentence rather than just consideration of its mood (e.g., declarative, interrogative) or the meaning of its performative verb. The functional meaning-in-conversation analyses extend, when necessary, this fairly broad view of pragmatic meaning to include, in the determination of speaker intent, equally relevant aspects of verbal and nonverbal context surrounding the occurrence of a particular utterance (cf. Searle, in press-b). For example,

---

[3] We consider only instances of *that* and *wh* complements that occurred in utterances containing at least five words. We do this so as to be able to compare the results of the functional analyses of these complements with those reported in Shatz and Gelman (1973). The original Shatz and Gelman analyses were for long utterances, containing five or more words.

[8] *Do you think this door goes to this car?*

can be intended by its 4-year-old speaker as a request for an opinion about the appropriate pairing of one toy part to another or as an indirect request for the listener to attach the door to the toy car. In this case the actual functional meaning-in-conversation can be determined only by reference to extrasentential considerations. A description of our decision process in assigning functional meanings will clarify the role that extrasentential considerations played.

The actual assignment of the functional meaning-in-conversation of the target utterances was done as follows. First, the authors together assigned a functional meaning to each target utterance by considering it in relation to the following information: the speech that preceded the target utterance, the listener's responses to the utterance, the speaker's subsequent response to his listener's response, what the participants in the interaction were doing, and what the topic of conversation was. The degree to which we relied on any of these contextual features varied. In some cases we were able to rely primarily on the content of the target utterance itself to assign functional meaning and then to use the context as a source of confirmation of our judgement or intuition. For example, it is clear that the use of an utterance like

[9] *I'll show you how to do it.*

served to announce the 4-year-old speaker's intent to demonstrate something. That he actually went ahead and demonstrated a toy to a 2-year-old was taken as support for our interpretation of the functional meaning of such an utterance.

In other cases we found it necessary to use the context to determine which of two (or more) functions a particular utterance served. For example, out of context one cannot determine in which of three ways

[10] *Do you know what this is?*

is being used: to introduce a topic that the speaker wants to talk about, to ask a listener for information that the speaker himself lacks, or to test the listener's knowledge. For such utterances, the assignment of functional meaning depended mainly on context. For example, the child's activities that accompanied the speech in Protocol A would lead to the judgment that [10] served to introduce a topic.

PROTOCOL A: (Child building a structure with blocks; adult present.)
CHILD: Do you know what this is?

ADULT: What?
CHILD: A airport. For helicopters to go in.

In Protocol B the child's earlier speech would dictate the assignment of [10] to the second type of functional meaning, asking for information.

PROTOCOL B: (Child playing with die-cut faceless wooden animals; adult present.)
CHILD: I can't tell if this is a bird. Maybe it's a bunny. Do you know what this is?
ADULT: I think it's a bird.

In Protocol C the speech following [10] would indicate the functional meaning of testing the listener's knowledge.

PROTOCOL C: R. M., a 2-year-old, and her mother are playing with blocks.)
MOTHER: Do you know what this is?
R.M.:   What?
MOTHER: What it is? Can you tell by looking at it?
R.M.:   Um . . .
MOTHER: What does this thing look like?

Having assigned a *functional meaning* to each of the target utterances, we then organized these meanings into categories (Tables 2 and 7). As a check on the extent to which our initial judgments were sound, we once again assigned a functional meaning to each utterance that had been "coded." This check was done several months after the first step in the procedure so as to minimize the chance that we remembered exactly how we had first treated each utterance. Our final judgments agreed with 91% of our initial assignments of functional meaning. Disagreements were resolved by further discussion.

RESULTS AND DISCUSSIONS OF THE ANALYSIS OF FOUR-YEAR-OLD SPEECH

Data Source

The data for 4-year-olds were drawn from some of the corpora we used in our initial monograph. In particular we used the corpora from the two studies in which 4-year-olds talked individually to both an adult and a 2-year-old. In the first study (hereinafter referred to as the "toy explanation study"), children were explicitly instructed to talk about the workings of a toy (either an ark with animals or a dumping station with trucks and marbles) to each of their two listeners. In all there were 24 sessions, each consisting of time spent talking separately to an adult and to a 2-year-old. Eight children each having a 2-year-old sibling, participated in two sessions, one involving the sibling and an adult and one involving a nonsibling and an adult. Another eight children who did not have 2-year-old siblings were run in one nonsibling–adult session. For this chapter we have pooled sibling and nonsibling sessions since separate analyses (reported in Shatz & Gelman, 1973) revealed no effect of the sibling–nonsibling variable on subjects being run twice.

In the second study (hereinafter referred to as the "unstructured study"), the situation was not constrained by the introduction of specific toys or explicit instructions. Instead, five 4-year-olds were allowed to play with each listener and to talk about almost any topic that came to mind (the adults, however, were asked to refrain from reading books).

Thus, in the toy explanation task, the focus of the situation (talking about the workings of a toy) was the same regardless of listener. In the unstructured study, on the other hand, the focus was uncontrolled. We can then compare the effect of setting as well as listener, a feature which makes it possible for us to ask whether the selection of messages was constrained by two variables that are important in discussions of conversational constraints: the kind of listener and the type of situation.

Functions of Speech Containing Predicate Complements

The first question, of course, is what functions do *wh* and *that* predicate complements serve for the 4-year-old speaker, no matter to whom he talks and what he talks about? These functions are as follows (see Table 2 for a summary).

Directing the Interaction, or "Show and Tell" Speech • A variety of utterances containing *that* and *wh* predicate complementizers were grouped together here because they all served essentially to focus the conversation on the speaker's activities and interests. Utterances like

[11] *This is how we do it.*
(Said as the speaker positioned toy animals on the ark.)

used deictic devices to accompany demonstrations with the toy. Also included were utterances like

[12] *I'll show you how to get gas.*
(Said just before the speaker "pumped" gas into a toy car.)

where the announcement of an imminent demonstration and its subsequent execution served as the criteria for classification.

TABLE 2.   Functional Meaning-in-Conversation of 4-Year-Olds' Utterances   on-taining *That* or *Wh* Predicate Complement Constructions

Function	Description of Function
Directing the interaction	Can: Accompany a demonstration. Indicate intent to demonstrate. Call for attention. Serve to initiate or terminate a topic. Suggest an activity.
Mental state	Can: Serve to relate speaker's own mental state or knowledge. Be used to talk about another's mental state or knowledge.
Modulation of assertion	Marks speaker's degree of doubt or certainty about an assertion that he or his listener advances.
Clarification	Serves to explain what has just been said or done by a listener or speaker.
Requests for new information or clarification	Asks listener to provide information or seeks listener's agreement.

There were also utterances such as

[13] *Look at what we've got.*
(Pointing out the ark to the younger child who had just entered.)

which served to call attention to something the speaker found interesting. Utterances like

[14] *Know what little deers do?*
(After which the speaker continued, "And they do a little trick. He can stand on his head.")

and

[15] *Well, I don't really know what they are.*
(Said in response to a request from the experimenter to tell the 2-year-old about the toy animals. The speaker did know what the animals were, ts revealed in her prior conversation with the adult listener.)

were also included since they served to introduce topics of interest or to close discussion of a topic the child did not want to pursue. Finally, there were utterances like

[16] *I think we'll get washed.*
(Said to 2-year-old whom speaker was trying to interest in taking a "pretend" bath.)

which served to *suggest* an activity. Note that although [16] serves to tell the listener what to do, it also indexes flexibility by using the verb *think* parenthetically (Urmson, 1963).

Mental State ● Utterances in this category functioned to communicate the thoughts, wishes, memories, or states of knowledge of the speaker, his listener, or another person, as in

[17] *Perry doesn't know how to put the animals on the ark.*
(Comment to adult as speaker watched the 2-year-old fumble with toy animals.)

and

[18] *Before, I thought this was a crocodile.*
(Speaker was playing with a small model of a reptile when he volunteered [18], followed by "Now I think it's an alligator" to an adult listener.)

In utterances sorted into this category, not only were verbs of thinking (Vendler, 1972) utilized as main verbs, but also the context had to support the conclusion that the child was indeed making a statement about someone's thoughts or feelings rather than using verbs of thinking for some other purpose, as in [14] to [16].

Modulation of Assertion ● Utterances classified here served to make explicit the degree of certainty with which the speaker advanced an assertion. Utterances so classified contained a complement clause that was introduced by a parenthetical or hedge verb (Urmson, 1963; G. Lakoff, 1972), that is, a verb phrase that indexed the speaker's degree of certainty about his statement. Thus

[19] *I'm sure this fits too.*
(Said after adult listener challenged the possibility of putting all the animals in the ark.)

explicitly marks the speaker's belief that the assertion "this fits too" is true, and

[20] *I think this is a lamb.*
      (Said just after the speaker asked the experimenter, "What's this?"
      as he played with a small toy animal.)

explicitly marks the speaker's belief that there is room to doubt his identification of the toy.

As already noted, some utterances, such as [16], classified as "show and
tell" speech, indexed the feature of flexibility. Insofar as they did so, they
are somewhat like those classified here. Both sets of utterances index the
extent to which the listener is expected to accept what the speaker says.
What distinguishes such utterances is the nature of the proposition the
listener is being asked to accept. In one case, the speaker is asserting a fact;
in the other, he is suggesting a particular activity. The introduction of flexibility markers in the first case addresses the possibility that the truth of the
proposition can be questioned; in the second case it allows for the possibility
that the listener will reject the suggested course of activity. The separate
classification of these two types of modulated utterances is based on the
assumption that the purpose of the speaker was to make an assertion in one
case and to direct the interaction by suggesting an action in the other.

Clarifications • Predicate complements were also used in utterances that
served to clarify a previous utterance or action. Again, context was used to
support this interpretation of the target utterance. Thus the statement

[21] *I mean that my red one is like this.*
      (Speaker was trying to explain why a rectangular shape would not fit
      into a triangular hole. He was tracing the shape with his finger as he
      spoke.)

is an example of a clarification.

Requests for Information or Confirmation • Finally, predicate complements
were used in utterances that served to request specific information, as in

[22] *What do you s'pose this could be?*
      (Speaker held up a toy animal and waited for the listener to identify
      the object.)

and

[23] *Tell me, what does the scarecrow scare away?*
      (Asked after the speaker identified a picture of a scarecrow. After the

listener's answer, the speaker went on to ask, "Why don't they" (scarecrow) want 'em (birds) to eat corn?")

Predicate complements were also used to ask the listener to confirm something the speaker did or said, as in

[24] *Is that how it goes in?*
(Said after placing a truck in the dumping station.)

Again, the context made clear that the child was seeking some specific information or that he wanted something specific checked.

One utterance containing a *wh* complement construction remained a puzzle as to functional meaning even after considering it in context. It was scored as indeterminate.

Table 3 shows the effects of both the listener and situation variables on our subjects' tendencies to use predicate complements to convey each of

TABLE 3. Percentage of All *That* and *Wh* Long Utterances in 4-Year-Old Speech Which Served Each Functional Meaning-in-Conversation in Each Listener Class

	Situation	
Function and Listener Class	Toy Task[a]	Unstructured[b]
Directing the interaction		
Adults	25	59
Two-year-olds	95	82
Mental state		
Adults	28	22
Two-ycar-olds	5	14
Modulation of assertion		
Adults	31	13
Two-year-olds	0	4
Clarification		
Adults	6	0
Two-year-olds	0	0
Requests for new information–confirmation		
Adults	9	6
Two-year-olds	0	0
Indeterminate		
Adults	1	0
Two-year-olds	0	0

[a] Based on 81 predicate complement constructions to adults and 21 to 2-year-olds.
[b] Based on 32 pedicate complement constructions to adults and 28 to 2-year-olds.

the five functional meanings-in-conversation. Not surprisingly, with 2-year-olds predicate complements were used mainly to direct the interaction. In the structured situation, 95% of the predicate complement constructions occurred in such "show and tell" utterances. In the unstructured situation, 82% of these types of constructions were so used. Both modulation of assertion and comments about mental state rarely occurred; they appeared almost exclusively in the unstructured situation. Clarifications and requests for information or confirmation never occurred.

The functions of the adult-directed utterances containing the predicate complement constructions shifted considerably from one situation to the other. During the toy explanation task, the children made relatively little effort to direct the interaction—at least with utterances containing predicate complement constructions. Instead, predicate complement constructions occurred mainly in statements about mental state and modulated assertions. They also served to some extent to request information or confirmation and to provide clarification. In the unstructured situation, however, similar syntactic forms were used much more often to direct the interaction and less often to modulate assertions. Thus we see that 4-year-olds used predicate complements to serve different functions. Moreover, the choice of functions was systematically determined by the nature of their listeners and the settings in which these listeners were addressed. Given these results, we can now ask whether the speech involving these predicate complement constructions was appropriate.

Are Four-Year-Olds' Speech Adjustments Appropriate? We Think So

In Section I we defined speech as appropriate if in context it (a) reveals an attempt to select content the listener *might* understand or respond to; and (b) shows evidence of using conversational devices to honor social conventions. With these criteria in mind, we examine the results of the functional analyses reported in Table 2.

Recall that in the toy task the children were explicitly given the task of explaining a toy to both an adult and a 2-year-old. As noted in Shatz and Gelman (1973), the children stayed on the topic of the toy to both sets of listeners. Witness Protocols D and E:

PROTOCOL D: (J.K. to mother about dumping station.)
      J.K.:   You put it in here.
            (Question from mother.)
      J.K.:   And then push it all the way in, and then you get marbles out here. You'll need gas. It only has enough gas to go to the gas station. It backed in here. That's good.
            (Question from experimenter.)

J.K.: You have to make it go back up here. Then you pick it up and it goes back in.

PROTOCOL E: J. K. to 2-year-old about dumping station.)

J.K.: I gave you it. You want to have something funny? Put the marbles in here. Put the marbles in here. I'll give you the marbles. Now pour them in here. Go up here. And pour them in here. Now we have to dump it. Dump it. No, not in here. Pour it in here. Pour it in here, OK? That's funny. No, not like that. I'll do it. See, Sara?

But the children did more than stay on topic: they treated their listeners quite differently, in terms of the range of topics they introduced, the style in which they did so, and what they requested of their listeners in response to their speech. With 2-year-olds, they focused on directing the interaction and demonstrating the toys. They did not talk about mental state, they did not ask their 2-year-old listeners to provide information, they did not modulate their statements, nor did they make suggestions about possible actions—they said, "Do it!" In short, their goals seemed to be to get the 2-year-olds to pay attention, to demonstrate the toy, and to tell the younger child what to do with the toy. In many ways they acted appropriately. Knowing that 2-year-olds are not very knowledgeable listeners, the 4-year-olds apparently were unconcerned about the vulnerability of their statements to challenge and did little hedging. They could reasonably expect that the 2-year-olds would not challenge the veracity of their statements. Also, a situation in which information must be transmitted to 2-year-olds does not call for maximizing the speaker's flexibility with regard to topic or activity. Rather, it is a situation where wisdom dictates emphasizing clear, simple, and basic statements about the topic under consideration. As we have seen, when the 4-year-olds talked to the 2-year-olds in the toy task setting, they seemed to be doing just that. They concentrated on the use of short, repetitive utterances, as well as a variety of demonstrative and attentional devices. Such techniques, together with the absence of conversational devices for offering the listener the option to change or ignore the topic or to challenge the listener, presumably enhanced information transmission to a poor receiver and were appropriate to the demands of the situation.

Now consider the 4-year-old talking to an adult about the toy. The task was still one of information transmission, but the receiver's capacities were no longer poor. Adults are knowledgeable and high in status. And it is appropriate for a speaker to use assumption-of-truth modulators when he makes assertions to someone who—by virtue of status or knowledge—can call into question his statements, for the speaker who himself questions or defends the truth value of his assertions is explicitly recognizing that there is an issue of supporting evidence and is less likely to lose face should his listener contradict or reject a particular statement. As previously noted, 4-year-olds did modulate their assertions to adults. Also, the increased competence of the adult listener presumably served to adjust the determination of what was relevant to the conversation. A wider range of topics could be introduced appropriately without being irrelevant, and this indeed happened, as shown in talk about mental state. It is also appropriate to seek information from a knowledgeable listener. Again, witness the introduction of requests for information or confirmation in speech to adults. Finally, in the toy task situation, the adult listener was either an experimenter or a parent who had been made aware of the child's task. These persons were, on the whole, solicitous attenders to the child's explanations. Thus there was little need for the speaker to try to direct the interaction by calling for attention.

Now consider the unstructured study. For both sets of listeners, the conversational constraints shifted with the change in situation. It was no longer quite so important for the older child to maintain the younger child's interest in the speaker's activities. The 4-year-old may still have directed the interaction, but he could be more tolerant of the younger child's unwillingness or inability to follow him, for he no longer had to prove his teaching ability to an experimenter. Therefore, although the 4-year-old still directed the interaction, he could now afford to do so more flexibly, allowing his listener (and himself) the option of not following up the introduction of topics. Accordingly, the direction of the interaction was sometimes accomplished with the aid of utterances like [16] which were marked for flexibility.

On the other hand, the adults presented more of an attentiveness problem in the free situation than in the constrained one. The free situation is a more natural one in that it allowed for the mother to be distracted by activities that normally take her attention away from her child. It is not surprising, then, that predicate complement constructions were often used in this situation in calls for attention and other attempts to direct the interaction. Although statements about mental state and modulation of assertions still occurred, the prime focus was on getting the mother into the action. Thus, with a change in the conditions under which interaction takes place, initiation and maintenance of the interaction become paramount, and the rates at which different functional meanings-in-conversation occur reflect this reweighting of the conversational constraints. In the layman's (or the 4-year-old's) terms, the rule might be, "Get Mom interested first. Then worry about whether she'll question what you're saying."

In sum, then, predicate complements generally served to convey messages appropriate for both kinds of listeners. Given this finding, it is now possible to explain the variable use of the two types of complement constructions (Table 1 summarizes the variable use of the constructions). Table 4 sum-

marizes the extent to which subjects used *that* or *wh* complement constructions when expressing the various functional meanings to each of their listeners in the structured and unstructured situations. No matter what the
nature of the situation or who the listener, the speaker *always* used *that* constructions when he *modulated his assertions* or wanted to clarify something.
Expressions of *mental state* were formed primarily with *wh* constructions.

TABLE 4. Percentage of Time 4-Year-Olds Expressed Each Functional Meaning
through a *Wh* or *That* Construction

| | Situation and Construction | | | |
| | Toy Task | | Unstructured | |
Function and Listener Class	*That*	*Wh*	*That*	*Wh*
Directing the interaction				
Adult	20	80	11	89
Two-year-olds	10	90	52	48
Mental state				
Adults	30	70	14	86
Two-year-olds	0	100	25	75
Modulation				
Adults	100	0	100	0
Two-year-olds	100	0	100	0
Clarification				
Adults	100	0	...	...
Two-year-olds	...	...	...	...
Requests for information–confirmation				
Adults	57	43	0	100
Two-year-olds	...	...	...	...

Requests for information or *confirmation* were about as readily expressed
with a *wh* as a *that* construction. Finally, the form in which the function of
directing the interaction was expressed varied; the expression of such a function with an adult listener occurred primarily in *wh constructons*, whether
or not the setting was structured. Similarly, *that* constructions served to direct
the interaction. Inspection of the *that* utterances sorted into this category
revealed that they always included flexibility markers, as in [16].

Since our speakers had little, if any, reason to mark their utterances to
2-year-olds with flexibility and since *that* constructions served this function,
we now see why so few occurred in child-directed speech during the toy
explanation task. And since there was reason to hedge statements with

adults, *that* constructions should have occurred in the speech to them—as indeed these constructions did.

The increased tendency to direct *that* constructions to 2-year-olds in the unstructured setting can be explained because such constructions serve to direct the interaction in a flexible way. Moreover, it was appropriate for our subjects to modulate directions when talking to 2-year-olds in a more relaxed unstructured situation. But the unstructured setting placed different constraints on the 4-year-old, depending on whether he talked to a 2-year-old or an adult. With the younger child he could let his guard down; with the adult he faced the problem of attracting his listener's attention before he could make statements which may have required hedging or clarification. As a consequence, there should have been relatively fewer *that* constructions, since these serve the hedging and clarification functions. Again, this was the case.

Just as we have shed light on the variable use of *that* constructions by considering the role of conversational constraints and the way in which these influence speech selections, we can do so for the *wh* construction results summarized in Table I. As shown in Table 4, *wh* constructions were most often used to direct the interaction. The toy explanation task made it necessary for the speaker to attract and direct the 2-year-old's attention to the speaker's activity with the toy. The fact that *wh constructions* serve this purpose makes clear why such constructions were used with the 2-year-olds. Since it was necessary to attract the adult's attention in the unstructured setting, we have a clue as to why the rate of occurrence of this construction with adults increased with a change from the toy task to the free situation.

What remains to be explained is why *wh*'s occurred as frequently as they did in adult-directed speech in the toy task. Recall that here the children talked about mental state with adults and requested information or confirmation from them. As shown in Table 4, *wh* constructions can be used for such purposes as well as for directing the interaction. Since there was some tendency to direct the interaction, and since it also was appropriate to mention mental state or request information, there were several reasons for choosing a *wh* construction when talking to adults during the toy task. In other words, *wh* constructions appeared quite often in adult-directed speech in the toy task because the situation made it acceptable for the child to use them for the various functions they can serve.

We see that the variable use of *that* and *wh* constructions was systematically controlled by the conversational constraints with which the children had to deal. What the children chose to say when they used such constructions was constrained by their listeners' status, cognitive capacity, and attentiveness and by the flexibility of the setting. From our point of view, then, the children were trying to produce messages that could be understood or responded to by the different listener classes. They adjusted the content of their messages. Likewise, they varied their use of conventional linguistic devices in response both to setting and to listener. In short, their speech was appropriate.

Further Evidence for the Claim of Appropriateness

Our argument that the 4-year-olds' speech was appropriate rests extensively on the analysis of the differences in the functional meanings of utterances with *that* and *wh* predicate complement constructions. If the argument is correct, one should be able to make it more generally. In other words, although clearly no claim is made that *all* functional meanings of conversation have been identified, those that have may be expressible in constructions other than the ones already analyzed. And the use of other constructions should distribute according to listener- and situation-dependent functions in much the same way as the long complement utterances. Inspection of the utterances that formed the basis of the functional analysis of predicate complements suggests a test of generality—the way the children used verbs of thinking or what we call "psychological" verbs.

Recall that the determination of the functions of the long utterances containing the predicate complement constructions rested on an examination of the full utterance and the context in which it occurred. A necessary, although not sufficient, part of that determination included the type of container verb used to introduce the complement clause, where *think*, as in

[25] *I think I'll get these.*

is a container verb. Two broadly defined types of container verbs, indicatory and psychological, were found in the 4-year-old's speech. In terms of a contextual word meaning, the indicatory verbs such as *look* and *show* carry a sense of pointing out or defining. The psychological verbs such as *think*, *know*, and *remember* involve reference to more internal types of mental activity. Table 5 lists the container verbs and verb phrases used by the 4-year-olds.

In the 4-year-old's speech, indicatory verbs commonly took complement constructions introduced by *wh* complementizers. As would be expected, they functioned almost exclusively in utterances that served to direct the interaction. Psychological verbs, on the other hand, took both types of complementizers and functioned in utterances expressing a wider range of functional meanings-in-conversation. Since a wider range of meaning was directed to adults than to 2-year-olds, more psychological verbs were directed to adults. However, there was no general prohibition against the lexical selection of psychological verbs for 2-year-olds, for they did occur in utterances that directed the conversation, as in [14]. Their relatively limited occurrence in 2-year-old-directed speech was the result of listener-dependent limitations on the expression of modulation and mental state, for the expression of such meanings by means of predicate complementation overwhelmingly involved the use of psychological verbs. If the conclusions we draw from the meaning-in-conversation analysis have any generality, the occurrences of psychological verbs in other than long predicate complement utterances should follow the same listener-dependent patterns of functional meaning as those in long utterances.

TABLE 5.   *That* and *Wh* Predicate Complement Container Verbs and Verb Phrases Used by 4-Year-Olds

Verb Type		
Indicatory	Psychological	
Be	Be glad	Remember
Do	Be right	Say
Look (at)	Be sure	See[a]
See[a]	Can tell	Seems
Show	Guess	Suppose
Teach	Hope	Think
Tell	Know	Wish
Say	Mean	Wonder
	Pretend	

[a] *See* was used both in the sense of viewing something and as an "apprehensive" (cf. Vendler, 1972).

Psychological verbs can help express the functional meanings previously presented without necessarily introducing the use of a full-blown predicate complement clause. For example,

[26] *I think I did.*
     (Said in response to a question as to whether the child had ever before played with a toy like the one just presented to him.)

is an instance of a short, elliptical predicate complement utterance involving modulation that was not previously considered because of its length. On the other hand,

[27] *She doesn't know all this.*
  (Said about a 2-year-old after speaker was told the younger child would be coming to play with the ark.)

TABLE 6.   Percentage of Psychological Verbs Used by 4-Year-Olds to Serve Each Meaning-in-Conversation Function for Each Listener Class and Situation

| | Situation and Construction | | | |
| | Toy Task | | Unstructured | |
Function and Listener Class	Container Verb for *That* and *Wh* Con- structions[a]	All Other Con- structions[b]	Container Verb for *That* and *Wh* Con- structions[c]	All Other Con- structions[d]
Directing the interaction				
Adults	18	27	47	63
Two-year-olds	83	100	74	67
Mental state				
Adults	33	44	32	12
Two-year-olds	17	0	21	11
Modulation of assertion				
Adults	35	20	21	19
Two-year-olds	0	0	5	11
Clarification				
Adults	7	3	0	0
Two-year-olds	0	0	0	11
Requests for information				
Adults	7	3	0	0
Two-year-olds	0	0	0	11
Indeterminate				
Adults	0	6	0	6
Two-year-olds	0	0	0	0

[a] Based on 71 instances of psychological verbs to adults and 6 to 2-year-olds.
[b] Based on 70 instances of psychological verbs to adults and 4 to 2-year-olds.
[c] Based on 19 instances of psychological verbs to adults and 19 to 2-year-olds.
[d] Based on 16 instances of psychological verbs to adults and 9 to 2-year-olds.

is an instance of the expression of mental state in an entirely different sort of construction. Accordingly, utterances that contained psychological verbs but were not previously considered were sorted according to their function in conversation.

Table 6 presents the results of sorting these utterances for each set of listener and each study. For the sake of comparison, the percentage of psychological verb utterances serving each function is listed separately for psychological verbs used as container verbs in the previously described long predicate complement utterances and for the remaining instances of psychological verbs used in other constructions.

Despite the small number of instances represented in some of the columns, the results of the psychological verb analysis support the results of the functional meaning-in-conversation analysis reported above. In the toy task study, psychological verbs addressed to adults served mainly in expressions of modulation or mental state, even when they were not used as container verbs in long utterances. The use of such verbs to 2-year-olds was rare, no matter what the construction, and the function most often served with 2-year-olds was directing the interaction.

The unstructured study results also support the analyses described earlier. Again, the situation compels the speaker to try to get the attention of the adult listener, and to be less concerned about modulating assertions or talking about mental states. Thus the types of functional meanings and the constraint-governed conversational system they imply are shown to have validity for a wider range of linguistic phenomena than predicate complements in long utterances.

MOTHERS' SPEECH TO TWO-YEAR-OLDS

We started with a consideration of "Motherese" as spoken by mothers, as well as by 4-year-olds. Here a reminder is in order: For both sorts of speakers, our position is that, in general, speech addressed to 2-year-olds is guided by an intent to communicate messages that are likely to be understood and/or responded to. The primary evidence offered in support of this view comes from our functional analyses of long utterances containing *that* and *wh* predicate complement constructions. We focused on these because we sought to determine whether such utterances carried conversational meanings that one might judge to be appropriate for 2-year-olds, despite the fact that they were syntactically complex. Like 4-year-olds, mothers used utterances that contained *wh* and *that* constructions, as in [28], [29], and [30]:

[28] *And then I'll show you what we can do with those pieces.*

[29] *You know what we've got here?*

[30] *I don't think it will fit in that hole.*

Can we conclude that such utterances are appropriate from the vantage point of intended communications? To find out, we performed a functional meaning-in-conversation analysis like the one described for 4-year-old speech.

Data Source

Data come from transcripts of videotaped sessions of ten white, middleclass mothers and their 2-year-old children. The children's ages ranged from 22 to 35 months, representing a mean age of 28 months. Half of the children were younger than 29 months; half were 29 months or older. The session consisted of the mother and child playing with and talking about a complicated toy (a farm setting with buildings, animals, people, and vehicles), and it lasted about 15 minutes. An assistant ran the equipment; author M. S. observed.

The methods for transcribing the speech were much like those described in Shatz and Gelman (1973); the main difference in the nature of the transcripts derives from the fact that videotapes were obtained here, allowing us to utilize considerably more detailed descriptions of the context. The criteria for marking utterance boundaries and computing mean length of utterance in words (MLU) were as described in Shatz and Gelman (1973). Mothers varied in the amount of speech they produced (90 to 310 utterances): the average number of utterances to children who were younger than 29 months was 210; to children who were 29 months or older, 144. Based on the first 75 utterances in the session, the corresponding mean MLUs were 3.68 and 4.38. All but one of the mothers represented in the latter group produced MLUs that were longer than any of those produced by mothers who talked to children younger than 29 months. These results are much like those reported by other investigators of "Motherese." Not only is the average utterance length relatively short, but also the younger the child, the shorter is the length. Furthermore, these statistics are comparable to the ones we reported previously for the 4-year-olds. Four-year-olds produced a mean MLU of 3.7 to listeners under 28 months of age and a mean MLU of 4.9 to those 28 months and older (Shatz & Gelman, 1973).

Functional Analysis of Predicate Complements in Long Utterances

As already noted, mothers' speech to 2-year-olds contained utterances with *that* and *wh* predicate complements. The rate at which these occurred varied; *wh* constructions appeared twice as often as *that* constructions. These differential rates are much like those we found in 4-year-olds' talk about the workings of a toy in a setting that was quite comparable to the one under consideration. The question is whether the use of the predicate complements reflected a comparable tendency to use such utterances to express similar functional meanings.

Table 7 summarizes the mothers' tendency to use *that* or *wh* predicate constructions to serve a variety of functions. In can be seen in the table that the predicate complements in mothers' speech served all the functions we described for 4-year-olds and some additional ones. Three functions appear in mothers' speech that were not present in 4-year-old speech.

TABLE 7. Functional Meaning-in-Conversation of Mothers' Long Utterances Which Contained *That* or *Wh* Predicate Complement Constructions

Function	Description of Function
Directing the interaction	Same as given in Table 1 for 4-year-olds.
Suggesting a chance of activity	Serves to tell listener not to do what he is doing and to do something else instead.
Mental state	Same as given in Table 1 for 4-year-olds.
Modulation of assertion	Same as given in Table 1 for 4-year-olds.
Clarification	Same as given in Table 1 for 4-year-olds.
Requests for new information or clarification	Same as given in Table 1 for 4-year-olds.
Confirmation	Can: Serve to indicate that the listener has performed the right action. Serve to indicate that the listener has given the right verbal response.
Testing	Serves to elicit answers or responses speaker knows are in the listener's repertoire.

Suggesting a Change of Activity ● Utterances in this category functioned much like those in the directing the interaction category, for they did serve to direct the child's activities. We classify them separately, however, in part because they did not occur in 4-year-old speech, but mainly because they did more than start, maintain, or complete interactions. They served to tell the child that he was doing something that he should *not* do and to suggest that *he might do something else*. As illustrated in [31], such directions were subtle (cf. Ervin-Tripp, 1976).

[31] *You think it goes in there?*
(Said by mother to 2-year-old who was involved in a sequence of placing objects on or in containers. The child said, "Here, here it go," while trying to fit a block in a hole—which was impossible. The mother then said [31] while watching the child. Subsequently, the mother asked, "What shape is that?")

As Ervin-Tripp points out, the young child is not very good at producing such subtle, hinting directives, an observation which possibly accounts for our failure to find such utterances in 4-year-old speech.

Testing • Utterances that served to elicit an answer or response the child could provide, as in [32], were classified under this function.

[32] *Do you know what that is?*
(Said while child was picking up a boat. Child answered mother with "Um, boat.")

Such utterances are called test questions (Holtzman, 1972) and serve to provide opportunities for the expression of the young child's knowledge. This function is reminiscent of the teacher who asks such questions when reviewing material.

Confirmation • Recall that 4-year-olds sought information or confirmation only from adults, individuals who might be able to meet the request. We now see that adult speech contains the reciprocal function to the request for information or confirmation: the provision of information or confirmation. Such predicate complement utterances functioned to tell the listener that he had performed correctly, as in [33] and [34]:

[33] *That's where it goes.*
(Said after child correctly placed an object.)

[34] *That's how you do it.*
(Child was playing with barn door and trying to close it. Mother's

TABLE 8. Percentage of All *That* and *Wh* Utterances in Mothers' Speech Which Served Each Functional Meaning-in-Conversation with 2-Year-Old Listeners

Function	Percentage of Time Served[a]
Directing the interaction	48
Suggesting a change of activity	13
Mental state	7
Modulation of assertion	6
Clarification	2
Requests for new information or confirmation	3
Confirmation	3
Testing	15
Indeterminate	3

[a] Based on 119 utterances, the total number that occurred throughout the 10 corpora.

utterance occurred as the child moved toward a successful termination of the act.)

Table 8 shows the rates at which these functions occurred in mothers' speech to 2-year-olds. It can be seen that almost half of the predicate complement utterances served to direct the interaction. The only other two functions that appear with some regularity are the *testing* and *suggesting-change* ones. Together, these three functions account for 75% of the speech. What emerges is a picture of mothers who direct the interaction, sometimes by being explicit, sometimes by hinting, and sometimes by acting as teachers. (Note the limited occurrence of the confirmation function as expressed in predicate complement constructions; we will return to this later.)

Recall that our 4-year-olds' use of predicate complements in long utterances was considered with regard to the use of a particular complementizer (a *that* or *wh*) for each of the functions. A functional analysis was also performed on *psychological* verbs that appeared in utterances not scored in the earlier long utterance analysis. In the next two sections, we do the same for mothers' speech.

TABLE 9.   Percentage of Time That Mother Used a *Wh* or *That* Construction to Express each Functional Meaning

Function	Percentage of *Wh*'s[a] Used for the Function	Percentage of *That*'s[b] Used for the Function
Directing interaction	56	32
Suggesting	9	21
Mental statements	5	11
Modulation of assertions	1	19
Clarifications	2	0
Requests for new information of confirmation	0	8
Confirmation	2	3
Testing	21	11
Indeterminate	4	0

[a] Based on 38 utterances.
[b] Based on 81 utterances.

Form versus Function of the Predicate Complements in Mothers' Speech

Table 9 breaks down the mothers' tendency to use *that* or *wh* constructions for each of the functions summarized in Table 7. Note that, when *wh*'s were used, they appeared primarily in utterances serving to direct the interaction and to test. *That*'s were employed for a wider variety of functions. Recall that *wh*'s were used twice as often as *that*'s. We now see why. As indicated, predicate complement constructions generally served to direct the interaction and to test. Some of the direction took the form of subtle hints. The directing and testing functions were most likely to be mapped into *that* constructions. But, except for the occurrence of subtle hints, these other functions seldom occur. Therefore, once again, considering the functional meaning of the utterances allows us to gain insight into the nature of the variable use of these syntactic constructions.

Functional Analysis of Psychological Verbs

An inspection of the list of all psychological verbs used by mothers— whether as container verbs for predicate complements or in other ways— revealed a great deal of overlap with the list we presented for 4-year-olds (Table 5). The verbs or verb phrases *be glad, hope, pretend,* and *wish* did not occur in mother's speech; the verbs (verb phrases) *bet, believe, looks like,* and *decide* were unique to the mothers' speech. Otherwise, the verbs used were the same.

The extent to which mothers used such verbs other than as container verbs in *that* and *wh* constructions was vanishingly small. In all, we found 30 additional occurrences in corpora that, all together, contained 1768 utterances. Still, when these verbs *were* used, they occurred in utterances that served the functions of directing the interaction ($N = 6$) and testing ($N = 7$). The remaining 11 cases distributed across the other functions, showing up no more than once or twice (if that) in a particular category.

Discussion of Mothers' Speech

We began with the position that "Motherese" is an example of the general phenomenon of speech adjustment, a phenomenon that is considered to be related to the constraints a conversational setting places on a speaker's selection of messages. In this context we suggested that the function of "Motherese" was to convey messages that are suitable in terms of content and social convention for the beginning language learner. Such a framework allows for the occurrence of long and complex utterances if they serve functions that seem appropriate for a 2-year-old. The functional analysis of the long utterances which contained predicate complement constructions lends some support to this view. Despite their length and complexity, these constructions served to direct the interaction, to test the children's vocabulary, and to teach about the workings of the toys. Furthermore, they were used to hint at ways in which a child might shift his focus of attention or action. We take such results to show that the utterances with predicate complement constructions were appropriate, despite their length. Young children require direction, and surely they need to practice vocabulary as well as learn how to work objects in their environment. They presumably do not have the ability to provide information to an adult who herself lacks the information, to know that an adult's assertions might be questionable, or to engage in talk about mental events. Accordingly, the full range of functions that can be mapped onto the syntactic constructions under consideration should not occur in "Motherese." The very ones that did occur most often make sense in terms of the relative abilities of the participants in the interactions we studied.

The occurrence of utterances with predicate complements that hint at new directions an interaction might take deserves some comment. We see this function in adult speech but not in 4-year-old speech to 2-year-olds. One reason has already been offered: the use of such a function is probably out of the range of the 4-year-olds' competence. But we think there is more to say. Adults did not have to use this function; they could communicate the same message more directly by saying, "Don't do this. Do that." How can the use of the subtle style be justified? Other investigators have noted the use of a variety of linguistic devices to mitigate status differences between listener and speaker (e.g., Labov & Fanshel, in preparation; R. Lakoff, 1973). In particular, Ervin-Tripp (1976) has drawn attention to the use of modified directives to mitigate the lower rank of children. Visitors to nursery schools will recognize the ubiquitous use of "Now, children, I think we'll ———." In other words, convention dictates that it is appropriate to mitigate one's power and authority when communicating with young children. Since the utterances with predicate complements (especially *that*'s) can be used in this way, their occurrence makes sense. It indicates that middle-class mothers do more than select messages that convey appropriate information: they talk in a style that our society recognizes as appropriate for dealing with young children.

Before turning to a summary and discussion of the general issues raised in this paper, we wish to make one further point about our analyses of the mothers' use of predicate complements. Table 7 shows that such constructions can be used to tell listeners that they are right, that is, to confirm an action or verbal response. Yet on the basis of Table 8 we see that this function was hardly ever used. This seems surprising, in view of all we have said about the skill mothers show in directing and teaching their children. We would expect them to tell their children when they have done something right or have given a correct answer. A further inspection of the protocols indicated that mothers do in fact confirm, although they do not often use predicate complements to do so. Instead, they employ other, more straightforward devices. A predominant method is to say simply, "That's right" or "Right, good." Other techniques employ something akin to the cheerleader style, involving the use of clapping and cheering ("Yeah!"). We suspect that this too is an issue of appropriate speech style. It is acceptable to jump up and down to tell 2-year-olds they are on the right track, but not acceptable to do so with any but the most familiar adults or in "fun" settings like charades.

GENERAL ISSUES

We began by asking how to account for "Motherese," be it spoken by mothers or other reasonably competent speakers of the language. To arrive at an answer to this question we considered the function that speech serves in a given setting and performed functional meaning-in-conversation analyses. The choice of utterances that we analyzed was originally motivated by a concern for determining why certain complex and long utterances occur in speech to beginning language learners. Accounts of "Motherese" that focus solely on the syntactic level of analysis have difficulty with the occurrence of such utterances and their variable use with 2-year-olds. Some syntactically based accounts assume that "Motherese" functions to teach the rules of syntax and that it does so by using syntactically simple utterances. We do not take this kind of account of "Motherese" to be entirely wrong; much of the language that is spoken to beginning language learners *is* syntactically simple, and, in general, most utterances are short. Our view that speakers select utterances that a 2-year-old will understand and/or respond to leaves room for the possibility that one way to do this is, in fact, to select syntactically simple utterances. Our main point is that this is not the *only* way to do so. To focus only on the syntax is to ignore other variables that are involved in the construction of "Motherese." We have identified some additional variables, that is, conversational constraints and their relation to the content and style of speech. Surely there are others. In a similar vein, Newport (1975, 1976) discusses a variety of information-processing factors that may influence the form of "Motherese." We suspect that the selection of syntactic form is secondary to such variables, but this view is based more on plausibility than on fact. The ultimate answer to this question must await further investigations on the interaction between a speaker's knowledge of syntax, conversational conventions, and processing constraints (cf. Bever, 1974).

Our approach to "Motherese" required a consideration of the problem of appropriateness. We chose to define speech as appropriate if (*a*) it contained content a 2-year-old might understand and/or respond to, and (*b*) its style conformed to conventional standards. In general, we concluded that the speech of 4-year-olds and mothers was appropriate. But now we ask whether 4-year-olds' speech was as appropriate as mothers'. Both talked about things that seem appropriate, given what we know about 2-year-olds (Shatz, 1975a). However, their speech styles were not quite the same, especially when the setting was structured and required the speakers to talk about toys and demonstrate them. Mothers hinted; 4-year-olds did not. Furthermore, 4-year-olds did not make polite suggestions in the toy task. As reported in Shatz and Gelman (1973), the 4-year-olds made use of bare imperatives (see Protocol B), despite the fact that they mitigated their directions to adults. In short, the style of the 4-year-olds' speech tended to be abrupt and curt. When considered in terms of cultural norms, it was not as appropriate as the style of the mothers' speech. We can think of two reasons that might account for the 4-year-olds' abruptness. One is simply that they have yet to learn some of the sociolinguistic conventions of their language—and surely this is part of the story (cf. Ervin-Tripp, 1976). The other involves a consideration of the task they confronted. The 4-year-olds did not take very kindly to being placed in the structured play situation with 2-year-olds; they would have preferred to play alone with the adult. If we try to take the viewpoint of the 4-year-olds, we might conclude that they communicated as best they could their annoyance at having to include the 2-year-olds in their play. The style served to index to the adults in the room that these children were less than ecstatic about having to interact with 2-year-olds when an interesting adult (the experimenter) was around. From their point of view, then, the style was appropriate for *them* if not for the 2-year-olds.

If such a view is correct, what emerges is still another consideration in the definition of appropriateness: the speaker's perceptions of his own role in the setting. Such perceptions can influence the speaker's own goals in a given conversation. We have already noted the possibility of conflict in the selection of speech style and content for a given conversation. Likewise, the speaker's perceptions of his own role in a given context and the extent to which he reflects his feelings about this role may very well conflict with the need to honor conventions and select appropriate content. In the case of our 4-year-olds, to the extent that they chose to convey their displeasure about talking to 2-year-olds, they made clear their dissatisfaction with the role assigned to them and thereby failed to honor the convention of mitigating status with very young children. All these considerations about the determination of appropriateness point to the complexity of conversational skills. They emphasize that the development of conversational skills involves the acquisition and coordination of a host of capacities, for example, an ability to communicate one's feelings by speaking in certain ways, a knowledge of the linguistic devices that index social conventions, and an understanding of one's listener's capacities.

We close with what may be an obvious point. We have been saying that, in a given context, speech addressed to a 2-year-old is appropriate if, in part, it contains messages the child can understand and/or respond to. We do not for a moment intend to say that beginning language learners necessarily understand the literal meaning of the long and complex utterances we have considered. Indeed, Shatz (1975a, 1975b, 1975c) has suggested that beginning language learners code very little in the way of literal meaning. Remember that we determine the intended meaning of utterances not only on the basis of what was said but also in terms of the context. Context was broadly defined to include ongoing activity, what was said when and by whom. Likewise, the listener's process of interpretation proceeds not only in terms of linguistic understanding but also in combination with readings of context (Bloom, 1974; Shatz, 1975b). In a given context, the general sound of an utterance, along with one or two content words, may suffice to communicate that the speaker expects a certain response. If this is an obvious point, then we have accomplished what we set out to do: to show that "Motherese" comes about as a function of the speaker's intent to convey certain messages in certain ways and according to conversational constraints. A competent communicator will use whatever devices he has available for these purposes, be they syntactic or nonsyntactic.

References

Austin, J. *How to do things with words.* Cambridge, Mass.: Harvard University Press, 1962.

Baldwin, A. L., & Frank, S. M. *Syntactic complexity in mother–child interactions.* Paper presented at the meetings of the Society for Research in Child Development, March 1969.

Bever, T. G. The ascent of the specious: There's a lot we don't know about mirrors. In D. Cohen (Ed.), *Explaining linguistic phenomena.* Washington, D.C.: Hemisphere Publishing Corporation, 1974.

Bloom, L. Talking, understanding and thinking. In R. L. Schiefelbusch & L. L. Lloyd (Eds.), *Language perspectives: Acquisition, retardation and intervention.* University Park, Pa.: University Park Press, 1974.

Broen, P. A. The verbal environment of the language-learning child. *ASHA Monographs*, 1972, No. 17.

Brown, R., & Bellugi, U. Three processes in the child's acquisition of syntax. *Harvard Educational Review,* 1964, **34**, 133–151.

Ervin-Tripp, S. An analysis of the interaction of language, topic and listener. In J. A. Fishman (Ed.), *Readings in the sociology of language.* The Hague: Mouton, 1968. Pp. 191–211.

Ervin-Tripp, S. Wait for me, roller-skate. In Mitchell-Kernan & S. Ervin-Tripp (Eds.), *Child discourse.* New York: Academic Press, 1976.

Gordon, D., & Lakoff, G. Conversational postulates. *In Papers from the Seventh Regional Meeting of the Chicago Linguistic Society.* Chicago: Linguistics Department, University of Chicago, 1971. Pp. 63–84.

Grice, H. P. *The logic of conversation.* Unpublished manuscript, Berkeley, 1957.

Holtzman, M. The use of interrogative forms in the verbal interaction of three mothers and their children. *Journal of Psycholinguistic Research*, 1972, **1**, 311–336.

Katz, J. *Semantic theory.* New York: Harper & Row, 1972.

Labov, W. The study of language in its social context. In W. Labov, *Sociolinguistic patterns.* Philadelphia: University of Pennsylvania Press, 1972.

Labov, W., & Fanshel, D. *Therapeutic discourse.* Manuscript in preparation, University of Pennsylvania.

Lakoff, G. Hedges: A study in meaning criteria and the logic of fuzzy concepts. In *Papers from the Eighth Regional Meeting of the Chicago Linguistic Society.* Chicago: Linguistics Department, University of Chicago, 1972. Pp. 183–228.

Lakoff, R. Language in context. *Language*, 1972, **48**, 907–927.

Lakoff, R. The logic of politeness; or, minding your p's and q's. In *Papers from the Ninth Regional Meeting of the Chicago Linguistic Society.* Chicago: Linguistics Department, University of Chicago, 1973. Pp. 292–305.

Newport, E. L. *Motherese: The speech of mothers to young children.* Unpublished dissertation, University of Pennsylvania, 1975.

Newport, E. L. Motherese: The speech of mother to young children. In N. J. Castellan, D. B. Pisoni, & G. R. Potts (Eds.), *Cognitive theory.* Vol. II. Hillsdale, N. J.: Lawrence Earlbaum Associates, 1976.

Newport, E. L., Gleitman. L. R., & Gleitman, H. Contributions to the theory of innate ideas from learning: A study of mothers' speech and child language acquisition. *Papers and Reports on Child Language Development*, No. 10. Palo Alto, Calif.: Stanford University Press, 1975.

Phillips, J. R. Syntax ad vocabulary of mother's speech to young children: Age and sex comparisons. *Child Development*, 1973, **44**, 182–185.

Piaget, J. *The language and thought of the child.* New York: Harcourt Brace, 1926.

Remick, H. *The material of linguistic development.* Unpublished dissertation, University of California, Davis, 1971.

Sachs, J., & Devin, J. *Young children's knowledge of age: Appropriate speech styles.* Paper read at meeting of the Linguistic Society of America, San Diego, December 1973.

Searle, J. *Speech acts.* Cambridge, England: Cambridge University Press, 1969.

Searle, J. A classification of illocutionary acts. In K. Gunderson (Ed.), *Minnesota studies in the philosophy of science.* Minneapolis: University of Minnesota Press, 1975.

Searle, J. Indirect speech acts. In P. Cole & J. Morgan (Eds.), *Syntax and semantics.* Vol. III. New York: Academic Press (in press).

Shatz, M. *On understanding messages: A study in the comprehension of indirect directives by young children.* Unpublished dissertation, University of Pennsylvania, 1975. (a)

Shatz, M. The comprehension of indirect directives: Can two-year-olds shut the door? *Pragmatics Micofiche*, December 1975. (b)

Shatz, M. How children respond to language: Procedures for answering. *Papers and Reports on Child Language Development,* No. 10. Palo Alto, Calif.: Standford University Press, 1975. (c)

Shatz, M., & Gelman, R. The development of communication skills: Modifications in the speech of young children as a function of listener. *Monographs of the Society for Research in Child Development,* 1973, **38**, 5, 1–37.

Shatz, M., & Gelman, R. Beyond syntax: The influence of conversational constraints on speech modifications. In C. Ferguson & C. Snow (Eds.), *Talking to children: Language input and acquisition.* Cambridge: Cambridge University Press, 1977.

Snow, C. E. Mothers' speech to children learning language. *Child Development,* 1972, **43**, 549–565.

Urmson, J. Parenthetical verbs. In C. E. Caton (Ed.), *Philosophy and ordinary language.* Urbana: University of Illinois Press, 1973. Pp. 220–240.

Vendler, Z. *Res cogitans.* Ithaca, N.Y.: Cornell University Press, 1972.

Weinreich, U. On the semantic structure of language. In J. H. Greenberg (Ed.), *Universals of language.* Cambridge, Mass.: M.I.T. Press, 1963. Pp. 142–216.

CHAPTER 3

The Contingent Query:
A Dependent Act in Conversation[1]

CATHERINE GARVEY
The Johns Hopkins University

INTRODUCTION

From a period of intense concentration on the acquisition of the syntactic and the phonological systems, the study of children's language has expanded rapidly to include the investigation of semantic structures (Clark, 1973) and the development of pragmatic competence (Ervin-Tripp, in press). Several chapters in this volume, especially those of Bates et al., Gelman and Shatz, and Ervin-Tripp and Miller, represent the growing concern with speech as an aspect of social behavior. One construct of linguistic pragmatics, the speech act, has proved particularly attractive to students of language development (e.g., Bates, Camaioni, & Volterra, 1973; Dore, in press), possibly because that construct promises to relate the functional and the formal aspects of language. The construct links the motive force (the communication of social intentions) with the development of a systematic means (the linguistic code) for the expression of meaning.

Studies (Garvey & Hogan, 1973; Keenan, 1974) have shown that preschool children do, indeed, converse (as well as hold forth in "collective monologues," as observed by Piaget, 1955). Pairs of young children can and do engage in connected, coherent discourse, not only in playful encounters, but in more goal-oriented, or reflective, ones as well (Garvey, 1974). An important question to be asked is: If the ontogeny of speech acts can be traced to the beginnings of speech and to its precursors, as Miller (1970) and Bruner (1975) have suggested, how are speech acts related to conversation or discourse? In the absence of a general theoretical framework for the structure of discourse, no comprehensive answers will be forthcoming.

The objective of this chapter is to relate the form and structure of a linguistically encoded social gesture to the flow of conversation and to examine

[1] Research was supported by Research Grant 5–RO1–23883–02 from the National Institutes of Mental Health. Paper was presented at the conference on The Origins of Behavior: Communication and Language, Princeton, New Jersey, October 1975.

this phenomenon as a feature of developing communicative competence. The chapter will describe a modular component of discourse as it occurs in young children's conversations. This modular component will be called a contingent query. It is a small but important building block that serves a vital function in the regulation of verbal interaction. It may also be viewed as a dependent speech act, possibly related to the potentially independent speech act, the request for information.

The chapter will first describe the distribution and structure of the contingent query in discourse and offer an analysis that will organize empirical data from dyads of young conversationalists. The chapter will also describe a technique for elicitation of contingent queries and will suggest what their structure can reveal concerning children's processing of spontaneous speech. Finally, the relation of this discourse component to the structure of speech acts will be discussed.

An example in which there are two well-formed and successful contingent queries will illustrate the phenomenon. (In example 1 the contingent queries and their responses are underlined. The direction of phrase final intonation in the queries is indicated where relevant by a slanting arrow. Utterances, which are numbered, are defined as a stretch of speech by one speaker bounded by the other speaker's speech or by a within-speaker pause exceeding 1 second. The speaker who produces the first query is designated as X, the other speaker as Y.)

1

Y	X
1. This is a nice place.	
	2. What?
3. This is a nice place.	
	4. What's a nice place? $\searrow$
	5. This room? $\nearrow$
6. Yup.	
	7. Oh, yeah.

The first query elicited a repetition, and the second—a complex query—elicited an assent. Furthermore, the final utterance appears to be a response, not to its immediate antecedent, but to the initial assertion plus the information elicited by the queries. The queries seem to be embedded in some other sequence, and different kinds of queries appear to elicit different kinds of replies.

CONTINGENT QUERIES IN THE STRUCTURE OF DISCOURSE

Discourse is not, of course, an undifferentiated stream of utterances. It may be useful to consider the notion that a discourse is composed of illocutionary acts or speech acts (Austin, 1962). Its structure incorporates speech acts, just as, at a lower level, the structure of speech acts incorporates propositional content. Discourse is a higher level of organization than is the speech act. As a higher level, discourse has its own dynamics and regulatory mechanisms. For example, the temporal distribution of speech and pause in the conversations of adults reveals a consistent synchrony (Jaffe & Feldstein, 1970). Similarly, a mother's playful talk to a preverbal infant reveals remarkably consistent patterns of speaking and pausing. Discourse also has its own principles for organization of content and for demarcation of component structures. We can probably no more understand discourse by assuming it to be composed of propositions or sentences (rather than acts) than we can understand speech acts by assuming them to be composed of words (rather than of propositions, clause structures, and illocutionary forces).

The speech act is the basic unit of human communication (Searle, 1969). It will be defined here as a linguistically encoded social gesture by means of which a speaker is able to convey to a hearer a possible message. There has been little empirical work that tests the theories of speech acts (but see Mohan, 1974). Most discussions of speech acts have focused on robust, potentially independent linguistic acts, either institutional ones such as baptizing or christening or vernacular ones such as blaming or promising (Fraser, 1974).

In a study of requests for action (RA), which are potentially independent linguistic acts, Garvey (1975) proposed that speech acts play a role in the structuring of discourse. It was shown in that study that responses to RAs often invoked the same meaning factors (or conditions) that are postulated to underlie such requests. Furthermore, the same factors could be expressed to convey an RA indirectly.

Figure 1 presents a summary of the factors, or conditions, relevant to a request for action. It follows Searle's (1969) analysis but includes some general conditions required to account for data obtained from the spontaneous conversations of young peer dyads. The request for action (RA) illustrated is "Hand me the flashlight."

Figure 1 shows that the belief conditions (section a) postulated for the RA are reflected in indirect variants of the RA (section c). Some typical types of responses are shown in section d. These responses particularly the noncompliant ones, also reflect the belief conditions and the general conditions (section b).

On the basis of this patterning of expressed meanings in a corpus of dyadic speech, Garvey (1975) suggested that these $3\frac{1}{2}$- to $5\frac{1}{2}$-year-old children were cognizant, in some way, of the revelant conditions that underlie the RA in the speech of adults. Inspection of the antecedents and consequences of direct and indirect requests made it possible to postulate a structure for this speech act *as it occurs in discourse*. In discourse it is possible to see the difficulties that often befall speech acts and the ways in which speakers go about clearing up these difficulties.

RA = Request [S, H (H will do A)]: "Hand me the flashlight."

a. Conditions on RA
   1. S wants H to do A.
   2. H is willing to do A.
   3. H is able to do A.
   4. H would not do A in absence of RA.

d. Responses to RA
   ...
   I don't want to.
   I can't.
   I was just going to.

b. Some General Conditions on Speech Acts
   1. S and H are appropriate participants in RA.
   2. The A is reasonable.
   3. H may have conflicting rights or needs.

   Don't you tell me what to do.
   Why should I?
   I got it first.

c. Indirect RA
   1. I need that flashlight, too.
   2. Can you give me that flashlight, Buddy?
   3. Want to hand me that flashlight?

FIGURE 1. Factors in performing a request for action. (*a*) Conditions or beliefs enabling the RA; (*b*) some general conditions on speech acts; (*c*) examples of indirect RAs; (*d*) sample responses to RAs reflecting the conditions. (S = speaker; H = addressee; A = the specific act requested; RA = request for action.)

Figure 2 illustrates the structure of the RA in discourse. This scheme suggests that there are optional as well as obligatory components of a speech act in discourse and that the components occur in more or less fixed order. This scheme gives a picture of a speech act as a sort of accordion, an object that can be expanded or contracted as necessary—and, to pursue this analogy, one that can be played with.

Figure 2 shows the request by the speaker (S) and acknowledgment by the addressee (H), which can be verbal or nonverbal, as the minimum obligatory components of a well-formed RA sequence. The other optional components enter the sequence under different discourse conditions and contribute to the success of the RA in different ways. For example, S might prepare the stage for his request, "Hand me the flashlight," by asking, "Do you see that tool belt over there?" When H indicates that he does, S can go on to produce the request proper.

The following discussion will employ two terms that deal with the effects of speech acts. The intended illocutionary effect (IIE) of a successful RA is that the addressee recognizes that the speaker intended to issue an RA. The intended perlocutionary effect (IPE) is that the addressee is moved to comply with the RA. Thus, to continue the example in Figure 1, the IIE is that the addressee understands the illocutionary act, that is, understands that "Can you give me that flashlight?" is intended to count as an RA. The IPE is that the addressee performs the act requested by the RA, that is, gives the speaker the flashlight. Nothing in the speech act itself requires the addressee to also say, "Sure, here," as he performs the act of giving S the flashlight. An RA does not request a verbal acknowledgement, it seeks only a compliant act. It is some other type of rule, one that comes from the book of discourse etiquette, that leads the addressee to respond verbally as well as to perform the desired act.

S and H	(Ia)	Preparation of propositional content
S	(Ib)	Adjunct to request
S	II	Request
H and S	(III)	Clarification = contingency query
H	IV	Acknowledgment of II

....

....

| S | (V) | Acknowledgement of IV |

FIGURE 2. Structural domain of request. (S = speaker, H = addressee. Optional elements are enclosed in parentheses. Dotted lines indicate potential location of repeated request if IV is other than compliant acknowledgment.)

Some speech acts such as assertions (e.g., "That fellow is my brother") require no *overt* response from the addressee, although their IPE may be something like "Addressee believes that what was asserted is the case." In discourse, however, it is evident that many assertions are followed by some sort of acknowledgment. The speech act that is a request for information (RI) (e.g., "Is that fellow your brother?") does require an overt response. It has the IPE of moving the addressee to satisfy the request for information, generally, but not always, by constructing some linguistic instrument—one that is called an answer. The contingent query is also that kind of speech act. It requests a verbal response. We can say that the IIE of a contingent query is that the addressee understands that the speaker has made a request for information of some sort, and that the IPE is that the addressee attempts to comply with the particular request.

One optional component represented in Figure 2 was designated as clarification (III). It is also a contingent query, contingent in the sense that it occurs in the domain of another speech act. It is a component to which both participants contribute. If it occurs, it is initiated by the recipient of the dominating speech act—in Figure 2, the RA. The issuer of the dominating speech act then responds to the contingent query. After this minor diversion, the RA, which remains in effect, receives its acknowledgment. The interesting thing about this sort of "side sequence," as it has been called by Jefferson (1972), is that it does not affect the turn-at-speaking. By issuing a contingent query the addressee does not take the floor and the speaker does not lose the floor. As soon as the contingent query has accomplished its IPE, the turn-at-speaking goes to the person who would have had it *if* the contingent query sequence had not occurred. Apparently, the obligation imposed in the discourse by the dominant speech act remains in effect. The addressee of the dominant act, whether it is an RA, an assertion, or even an independent RI, goes on to acknowledge in some way the act originally addressed to him, if such acknowledgment is appropriate, and if it is not, the original speaker continues.

Figure 3 illustrates contingent queries (CQ) embedded in dominant speech acts, RAs on the left, assertions on the right. The examples are taken from conversations of preschool children. The speaker who produces the query is designated as X. The speaker responsible for the initial utterance on which the query follows is designated as Y. In each example, the first utterance is the dominant act, and the final utterance or nonverbal act is one that would be appropriately responsive to that dominant act if the CQ had not occurred.

a. RA Sequences

Y: Would you get that thing?
    [points at stool]
X: Which?↘
Y: The one with the glass on it.
X: All right. [fetches stool]

Y: Why don't you try this on, okay?
    [holds up hat]
X: What?↗
Y: Try this on.
X: [puts on the hat]

b. Assertion Sequences

Y: This is a nice place.

X: What's a nice place?↘ This room?↗
Y: Yup.
X: Oh, yeah.

Y: Maybe it's going right through
    microphone.
X: What?↘
Y: Our talking.
X: Yeah.

FIGURE 3. Examples of (*a*) RA sequences and (*b*) assertion sequences. (Embedded CQ components are underlined. X and Y indicate the two speakers. Nonverbal actions are in brackets.)

Figure 3 illustrates that in discourse not all speech acts are created equal. A certain act may dominate a sequence, creating a domain of structure and meaning. Other acts may be embedded as subordinate, or contingent, acts. Turns-at-speaking seem to be distributed, in part at least, according to the speech act roles set up by the dominant and subordinate acts, roles such as requester and questioner. The embedded CQ module is truly embedded in the sense that, if it were removed, the dominant act and the response would remain intact and well formed.

TYPES OF CONTINGENT QUERIES

There are two principal types of contingent queries: solicited and unsolicited. A solicited contingent query follows on a speech act that has as its IPE just the elicitation of the query. An unsolicited contingent query follows on a speech act that has some intended effect other than the elicitation of the query. Both types may be considered as three-step sequences composed of some utterance. M0, which is the occasion for the query. Utterance M0 is followed by M1, the query proper, which is followed in turn by M2, the response to the query. In the case of unsolicited contingent queries, which will be examined first, M0 can be anything, that is, any sentence or act type. Query M1 is of several different types. Response M2 represents the IPE of M1, and its form is largely determined by M1. But what are the relations that hold among these three steps? Figure 4 presents an outline of the relations that obtain between the components of the sequence.

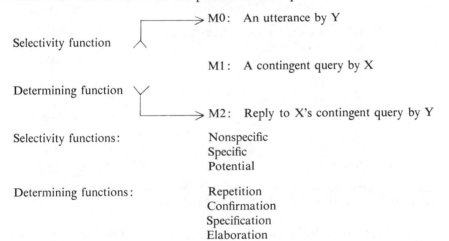

FIGURE 4. Structure of a contingent query sequence.

The query proper, M1, can be said to exercise a *selectivity* function in respect to M0. That selectivity function is nonspecific, specific, or potential in respect to the content of M0. The query proper, M1, exercises a *determining* function in respect to M2; it requests a particular type of M2. The kinds of determining function exercised by M1 on M2 are requests for repetition, for confirmation, for specification, and for elaboration. Figure 4 presents the structure of the sequence with the selectivity and determining functions of M1. It is the form in which M1 is encoded that selects the particular content of the query and determines the manner in which it will be responded to in a well-formed sequence. There may be still other determining functions exercised by M1, but, if so, they cannot be examined in this chapter.

	Code				*Function*
1.		M0:	Joe Glick knows a friend of yours.	S:	Nonspecific
	NRR	M1:	What? ↗	= E	
		M2:	Joe Glick knows a friend of yours.	D:	Repetition
2.		M0:	Joe Glick knows a friend of yours.	S:	Specific
	SRR	M1:	A what? ↗	= E	
		M2:	A friend of yours.	D:	Repetition
3.		M0:	Joe Glick knows a friend of yours.	S:	Specific
	SRR	M1:	Who? ↗	− E	
		M2:	Joe Glick.	D:	Repetition
4.		M0:	Joe Glick knows a friend of yours.	S:	Specific
	SRC	M1:	A friend of mine? ↗ *or* He does? ↗	= E	
		M2:	Yes.	D:	Confirmation
5.		M0:	Joe Glick knows a friend of yours.	S:	Specific
	SRS	M1:	Who? ↘ *or* Which one? ↘	= E	
		M2:	That Greek fellow.	D:	Specification
6.		M0:	I hear a noise.	S:	Potential
	PRE	M1:	Where? ↘	= E	
		M2:	Outside.	D:	Elaboration
7.		M0:	I hear a noise.	S:	Potential
	PRC	M1:	Where? ↘ Outside? ↗	= E	
		M2:	Yes.	D:	Confirmation

FIGURE 5. Several common types of unsolicited contingent queries. (S = selectivity function; E = encoding of M1; D = determining function.)

Some examples will illustrate the operation of these functions and show how M1 is variously encoded. A constructed example will be used to point out the subtle differences and the similarities among contingent queries. Figure 5 shows constructed examples of unsolicited contingent queries. The part of M0 that M1 selects is underlined in the figure.

The two major functions are, to some extent, independent. In examples 1 and 2 of Figure 5, the selectivity functions are nonspecific and specific, respectively. However, the determining function (repetition) is the same. Examples 2 and 3 show the same selectivity function (specific) and the same determining function (repetition); however, the encoding of M1 further selects precisely the segmental component which is being queried. Both examples 3 and 4 have the same selectivity function (specific), but the determining function differs. The query in example 3 requests a repetition, but in example 4 the query requests confirmation, that is, a "yes"/"no" reply or its equivalent. The selectivity function label on example 5 is, indeed, specific, but the encoding of M1 indicates that the specific segment selected for the query is not adequately specified. Comparison of examples 3 and 5 illustrates the critical role that intonation can play in the contingent query sequence. Depending on whether the final intonation of the query "Who?" rises or falls, a request for repetition or specification, respectively, is communicated.

Examples 6 and 7 illustrate rather interesting types of contingent queries. Although no data will be presented here on these types, a few speculations are in order. The potential selectivity type identifies some element that is missing from the surface form of M0. But what it selects is potentially available. Where, then, does it come from? There are several possible sources. One source is the potential case arguments of a verb, those that are possible but may not be expressed in a given utterance. For example, if the verb *give* has the potential arguments agent, object, and beneficiary, and only agent and object are expressed in M0, then a contingent query may select the potential argument of beneficiary, for example, Y: "I'm giving a birthday present." X: "To whom?" This is material that Leech (1974) has called "null arguments."

Another source of potential contingent query is the material that Chafe (1972) has suggested is relevant to many verbs, that is, the cause, accompaniments, and results of an event denoted by the verb. For example, if Y says, "My neighbor's house burned down." X can reasonably ask, "What caused the fire?" *or* "Did you see the flames?" Either query would be interpreted as intelligible, even though the topic "fire" or "flames" had not been expressed as definite in M0.

Another source for contingent queries is, of course, the underlying condition structure of speech acts. Thus one necessary condition on the performance of an RA is that the speaker wants the addressee to carry out the act specified (see Figure 1). A contingent query of the potential selectivity type could select that condition, for example, Y: "Tell me what he said." X: "Do you really want me to?" The condition is not explicit in M0 but is pragmatically presupposed by the M0 act type.

Still another source of "potential" material is attributable to the mode of the discourse. Young children often question whether their partners are speaking in a play (pretend) or nonplay mode. Verification of the mode of a partner's action is obviously important in deciding what kind of response is expected and should be forthcoming. For example, a 4-year-old speaker, picking up a toy telephone, said to his playmate, "I'm going to call my daddy." The playmate queried, "Are you really?" The first speaker replied, "No, just pretend."

Determination of the various sources of potential material selectable by a contingent query would, obviously, advance our knowledge of what constitutes a relevant reply. This chapter must be restricted, however, to the simpler types of contingent queries.

Comparison of M2 and M0 will, in most cases, reveal how well the addressee of the contingent query has responded to it. When M1 is a request for repetition, the expected reply is a repetition of part or all of M0, plus or minus optional elaboration. However, M2 may be a paraphrase rather than a verbatim repetition. When M1 is a request for specification, the expected reply provides a more precise version of the queried segment. The content of M2 is often, in this case, material that could be incorporated into the form of the M0 in apposition to the segment selected as underspecified; for example,

M0: I know a friend of yours.
M1: Who? ↘
M2: That Greek fellow.

could form the utterance "I know a friend of yours, that Greek fellow." When M1 encodes a request for elaboration, M2 could be added to M0 to form a more complex utterance, for example,

M0: I hear a noise.
M1: Where ↘
M2: Outside.

could form the utterance "I hear a noise outside" *or* "I hear a noise, and I think it is outside."

One further phenomenon in Figure 5 should be noted. In example 7, M1 is made up of two queries. The first alone would determine a request for elaboration, but the second determines a request for confirmation. In all the cases observed of such complex queries, the request for confirmation comes second and appears to override any first query of a different determining type. Thus the M2 furnished in such cases is always equivalent to a "yes"/ "no" reply.

CONTINGENT QUERIES IN A CORPUS OF CHILDREN'S SPEECH

Examples from a corpus of spontaneous conversations between same-age dyads of nursery school children will illustrate contingent queries in use and will indicate how the queries were assigned to the code types listed in Figure 5. In example 2 one girl pointed out to another a stuffed parrot hanging in the center of the playroom.

2

Y	X
1. Look it. We found a parrot in our house.	
	2. A what? ↗
3. A parrot.	
4. A bird.	
	5. Wow!

The first utterance in example 2 is the M0, which is an assertion preceded by an attention-getting device, "Look it." The query is a specific request for repetition. It receives the expected response and, after a pause of slightly more than 1 second, a further response. The final comment, "Wow!" is an appropriate discoursal acknowledgment of the now-clarified initial utterance.

In example 3 two girls were conversing. At utterance 6, one pointed out a shiny metallic surface on the wall, near the ceiling.

3a

Y	X
1. Then you're not scared.	
2. If you're not a scaredy-cat.	
	3. Scaredy-cat? ↗
4. Uh-huh.	
	5. Well I'm scared because I don't see my teacher (short pause).

3b

X	Y
	6. Look at that little mirror up there.
7. Where? ↘	
	8. Up there. [pointing]
9. Where? ↘	
	10. Up up. [pointing]
11. Where? ↘	
	12. Do you see it over there in that corner? [pointing]
13. No. Oh.	

The contingent query in example 3a is a specific request for confirmation. It predictably reecived a "yes"/"no" response. In example 3b the three queries (utterances 7, 9, and 11) are specific requests for specification. The first two received some specification in that the child added pointing to her verbal reply, but the third received a fuller verbal specification (plus more pointing) in the form of a still further embedded query (which we do not analyze here). The final "Oh" acknowledged X's understanding as she saw the little mirror.

Example 4 was taken from a role enactment episode. "Father," a 4-year-old boy, was preparing to drive away on a wooden car, and "Mother," a girl, wanted to come along and bring the (imaginary) baby.

4

Y	X
1. Father, can I come?	
	2. What ↗
3. Can I come?	
	4. What ↗
5. Can I come?	
	6. Call? ↗
7. Come.	
	8. Yes.
9. I have to watch the baby.	

Example 4 shows two nonspecific requests for repetition (utterances 2 and 4) which did receive the expected repetitions. The third contingent query (utterance 6) is a specific request for confirmation. Since it was erroneous, it was met with a "no" reply in the form of a correction. That correction was produced with emphatic stress and exaggeratedly clear pronunciation. (The final consonant was released.) Utterance 8 was a response to the request for permission that was first issued in utterance 1. Thus this multiple contingent query sequence is embedded within the speech act pair consisting of request for permission–granting of permission.

Example 5 (identical with example 1) was excerpted from a boy's and girl's discussion of the playroom.

5

Y	X
1. This is a nice place.	
	2. What? ↗
3. This is a nice place.	
	4. What's a nice place? ↘
	5. This room? ↗
6. Yup.	
	7. Oh, yeah.

Utterance 2 is a nonspecific request for repetition which was correctly satisfied in utterance 3. Utterances 4 and 5 are, respectively, a specific request for specification (SRS) and a specific request for confirmation (SRC). Here the SRS failed to elicit a reply and was followed after a pause slightly greater than 1 second by the SRC. The reply was one appropriate to the SRC. Again, as in example 4, once the contingent query sequence was completed, the addressee of the initial act in whose domain the contingent query occurred replied to the now-clarified assertion, which may be represented as "This room is a nice place." Thus this example, like examples 2 through 4, shows embedding.

It is tempting to recruit one more character to the cast of hypothetical beings that people the social sciences. The ideal speaker–listener, whose grammatical competence has been exhaustively examined by practitioners of generative transformational linguistics, is the most familiar. A standard receiver who interprets utterances in a straightforward way has been proposed by Mackay (1969). There is also a rational actor who makes reasonable decisions on the basis of relevant information. We now propose an ideal cooperative conversationalist. He would be the perfectly responsive conversational partner. He might not fully observe the maxims that follow on Grice's (1967) cooperative principle, and he might not even be entirely rational, but he would unfailingly respond with relevant acts to his partner's acts, whether they were playful or serious. One more example will show that two $3\frac{1}{2}$-year-olds came close to realizing the ideal cooperative conversationalists. This dyad may hold the record for multiple embedded contingent queries. It was not until utterance 17 that Y's patience was exhausted. That last M2 was almost screamed.

6

Y	X
1. Going to camp.	
	2. What? ↗
3. Going to camp.	
	4. What? ↗
5. Going to camp.	
	6. What? ↗
7. Going to camp.	
	8. Can? ↗
9. Camp.	
	10. Campin'? ↗
11. Campin'.	
	12. Campin'? ↗
13. Yes.	

14. What? ↗

15. <u>Go to campin'.</u>

16. <u>You go campin'?</u> ↗

17. <u>Yes!</u>

18. Oh.

RESULTS FROM OBSERVATIONAL DATA

We were interested in seeing how same-age dyads of nursery school children whose free-play sessions we had previously videotaped used contingent queries and responded to them. The youngest dyads ranged in age from 34 to 39 months, the young dyads from 42 to 52 months, and the older dyads from 55 to 67 months. There were 12 children in the first two groups, and 24 in the group of older dyads. All pairs were previously acquainted, and each group contained both same and mixed-sex dyads. Each videotaped session lasted about 15 minutes. Details of the observation and transcription procedures have been reported elsewhere (Garvey, 1974).

The recordings were examined to identify and code nonspecific and specific requests for repetition, specific requests for confirmation, and specific requests for specification. The analysis did not include potential selectivity types. Responses to contingent queries were coded as expected-predicted replies (ER) if they conformed to the model presented above. Other replies that appeared to be responsive to the query but employed, for example, paraphrase rather than repetition as a response to a request for repetition were coded as other relevant responses (OR). No response or some utterance that did not recognize the query as such was coded as no response (NR). Two coders worked independently, and judgments on direction of intonation and on code categories of M1 and M2 were virtually unanimous. The results for the nonspecific requests for repetition for the three age groupings of dyads are presented in Table 1. The expected response for this type is a complete or partial repetition, plus or minus elaboration.

Table 1 includes three cases of "What?" and two cases of "Huh?" with level rather than rising intonation. Four of the five cases elicited repetition responses, and one received no response. Thus it was assumed that level intonation, though rare in a request for repetition, is a variant of rising intonation and contrasts with falling intonation. Excluded from the table were three cases of "Huh?" ↘ with falling intonation, since all were produced by the youngest dyads. Two of the excluded cases elicited a repetition; the third, no response. Table 1 indicates that "What?" ↗ is the preferred variant for the nonspecific request for repetition for young and older dyads, though the youngest dyads use "Huh?" ↗ more often. The table also indicates that these queries were met with the expected response in 66% of

TABLE 1. Nonspecific Requests for Repetition Produced by Youngest, Young, and Older Dyads and the Response Types

Group	Request Type M1	Response Type: M2				Subtotal M1
		ER	OR	NR		
Youngest (N = 12)	What?↗	10	1	3	=	14
		13	0	13		26
	Huh?↗	—	–	—	=	—
		23	1	16		40
Young (N = 12)	What?↗	28	8	2	=	38
		12	6	4		22
	Huh?↗	—	—	–	=	—
		40	14	6		60
Older (N = 24)	What?↗	41	15	2	=	58
		25	10	3		38
	Huh?↗	—	—	–	=	—
		66	25	5		96
Total M2:		129	40	(27)		196

their occurrences and that 20% met with some other relevant reply. Only 14% failed to elicit a reply to the M1. The highest percentage of ineffective queries occurred among the youngest dyads. They failed to respond to 40% of the queries.

Table 2 presents the results for the rather infrequent specific request for repetition and for the specific requests for confirmation and for specification for the three groups of dyads. Together, the three types met with expected responses in 74% of their occurrences, 6% received some other relevant response, and 20% failed to elicit a reply. All groups had about the same percentage of no response.

It is worth mentioning that nonsense responses were not observed; for example, no cases occurred in which requests for repetition or for specification were met with a "yes"/"no" reply. The low incidence of other relevant responses suggests that the determining function of these queries is fairly efficient.

The data indicate that children do issue and respond appropriately to a

TABLE 2. Specific Requests for Repetition, Requests for Confirmation, and Requests for Specification Produced by Youngest, Younger, and Older Dyads with Response Types

Group	Request Type M1	Response Type: M2				Subtotal M1
		ER	OR	NR		
Youngest	SRR	2	0	2	=	4
(N = 12)	SRC	25	0	5	=	30
	SRS	10	1	3	=	14
		—	—	—		—
		37	1	10		48
Young	SRR	2	0	0	=	2
(N = 12)	SRC	29	2	8	=	39
	SRS	12	0	2	=	14
		—	—	—		—
		43	2	10		55
Older	SRR	3	0	1	=	4
(N = 24)	SRC	20	2	8	=	30
	SRS	26	6	5	=	37
		—	—	—		—
		49	8	14		71
Total M2:		129	11	(34)	=	174

number of rather subtly different contingent queries, some differentiated in the M1 element *solely by direction of final intonation.*

These unsolicited contingent queries appear to serve the function of discourse regulation. Although speaker Y has perhaps failed to premonitor his speech for X and has thus produced a less than completely intelligible or less than adequately specifying utterance, he appears willing to correct the failure when requested to do so. And although X may not have been attending carefully to Y's initial utterance, his query indicates that he *is* attending to Y and sometimes carefully enough to specify exactly what segment he failed to hear or comprehend. The cooperative conversationalist needs to understand at least as much of his partner's contribution as he requires to formulate an appropriate response. Within a discourse that appropriate response may be an obligatory second member of an act pair such as an answer to a request for information; it may be a discourse-appropriate behavior, such as an acknowledgment of an assertion (e.g., "I like it here." "So do I") or merely a signal of attentive or receptive participation, such as "uh-huh" or a head nod. The unsolicited contingent query is a major technique which a cooperative conversationalist can use to acquire what he needs in order to respond. This argument should not be taken to imply that "discourse regulation" is itself a simple function or that the flow of factual information is the only aspect of exchange that is subject to participant monitoring and adjustment.

Relatively few published reports on language acquisition have provided examples of speech in context. In most cases the linguistic forms of interest are discussed as isolated or independent utterances. The few available examples of spontaneous conversation support the notion that the contingent query sequence is an important part of child–caretaker conversations. Examples given by Miller and Ervin-Tripp (1964) show that at 27 months Harlan was an experienced processor of contingent queries:[2]

7. HARLAN: I go boom boom.
   ADULT: What'd you go? (SRR)
   HARLAN: I went boom.

8. HARLAN: Want d'you policeman?
   ADULT: Hm? (NRR)
   HARLAN: Want . . . want d'you policeman?

Lewis (1936) provides an example of what appear to be negative and affirmative responses to specific requests for confirmation by a child of 24 months:

9. CHILD: /mouka/
   ADULT: Motor-car? (SRC)
   CHILD: No.
   ADULT: Moo cow? (SRC)
   CHILD: /muka/

Transcripts of Roger Brown's Adam at 26 months are literally peppered with such queries, most of them issued by the mother but some by Adam himself, for example:

10. ADAM: Radio.
    MOTHER: No, that's a tape recorder.
    ADAM: Tape corder? (SRC)
    MOTHER: Yes, tape recorder.

[2] The intonation contour of the queries in examples 7 to 10 was not provided; thus it is assumed that the intonation conformed to that predicted by the proposed model (see Figure 5).

The usefulness of this technique to the language learner is twofold. On the one hand, a contingent query from an adult provides the child with immediate feedback on the intelligibility or acceptability of his last utterance. On the other hand, he himself can employ the query to check his understanding of all or part of the adult's message, as Adam did in example 10.

The data presented in Tables 1 and 2 account for almost all the unsolicited contingent queries in the corpus, with the exception, as noted, of the numerous potential requests for elaboration or confirmation. There is, however, another type that is relatively rare but interesting. It is illustrated in example 11.

11.

Y	X
1. Somebody just buyed this.	
	2. Somebody just $\searrow$ buyed $\nearrow$ this? $\searrow$
3. Yes.	

In this type the M1 selects all or part of the M0, marking the selected segment with a (optional) falling and then rising–falling intonation. The M2 type determined by this query is a "yes"/"no" response or its equivalent; thus the type resembles a request for confirmation. It is, however, obviously marked for some special meaning, which in adult speech is one of surprise or incredulity. The corpus does not provide enough instances to permit classification of these tokens as either a separate type of query or as an affectively marked variant of a request for confirmation. It does show intonation characteristics which are associated with certain *solicited* contingent queries. This type can now be examined.

SOLICITED CONTINGENT QUERIES

The unsolicited contingent query is a fairly powerful device. In this corpus it accomplished its IPE about 80 to 85% of the time. The unsolicited contingent query serves the needs of one speaker in regulating the stream of conversation. That speaker is the addressee of a speech act in the domain of which the contingent query occurs.

The speaker who is executing or is about to execute a major speech act (the one designated here as Y) can use the structure of the contingent query to ensure the success of his act; that is, he can produce an utterance whose IPE is *just* the elicitation of a contingent query. A contingent query that has been intentionally evoked will be called a *solicited* contingent query.

Three kinds of solicited queries will be mentioned here; each can be analyzed according to the proposed three-step model. In two kinds, the query (M1) is identical in encoding form to the "What?"$\searrow$ variant of the specific request for specification. These are the summons-answer routine (originally described by Schegloff, 1968) and the rhetorical gambit. Both were examined previously in a subset of the present corpus (Garvey & Hogan, 1973). In both types Y produces an utterance (M0) that is calculated to elicit a contingent query. In effect, Y has maneuvered X into asking him just what he wanted to say anyway. Example 12 is from a role enactment episode.

12.

Y	X
1. Wife? ↗	
	2. What? ↘
2. I think I better go out for a place	
where I can find something good that we'll	
need—so bye.	

Example 12 represents a typical summons-answer sequence. The M0 is simple: "Wife?" ↗. The solicited contingent query is identical in all segmental and prosodic respects to an encoding of the specific request for specification, that is, "What?" ↘. The M2 is indeed a specification of what Y had wanted to say. It is, presumably, the reason he uttered the summons in the first place.

Example 13 shows a slightly different kind of solicited query.

13.

Y	X
1. What are you, a policeman?	
	2. I'm a fireman and a police. Do you
	know what I want to be when I grow up?
3. What? ↘	
	4. I wanna be a fireman.
5. Oh.	

Example 13 illustrates a typical rhetorical gambit, which is often realized with the phrases, "You know what?" "Guess what?" or "I'll tell you what." Here the M0 is, "Do you know what I want to be when I grow up?" The cooperative conversationalist did not answer the utterance with "No" ↘, as he might have if he had taken it to be a request for information. Rather, the M1 is "What?" ↘, which enables Y to proceed with the assertion of M2, which he had evidently wanted to say anyway. The solicited query, however, has set the stage for his assertion, and he can proceed with more confidence that he has his partner's attention.

A third type of solicited query, the appreciation sequence, is illustrated in example 14. Here the M0 is an utterance that Y sets forth as "funny." Four-year-olds take great delight in breaking language rules and conventions. A shift or distortion of normal sound-meaning correspondence can be funny. Here the funny material is ridiculous proper names.

14.

Y	X
1. Mommy, mommy, I got new friends called dool, sol, ta.	
	2. Dool, sue and ↘ta?↗↘
(both laugh)	
3. <u>Those are funny names aren't they?</u>	
	4. No, it's Poopoo, Daigi and Dia . . . Diarrhea.
(both laugh)	

15a.

Y	X
1. You're you—you want to know your nickname?	
	2. <u>What?</u>↘
3. <u>Lisa.</u>	

15b.

Y	X
	4. No, Melissa.
↘ ↗ ↘ 5. <u>Melissa?</u>	
	6. <u>Yeah. Melissa.</u>
7. Well, Lisa, Melissa. Well, Lisa, teacher calls you Lisa.	

The solicited M1 in example 14 repeated the specific segment and marked it with falling-rising-falling intonation. After the query Y and X laugh together. Then the M2 (utterance 3) affirms the M0 assertion as an intended joke, and the playful conversation continues.

The marked intonation of this solicited contingent query is virtually identical to the surprise or incredulity marker mentioned above as a rare variant of the request for confirmation. It is clear that in occasional cases it is difficult to decide whether or not an M0 preceding an M1 having this intonation was directed toward this effect, that is, was solicited or unsolicited. Example 15b appears to contrast with example 14. (Example 15a, which immediately preceded 15b in the corpus, contains a solicited query in a rhetorical gambit sequence.)

Utterance 5 of example 15b appears to be an *unsolicited* request for confirmation, and it does, indeed, receive a confirmation. It is marked, however, by the falling-rising-falling intonation contour employed in the solicited query in utterance 2 of example 14. At this time we can only propose that this particular intonation, when combined with repetition of a segment of the preceding utterance, has special affective value.

ELICITATION OF CONTINGENT QUERIES

The 48 children observed seemed both willing and able to use these modular components to serve, in part at least, the objectives of discourse regulation and maintenance. Furthermore, the components were formed and used according to adult rules. A limited test of the model in an experiment with adult subjects has confirmed the predictions from the model that were examined (BenDebba & Garvey, manuscript). Many conversations in the corpus, though using contingent queries normally, differed in other respects from adult discourse. The modular components examined here, however, performed quite effectively and in a normal fashion.

If the rules that structure these components are well learned, and if the structure proposed here is correct, then it should be possible to elicit contingent queries in a more systematic way. In a pilot study, still in progress, we have succeeded in eliciting minimally different types of contingent queries from a different sample of children ranging in age from 38 to 49 months. These children were from nursery schools and were exploring the laboratory playroom for the first time in preparation for dyadic play sessions in another study. Each child entered the playroom with an adult male whom he or she had met at least once before. The "elicitor" was instructed to put four types of contingent queries to the child, as appropriate. First, he was to use the nonspecific request for repetition ("What?" ↗), which may be inserted after virtually any utterance. Second, he was to use the specific request for repetition where appropriate. For example, following an utterance with a proper name, he might ask, "Who?" ↗.[3] Third, he was to use the request for confirmation after informative utterances, where it seemed natural. For example, after a child's assertion "I'm 4 today," he might ask, "You are?" ↗. Finally, he was to listen very carefully for utterances that contained an underspecified element which he could query with a request for specification (e.g., Child: "I see something in the corner." Adult: "What?" ↘) or a request for elaboration (e.g., Child: "I'm going to Robby's house." Adult: "When?" ↘). At the

---

[3] Any major component of an M0 can be selected for repetition. For example, the utterance "My brother gave me a birthday present" can be queried as follows: "Who?" ↗, "Did what?" ↗, "Gave who a present?" ↗, "Gave you what?" ↗, or "A what?" ↗".

same time he was to conduct a normal adult-child conversation, showing the child the toys and responding to any conversational topic the child might introduce.

The results were interesting in a number of ways. First, it was observed that an adult who is being responsive to a child almost automatically queries many of the child's utterances. Berko Gleason (1973) has also noted this behavior in adult speech to children. Thus, even as the elicitor grew more skilled, he produced a great number of requests for confirmation that were probably involuntary. Second, we found, not entirely by accident, that a sympathetic and playful elicitor can engineer ritual play sequences with a child if he uses familiar patterns. The repetitive verbal play sequence built on assertion–counterassertion, which is a favourite with peer dyads (Garvey, 1974), could be set up and maintained in the adult–child dyad. Third, we found that not only could responses to contingent queries be elicited from the child, but also an M1 could be elicited by addressing to the child an unintelligible segment in an otherwise intelligible and interesting utterance. One example of adult elicitation will suffice:

	Child	Adult
16.	I have a bean bag dolly but not that color. I have a all different color one.	
		What? ↗ (NRR)
	I don't have that color of a bean bag doll.	
		You don't? ↗ (SRC)
	No, not that color.	
		What color? ↘ (SRS)
	A different color.	
		What different color? ↘ (SRS)
	All those different colors.	
		Oh, I see.
	I don't have a black . . . I'm stupid. I wish I had a black one.	
		A what? ↗ (SRR)
	A black bean bag doll.	

We found also that all types could be responded to appropriately, but that occasionally a child would respond to the segmental form of the query, apparently ignoring the important intonational cue. Such inappropriate replies were more common to an adult questioner than to a peer. This result needs further investigation.

SOME RESEARCH USES OF CONTINGENT QUERIES

Well-formed contingent query sequences produce two utterances from the same child, M0 and M2. The relation between these utterances is one of repetition, confirmation, specification, or elaboration, depending on the determining function of M1. Comparison of M0 and M2 can thus provide a natural set of data that reflects the child's ability to segment surface strings (i.e., to produce partial repetitions) and to substitute functionally, semantically, or formally equivalent phrases (i.e., to produce different kinds of paraphrase). Such a comparison can also reveal a child's ability to isolate propositions from the act and discourse features that transform the propositional content into situated, interactive speech behavior. It may be useful, then, to indicate briefly some of the relationships that are revealed by a comparison of M0 and M2.

First, on the phonological level, M2 is generally marked prosodically or paralinguistically as a *repeated* utterance. One or more of the following features generally co-occur with M2 and are quite salient when M2 is compared with M0:

1. Reduction in tempo, often with clear separation of syllables.
2. Increase in precision of articulation, for example, release of final consonants.
3. Increase in volume.
4. Widening of pitch range.
5. Use of contrastive stress on some portion of the selected segment.

Second, on the clause level, M2 often displays either a reduction or an expansion of M0. The reductions involve omission of a connective, a response constant, a tag, a vocative term, an attention-getting device, or the topic (as opposed to the comment). With the exception of the topic, perhaps, all these elements are peripheral to the propositional content of M0 and serve various kinds of discourse functions. Below are examples in which the utterance including the bracketed material is the M0. The M2 is a partial repetition that omitted the bracketed material. In all these examples the M1 was a nonspecific request for repetition, that is, "What?" ↗ or "Huh?" ↗.

Segment Omitted
17.   Connective: [On account of] I don't like these trains of the world.
      Response constant: [No. no] I won't take my fish.
      Response constant and tag: [Oh, well] We'll stay little [right?]

Vocative: [Father] Can I come?
Attention-getting device: [Hey] Where's the iron?
Topic: [This] Don't turn on.

These representative cases clearly indicate a tendency to omit material from M2 that serves to tie M0 to its conversational context and to offer instead repetition of essential propositional content. It can also be noted that, if M0 was composed of several clauses, generally only the last clause was subject to repetition, for example:

Segment Omitted
18.   Nonfinal clause:
    M0: It's not stupid. Know why? The other one's stupid.
    M1: What? ↗ (NRR)
    M2: The other one's stupid.

In other cases M2 represented an extension of M0, usually in the form of further relevant material. Example 19 provides two cases of extension of propositional content; the first is embedded and suffixed to the M0 form, and the second is only suffixed to the M0 form. (Added material is underlined in examples 19 and 20.)

19.   M0: All the noise is going in.
    M1: What? ↗ (NRR)
    M2: All the noise that we're making is going in the microphone.

20.   M0: Call the police, ok?
    M1: What ↗ (NRR)
    M2: Call the police to get that snake.

In example 20 the tag M0 ("OK") is omitted from M2, and the propositional content is expanded to add a result clause (i.e., "to get that snake") to the original imperative utterance of M0.

Third, on the speech act level of analysis, comparison between M0 and M2 may provide evidence of the relation between variants of speech acts and of the kinds of paraphrase relations that may obtain among speech acts in discourse. These types of M0–M2 relations require cautious interpretation, and only a few possibilities can be suggested here.

M0 and M2 may represent direct and indirect variants of a given speech act type, for example:

21.   M0: Why don't you try this on, OK? (Indirect RA)

M1: What? ↗ (NRR)
M2: Try this on. (Direct RA)

Or M2 may repeat M0 and add explicit marking of its act type, for example:

22. M0: I'm under here. (Assertion)
M1: What? ↗ (NRR)
M2: I said, I'm under here. (Report of assertion)

Finally, M2 may represent what might be called a different but related act type, for example:

23. M0: Let's open this. (Suggestion for joint action)
M1: What? ↗ (NRR)
M2: Open this. (RA)

A broader and more detailed examination of such comparisons, whether of spontaneous or of elicited contingent queries, should prove useful for the study of children's ability to deploy linguistic resources in communication. The CQ sequence is, as was shown above, a quite consistent and reliable phenomenon. The M0 of a solicited query (e.g., "Guess what?" ↘) is virtually irresistible to an addressee, and the M1 segments of unsolicited queries are very powerful in determining the occurrence of an appropriate M2. Thus the technique is a promising one for elicitation of conversational responses.

DISCUSSION

The objective of this chapter has been to describe a small part of the nature of what the ideal 3- to 5-year-old conversationalist must know in order to function as a competent member of his speech community. Solicited and unsolicited contingent queries constitute a part of the mechanics of discourse. The unsolicited queries serve, in cases of failure in comprehension, to adjust the information required by a speaker in order to respond appropriately. The solicited queries discussed above serve the function of assuring attention or of registering appreciative participation. Thus these embedded acts meet the conversational essentials (illusory or real) of mutual understanding and attention.

Competence in the performance of these modular components requires at least the following knowledge:

1. The performance of a contingent query does not shift the floor from Y to X.

2. The performance of a contingent query does not relieve X from responding to the speech act in which the query is embedded.

3. X's needs (or whatever motivated his query) may be quite broad or relatively specific in relation to the contingent of M0.

4. Y must satisfy X's needs before proceeding with any further talk, and should do so in the manner that X's query has determined.

This kind of knowledge belongs to the realm of discourse, the organization of verbal exchanges. It is possible to describe contingent queries in relation to their occurrence in elements called speech acts, which, in actual discourse, have a structure that can accommodate embedded modular components. Although they are dependent acts, they nevertheless appear to convey conventional messages that elicit remarkably consistent and predictable responses from an addressee. Searle (1969) states that the illocutionary force of an utterance (the intended, social message it conveys in a particular situation) rests on a unique combination of belief conditions specific to the speech act. He also notes that more general conditions hold for the correct performance of many different speech acts. In Figure 1, section *a* shows the unique combination of conditions enabling performance of an RA, and section *b* proposes more general conditions that an RA shares with other speech acts. What conditions underlie the correctly executed contingent query?

Contingent queries bear a close family resemblance to requests for information (RI), though the latter are potentially independent acts. The following set of conditions has been listed by Leech (1974) for an RI. The first two are identical to what Searle (1969) called the preparatory and the sincerity condition for an RI.

a. There is a piece of information (I) of which S is ignorant (Searle—preparatory).

b. S wants to know I. (Searle—sincerity).

c. S believes that H knows I.

d. S is in a position to elicit I from H.

These conditions are, Leech claims, at least necessary for a well-formed RI. He omits the "nonobviousness" that Searle includes as a preparatory condition, perhaps rightly, since this is a general condition on the use of speech acts in discourse rather than a condition limited to RI. But Leech is, perhaps not correct in including the relative status or positions of S and H in the conditions for RI. Though this condition is necessary to the acceptable performance of an RI, it is broadly relevant to other acts as well. Thus it, too, is probably a general condition on the use of speech acts in situated discourse. Furthermore, knowledge external to the speech situation itself is often needed to assess the appropriateness of the realizations of this condition in any given situated conversation. But there is no question that Leech's condition *d* is a relevant factor, since an appropriate reply to an RI is "None of your business" or "I don't have to tell you." Whether the necessary conditions of a speech act should include factors that depend on extra-speech-act information *or* factors that are so very general is still an open issue in speech act theory. The importance of the latter point is that, when rules for speech acts and the derivations of speech acts are written, it may prove more convenient notationally to specify when a general condition does not hold for a particular act than to write it almost everywhere as a necessary condition for a number of distinct acts.

In view of these considerations, then, the minimal set of necessary conditions for the performance of an RI as a speech act type can be proposed as follows:

a.   S does not know the "answer" (or piece of information).
b.   S wants to know the answer.
c.   S believes that H is able and willing to divulge the answer.

These three conditions also hold in respect to the unsolicited contingent query. The issuer of the query wants to know the information selected by the M1. He does not know that information, and he has, of course, good reason to believe that the person who has issued the M0 can indeed repeat, confirm, specify, or elaborate what he has just said, thus providing this information.

Two other conditions on which Leech and Searle do not agree are:

d.   It is not obvious to S and H that H will provide the answer at that time in the absence of the RI.
e.   S is in a position to elicit the answer from H.

These conditions, the "nonobviousness" condition and the "participant status or relation" condition, respectively, are in some way different from *a* to *c*. They relate more directly to the situational context than to the internal structure of the speech act; they appear to be relevant to a large number of speech acts and, furthermore, the realization of these factors in a given token of a speech act type is dependent on very specific features of the speech situation. It is proposed here that these conditions are a property of the discourse context and are not intrinsic to the definition of the speech act type in isolation.

In respect to the "nonobviousness" condition in unsolicited contingent queries, it is *within the discourse* that the information desired by S is not forthcoming. In the absence of the query, the issuer of the M0 would either continue talking or would wait for a response to the major act that the M0 represents—an answer to his RI, compliance with his RA, a granting of his request for permission, and so on. In respect to the participant relation, S is, *within the discourse*, indeed in a position to elicit an answer to his contingent query, since it is clear to both parties that X needs a reply in order to respond to the major act within whose domain the contingent query falls. It is the discourse role that justifies an adequate response to the contingent query, rather than some status relation between the speakers. (Status relations external to the discourse itself may, however, influence the encoding form of M1. "I beg your pardon?"↗ or "Pardon?"↗ can function as an NRR but has, of course, a different situational distribution from "Huh?"↗.) The point of these speculations is that it may not be possible to extricate the conditions essential to defining or discriminating among speech acts until the way in which discourse context contributes to the operation of these conditions is taken into account.

It may be worth while to examine more closely what Searle (1969) has called the "sincerity" condition (S wants to know the answer). This condition has a rather general aspect common to most speech acts and a more specific aspect essential to the definition of a request for information. The more general aspect might be called "good faith." This aspect leads participants to expect that a speech act is produced sincerely rather than facetiously or in jest. In relation to the contingent query, the participants believe that the antecedent to the query, M0, was uttered in good faith, that is, was motivated by the intent that it purported to have. In other words, its ostensible IPE was genuinely intended. The more specific aspect of good faith is, of course, that the one who puts the query sincerely wants to know what he asked. In the case of unsolicited contingent queries, both aspects of the sincerity condition seem to hold. The M0 is uttered in good faith; the issuer of the contingent query believes this is so and can thus sincerely request the information he needs in order to furnish a response appropriate to the M0.

In the case of *solicited* contingent queries, however, these two aspects are distorted in subtle ways. The M0 in solicited queries has *only* the IPE of eliciting a contingent query. This objective appears not only in summons-answer routines and in rhetorical gambits, but also in highly structured routines such as riddles (Y: "What does a kangaroo have that no other animal has?" X: "I don't know. What?"↘. Y: "Baby kangaroos."). As to the sincerity of the query itself, there is something distorted in it as well. In effect, X is led to produce the contingent query *as if* he sincerely wanted to know the answer. But in actual fact he is only being a good conversational sport. It could be said that X asks a discoursally sincere question (and that at his partner's behest), but it is a question that, in respect to the speech act itself, is not somehow entirely sincere. It looks as if the basic form and function of the unsolicited contingent query are employed, in the case of solicited queries, as a special discoursal strategy, and that this strategy builds on a distortion of the underlying conditions.

CONCLUSIONS

The objective of this chapter has been to describe the structure and use of a dependent speech act. The description has implications for the study of discourse and for the study of the development of communicative competence. The rather complex forms of the contingent query were shown to be well learned by the time that speech is fluent, that is, by about 3 to $3\frac{1}{2}$ years of age. Its proper functioning requires some knowledge of the rules of discourse and some expertise in the analysis of utterances. It is probable that this modular component is learned at a still earlier age and that its operation may be an important technique for subsequent language learning.

The interpersonal function of unsolicited queries appears to be the maintenance of mutual understanding; the function of solicited queries, the promotion of mutual attention or rapport. The operation of this component is, in some of its variant types, dependent on a single intonational cue. The contingent query is, thus, not the sort of phenomenon that could be considered characteristic of "egocentric" speech. It is certainly not a conversational refinement that is learned sometime after the basic syntactic features of the linguistic code are learned. On the contrary, it seems to be acquired as part of learning to talk and to listen and to talk.

The contingent query is related to discourse as a dependent speech act. The unsolicited query rests on a set of conditions similar to that postulated for the independent act, request for information. The solicited query appears to operate by means of a subtle distortion of those conditions. It was suggested that the study of acts in the context of discourse may influence the statement of the condition structure of speech acts. The process by which the contingent query is incorporated in a conversation is most commonly that of embedding. In the majority of cases, the removal of the query and the response to it results in an intact speech act and response (e.g., example 4). However, as in example 4, the formal rule that inserts the contingent query can be applied recursively, forming an extended series of contingent queries, dependent on a single speech act. These facts suggest an analogy with syntactic aspects of sentence formation, of which embedding and repeated applications of a single rule are important processes.

References

Austin, J. L. *How to do things with words.* Oxford: Oxford University Press, 1962.

Bates, E., Camaioni, L., & Volterra, V. The acquisition of performatives prior to speech. *Merrill-Palmer Quarterly,* 1975, **21,** 205–226.

BenDebba, M., & Garvey, C. *An experimental investigation of the contingent query sequence.* Unpublished manuscript, 1975.

Berko Gleason, J. Code switching in children's language. In T. E. Moore (Ed.), *Cognitive development and the acquisition of language.* New York: Academic Press, 1973. Pp. 159–167.

Bruner, J. The ontogenesis of speech acts. *Journal of Child Language,* 1975, **2,** 1–20.

Chafe, W. L. Discourse structure and human knowledge. In J. B. Carroll & R. O. Freedle (Eds.), *Language comprehension and the acquisition of knowledge.* Washington, D.C.: Winston, 1972. Pp. 41–69.

Clark, E. V. What's in a word? On the child's acquisition of semantics in his first language. In T. E. Moore (Ed.), *Cognitive development and the acquisition of language.* New York: Academic Press, 1973. Pp. 65–110.

Dore, J. *The development of speech acts.* The Hague: Mouton (in press).

Ervin-Tripp, S. Is Sybil there: The structure of American–English directives. *Language in Society,* 1976, **5,** 25–66.

Fraser, B. *An analysis of vernacular performative verbs.* Reproduced by the Indiana University Linguistics Club, Bloomington, 1974.

Garvey, C. Some properties of social play. *Merrill-Palmer Quarterly,* 1974, **20,** 163–180.

Garvey, C. Requests and responses in children's speech. *Journal of Child language,* 1975, **2,** 41–64.

Garvey, C., & Hogan, R. Social speech and social interaction: Egocentrism revisited. *Child Development,* 1973, **44,** 562–568.

Grice, H. P. *Logic and conversation.* Unpublished manuscript of William James Lectures, Harvard University, 1967.

Jaffe, J., & Feldstein, S. *Rhythms of dialogue.* New York: Academic Press, 1970.

Jefferson, G. Side sequences. In D. Sudnow (Ed.), *Studies in social interaction.* New York: The Free Press, 1972. Pp. 294–338.

Keenan, E. O. Conversational competence in children. *Journal of Child Language,* 1974, **1,** 163–183.

Leech, G. *Semantics.* Middlesex, England: Pelican, 1974.

Lewis, M. M. *Infant speech: A study of beginnings of language.* London: Routledge & Kegan Paul, 1936.

Mackay, D. M. *Information, mechanism, and meaning.* Cambridge, Mass.: M.I.T. Press, 1969.

Miller, G. Four philosophical problems of psycholinguistics. *Philosophy of Science,* 1970, **37,** 183–199.

Miller, W., & Ervin-Tripp, S. The development of grammar in child language. In R. Brown & U. Bellugi (Eds.), the acquisition of language. *Monographs of the Society for Research in Child Development*, 1964, **92**, 9–34.

Mohan, B. Do sequencing rules exist? *Semiotica*, 1974, **12**, 75–96.

Piaget, J. *The language and thought of the child.* New York: World, 1955.

Schegloff, E. A. Sequencing in conversational openings. *American Anthropologist*, 1968, **70**, 1075–1095.

Searle, J. R. *Speech acts: An essay in the philosophy of language.* Cambridge, England: Cambridge University Press, 1969.

CHAPTER 4

Sensory Templates, Vocal Perception, and Development: A Comparative View

PETER MARLER

The Rockefeller University

The ability to modify vocal production with experience, and to produce sounds with a novel morphology as a result of auditory stimulation with acoustical models for imitation, is fundamental to the normal employment of speech language. This ability is restricted to vertebrate animals and is rare among them, being adequately documented only in birds and man. This chapter reviews comparative evidence on mechanisms of vocal learning, including the human case (Marler, 1975). The central concept advanced to explain the process of vocal learning is that of sensory templates, to which vocal output is matched by auditory feedback. The approach relates to the classical ethological concept of "innate release mechanisms." This term was coined by Lorenz (1935; see translation, 1970) to conceptualize the inherited responsiveness of organisms to particular patterns of external stimulation without prior exposure to such stimuli from the environment. The evolution of innate release mechanisms depends on the assumption in phylogenetic history of particular valence by certain external stimuli important for the survival of a species. Although a predisposition to be especially responsive to such stimuli is physiologically preordained, responsiveness is also modifiable through experience. This potentiality for change is inherent in the original conception, as, for example, in "imprinting," where responsiveness to an acquired schema of conspecifics replaces a less specific "innate schema" to which a duckling or gosling originally gives its following response. The sequence visualized here for vocal learning resembles that for imprinting in that an organism begins with inherited responsiveness to patterns of external stimulation. In the course of responding to them, it acquires more selective responsiveness to a particular subset, with more specific attributes, generalized from the particular stimulus situation that the individual has experienced (Lorenz, 1935; see translation, 1970).

SENSORY TEMPLATES AND LORENZIAN
INNATE RELEASE MECHANISMS

Emphasis in original concept retained	Selective filtering of external stimuli
Development of initial selectivity without prior experience of a model	Modifiability of selectivity by external stimulation
Development of concept required	Incorporation in motor development

FIGURE 1. The relationship between "sensory templates" and ethological "innate release mechanisms".

The original concept is changed to involve "sensory templates" in the development of motor behavior (Figure 1). As motor activity is performed, sensory feedback is generated; and as long as the appropriate sensory channels are intact, the organism proceeds to match the feedback to the dictates of the sensory template, either in its innate form or as modified by experience. Such a process is believed to lie at the heart of the acquisition of learned song in certain songbirds. It is also generalizable to the acquisition of speech by human infants.

VOCAL LEARNING IN MALE BIRDS

Studies by Konishi (1963, 1964, 1965a, 1965b) on the effects of deafening on avian vocal development have lent support to the hypothesis that the ontogeny of song in certain bird species is based on species-specific auditory templates. One consequence is the imposition of constraints on the processes of avian vocal learning, underlying the development in many bird species of both male song and female responsiveness to conspecific song. One of the better studied species, the white-crowned sparrow, will serve as an illustration of the kind of evidence implicating a sensory template mechanism in song development (Marler & Tamura, 1964; Konishi, 1965b; Marler, 1970).

A young male white-crowned sparrow usually begins to sing, first at irregular intervals and then more continuously, at about 100 days of age, with full song usually emerging before 200 days of age. Konishi demonstrated that, if such a bird is deafened between 40 and 100 days of age before singing behavior has developed, it will subsequently begin singing on a normal schedule, but with a highly abnormal song. Such an early-deafened male has a song with a scratchy or buzzy tone, amorphous and variable in structure with components that change suddenly and erratically. The contrast with the tonal structure of normal singing is evident in Figure 2.

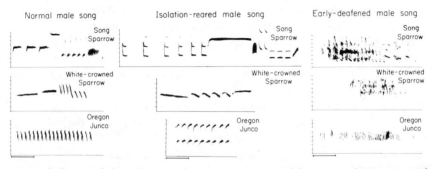

FIGURE 2. Songs of three bird species—song sparrow, white-crowned sparrow, and Oregon junco—in normal wild-type form (left), when reared in social isolation (center), and when deafened early in life (right).

The songs of two close relatives of the white-crowned sparrow, the song sparrow (top) and the Oregon junco (bottom), are also illustrated in Figure 2. Normal songs of these three species are highly species specific, being distinctly different both from one another and from sympatric songbirds.

Examples of songs produced by males of these same species deafened early in life, illustrated on the right of Figure 2, lack most of these species-specific traits, only the duration and range of frequencies remaining approximately normal (Konishi, 1964, 1965b; Mulligan, 1966). Thus audition plays a critical role in the development of the species-specific characteristics of sparrow song. Similar gross abnormalities have been demonstrated in the songs of early-deafened chaffinches, cardinals, robins, black-headed grosbeaks, red-winged blackbirds, and canaries (Nottebohm, 1967, 1968; Dittus & Lemon, 1970; Konishi, 1965a; Marler, Mundinger, Waser, & Lutjen, 1972; Marler & Waser, in press).

Further study reveals that audition is important in song development, both to permit the young male to hear his own voice and to enable him to hear conspecific song from others as models for imitation (Marler & Tamura, 1964; Marler, 1970). A young male white-crowned sparrow taken from the nest before fledging and raised by hand with hearing intact, so that it can hear its own voice but has no further opportunity to hear conspecific song, develops a song less abnormal than that of an early-deafened bird. The song has a definite, patterned morphology, made up of relatively pure and sustained tones, which are longer in duration at the beginning than at the end of the song. Thus the song of such an intact male reared in isolation from conspecific song after the early nestling phase shares some normal characteristics with wild, white-crowned sparrow singing (Figure 2). However several significant normal singing characteristics are lacking.

As Figure 2 shows, the three illustrations of white-crowned sparrow song —first, the normal wild type; second, that of a hearing bird reared in isolation from conspecific song; and, third, that of an early-deafened male—represent a series with progressive loss of species specificity. The same is true of the Oregon junco, although the abnormality of the song of an intact isolate is less marked than in the white-crown. The loss of species specificity by an early-deafened bird is, however, equally marked. The same is true of the song sparrow (Figure 2), in spite of the ability of an intact, isolated song sparrow to approximate much more normal singing than the other two species (Mulligan, 1966; Kroodsma, in press).

In addition to allowing auditory feedback from vocalization, the sense of hearing also gives a bird access to patterned acoustical stimulation from other individuals. This stimulation may have both generalized and highly specific effects on subsequent singing behavior depending on the species (Marler & Mundinger, 1971). An illustration of the former type of effect is provided by the Arizona junco. Early-deafened birds produce highly abnormal song (Konishi, 1964). Intact birds reared in isolation from conspecific song develop more normally, but several species-specific features are lacking from the song. These are restored, however, if a young male is given access either to adult conspecific song or to the vocalizations of sibling males (Marler, 1967). Typically the elimination of abnormality in juncos by experience of the sounds of others is not the result of imitation of the sounds heard. Instead more complex songs, incorporating all normal species-specific features, result from provocation to an increased level of vocal invention or improvisation. Such generalized effects of external stimulation on subsequent vocal development may be more widespread than is presently realized, and can be intriguingly difficult to distinguish from more specific ontogenetic effects of auditory stimulation such as imitation.

To illustrate specific consequences of auditory stimulation for subsequent vocal development, the white-crowned sparrow will again serve. The absence of certain properties of normal conspecific song in isolated males is illustrated in Figure 3, showing the songs of nine male white-crowns reared together as a group but in isolation from normal conspecific song after the first few days of life (Marler, 1970). They came from three different areas in California. Examples of normal song from each area are illustrated in the insets. A comparison of these with the songs of the intact but isolation-reared males reveals two kinds of abnormalities in the latter, especially in the second part of the song. Although the second part of a typical "isolate"

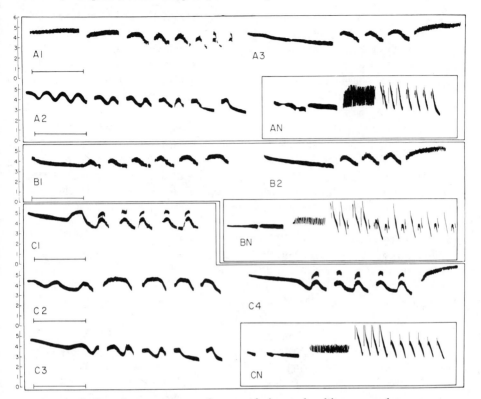

FIGURE 3. Sound spectrograms of songs of nine male white-crowned sparrows taken from three different areas and reared in one group. The three inserts, AN, BN and CN illustrate local dialects where the birds were taken. The time marker indicates 0.5 sec. and the vertical scales are marked in RHz.

song is broken into a train of separate notes that are shorter in duration than the introduction, the notes are longer than in normal song and lack all of the fine detail usually present. In nature these details reveal local dialects, each unique to an area. The second or "trill" portion of the song is especially diagnostic of the local dialect. Thus every wild white-crowned sparrow song exhibits some dialect characteristics and other species-specific features shared with all populations of the species. Both are lacking from the song of an intact male reared in isolation from normal song after the nestling phase.

If a young male white-crowned sparrow taken as a nestling is placed in individual isolation and allowed to hear 25 normal conspecific songs per day for 3 weeks some time between 7 and 50 days of age, his song will subsequently develop normally and will be a copy of the model to which he was exposed. This copy will include the dialect characteristics of the model. It may differ in some properties of the first part of the song, which tends to be individually distinct (Marler, 1970).

The process of song learning exhibits a sensitive period. Equivalent exposure to a model between 50 and 71 days of age had only minor effects on the subsequent singing of male white-crowns, and exposure after about 100 days of age had none at all. Other birds known to exhibit sensitive periods for song learning include the chaffinch and the zebra finch (Thorpe, 1958; Immelmann, 1969; Nottebohm, 1969; Arnold, 1975a, 1975b). In both species a male reared without exposure to normal song will sing abnormally. Exposure to normal song during the sensitive period not only restores the general characteristics of normal conspecific singing, but also results in imitation of the particular model used. In chaffinches, as in white-crowned sparrows, song dialects result (Marler, 1952). Their existence in songs of the Australian zebra finch is predictable, though this has yet to be studied.

THE SELECTIVITY OF LEARNING

The song-learning ability manifested by some birds during sensitive periods has the further characteristic that it is selective with regard to which models are most acceptable. If a male white-crowned sparrow is given playback of both conspecific song and song of another species during the sensitive period, it will learn only the conspecific song. Exposed to the alien song and nothing else at this time, it will develop songs like those of untrained social isolates (Marler, 1970).

Further reflection on the natural history of song learning suggests the likelihood of such selectivity. Many other birds are present in the environment where a young male white-crowned sparrow grows up, all producing sounds that the young male can hear. Songs of these other species are rarely imitated in nature, and interspecific learning would seriously reduce a male's fitness.

Females probably base their initial selection of a mate on song recognition, so that a male learning the song of another species would experience communicative and reproductive difficulties. It is to be anticipated that the evolution of the capacity for song learning will be coupled with genetically based constraints that restrict the learning to conspecific models.

The existence of such inherited constraints on vocal learning was anticipated more than 40 years ago by Konrad Lorenz (1932). In reviewing evidence that young European goldfinches learn one of their calls from adults, Lorenz suggested that *recognition* of the call might nevertheless be innate "to the extent that the juvenile bird selects and imitates the species-specific call among the babble of vocalizations to be heard in its natural environment" (Lorenz, 1932, translated 1970, p. 77). He concluded that this "amounts to the same thing as an innate response to non-innate vocalizations." The song template hypothesis provides a potential explanation for this selectivity.

SENSORY TEMPLATES AS MECHANISMS FOR GUIDING VOCAL LEARNING

Various lines of evidence point to the existence of constraints on the process of song learning. There are constraints in time with sensitive periods during which learning takes place most readily. There are also stimulus constraints, with some acoustical patterns learned more readily than others. Some species also exhibit contextual constraints, as will be mentioned later. In birds such as the white-crowned sparrow and the chaffinch (Thorpe, 1958), however, there are no binding contextual restrictions on sounds that are learned, such as might be imposed by the social situation. Selectivity is manifest in response to sounds coming from a loudspeaker. Here there must be constraints that are endogenous to the male bird. Of the two kinds of contraints most readily imaginable, motor and sensory, the latter are believed to be dominant in the present case.

The structure of the sound-producing equipment of birds, involving the respiratory machinery, the syrinx and its associated membranes, muscles, and resonators, clearly imposes restrictions on the sounds that can be produced. The mechanisms involved have been clarified by recent research on the functioning of the avian syrinx (Nottebohm, 1975). Whereas the syringes of distantly related birds operate in different ways, those of close relatives seem to be very similar in both morphology and mode of operation. The structure of the avian syrinx is, in fact, so conservative that its slow rate of evolutionary change has led to its extensive use as a taxonomic character at higher levels of classification.

The likelihood that differences in syringeal structure are responsible for the differences in learning selectivity of juncos, white-crowned sparrows, and song sparrows is reduced by the resemblance we have already noted in the songs these birds produce after early deafening. The outputs of the syringes of these three species seem very similar when freed from auditory control. Also it is known that species with similar syringeal structures, such as a chaffinch and a bullfinch, can produce very different vocalizations. The latter, a species in which song learning seems to be guided by social constraints, can be trained by a person who assumes the appropriate social role, and will imitate a great variety of unnatural sounds, including musical instruments (Thorpe, 1955; Nicolai, 1959). I conclude that limitations on the sensory side, such as are implied by the sensory template hypothesis, provide a more plausible explanation of the selectivity of song learning in these species, although restrictions on the motor side require further study.

The loss of species specificity in singing behavior resulting from auditory deprivation, partial after isolation from stimulation by conspecific song, and extreme after early deafening, points to a sensory mechanism in control of song species specificity. It is in this context that auditory templates have been invoked. These are conceptualized as involving the neural pathways for auditory processing, having the consequence of sensitizing the organism to certain patterns of stimulation. As such, they embody information about the structure of vocal sounds and possess the capacity to guide motor development. According to this view, the young male starting to sing gradually strikes a closer and closer match between his vocal output and the dictates of the auditory template. The progression from subsong through plastic song to full song is viewed as a reflection of the gradual acquisition of skill in using the motor equipment for sound production and the process of bringing it under full auditory control.

In certain birds the initial sensory phase of song learning is separable in time from the start of singing. This occurs normally in the white-crowned sparrow and can occur in the zebra finch (Immelmann, 1969). Thus there is a sense in which these two species learn to sing from memory, and the sensory template, enriched and modified from its innate primordium as a result of the experience of conspecific song, is viewed as a mechanism for bridging the intervening time span.

Conceived as sensory mechanisms embodying species-specific information that guides vocal development, auditory templates vary from species to species in their competence to generate fully natural song without access to a model. The template of the male white-crowned sparrow is the least competent of the three species shown in Figure 2 in the sense that the song of an intact male isolated from the fledgling phase differs radically from the natural conspecific song.

By contrast, an isolated, intact male song sparrow produces songs which, though somewhat variable and often longer than normal, are often difficult to distinguish from those of wild birds (Mulligan, 1966; Kroodsma, in press). A more competent auditory template than that of the white-crown is implied, the auditory nature of the mechanism being inferred from the radical loss of these conspecific features after early deafening. Unlike the template of a white-crowned sparrow, which must be extensively modified by environmental learning to produce natural song, a song sparrow template is capable of guiding virtually normal development without a model. Song sparrows are nevertheless capable of imitating conspecific song when given the opportunity (Mulligan, 1966), although learning plays a less intrusive role than in the white-crowned sparrow, as is implied by the lack of emphasis in their natural song on local dialects (Harris & Lemon, 1972), marked in songs of the white-crowned sparrow (Marler & Tamura, 1962).

The Oregon junco shares with the song sparrow a lack of emphasis on dialects in its natural song. Correspondingly, a male Oregon junco reared in isolation from conspecific models produces a song which, although abnormal in several respects, is closer to the natural pattern than that of a white-crowned sparrow reared in similar circumstances (Marler, Kreith, & Tamura, 1962). One might think of the naive sensory template for junco song, as manifest without exposure to a model, as intermediate between the other two species in its competence to generate normal song. Again, it is modifiable through experience of song stimulation, though usually only the general pattern has an influence. Thus juncos are less prone to slavish imitation of a song model they experience than are white-crowns. Instead, each male tends to produce songs made up of notes with individually specific morphology, while species specific in overall pattern (Konishi, 1964; Marler, 1967). Within the rather broad limits set by the auditory template, each male seems to improvise his own individual set of patterns. Thus dependence on a sensory template in song development is not incompatible with a significant role for the "invention" or "improvisation" of individualistic patterns of motor activity.

The hypothesis advanced here is that species differ in the particular pattern of auditory stimulation specified by the auditory template of a naive individual. In some it is sufficient to generate virtually normal song. In others it requires more or less extensive learned modification before normal singing can develop, through stimulation by a model. In the latter case, the template is still sufficiently specific to focus the learning bird's attention on conspecific models. Species also differ in the latitude allowed for motor development within the constraints set by the sensory templates. In some the constraints are narrow, although even in this case, as in the white-crowned sparrow, in which the particular song dialect heard during the sensitive period is precisely imitated, there is often individuality in the introductory part of the song

(Marler and Tamura, 1964). In species with broader constraints there is less conformity to models experienced, and correspondingly more latitude for individuality. This is a significant point, for individualistic characteristics are prominent in many bird songs, and there is ample evidence that these serve an important function in mediating individual recognition in nature.

SENSORY TEMPLATES AND SPEECH DEVELOPMENT

Human infants manifest an ability to discriminate between conspecific, communicative sounds and others that impinge on them from the environment at a very early age, probably within a few days after birth (Moffitt, 1971; Morse, 1972; Trehub, 1973; Palermo, 1975). Present evidence suggests that this ability is not dependent on prior experience of speech sounds by the infant, although further work is needed on the possibilities of intrauterine speech perception (Bradley & Mistretta, 1975) and rapid postnatal learning. Nothwithstanding, much as a white-crowned sparrow is able to discriminate conspecific song from other sounds without prior song experience, the ability of a human infant to recognise speech sounds as a class before the development of speaking is well established.

Other lines of research have specified some of the critical acoustical properties that underlie an infant's recognition of speech sounds. Studies of the responses of adults to synthetic speech in which gradually changing series of phoneme-like sounds are presented to listeners, each one differing from its neighbors by small changes in one parameter, reveal that such speech continua are segmentalized at particular boundaries.

Presented with pairs of sounds that fall on the same side of the normal boundary that separates such speech sounds as [ba] and [pa], a listener finds it difficult even to discriminate between them (Liberman, Harris, Hoffman, & Griffith, 1957; Liberman, Harris, Kinney, & Lane, 1961; Liberman, Cooper Shankweiler, & Studdert-Kennedy, 1967). The same point can also be made with recorded sounds of natural speech, but speech varies in so many respects that experiments with synthetic stimuli are easier to interpret.

Confronted with a graded series of synthetic speech sounds ranging from [pa] to [ba], with the so-called voice onset time varying between extremes of $+100$ milliseconds and -100 milliseconds in ten millisecond steps, an adult asked to identify such sounds divides the continuum into two categories. In this case all sounds with a voice onset time longer than 25 milliseconds are identified as [pa], and those on the other side of this boundary, with shorter or negative voice onset times, as [ba]. This is what we do in listening to normal speech, making allowance for the great variation of voice onset times, both within and between speech sound categories.

Such an experiment demonstrates a tendency toward categorical labeling of such a graded series of speech sounds, but does not deal with the issue of discriminability. Here another approach is commonly used, the so-called ABX paradigm, with one sound presented first, then its neighbor in the series, and finally a third. The subject has to decide whether the third stimulus (X) is identical with the first (A) or the second (B). In practice, X will be either A or B; and if these cannot be discriminated, a chance score will result. This is, in fact, the probable outcome, with an untrained listener, if A and B come from within the same speech sound category. On the other hand, as one approaches the set of values for voice onset time that normally constitutes the phonemic boundary, adjacent pairs are readily discriminable with a high degree of accuracy (Liberman et al., 1961).

Although such categorical perception of points along a stimulus continuum is not unique to speech sounds (e.g., Miller, Pastore, Wier, Kelly, & Dooling, 1974), it is especially involved in speech sound discrimination. Parallel experiments with sounds not identified by subjects as speech, yet differing from each other in essentially the same way and by similar amounts as speech stimulus series, reveal no increase in discriminability at stimulus values in the region of the phoneme boundary. Interestingly, the discriminability of control stimuli is lower than that of speech sounds close to an intercategory boundary, suggesting that the perceptual distinctness of small variations at this part of the stimulus continuum is especially emphasized.

The implication is that the physiological mechanisms underlying the perception of at least some speech sounds are, to a degree, different in their mode of operation from those involved in the auditory perception of other kinds of sounds. It is not yet clear whether one should think of categorical speech sound processing as expressly evolved for this function, or whether, as some animal studies of speech sound perception suggest (Sinnot, 1974; Kuhl & Miller 1975; Morse & Snowdon, 1975; Sinnot, Beecher, Moody, & Stebbins, in press), we are dealing with a characteristic of the generalized mammalian auditory system, used to advantage in human speech perception (Liberman, 1976). Evidence pointing to the former conclusion derives from other sources (Liberman et al., 1967; Studdert-Kennedy, 1975). Dichotic listening studies in which competing sounds are presented to the two ears revealed that speech sounds are more readily perceived when they arrive at the right ear rather than the left, whereas there is dichotic equivalence or left-ear dominance for nonspeech sounds (e.g., Kimura, 1961, 1964; Studdert-Kennedy & Shankweiler, 1970). Electrophysiological studies, using averaged evoked potentials as a measure of responsiveness to speech and nonspeech sounds, also indicate a tendency for separation of the processing of speech and nonspeech in the two hemispheres (Wood, Goff, & Day, 1971; Molfese, 1972). The same method can also be used to demonstrate categorical processing (Dorman, 1974). Even in infants as young as 1 week of age, stronger responsiveness of the left hemisphere to speech sounds has been demonstrated by dichotic testing (Molfese, 1972; Molfese, Nunez, Seibert, & Ramanaiah, 1976). Thus the distinctive attributes of the perceptual processing of speech sounds as compared with other kinds of auditory stimuli include not only a tendency toward categorical rather than continuous processing, but also an association of processing with the left hemisphere of the human brain.

In itself, the demonstration of special sensitivity to variation in speech sounds close to critical boundaries is not unexpected, and perhaps is of more interest to psychologists than to biologists. Two further findings, however, draw the phenomenon firmly into the biological realm. Abramson and Lisker, having defined the critical boundaries for some acoustically related sounds, have demonstrated in comparative studies the recurrence of approximately similar boundaries in speech sounds of one language after another. This proves to be the case however different the languages may be in other respects. Thus one may begin to think of some of these critical boundaries as universals in all human speech (Abramson & Lisker, 1965, 1970; Lisker & Abramson, 1964, 1970).

In addition to the features of grammar that structural linguists and students of early speech development believe to be shared by all languages (e.g., McNeill, 1966; Chomsky, 1967; Lenneberg, 1967; Brown, 1973), more superficial aspects of the acoustical structure defining categorical boundaries in speech seem also to be shared by all human speakers. The universality of such species-specific features invites the speculation that genetic factors play a significant role in their determination.

The research cited thus far on speech perception derives from experiments with adult subjects. The work of Eimas and his colleagues (Eimas, Siqueland, Jusczyk, & Vigorito, 1971; Eimas, 1975; Cutting & Eimas, 1975) demonstrates, however, that similar segmental processing of speech sounds, with roughly similar boundary values, occurs in infants as young as 1 to 4 months of age. The ability is manifest long before they have begun to speak or even to babble.

Working with several speech sound series, distinguished by adults on criteria broadly similar in all languages studies thus far, infants have been found to process them in essentially the same way as adults. The demonstrations rest on habituation of a sucking response, with repetitions of playback of a recorded speech sound contingent upon sucking. Evidently the infant is prone to react by sucking on a nipple in response to sounds that catch his attention. Repetitions of one sound pattern result in habituation, which is taken to a criterion value. Then the first sound is replaced by a second, and the extent of revival of the sucking response is used as a measure of the degree of contrast between the first and second sounds. Working in this way, along series of synthetic speech sounds, each different from its neighbors by a small amount in some measure such as voice onset time, Eimas found little or no evidence of contrast between within-category sound pairs. However, as he approached the part of the stimulus continuum where an adult discerns a boundary, the infants showed a sudden revival of response. Heightened responsiveness to stimulus variation has been demonstrated, at several speech sound boundaries, in infants young enough that it becomes plausible to invoke appropriate categorical processing without the need for prior exposure. There is thus a suggestive analogy with the auditory templates postulated to explain the selective perception of bird song.

Auditory templates for certain speech sounds could serve a prespeech child in two ways. First, they would focus the infant's attention on a class of external stimuli appropriate for particular social responsiveness. Second, auditory templates for certain speech sounds could serve as an orderly frame of references for the infant's developing responsiveness to speech patterns of the culture in which he is growing up. In view of the myriad of complex and highly variable properties of normal speech, there would be value in drawing the naive infant's attention to a particular subset with some universal significance (Mattingley, 1972). Although auditory templates for speech sounds would become highly modified and multiplied in the process of learning a language, guidance while taking some of the initial steps in the perceptual analysis of speech would favor the abstraction of similar rules for speech perception in all users of the language.

The capacity for categorical perception of certain speech sounds develops in infants long before speaking. There is a general tendency for speech recognition and comprehension to precede production in the developing child (Fry, 1966; Lenneberg, 1966). One may view the emerging ability to discriminate and appropriately classify speech sounds as underlain by the multiplication, and the changing specifications, of auditory templates for speech sounds that are to some extent perfected in advance of speaking. Extrapolating from the model provided by bird song learning, one may postulate that early stages of speech development depend on a process of matching vocal output to auditory templates by auditory feedback.

Fry (1966) has proposed:

"A word that is recognised means an auditory pattern stored in the child's memory. When the child utters a word, he links this auditory memory with a very complex pattern of activity. The muscles receive their operating instructions from the brain, and the course of their activity is controlled through the kinesthetic and the auditory feedback loops. Learning on the motor side includes the training of the muscle systems as well as the accumulating of memory patterns in the brain. What the child is doing in the process of modifying his speech is to set up habits of movement with the aid of kinesthetic and auditory information. He arrives at a satisfactory movement by using his ears to judge the resulting sounds, and thus the motor learning in speech is very largely dependent on hearing; the child must be able to hear the results of his own speech movements if he is ever to acquire normal speech or something approaching normal speech. When habits are established, they form the memory store of kinesthetic patterns that are the basis of all future speech movements." (pp. 192-193).

Attention has been drawn earlier to the special interest of the early stage of bird song development known as "subsong." It has been interpreted as the phase of development in which the young bird is acquiring skill in the control and coordination of the motor equipment for sound production and in matching vocal output to sensory templates by auditory feedback. Fry (1966) has placed a similar interpretation upon the babbling stage of speech development:

"At this period two very important developments are taking place. First the child is discovering the possibilities inherent in the phonatory and articulatory muscle systems. He learns to combine articulation with phonation in a variety of ways. Although he certainly does not acquire all the articulations that he will later need, he does produce some classes of sound that will not be required by the phonemic system of his language. . . . The second important development at this time is the establishment of the auditory feedback loop. As sound-producing movements are repeated and repeated, a strong link is forged between tactual and kinesthetic impressions and the auditory sensation that the child receives from his own utterances." (p. 189).

Although more study is needed, the parallels between babbling and subsong are striking. We have noted the gradual progression of song development in a bird like a white-crowned sparrow as motor performance gradually comes to match closely the sound of the conspecific model heard earlier. Similar progressions have been recorded in speech. Eguchi and Hirsh (1969) show how the variability of critical temporal features of speech sounds, such as the voice onset time of the sounds b, p, and t, as measured by standard deviations, decreases with age to stabilize at "an adult-like minimum value at 7 or 8 years." Kewley-Port and Preston (1974) have documented the gradual changes in the distributions of voice onset times with the phonemic categories [d] and [t] between the ages of 6 months and $4\frac{1}{2}$ years. The "apical stop consonants" were recorded first around 6 months of age, at which time the "voice onset time distributions had a wide range of randomly distributed values. Some months later a concentration of apicals in the short voicing lag category is observed. Apical stops in the long voicing category are then gradually added." This is the kind of progression one would expect to see if the child is gradually acquiring skill in matching vocal output to the dictates of auditory templates.

According to the view developed here, there are parallels between the processes of vocal learning in birds and in man. Both can be interpreted as employing sensory templates extensively, both for selective perception of auditory stimuli and for shaping vocal development. Whereas birds use the ability for selective auditory perception to distinguish between acceptable and nonacceptable models for vocal development, children use auditory templates both for this purpose and for the multiple classification of acceptable sounds into subcategories. It is likely that birds also have several distinct auditory filtering mechanisms for vocal signals involved in different behavioral systems (e.g., Gottlieb, 1971), but I do not know of a case where more than one is involved in the development of the song of an individual.

Although one may conceptualize auditory templates, in both birds and man, as distinct functional entities, they may, in fact, involve several separate physiological components that together serve as stimulus filters. Components that are modifiable might be separate from those that underlie the selective perception of a naive, as yet untrained subject. The two sets might operate in series or in parallel, with control shifting from one to the other after training. As with other "feature detectors," one should be prepared for the likelihood that similar behavioral ends may be achieved by different physiological mechanisms.

The parallels between human and avian vocal learning are so many and varied that it is hard to regard them as mere coincidence. Rather, the evidence suggests that there are general rules, shared by man and birds, for the efficient acquisition of appropriate responsiveness to conspecific communi-

CHARACTERISTICS OF THE LEARNING OF

AVIAN SONG AND HUMAN SPEECH.

1. LEARNING HAS A DOMINANT ROLE IN DEVELOPING SONG/SPEECH, EXHIBITING SENSITIVE PERIODS WHEN LEARNING OCCURS MOST READILY, AND RESULTING IN DIALECTS.

2. ALTHOUGH SONG/SPEECH SHOWS GREAT INTRA-SPECIFIC VARIATION THERE ARE NEVERTHELESS SPECIES-SPECIFIC "UNIVERSALS".

3. IN INFANCY THERE IS SELECTIVE INITIAL RESPONSIVENESS TO CONSPECIFIC SOUNDS PRIOR TO SINGING/SPEAKING.

4. THERE IS EVIDENCE THAT SONG/SPEECH DEVELOPMENT PROCEEDS BY A PROCESS OF MATCHING AUDITORY FEEDBACK TO MODIFIABLE SENSORY TEMPLATES.

5. CONVERGENCE ON PHYSIOLOGICAL MECHANISMS WITH SIMILAR FUNCTIONAL PROPERTIES IS INDICATED: E.G. THE OCCURRENCE OF CEREBRAL DOMINANCE IN THE CONTROL OF SPEECH AND SONG (NOTTEBOHM) AND SENSITIVE PERIODS FOR THE MOST RAPID LEARNING OF SPEAKING AND SINGING.

FIGURE 4. Features shared by processes of avian song learning and the development of speech.

cative stimuli, and for the development of motor patterns of signaling behavior conforming in some degree to those in use among conspecific companions. As indicated in Figure 4, the parallels extend even to principles of neural organization, such as the demonstration by Nottebohm of cerebral dominance in the control of the vocal behaviour of birds with learned songs (Nottebohm, 1971, 1972, in press; Nottebohm & Nottebohm, 1976; Lemon, 1973). These parallels add to my conviction that auditory template matching may indeed provide an accurate and heuristically productive approach to the acquisition of speech in children. In this view, the evolution of innate but modifiable auditory templates for speech sounds was perhaps the most critical single phylogenetic change in the developmental physiology of human or prehuman vocal behavior, both in sensory and in motor aspects.

References

Abramson, A. S., & Lisker, L. Voice onset in stop consonants: Acoustic analysis and synthesis. In *Proceedings of the Fifth International Congress on Acoustics, Liege.* Inp. G. Thone, A51, 1965.

Abramson, A. S., & Lisker, L. Discriminability along with voicing continuum: Cross-language tests. In Proceedings of the Sixth International Congress of Phonetic Sciences, Prague, 1967. *Academia,* 1970, 569–573.

Arnold, A. P. The effects of castration on song development in zebra finches (*Poephila guttata*). *Journal of Experimental Zoology,* 1975, **191**, 261–268. (a)

Arnold, A. P. The effects of castration and androgen replacement on song, courtship, and aggression in zebra finches (*Poephila guttata*). *Journal of Experimental Zoology,* 1975, 191, 309–326. (b)

Bradley, R. M., & Mistretta, C. M. Fetal sensory receptors. *Physiological Review,* 1975, **55**, 352–382.

Brown, R. *A first language: The early stages.* Cambridge, Mass.: Harvard University Press, 1973.

Chomsky, N. The formal nature of language. In E. H. Lenneberg (Ed.), *Biological foundations of language.* New York: Wiley, 1967. Appendix A.

Cutting, E. J., & Eimas, P. D. Phonetic feature analyzers and the processing of speech in infants. In J. F. Kavanagh and J. E. Cutting (Eds.), *The role of speech in language.* Cambridge, Mass.: M.I.T. Press, 1975.

Dittus, W. P., & Lemon, R. E. Auditory feedback in the singing of cardinals. *Ibis,* 1970, **112**, 544–548.

Dorman, M. F. Auditory-evoked potential correlates of speech sound discrimination. *Perception and Psychophysics,* 1974, **15**, 215–220.

Eguchi, S., & Hirsh. I. J. Development of speech sounds in children. *Acta Oto-laryingologica,* Supplement, 1969, **257**, 1–51.

Eimas, P. D. Speech perception in early infancy. In L. B. Cohen & P. Salapatek (Eds.), *Infant perception.* New York: Academic Press 1975.

Eimas, P. D., Siqueland, E. R., Jusczyk, P., & Vigorito, J. M. Speech perception in infants. *Science,* 1971, **171,** 303–306.

Fry, D. B. The development of the phonological system in the normal and the deaf child. In F. Smith & G. A. Miller (Eds.), *The genesis of language.* Cambridge, Mass.: M.I.T. Press, 1966.

Gottlieb, G. *Development of species identification in birds.* Chicago: Chicago University Press, 1971.

Harris, M. A., & Lemon, R. E. Songs of song sparrows (*Melospiza melodia*): individual variation and dialects. *Canadian Journal of Zoology,* 1972, **50,** 301–309.

Immelmann, K. Song development in the zebra finch and other estrilid finches. In R. Hinde (Ed.), *Bird vocalization.* Cambridge: Cambridge University Press, 1969.

Kewley-Port, D., & Preston, M. S. Early apical stop production: A voice onset time analysis. *Journal of Phonetics,* 1974, **2,** 195–210.

Kimura, D. Cerebral dominance and the perception of verbal stimuli. *Canadian Journal of Psychology,* 1961, **15,** 166–171.

Kimura, D. Left-right differences in the perception of melodies. *Quarterly Journal of Experimental Psychology,* 1964, **16,** 355–358.

Konishi, M. The role of auditory feedback in the vocal behavior of domestic fowl. *Zeitschrift für Tierpsychologie,* 1963, **20,** 349–367.

Konishi, M. Effects of deafening on song development in two species of juncos. *Condor,* 1964, **66,** 85–102.

Konishi, M. Effects of deafening on song development in American robins and blackheaded grosbeaks. *Zeitschrift für Tierpsychologie,* 1965, **22,** 584–599. (a)

Konishi, M. The role of auditory feedback in the control of vocalization in the white-crowned sparrow. *Zeitschrift für Tierpsychologie,* 1965, **22,** 770–783. (b)

Kroodsma, D. A re-evaluation of song development in the song sparrow and the *Junco-Zonotrichia-Melospiza* complex; *Animal Behaviour,* in press.

Kuhl, P. K., & Miller, J. D. Speech perception by the chinchilla: voiced-voiceless distinction in alveolar plosive consonants. *Science,* 1975, **190,** 69–72.

Lemon, R. E. Nervous control of the syrinx in white-throated sparrows (*Zonotrichia albicollis*). *Journal of Zoology London,* 1973, **171,** 131–140.

Lenneberg, E. H. The natural history of language. In F. Smith & G. A. Miller (Eds.), *The genesis of language.* Cambridge, Mass.: M.I.T. Press, 1966.

Lenneberg, E. H. *Biological foundations of language.* New York: Wiley, 1967.

Liberman, A. M. *Comments on the session: Perception and production of speech.* II: Annals of the New York Academy of Sciences 1976, **280,** 718–724.

Liberman, A. M., Cooper, F. S., Shankweiler, D. S., & Studdert-Kennedy, M. Perception of the speech code. *Psychological Review,* 1967, **74,** 431–461.

Liberman, A. M., Harris, K. S., Hoffman, H. S., & Griffith, B. C. The discrimination of speech sounds within and across phoneme boundaries. *Journal of Experimental Psychology*, 1957, **54**, 358–368.

Liberman, A. M., Harris, K. S., Kinney, J., & Lane, H. The discrimination of relative onset time of the components of certain speech and nonspeech patterns. *Journal of Experimental Psychology*, 1961, **61**, 379–388.

Lisker, L., & Abramson, A. S. A cross-language study of voicing of initial stops: Acoustical measurements. *Word*, 1964, **20**, 384–422.

Lisker, L., & Abramson, A. S. The voicing dimension: Some experiments in comparative phonetics. In Proceedings of the Sixth International Congress of Phonetic Sciences, Prague, 1967. *Academia*, 1970, 563–567.

Lorenz, K. Betrachtungen über das Erkennen der arteigenen Triebhandlungen der Vögel. *Journal of Ornithology*, 1932, **80**. Republished in English translation in *Studies in animal and human behaviour*. Vol. I. Cambridge, Mass.: Harvard University Press, 1970.

Lorenz, K. Der Kumpan in der Umwelt des Vogels. *Journal of Ornithology*, 1935, **83**, 137–213, 289–413. Republished in English translation in *Studies in animal and human behaviour*. Vol. I. Cambridge, Mass.: Harvard University Press, 1970.

Marler, P. Variations in the song of the chaffinch, *Fringilla coelebs. Ibis*, 1952, **94**, 458–472.

Marler, P. Comparative study of song development in sparrows. In D. W. Snow (Ed.), *Proceedings of the XIV International Ornithology Congress, 1966*. Oxford: Blackwell Scientific Publication, 1967. Pp. 231–244.

Marler, P. A comparative approach to vocal development: Song learning in the white-crowned sparrow. *Journal of Comparative Physiology and Psychology*, 1970, **71**, 1–25.

Marler, P. On the origin of speech from animal sounds. In J. F. Kavanagh & J. E. Cutting (Eds.), *The role of speech in language*. Cambridge, Mass.: M.I.T. Press, 1975.

Marler, P., Kreith, M., & Tamura, M. Song development in hand-raised Oregon juncos. *Auk*, 1962, **79**, 12–30.

Marler, P., & Mundinger, P. Vocal learning in birds. In H. Moltz (Ed.), *Ontogeny of vertebrate behavior*. New York: Academic Press, 1971.

Marler, P., Mundinger, P., Waser, M. S., & Lutjen, A. Effects of acoustical stimulation and deprivation on song development in red-winged blackbirds (*Agelaius phoeniceus*). *Animal Behavior*, 1972, **20**, 586–606.

Marler, P., & Tamura, M. Song dialects in three populations of white-crowned sparrows. *Condor*, 1962, **64**, 368–377.

Marler, P., & Tamura, M. Culturally transmitted patterns of vocal behavior in sparrows. *Science*, 1964, **146**, 1483–1486.

Marler, P., & Waser, M. S. *The role of auditory feedback in song development of the canary* (in press).

Mattingley, I. G. Speech cues and sign stimuli. *American Scientist*, 1972, **60**, 327–337.

McNeill, D. Developmental psycholinguistics. In F. Smith & G. A. Miller (Eds.), *The genesis of language.* Cambridge, Mass.: M.I.T. Press, 1966.

Miller, J. D., Pastore, R. E., Wier, C. C., Kelly, W. J., & Dooling, R. J. Discrimination and labelling of noise-buzz sequences with various noise-lead times. *Journal of the Acoustic Society of America,* 1974, **55,** 390(A).

Moffitt, A. R. Consonant cue perception by twenty- to twenty-four-week-old infants. *Child Development,* 1971, **42,** 717–731.

Molfese, D. L. *Cerebral asymmetry in infants, children and adults: Auditory-evoked responses to speech and noise stimuli.* Unpublished doctoral dissertation, Pennsylvania State University, 1972.

Molfese, D. L., Nunez, V., Seibert, S. M., & Ramanaiah, N. V. Cerebral asymmetry: changes in factors affecting its development. *Annals of the New York Academy of Science* 1976, **280,** 821–833.

Morse, P. A. The discrimination of speech and nonspeech stimuli in early infancy. *Journal of Experimental Child Psychology,* 1972, **14,** 477–492.

Morse, P. A., & Snowdon, C. T. An investigation of categorical speech discrimination by rhesus monkeys. *Perception and Psychophysics* 1975, **17,** 9–16.

Mulligan, J. A. Singing behavior and its development in the song sparrow, *Melospiza melodia.* University of California, *Publications in Zoology,* 1966, **81,** 1–76.

Nicolai, J. Familientradition in der Gesangsentwicklung des Gimpels (*Pyrrhula pyrrhula L.*). *Journal für Ornithologie,* 1959, **100,** 39–46.

Nottebohm, F. The role of sensory feedback in the development of avian vocalizations. In D. W. Snow (Ed.), *Proceedings of the XIV International Ornithological Congress,* 1966. Oxford: Blackwell Scientific Publications, 1967.

Nottebohm, F. Auditory experience and song development in the chaffinch, *Fringilla coelebs. Ibis,* 1968, **110,** 549–568.

Nottebohm, F. The "critical period" for song learning in birds. *Ibis,* 1969, **111,** 386–387.

Nottebohm, F. Neural lateralization of vocal control in a passerine bird. I. Song. *Journal of Experimental Zoology,* 1971, **177,** 229–261.

Nottebohm, F. Neural lateralization of vocal control in a passerine bird. II. Subsong, calls, and a theory of vocal learning. *Journal of Experimental Zoology,* 1972, **179,** 35–49.

Nottebohm, F. Vocal behavior in birds. In D. Farner & J. R. King (Eds.), *Avian biology.* Vol. 5. New York: Academic Press, 1975.

Nottebohm, F. Neural asymmetries in the vocal control of the canary. In S. R. Harnad & R. W. Doty (Eds.), *Lateralization in the nervous system.* New York: Academic Press (in press).

Nottebohm, F., & Nottebohm, M. Left hypoglossal dominance in the control of canary and white-crowned sparrow song. *Journal of Comparative Physiology,* Series A 1976, **108,** 171–192.

Palermo, D. S. Developmental aspects of speech perception: problems for a motor theory. In J. F. Kavanagh & J. E. Cutting (Eds.), *The role of speech in language.* Cambridge, Mass.: M.I.T. Press, 1975.

Sinnot, J. M. Human versus monkey discrimination of the /ba/ /da/ continuum using three-step paired comparisons. *Journal of the Acoustical Society of America*, Supplement, 1974, **55**, S55(A).

Sinnot, J. M., Beecher, M. D., Moody, D. B., & Stebbins, W. C. *A comparative study of speech sound discrimination in monkeys and humans* (in press).

Studdert-Kennedy, M. From continuous signal to discrete message: syllable to phoneme. In J. F. Kavanagh & J. E. Cutting (Eds.), *The role of speech in language*. Cambridge, Mass.: M.I.T. Press, 1975.

Studdert-Kennedy, M., & Shankweiler, D. P. Hemispheric specialization for speech perception. *Journal of the Acoustical Society of America*, 1970, **48**, 579–594.

Thorpe, W. H. Comments on "The Bird Fancyer's Delight" together with notes on imitation in the subsong of the chaffinch. *Ibis*, 1955, **97**, 247–251.

Thorpe, W. H. The learning of song patterns by birds, with especial reference to the song of the chaffinch, *Fringilla coelebs*. *Ibis*, 1958, **100**, 535–570.

Trehub, S. E. Infant's sensitivity to vowel and tonal contrasts. *Developmental Psychology*, 1973, **9**, 91 96.

Wood, C. C., Goff, W. R., & Day, R. S. Auditory-evoked potentials during speech perception. *Science*, 1971, **173**, 1248–1251.

CHAPTER 5

Language and Language-Type Communication: Studies with a Chimpanzee[1]

DUANE M. RUMBAUGH

and

TIMOTHY V. GILL

Georgia State University
and
the Yerkes Regional Primate Center of Emory University

INTRODUCTION

A Perspective of Language Origins

A number of dimensions clearly differentiate man from other primate species. Outstanding among these are his characteristic orthograde posture and bipedalism, his profound capacity for creative intelligence, and, perhaps most salient of all, his propensity for a seemingly unique mode of communication termed *language*. The roots of man's typical posture, his mode of locomotion and even his creative intelligence has been partially traced through comparative psychological studies, but the origins of his language remain relatively obscure.

One thing is clear: we cannot understand man's spoken language as a simple extension of the vocalizations of monkeys and apes. In nonhuman primates, vocalizations are essentially limbically controlled, closed, and species characteristic. In man, on the other hand, vocal capacity is subject to cortical control and has permitted the development of a relatively plastic, open, and highly variable array of utterances from which the many "natural" languages have been derived. The most salient characteristic of man's language, however, is speech itself, and thus, understandingly, human language

[1] This research was supported by National Institute of Health Grants HD–06016 and RR–00165. Send reprint requests to the first author at the Department of Psychology, Georgia State University, Atlanta, Ga. 30303.

115

has usually been defined primarily in terms of speech. Unfortunately, traditional definitions of language have emphasized speech as a public production to the near exclusion of the underlying psychological processes. The result of such circumscribed definitions has been the argument that, because language consists of human speech, no life form other than man can be linguistic. Although this argument ensures victory to those who cling to the anthropocentric perspective, it also serves to thwart attempts to define these fundamental operations that allow man's utterances to be packed with novel, well-defined information for social commerce. It is our thesis that fundamentally language consists of the covert psychological processes which allow man's utterances to be at once novel and informative. Speech, though perhaps the most "natural" channel of thought, is the product, not the essence, of language.

The comparative psychological perspective holds that evolutionary advancements in competence result primarily from the accretion and refinement of processes. On occasion, processes selected for one adaptive function may come to serve quite different functions, but this transition does not justify the unwarranted conclusion that a unique attribute has emerged as a mutation, a conclusion sometimes applied to the emergence of the human language system. Certainly man's larynx endows him with profoundly different capabilities for generating sound patterns than do the larynges of the apes—capabilities so different as to indicate a qualitative shift from ape to man—yet the organs in both ape and man share a relatively recent evolutionary root. Man's brain, furthermore, is probably a natural extension of the organization and attendant function of the anthropoid's. This is not to say that there have not been important refinements, for there have been many, the advanced lateralization of brain functions being perhaps one of the most significant, but the refinements that allowed for the emergence of man's language system in full bloom reflect fundamental processes which in rudimentary form are extant and operational in other primates, notably the great apes (Pongidae).

It follows from our thesis, then, that the *requisites* for language as an overt, public form of communication and also its fundamental parameters can be discovered only through the study of the covert processes of cognition, processes which we suspect are essentially linguistic in structure and function. This conclusion reflects the fact that chimpanzee language projects have succeeded far beyond expectations (Gardner & Gardner, 1971; Premack, 1971; Rumbaugh & Gill, 1976a, 1976b). Their success is probably due to the fact that the chimpanzees entered the projects already equipped with the covert linguistic operations from which man's public language has evolved. Consideration of the possible evolutionary roots of those processes is in order.

Primate Intelligence

To many educators and scientists the concept of intelligence has become an anathema, a concept that often appears to be as useless as instinct and may, in fact, be more counterproductive. Nevertheless, the reality is that, when confronted with a novel situation, individuals from apparently equivalent backgrounds will perform differently. Some, by solving complex problems or devising new tactics, will cope with the situation much better than others. In our attempts to understand these individual differences in performances, we will in all likelihood need to retain some construct that reflects this ability to adapt. It is not the purpose of this chapter to debate the relative merits of various concepts of intelligence. It is important to realize, however, that it is man's extraordinary ability to adapt innovatively to problematic situations through cognitive operations that most distinctly sets him apart from other forms of life. If we did not have this ability, he would, in fact, stand out in any distinctive way from the other species of primates.

If we compare man's cognitive operations with those of his nearest living relatives, the great apes (*Pan, Gorilla, and Pongo*), we initially find that in this respect the difference is one of quantity, not quality. Yet no one would deny that the quantitative difference is extreme; man's brain is physically three to four times larger than that of the apes, and its cognitive potential immensely greater. At what point, then, does *more* become *different*? We agree with Nissen (1951) that *quantitative* advances can be so significant as to permit the emergence of *qualitatively* new operations. It is quite possible that the initial testing of Nissen's proposition has already begun, as comparative explorations into development, cognition, and, more recently, the capacity for language acquisition of ape and man gather momentum.

It was the basic question of the relationship between complex learning skills and the evolution of the primate brain which induced the first author to undertake a series of comparative learning experiments with a variety of primates—prosimian, New and Old World monkeys, lesser and great apes (Rumbaugh & McCormack, 1967). Although the initial approach entailed great methodological risks regarding the equity of the test methods for the diverse species tested, it revealed marked differences between the performances of great apes and macaques (*Macaca*) and those of lesser apes (*Hylobates*) and squirrel monkeys (*Saimiri*). The great apes and macaques proved markedly superior to the lesser apes and squirrel monkeys, whose performance, in fact, often did not justify advancing them to the more demanding phases of the testing program. The equity of test methods for comparative assessment was subsequently enhanced by the development of the Transfer Index (Rambaugh, 1969, 1970). The Transfer Index, which grew out of the earlier work, is a variant of the discrimination-reversal paradigm and is believed to measure the capacity to acquire learning sets (Harlow, 1949) associated with the facile learning of problems of a familiar type or class. Measurements derived from this new test revealed an even more orderly relationship between varying degrees of brain evolution and cognitive ability as assessed through transfer tests.

We hold that transfer-of-learning skills are a fundamental dimension of man's intelligence. If he could not use the experiences of his past to solve the problems of the present, the variety of cognitive solutions to new problems would surely be restricted. This very premise was substantiated when Smith (1973) obtained correlations of $+.76$ between the mental ages of 30 $4\frac{1}{2}$-year-old children and their Transfer Index values. Since all primates manifest transfer-of-learning skills, we hold logically and empirically that the fundamental operations of human intelligence exist in nonhuman primates. It is therefore possible that the operational roots of intelligence can best be defined through the study of nonhuman primates rather than of man.

Our test for measuring transfer of learning, the Transfer Index, presents the subject with a series of problems. In connection with each problem, the subject is given a course of *acquisition* trials on which one object is correct (rewarded) and the other is incorrect (not rewarded). Training on the discrimination continues until an operationally defined criterion is achieved. The achievement of the criterion is relatively precise—the subject must be neither under nor over the predetermined level of learning/mastery. Upon achievement of the criterion, the cue values are rewarded: the initially correct and rewarded stimulus becomes incorrect and not rewarded, and the initially incorrect and not rewarded stimulus becomes correct and is rewarded if chosen. The trials subsequent to the alteration of relative cue values are termed *reversal test* trials. Through the course of these trials the subject can transfer either positively or negatively (with advantage or disadvantage) whatever he learned during the acquisition or prereversal trials in relatively specific amount.

Initial work involved only two criterion levels of acquisition—the 67% and 84% correct schedule (Rumbaugh, 1970). Interestingly, a marked interaction was obtained between these two levels and species in accuracy of reversal test performances. (These performances are used in relation to the prereversal criterion schedules to calculate the Transfer Indices: TI = % correct on reversal ÷ % correct required during criterion acquisition.)

Figure 1 portrays Transfer Index values for a variety of species. The higher the TI values, the more advantageous was the transfer of learning. The axes at the right of the figure reveal that reversal test performance increased, on the average, for the great apes as the prereversal criterion was advanced from 67 to the 84% level. In contrast, for the lesser apes, the vervet monkeys (*Cercopithecus*), and the lemurs (*Lemur*) there was no such increment in reversal performance accuracy. For the diminutive talapoin (*Miopi-thecus*) there was a profound decrement. Briefly, the greater the mastery/learning required in the initial discrimination, the more positive was the transfer test performance for the great apes; and, again, the same increment in learning level resulted in greater negative transfer by the talapoin monkeys. Presumably this interaction reflects pervasive differences in the brains of these species.

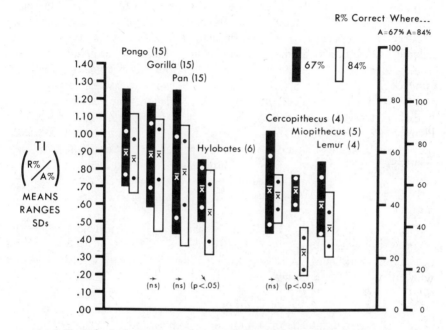

FIGURE 1. Transfer Index means and ranges (left axis) for groups of apes and monkeys where criterional training before cue reversal (A%) was to the 67 and 84% levels of correctness. Transfer index values were calculated on the basis of 10-problem blocks, with percentage responses correct on the reversal trials (R%, trial 1 excepted) divided by the appropriate A% value (either 67 or 84%). The two right axes indicate absolute R% values after training to the two criterional levels. (For instance, talapoin monkeys—*Miopithecus*—were, on the average, 41% correct on reversal trials after initial criterional training to the 67% level, but they were only 25% correct on reversal trials after criterional training to the 84% level.)

Related studies have revealed that, in terms of Transfer Index values, great apes are much more dependent on early enriched environments for normal cognitive development (Davenport, Rogers, & Rumbaugh, 1973) than are rhesus macaques (Rumbaugh & Gill, 1975). Other evidence (Rumbaugh, 1971) suggests that there are qualitative differences in the learning processes of great apes and talapoin monkeys, even though they master problems to a common criterion with equivalent facility. One explanation for the above phenomenon suggested by various reversal test conditions is the possibility that, whereas the great apes mastered the initial discrimination by abstractive/ideational processes, the talapoin monkeys mastered it by stimulus-response habit acquisition. In terms of our conceptual framework, it appears that elaboration of the brain through the course of evolution has provided for the emergence of new learning processes.

We have made the above review of the research on the relationships between brain evolution and cognitive competence because we believe that this research is germane (1) to the selection of apes rather than monkeys for language research with animals, (2) to the interpretation of the results of these studies, and (3) to the definition of the all-important term *language*. Elaborating on the first point above, we decided to work with apes rather than monkeys primarily because apes are cognitively more competent. Although we believe the various genera of great apes to be nearly equal in competence (Rumbaugh & Gill, 1973), we chose to work with chimpanzees because they seem to relate better to man than does either the orangutan or the gorilla. Too, it is quite possible that chimpanzees are more inclined to interact with mechanical contrivances of the type perfected in the Lan*a Project (Lan*a = *language analogue;* Lana is also the name of our first chimpanzee subject).

The rest of this chapter will be addressed to the Lan*a Project, a report of an experimental inquiry into certain parameters of conversation with our ape subject, and, finally, a consideration of certain implications of language-relevant research with chimpanzees to date. Through all of these considerations, a key premise is that cognitive competence, provided for through evolution of the hominian brain and hominian intelligence, provides the essence of covert linguistic operations and, consequently, the underpinnings for the overt, public production of speech and other modes of linguistic expression.

THE LAN*A PROJECT

Earlier reports by Gardner and Gardner (1971) and by Premack (1971) served to demonstrate that apes do, in fact, possess at least elementary linguistic abilities. Our primary objective (Rumbaugh, Gill, & von Glasersfeld, 1973) was to continue study of those abilities through the development of procedures which would enhance both the objectivity and the efficiency of inquiry.

The diverse aspects of the system (Figure 2) were designed by an interdisciplinary team, formed by the senior author and Harold Warner, which included a psycholinguist (Ernst von Glasersfeld), a computer specialist

(Pier Pisani), an infancy consultant (Josephine Brown), and behavioral and electronics specialists (Timothy V. Gill and Charles V. Bell, respectively). We wanted a system that would operate 24 hours a day and would permit the ape to control its environment through the use of linguistic skills. Basically, the entire system (Rumbaugh et al, 1973; Warner, Bell, Rumbaugh, & Gill, 1975) contained three main features: the computer, the language, and the hardware involved in Lana's testing chamber. The computer involved

FIGURE 2. Lana (at age 4½) at the keyboard. Each key has on its surface a geometric pattern (lexigram) that designates its function or meaning. Depression of a key results in a production of a facsimile of the key's lexigram on a projector above the keyboard. The locations of the keys are changed frequently to ensure that the keys are selected on the basis of their lexigrams, not their positions.

was a PDP8-E/CA (Digital Equipment Corp., Maynard, Mass.), which served as the intermediary between Lana and the outside world. It functions simultaneously as a language analyzer, an agent that dispenses requested items, and a recorder of all language interactions between Lana and the outside world.

The grammar of the language involved, called *Yerkish*, was derived from the correlational grammar developed for computer applications in the area of automatic language analysis and machine translation (von Glasersfeld, 1975). Briefly, each word of Yerkish, termed a *lexigram*, is assigned to a class and is restricted, in general, to one and only one meaning of a corresponding English word (or words), to avoid as many ambiguities as possible. There are a number of different lexigrams in most classes, and, within each class, members are treated as equivalents by the language system. Classes are restricted on a conceptual level as to the other classes with which they may be correctly correlated. For example, the sentence *Machine drink(s) juice*, which in English would be grammatically correct but semantically deviant, would be ungrammatical in Yerkish because the lexigram *machine* does not belong to a class of items that can function as the subject of the verb *drink*. The grammar involved in Yerkish is of the general form subject–verb–object, with sentence markers corresponding to intonations in spoken English coming at the beginning of the sentence.

Lana's four keyboards were each 1 foot square and contained 25 rectangular acrylic keys with specific lexigrams embossed on their surfaces. Each lexigram was composed of a combination of one or more of nine distinct stimulus elements and had a particular background color signifying its conceptual class. When a key was depressed, a likeness of the lexigram chosen was displayed on one of a series of rear-projection screens located both above Lana's keyboards and outside of her room in the experimenter's area. Outside of Lana's chamber was a functionally equivalent keyboard which the experimenter used in attempting conversation with Lana. Two sets of projectors were involved, one to send messages and the other to receive them. It was through these projectors that interactions of a linguistic nature would, we hoped, eventually occur.

An initial concern was that Lana might never attend to, let alone read, the lexigram facsimiles produced in the rows of projectors. Eventual conversation with her would not only require that she discern similarities between the lexigrams embossed on the keys' surfaces and the facsimiles produced therewith on the projectors, it would also require that she differentially perceive various sequences of lexigrams as serially ordered to form sentences. Too, she would have to be attentive to the grammatical constraints of the Yerkish language if novel and productive exchanges were to transpire. To our delight, we observed that Lana learned all of these things quite by herself. Very early in her formal training we found her erasing her own errors and building upon sentence beginnings. With about 90% accuracy she completed sentences validly started for her and rejected, via prompt erasure, invalid sentence beginnings that could not possibly be completed to the system's satisfaction. Too, it was determined that she would complete "stock sentences" begun by the experimenter with a high degree of accuracy, regardless of how much of the sentence was left for her to complete. Through these studies, we concluded that Lana had at least rudimentary "reading and writing" abilities (Rumbaugh, et al., 1973).

A word regarding "stock sentences" is in order. These were sentences taught to Lana through basic operant conditioning procedures. Details of the training procedure have been provided elsewhere (Rumbaugh & Gill, 1975). Briefly, Lana first learned to press single keys to get different foods and drinks. She then learned through a modified holophrastic-type training, suggested by Ernst von Glasersfeld, to compose standard stock sentences that resulted in the reliable dispensation of incentives. Examples are PLEASE MACHINE GIVE PIECE OF CHOW, PLEASE MACHINE MAKE MOVIE, and PLEASE TIM TICKLE LANA. Because these word strings were cultivated through procedures that were basically operant conditioning, they were not *linguistic* productions by Lana and should *not* be so viewed by the reader. They were the beginning point, however, from which she has mastered and developed on her own initiative increasingly sophisticated linguistic-type skills.

Shortly after Lana became proficient in her use of various stock sentences to obtain food, drink, outings, music, movies, and social interactions, she extended the meaning of (or redefined) NO from a response of negation to one of protest, learned through the course of systematic training that things have names (Gill & Rumbaugh, 1974) and extended her use of stock sentences to cope with novel problem situation. Specifically, she spontaneously asked for technicians to "move behind the room" when the vending devices were not dispensing the foods requested, though her initial training with that request was to get someone positioned behind a closed window so that he might be viewed after the use of another stock sentence, PLEASE MACHINE MAKE WINDOW OPEN. About 10 weeks after Lana innovatively used stock sentences for other than the intended purpose (Rumbaugh & Gill, 1976a), she initiated productive conversations with the second author of this chapter. In her first conversation she formulated a new sentence to request that she be allowed to drink some of "this" (Tim's coke) out of her room. When asked what "this" was by name, she altered her novel sentence, ? LANA DRINK THIS OUT-OF ROOM PERIOD, to ? LANA DRINK COKE OUT-OF ROOM. Other representative conversations that signal possible hallmarks in the development of her linguistic competence have been detailed in other reports (Rumbaugh, Gill von Glasersfeld, Warner, & Pisani, 1975; Rumbaugh & Gill, 1976b). Reflection upon their dynamics and parameters gave rise to the casting of the following study, which is also the second author's dissertation (Gill, 1977).

AN EXPERIMENT WITH CONVERSATION

A Perspective Regarding Conversation

Conversation provides for an efficient exchange of information between individuals. For a conversation to progress efficiently, its topic or goal must be known by all participants. Only with this mutual understanding can the participants reject irrelevant information and pursue relevant leads.

Despite its prominence in human communication, there has been surprisingly little research on the parameters of conversation, and most of the research on conversation which has been done has focused on syntactical structure, not flow of themes. Virtually no work at all has been done on such important aspects as the variables which influence the probability that a conversation will ensue, topics of conversation, and changes in direction, pace, and duration. Nevertheless, common experience suggests that conversation is primarily a problem-solving activity (though we do not wish to discount the importance of "idle" conversation). It seems reasonable to assume, therefore, that if two or more individuals perceive a common problem, the likelihood that a conversation will be initiated is high. Once the problem is solved or the goal achieved, that conversation will probably cease.

Typically, we think of conversation as vocal activity, an exchange of vocally produced statements between individuals. In accordance with the ideas outlined above, however, we hold that visually produced messages, similarly organized and exchanged, can just as well constitute a conversation. Had we not admitted that conversation can consist of visual as well as vocal messages, we could not, of course, have proceeded with the Lan*a Project. Our working definition of conversation contained three criteria: (1) a conversation must be a linguistic type of exchange, (2) each party must produce at least one novel message, and (3) the topic of the exchange must be relatively stable across time.

From the inception of the project, we hoped to engage Lana in conversation with regard to a number of topics. This goal has not yet been reached. Before beginning the present experiment, however, Tim had succeeded in engaging Lana in a number of conversations about one topic only. That single topic was the procurement of food and drink, items which seem to have enduring incentive value for her (Rumbaugh and Gill, 1976a, 1976b). All of these conversations were impromptu, all were initiated by Lana, and all centered around things she apparently wanted. The question then arose: Could we achieve experimental control over the probability, topic, and duration of conversations with Lana? To this end, a study was conceived to make systematic inquiry into the possibility that certain parameters of conversation with Lana could be defined. Success not only would serve to help us understand the essence of conversational phenomena, but also would provide support for our thesis that man is not alone in his ability to communicate linguistically.

The Experiment

Lana was 4.5 years old at the time of this experiment. The system used for the study was described in an earlier section of this chapter. The experimental manipulation involved three alternative forms to entice Lana into conversation: (1) the experimenter, through use of his keyboard, asked ? LANA WANT WHAT DRINK; (2) he simply stood in full view of Lana holding a known food or drink; or (3) again, with the use of his keyboard, he asked ? LANA WANT WHAT EAT. Only one of these enticement alternatives was employed in a given daily session (9:30 A.M. and 4:30 P.M.). An important notation is that Lana was normally given milk at 9:30 A.M. and her main ration of Purina Monkey Chow at 4:30 P.M. Consequently, the question ? LANA WANT WHAT DRINK was appropriate to her routine receipt of milk in the morning, and the question ? LANA WANT WHAT EAT was appropriate to her receipt of monkey chow in the afternoon; however, on half of the sessions in which either of these two questions was presented, Lana was, in fact, asked what she wanted to drink when it was 4:30 in the afternoon and what she wanted to eat when it was 9:30 in the morning. This manipulation was made to determine whether she would attend primarily to the question of what it was she wanted to ingest or, on the other hand, to the time of day and to what would normally be available to her in the way of food or drink.

Interestingly, Lana was very sensitive to the content of the question posed to her regardless of the time of day. It was an exceptional instance when her response was not a clear reflection of or response to the question posed. Of greater interest was the fact that she frequently negated the option offered by the question. For example, when asked what she wanted to drink in the late afternoon, when it was really time for monkey chow, she responded, NO LANA WANT DRINK. When asked what she wanted to eat when it was morning and time to drink, she responded, LANA WANT DRINK.

With the second type of enticement, where a known food or drink was held in her view, Lana very reliably asked that it be put into the machine, using its name. When that directive was carried out, she very reliably asked the machine, through use of appropriate sentences, to vend it.

In a subsequent part of the study, in which Lana was asked whether she wanted the machine to make music or open the window (both events which would, in effect, tie up the computer's operation for 2.5 minutes and preclude her working for the food or drink otherwise available to her through appropriate requests of the machine), she reliably rejected the option by re-

sponding NO. For example, on June 16, 1975, the experiment called for
Tim to enter the anteroom at 4:30 P.M. with a bowl of monkey chow, food
appropriate to the hour. The following conversation ensued:

LANA: ? You put chow in machine.   16:33
  TIM: Yes. ? Lana want machine make window open. (This would have
         tied up the computer.)
LANA: No open. (an ellipsis)   16:33
         (Tim then put a portion of the chow in the machine and left the
         room while Lana requested PLEASE MACHINE GIVE PIECE
         OF CHOW until all of it was consumed, from 16:34 to 16:36.
         Upon Tim's return to the room at 16:37, Lana continued the con-
         versation as follows.)
LANA: ? You put more chow in machine.   16:37
  TIM: Yes. (and he did so)
LANA: Please machine give piece of chow. (repeatedly)   16:39

In brief, Lana rejected the invitation to have the machine open the window
and did so by use of a self-formulated ellipsis, NO OPEN. With the initial
ration of chow exhausted, she asked for MORE CHOW. She remained goal
oriented throughout the conversation and appropriately used her linguistic
skills efficiently to avoid time-consuming diversions and to achieve the goal
of food.

Another part of the experiment entailed substituting a food or drink
other than what Lana asked for. For example, if Lana was asked what she
wanted to eat (or drink) and she responded with a request for monkey chow
(or milk), the experimenter would load into the vending device either a nonpreferred food (cabbage) or a nonpreferred drink (water). The question was
whether Lana would be attentive to these substitutes.

The results showed very clearly that she was. In one of the more striking
episodes, Tim substituted water for milk, requested by Lana, into the milk
dispenser and then asked Lana, ? WHAT NAME-OF THIS THAT'S IN
MACHINE. Lana replied, PLEASE MACHINE GIVE MILK, which resulted in some of the water being dispensed. (As she could not see the contents of the reservoir, she had to obtain a sample and taste it to get the
information for answering Tim's question.) She tasted it and then promptly
declared, WATER NAME-OF THIS.

The following conversations serve to illustrate Lana's sensitivity to sub-
stitutions of food and drink made by Tim through the course of the experiment. The first example, from June 11, 1975, entailed enticing her with a
bowl of monkey chow. Lana asked that it be loaded into the machine; however, the conditions of the test called for Tim *not* to comply, to load cabbage
for vending instead, and to declare falsely that chow was in the machine.

Although Lana might have asked the machine to vend "chow," she did not and appropriately so, since cabbage—and not monkey chow—was in the vendor. The dialogue was as follows:

LANA:	Please machine give piece of cabbage.	16:53
	? You (Tim) put chow in machine. (5 times)	16:54-16:55
TIM:	(lying) Chow in machine. (In response to each of the 5 requests)	
LANA:	? Chow in machine.	16:57
TIM:	(still lying) Yes.	16:57
LANA:	No chow in machine. (which was true)	16:57
TIM:	? What in machine. (repeat once)	16:57 and 16:58
LANA:	Cabbage in machine.	16:59
TIM:	Yes cabbage in machine.	16:59
LANA:	? You move cabbage out-of machine.	17:00
TIM:	Yes. (whereupon he removed the cabbage and put in the monkey chow)	17:01
LANA:	Please machine give piece of chow. (repeatedly until all was obtained)	17:01

Lana discerned what had, in fact, been loaded into the machine, did not concur with Tim's assertion that it was "chow," asked that Tim remove it, and then asked for "chow" once chow was loaded for vending.

In the second example, which occurred on the afternoon of June 12, 1975, Tim substituted water for the monkey chow requested and insisted that he had loaded monkey chow ("chow") into the vending device operated by the system.

TIM:	? Lana want what eat.	16:23
LANA:	Lana want chow.	16:23
	(At this point, Tim put water into the milk dispenser.)	
LANA:	Please machine give milk. (a response appropriate to the fact that she had seen Tim put something—water—into the milk dispenser)	16:28
LANA:	? You put chow in machine.	16:28
TIM:	Chow in machine. (which was, of course, not true)	
LANA:	? You put chow in machine	16:30
TIM:	Chow in machine.	
LANA:	? Tim put juice in machine. (a new tack on Lana's part)	16:31
TIM:	Juice in machine. (again lying)	
LANA:	No juice. (a declaration that there was, in fact, no juice in the machine)	16:32
TIM:	? What in machine. (repeated at 16:33)	
LANA:	Water in . . . (pause) . . . milk. (sentence completion delayed as she search among keys such as "machine," "milk," and "room")	

For the next 11 minutes, Lana persisted in attempting to get juice but to no avail. She then returned to her original request for monkey chow, at which time Tim finally complied. The entire conversation spanned 29 minutes. Throughout its course, the organization was clear, though there were shifts in topic initiated by Lana which were relevant to preceding exchanges and the conditions of that session.

The overview of some of the main results herein reported support the conclusion that for Lana conversation was indeed a problem-solving activity. The probability of a conversation being generated increased substantially if Tim refused to comply with any response she initially gave, either after being asked what she wanted to eat or drink or after seeing a preferred food or drink in his hand. She was clearly sensitive to the specific questions that were asked of her, regardless of the time of day and the routine normally associated therewith. She rejected options that would "tie up" the keyboard for her use in obtaining foods and drinks through the machine. Quite reliably, she exerted control over the topic of conversation, rejecting diversions of both activities and other incentives offered to her on a programmed basis as called for by the design of the experiment. Finally, Lana's achievement of the food or drink toward which she was oriented. Upon their receipt in part or in whole, the probability that the conversation would continue dropped sharply. Among other things, this study serves to support the conclusion that language serves instrumentally as a problem-solving activity to achieve goals appropriate to motivational states.

OVERVIEW

Chimpanzee projects which have focused on the acquisition of language-relevant skills are currently having a major impact on scientific thought regarding language, ape, and man. It seems clear to us that the success of these projects has been contingent primarily on cognitive skills which characterize the chimpanzee as an anthropoid ape just as much as do its skeleton, musculature, development, and overall close genetic and biological relationship with man (King & Wilson, 1975). The close sensory, perceptual, and cognitive relationship between man and ape has allowed for the building of a linguistic-type bridge through the implementation of Ameslan and artificial languages as employed by Premack and in the Lan*a Project. It has been the ape's readiness to project innovatively the development of basic linguistic-type skills beyond the limits of formal training that has allowed, we believe, for the achievements which have been reported to date.

It is our conclusion that the results of the Lan*a Project, in particular, point to a very close relationship between hominian intelligence and linguistic competence. It remains our thesis that, to the degree that form of intelligence is extant, its operations provide for the covert linguistic process which are fundamental to the encoding and decoding of public linguistic-type communications. These covert cognitive/linguistic processes and their patterns of operation are probably genetically dictated for the most part. Through the processes of learning, they can be extended in their effectiveness and use to the acquisition of skills that allow for *public* commerce of a linguistic type. But a clear requisite to that form of public commerce is a level of intelligence which is sufficient for two or more beings to reach agreement, by whatever means, as to the definitions of the signals/words/lexical items which form a common vocabulary. This perspective implies that, because the chimpanzee's intelligence is hominian, it has the basic covert processes of language. It lacks, however, the level of intelligence sufficient to develop a public language type of communication through which individuals come to concur about the meanings of the fundamentally meaningless stimuli that serve as the lexical items of public language systems. With man's assistance, however, and at his instigation, the chimpanzee can learn at least the general referents/meanings of items which serve as the functional equivalents of words.

The chimpanzee studies also serve to encourage a redefinition of language in terms of basic psycholinguistic processes rather than in terms of anthropocentric productions of speech (Rumbaugh & Gill, 1976b).

At present, we should continue to view the products of the chimpanzee projects as analogues to human language. Questions as to whether the processes in chimpanzee and man are homologous are so problematic as to require time and careful study for proper resolution. It is important to stress, however, that the necessary studies should be conducted to determine whether the optimal course of training apes in language-type skills parallels the course of language acquisition for the human child. To the degree that the two are similar, homologous (as opposed to analogous) processes supporting their functions would be suggested. And to the degree that homology is manifested, the more likely it is that new perspectives of man's language and attendant abilities can be gained through comparative studies of the apes.

References

Davenport, R. K., Rogers, C. M., & Rumbaugh, D. M. Long-term cognitive deficits in chimpanzees associated with early impoverished rearing. *Developmental Psychology*, 1973, **9**, 343–347.

Gardner, B. T., & Gardner, R. A. Two-way communication with an infant chimpanzee. In A. M. Schrier & F. Stollnitz (Eds.), *Behavior of nonhuman primates.* Vol. 4. New York: Academic Press, 1971. Pp. 117–184.

Gill, T. V. Conversations with a chimpanzee. In D. M. Rumbaugh (Ed.), *The Lan*a Project*. New York: Academic Press, 1977.

Gill, T. V., & Rumbaugh, D. M. Mastery of naming skills by a chimpanzee. *Journal of Human Evolution*, 1974, **3**, 483–492.

Harlow, H. F. The formation of learning sets. *Psychological Review*, 1949, **56**, 51–65.

King, M. C., & Wilson, A. C. Evolution at two levels in humans and chimpanzees. *Science*, 1975, **188**, 107–116.

Nissen, H. W. Phylogenetic comparison. In S. S. Stevens (Ed.), *Handbook of Experimental Psychology*. New York: Wiley, 1951.

Premack, D. On the assessment of language competence in the chimpanzee. In A. M. Schrier & F. Stollnitz (Eds.), *Behavior of nonhuman primates*. New York: Academic Press, 1971. Pp. 185–228.

Rumbaugh, D. M. The Transfer Index: An alternative measure of learning set. In *Proceedings of the Second International Congress of Primatology*. Basel: S. Karger, 1969.

Rumbaugh, D. M. Learning skills of anthropoids. In L. A. Rosenblum (Ed.), *Primate behaviour: developments in field and laboratory research*. New York: Academic Press, 1970. Pp. 1–70.

Rumbaugh, D. M. Evidence of qualitative differences in learning among primates. *Journal of Comparative and Physiological Psychology*, 1971, **76**, 250–255.

Rumbaugh, D. M., & Gill, T. V. The learning skills of great apes. *Journal of Human Evolution*, 1973, **2**, 171–179.

Rumbaugh, D. M., & Gill, T. V. The learning skills of rhesus monkeys. In G. H. Bourne (Ed.), *The rhesus monkey*. Vol. I. New York: Academic Press, 1976.

Rumbaugh, D. M., & Gill, T. V. Language and the acquisition of language-type skills by a chimpanzee (*Pan*). In K. Salzinger (Ed.), *Psychology in progress: An interim report*. Vol. **270**. New York: New York Academy of Sciences, 1976. (a)

Rumbaugh, D. M., & Gill, T. V. The mastery of language-type skills by the chimpanzee (*Pan*). In *Proceedings of the Conference on Language Origins and Evolution*. Vol. **280**. New York: New York Academy of Sciences, 1976. (b)

Rumbaugh D. M., Gill, T. V., & Von Glasersfeld, E. C. Reading and sentence completion by a chimpanzee (*Pan*). *Science*, 1973, **182**, 731–733.

Rumbaugh, D. M., Gill, T. V., & Von Glasersfeld, E. C. Warner, H., & Pisani, P. Conversations with a chimpanzee in a computer-controlled environment. *Biological Psychiatry*, 1975, **10**(6), 627–641.

Rumbaugh, D. M., & McCormack, C. The learning skills of primates: a comparative study of apes and monkeys. In D. Starck, R. Schneider, & H. J. Kuhn (Eds.), *Progress in primatology*. Stuttgart: Gustav Fischer, 1967. Pp. 289–306.

Rumbaugh, D. M., Von Glasersfeld, E. C., Warner, H., Pisani, P., Gill, T. V., Brown, J. V., & Bell, C. L. A computer-controlled language training system for investigating the language skills of young apes. *Behavior Research Methods and Instrumentation*, 1973, **5**(5), 385–392.

Smith, S. B. *Transfer Index testing in children.* Unpublished master's thesis, Georgia State University, 1973.

Von Glasersfeld, E. C. The Yerkish language for nonhuman primates. *American Journal of Computational Linguistics*, Microfiche 12, 1975.

Warner, H., Bell, C. L., Rumbaugh, D. M., & Gill, T. V. Computer-controlled teaching instrumentation for linguistic studies with the great apes. *IEEE Transaction on Computers*, 1976, **c-25**(1), 38–43.

CHAPTER 6

The Regulation of Exchange in the Infant-Caretaker System and Some Aspects of the Context-Content Relationship[1]

LOUIS W. SANDER

Boston University School of Medicine

INTRODUCTION

Language serves many different functions, one of these is the regulation of behavior in interpersonal interactions.[2] In turning to the area of early human development for clues to the acquisition of language, one is at once confronted with the changing characteristics of the interactions between the infant and the people about him over the first months and years of postnatal life. There is an ontogeny in the regulation of these exchanges, and it is difficult to imagine that language is acquired completely independently of this ontogeny. The aim of this chapter, then, is to provide a perspective on the regulation of interactions between the infant and the caretaker, generalizing some of the characteristics about these regulatory processes that one can observe and that form a matrix of behavioral exchange characteristics within which language emerges. There appears to be considerable current interest in defining the preverbal context, the interpersonal process, or the "structures" which underlie the acquisition of language and its semantic and syntactical organization. When viewed as an interactive regulative system, the infant and the caregiving environment show an organization of their interactions almost from the outset, but one which undergoes a process of change in ensuing weeks and months, shifting from a more prominently *biosocial* to a more clearly *psychosocial* level.

[1] The author is supported by U.S. Public Health Service Research Scientist Award 5-K5MH20505. Project support has been provided by the Grant Foundation–USPHS NCHD Grant HD01766 and University Hospital General Research Support Funds.

[2] We have taken for a simple meaning of "regulation" that of "governed exchange," attributed by Yamamoto and Brobeck (1965) to Lavoisier.

Joanna Ryan (1974), in her paper in Martin Richard's book, *The integra-tion of a child into a social world* (1974), has set the stage as specifically as possible for what I have to say. In this paper, "Early language development: towards a communicational analysis," Ryan has underlined the contributions of several investigators toward the conceptualization of "communicative competence," especially the contributions of Campbell and Wales (1970), Marshall (1971), and Habermas (1970), stressing in her discussion the im-portance of situational factors in the production of utterances, and the nature of adult–child interaction in explaining language acquisition. She describes Marshall as arguing that any adequate model of language use has to charac-terize the shared knowledge, "the semantic congruence between the contents of two minds," and Habermas as proposing that it is the "structure of inter-subjectivity" between speakers, capable of mutual understanding, that makes the application of linguistic competence possible. Ryan herself goes on to analyze some of the aspects of the adult–child interaction in terms of the adult's difficulties in interpreting the meaning of an utterance and in the understanding, at least in part, of the structure of intersubjectivity between participants in dialogue as being dependent on the mutual recognition of certain kinds of *intention*.

Links between the biosocial and the psychosocial begin to appear when we regard the developmental course of interactions between infant and care-taker from the point of view of regulation, inasmuch as this central concept of regulation in biology is basic to the understanding of the life process itself. The way we have drawn upon the concept can be summarized by a group of assumptions, which have both guided our work and evolved from it. The presentation of these assumptions will be followed by comment on illustra-tive data from our observations of the neonate–caretaker system, and the chapter will conclude with a discussion of the relevance of this viewpoint for a volume on communication and language.

ASSUMPTIONS

The sequence of assumptions which follows, then, represents a number of more or less familiar points of departure, which we will draw upon in apply-ing a conceptualization of regulation in a biological system to the ontogeny of exchange between the human infant and its caregiving environment.

1. In considering life processes, one always considers the organism to-gether with the environment of life support. When we speak of infant and caretaking environment, it is tempting to conceptualize the organism, and the apparently relatively stable organization of its variety of parts and func-tions, as a thing, a creation in itself, beholding it for the sake of thinking

about it, abstracted from any complex matrix. But if one is thinking of the *living* of the organism, immediately his consideration includes the surroundings and the exchanges ongoing between the organism and these surroundings. For the purposes of investigation, it helps to take one or the other of these two poles, the organism or the surround, for analysis, or to attend to transactions taking place back and forth between one and the other in the exchange; but if our concern is for the life process itself, we are always left with something which both includes the poles and the distinctions that separate them, but is always ongoing, organizing the dynamic field somewhere between them.

At any rate, organism, surround, and exchanges-between can be represented, or discussed, as a system—comprising the whole, its component parts, and their relationships.[3] Systems relevant to biology can be identified in a vast hierarchy, involving every level of complexity from subcellular to solar-planetary, each whole the *context* for its components and for the *content* of their exchanges. Organism and surround, whole and part, context and content, thus introduce the ubiquity of *polarities* or dualities, which seem so characteristic of the biological domain wherever we look.

We are confronted at the same time with the *ongoing processes* by which we recognize these *polarities* as being related. In fact, polarity or duality might be viewed as a basic property of matter providing a dynamic for which ongoing processes, including biological organization, provide a solution.

2. A second assumption is that biological processes, as far as we can understand them in the perspective of evolutionary adaptation, eventuate in increasing order (as well as complexity). (It is not settled whether the universe as a whole is, at the same time, gaining entropy or disorder.) In other words, life process involves *integration* or *synthesis*.[4] This is represented in the concept of adaptive process, whereby the exchanges between interacting components in a system, through mutual modification, reach a harmonious co-ordination consistent with the conditions for enduring existence of each. In other words, the components become *joined* in the system through the enduring stability of their harmoniously coordinated exchanges, upon which the regulation of their functions depends, and in terms of which we begin to describe the organization of the system. By virtue of the synthesis effected by these enduring coordinations, the organism has continued existence over time and the appearance of coherence or unity in its environment of evolutionary adaptation. Adaptation is as inseparable from organization as it is

[3] I am referring here to the "open system" as discussed by Bertalanffy (1968).

[4] Weiss (1970) has emphasized the mystery of the maintenance over time of individual unity or identity in the face of an almost infinite complexity of unstable macromolecular processes, this being one of the main "secrets of life" to which biology should be addressing itself in both education and investigation.

from regulation. As Piaget (1952) so succinctly put it. "From the biological point of view organization is inseparable from adaptation. They are two complementary processes of the same mechanism, the first being the internal aspect of the cycle of which adaptation concerns the external aspect." One might also add that synthesis at the level of the system is part and parcel of a process of synthesis or integration at the level of the individual organism. In the viewpoint we are proposing, the concept of integration is given a central role in relation both to the system and to the individual.

In regard to integration at the level of the individual, Von Bertalanffy pointed out in *Problems of life* (1952), that all living matter is characterized both by organization and by endogenous primary activity. Included in the endogenous activity of living matter is the idea of the organism's active self-regulation, carried on by an essential set of mechanisms interfacing inner and outer. In other words, a basic and essential function of ongoing active integration is to harmonize the existential flow of events in time, which are occurring within and between the organism and its surround.

The idea, that the components of a biological system, which are adapting to each other, are each already endogenously active and self-regulating, implies their semi-independence. In the process of adaptation between the components, one is not activated by the other, but the two, already complexly organized and actively generating behavior, must be *interfaced* with each other to reach an enduringly harmonious coordination. We are at once eager to know how exchange can be governed in the adaptive process between self-regulating elements so that this harmonious coordination not only can be achieved but also can endure. Furthermore, the fact that the interface must accommodate both *complexity* and *specificity* would appear to pose a formidable obstacle to the accomplishment of synthesis in the system. We shall be intrigued to learn nature's solution to the elusive function of integration, the harmonizing of polarities, and the mechanisms which make these accomplishments possible. What does integration really consist of? No one that I know of has more clearly defined the now-unsolved issues for the problem of "organization" in biology, which these two contrasting characteristics of complexity and specificity pose, than has Paul Weiss (1969, 1970).

The function of self-regulation and the "self" as a psychic structure furthermore should be related at some basic level of conceptualization.[5]

_____

[5] For the human being one should be able to trace a core function of endogenously active self-regulation and integration from the biological level through an ontogeny of exchange characteristics to the psychological level, where it would appear as the regulatory and integrative functions of a "self." The self is currently being formulated as a central organizing concept within psychoanalytic metapsychology (Gedo, 1975). On the basis of information-processing mechanisms, Basch (1975) proposes an "ordering function" to account for integration in personality organization. One can trace an

3.   The third broad set of assumptions that has guided our work is that it is the domain of *time* and the temporal organization of events that provides the framework for the resolution of the paradoxes and the polarities which confront the developing organism in the biological system, and the framework for the unscrambling of the difficulties in conceptualizing the interface between two ongoing organizations. One cannot contemplate life and life processes outside of time and the organization of events in time by which we describe living. As we will see, however, time in a properly organized system allows for a *meaningful co-occurrence of paradoxical elements, for example, of simultaneity and contingency, or of flow and segmentation, setting the stage for considerations of an ongoing context–content relationship.* Furthermore, in interfacing paradoxical dimensions, which we are too easily convinced to leave as opposites, substance is given to the present moment, so often a vanishing point in the sequence between past and future.

Provided *with the framework of the time dimension,* one can see active exchanges in the adapted system (of organism and surround) as representing *the integration* of events over time in their relation to a present moment. On the one hand, from the *viewpoint of the organism,* time seems curiously enough to demand resolution of complexity, in that the organism as a whole can commit itself to but one voluntary act in time in any one instant. On the other hand, from the viewpoint of the system, simultaneity in time allows the co-occurrence of a broad spectrum of events.

The motor efferent pathway constitutes the "final common path" of integration in the nervous system. An act cannot be taken back once it has actually occurred. The "schema," as proposed by Piaget, represents integration of goal-*directed* action *adapted* to a specific configuration within an assimilated context. In the adapted system in nature, prey capture illustrates the eventuation of integrative processes in the commitment of the organism to the contingent sequencing of events. Integration is built into the system in many ways. A basic level of integration is engineered in the very design of the nervous system. This is beautifully illustrated by the analysis of the frog's visual system worked out by Lettvin, Maturana, McCulloch, and Pitts (1959) in terms of four distributed operations on the visual image: (1) local sharp edges and contrast, (2) the curvature of the edge of a *dark* contrast, (3) the movement of edges, and (4) *local* dimmings produced by movement or *rapid* general darkenings. The "image" is transformed "from a space of simple discrete points to a congruent space where each equivalent point

ontogeny or "developmental line" of an organizing or integrating psychological structure such as the self, provided that such ontogeny can relate changes in interactive regulation over the first years of life to associated changes in the organization of the functions of attention, attention deployment, awareness, and self-awareness in relation to their roles in self-regulation and the guidance of the individual's behavior.

is described by the interaction of particular *qualities* in its neighborhood. Every point is seen in definite context. The character of the contexts genetically built up is the physiologic synthetic a priori." Time constants and rates of transmission of the four operations integrate an increasingly precise temporal sequence which sets the proper moment for the definitive strike of the frog's tongue to ensnare the prey.

From the system's point of view, however, the order begins with a fifth set of neurons that Lettvin labels as "others," which have no distinct receptive field but have a long time constant and a frequency of discharge that is greater the darker it is—in other words, with a decrease in the general level of background illumination dusk sets the stage for a *simultaneity* which provides the general conditions for both activation of the insect prey and activation of the frog. Time thus has the peculiar characteristic, because of the spectrum of rates for which it provides, of allowing the harmonizing of the two contrasting domains—simultaneity and contingency. From the viewpoint of the system, the commitment of the frog in its strike is thus a temporal integration of a broad *context* of states simultaneously characterizing the participating components, plus the highly specific content of the behaviors of reacting parts at a higher frequency in the contingent relation.

Current research reports now confront us with evidence for a certain receptivity or resonance between subsystems, whose broader states of readiness or reactivity are synchronized or entrained one with the other, especially in connection with the apparent simultaneity of high-frequency events generated by the two components. Recent work has stimulated increasing interest in the extent to which the human infant is preadapted for this simultaneity. For example, the looking preference of the newborn infant is for the organized, as contrasted to the scrambled, human face as a stimulus (Freedman, 1971). The imitation of complex facial gestures of the human adult by the 2-week-old neonate (Moore & Meltzoff, 1975) boggles the mind for explanation, as does the phenomenon of linguistic-kinesic synchrony in the newborn, as early as 12 hours postdelivery (Condon & Sander, 1974*a, b*). Condon's frame-by-frame segmentation of the acoustic boundaries in adult speech is found to match precisely the frame-by-frame segmentation of the movements of the awake, active newborn exposed to the sound of this speech. In this synchrony, should there be a pause, activation and sound onset both begin again in the same $\frac{1}{24}$th of a second. The work of Condon (1975) with the *asynchrony* of autistic, dyslexic, or aphasic children, showing fraction-of-a-second delays in their acoustic sensorimotor processing time, confirm his conceptualization of a preadapted neurophysiological basis for an essential and basic participation of infant and caretaker from birth in a mutually shared, high-frequency linguistic-kinesic synchrony. Byers (1975) provides further evidence of the role of events between the participants at the level of EEG frequencies (i.e., 10 cycles/second) governing both simultaneous and reciprocal behaviors in conversational and ritualistic exchanges in certain primitive cultures.

We can begin to propose, then, that these components of the system are interfaced at more than one temporal level—the broader background level of state, cycling at a lower frequency, in relation to a foreground of higher-frequency events. Furthermore, at both levels there can be both simultaneity and contingency. Shared or alternating contingency becomes reciprocation. From the perspective of a temporal organization interfacing the partners, we have the basis for the "structure of intersubjectivity." Negotiation of the specifically initiated intentions of one or the other of the participants in the *system* is given meaning by this context. This suggests an ontogenetic basis for the emergence of "meaning" in communication, referred to above by Joanna Ryan in her discussion of developmental studies of language.

4.   A fourth set of assumptions, which explicates further the dimension of time, centers about the notion that *biorhythmicity* and its related feature of phase control provide the mechanisms interfacing the active, self-regulatory organizations which are components of the adapted biologic system. Biorhythmicity consequently plays a central role in the regulation of exchanges between components. We have said that, from the systems point of view, the spectrum of different rates or frequencies allows the harmonizing of the contrasting domains of simultaneity and contingency. Rhythms exist in a spectrum of time levels from low frequency (macroscopic) to high frequency (microscopic), allowing further characterization of the context–content relationship, the longer periodicities providing context for the briefer ones.

The mechanisms involved in the entrainment of biorhythms provide the means for harmonizing the polarity of complexity and specificity. A highly specific cue locked to phasic variations of one rhythmic component of the system, within limits, shifts the phase in a second rhythmic component, receptive to the specific cue, so that synchrony between the two components is effected. The cue, being itself located in the flow of the first rhythm, is thus regularly recurrent and establishes a temporal background for continuity or stability in maintaining the phasic relationship with the rhythm of the second function. With a background, let us say for example, of states of activity and quiescence oscillating at a relatively slow frequency but locked together by a specific cue, the two complex organisms, infant and mother, can maintain the background of synchrony or simultaneity despite an otherwise complexly distracting foreground of great variation.

As was pointed out sometime ago by Halburg (1960), Pittendrigh (1961), Aschoff (1965), and others (e.g., Luce, 1970), both *adaptation* and *integration* of biologic systems can be resolved as features of phase synchronization.

Disturbances in this function of integration have been experienced by each of us in crossing time zones, with some individuals requiring 2 weeks or more in a so-called jetlag to regain full integration of all the different physiological subsystems. There is evidence of an interesting semi-independence of the rhythms of our many different physiological functions, inasmuch as some functions resynchronize more readily after a jetlag than do others.

Both the model of integration as phase synchronization and the semi-independence of physiological subsystems are confirmed as well in infancy research. In polygraphic studies of sleep, a crucial infant difference in sleep organization is the relative *coherence* or togetherness in the timing of fluctuations of physiological variables (such as vascular, respiratory, and neural) as the infant cycles through REM and quiet subphases of sleep (Prechtl, 1968). In regard to the semi-independence of physiological subsystems, it has been found that the first appearance of circadian rhythmicity occurs at different chronological points, over the first months of life, for the various physiological functions (Hellbrugge, Lange, Rutenfranz, & Stehr, 1964).

One other point should be mentioned: in relation to this fourth set of assumptions, biorhythmicity also provides for the harmonizing of another paradox, that of flow and segment. In the sine wave, the alternating of opposite positive and negative phases allows the flow to be segmented at the boundaries generated by this inflection in direction. Although he was not concerned with rhythmicity itself, it was by the notion of the juxtaposition of contrasts or opposites which break up the flow of speech that de Saussure, at the turn of the century, began the definition of phonemes and the systematic study of phonetics, which segments speech at naturally contrasting acoustic boundaries.[6] As mentioned above, segmentation of speech at the tenths-of-a-second level has been carried out by Condon and found to match with a synchronized segmentation of neonatal movement at an exactly similar level. Here he is dealing with frequencies of 0.04 to 0.20 second, roughly in the range of EEG alpha rhythms, as is Byers (1975) in his investigations of communicational behavior in primitive cultures. Stern (1974; Stern, Jaffe, Beebe, & Bennett, 1976) has demonstrated and beautifully documented the occurrence of simultaneous and reciprocal exchanges in the mother–infant

---

[6] De Saussure (1950) also had the idea of speech arising as an integrative act in a way similar to the notion of the adapted act as synthesis, which we have been describing. "The characteristic role of language with respect to thought is not to create a material phonic means for expressing ideas, but to serve as a link between thought and sound, under conditions that of necessity bring about the reciprocal delimitations of units. Neither are thoughts given material form nor are sounds transformed into mental entities; the somewhat mysterious fact is rather that 'thought–sound' implies division, and that language works out its units while taking shape between two shapeless masses" (p. 112).

dyad and has related the simultaneous exchanges to certain coincidences of state in the participants.

5.   A fifth set of assumptions, concerned as well with mechanisms of regulation, is that regulation of exchange in the biological system involves cybernetic or feedback control mechanisms. This is scarcely an assumption in the present day. However, to include the point that regulation of exchange involves cybernetic control allows us to include the information-processing model in building a viewpoint of early regulation which may underlie communicational process. Very briefly, this model suggests mechanisms whereby modifications in behavior necessary to realize goals become incorporated in the representation of the goal. Piaget's notion of the schema is a conceptualization of adaptive behavior which is in close agreement with information-processing theroy.

Ashby's cybernetic model (1952) also provides a way out of an additional major paradox confronting developmental conceptualization, namely, that posed by the contrasting tendencies of synchronization and differentiation. Although rhythm entrainment and phase synchronization help us to visualize mutual participation, simultaneity, and bonding between subsystems, they do not account for a concurrent tendency in development, namely, that of separation, differentiation, and individuation. If we are looking for "structures" in the sociobiological matrix to shed light on communicational processes and language formation, surely the synthesis demanded by the polarity of tendencies toward uniting versus tendencies toward separating cannot be omitted from our understanding of the regulation of exchange in the developing infant–caretaker system. Mention of two further sets of assumptions based on Ashby's model suggests mechanisms by which the former tendency provides context for the latter.

6.   The sixth set of assumptions attempts to follow Ashby, Piaget, and biorhythmicity further in proposing (1) that an *empirical* basis for "equilibrium" between adapting components in a system exists in the phase synchrony of their biorhythms (empirically certain allowable variation in values of variables will remain within the equilibrium, within the "regions of stability" characteristic of cybernetic control); and (2) that component subsystems of a complex system rich in such equilibria then can become loosely coupled and enter a temporary and relative independence in adaptive encounter with the surround. The loosely coupled subsystem can be said to be disjoined, or temporarily independent, in relation to the larger system. The effects of constancies on temporary independence of component functions within the system have been proposed by Ashby to describe the situation which exists in the presence of stability in a complex system having a great many subsystems in equilibrium (Ashby, 1952, pp. 164–166). Under such conditions, *perturbation* of the "disjoined" or partially independent sub-

system as a consequence of its adaptive encounter with the surround does not spread to the rest of the system. The subsystem is, in effect, insulated from the rest of the system as long as the general state of stability or richness of equilibria persists. On the other hand, when the system is tightly coupled and relatively poor in such states of equilibrium, perturbation of one subsystem preempts the function of the rest of the component subsystems to restore variables to their region of stability. For example, we see a limited spread of perturbation in an infant in a stable awake state, as he begins the process of differentiation by actively exploring a stimulus, or "groping" with eyes, ears, fingers, or other sensorimotor functions in the stabilizing of new operant schema relating him to some relatively low-intensity feature of his surround.[7]

The assumptions in this sixth set serve to harmonize the polarity of togetherness and separation through the necessary condition of richness of equilibria in the system which makes possible the "temporary independence" of actively self-regulating components in semi-independent adaptive encounter. In an earlier description of "adaptive issues," negotiated in the interaction between infant and caretaker, which bond them by an epigenetic succession of mutually harmonized coordinations (Sander 1969), we sought to represent the acquisition by the infant of a "requisite variety" of options, through acquisition of the succession of adaptive achievements. (For "requisite variety" see Ashby, 1956, pp. 206–213.) This same set of assumptions, furthermore, leads directly to the seventh set, concerned with conceptualization of the ontogeny through which the active self-regulatory mechanisms of the infant pass in the generation of the "self" as a psychic structure. This completes the conceptualization of a progression from biosocial to psychosocial, using the same set of assumptions and the same basic systems model.

7.   The seventh set of assumptions carries the general model to the level of psychic structure, but we shall have to leave this to a future, more detailed discussion. It is essentially concerned with the extension of the basic interactive-regulative model to the matter *first* of the consolidation and *then* of the partial independence of the self-regulatory function, associated with the advancing capacity for the representation of, and the "internal perception" of, intentions and aims and the differentiation of a core of self-awareness including that of own state, that is, proposing a beginning ontogeny of the self around 15 to 20 months modeled closely on that proposed by Spitz

_____

   [7] "It must not be overlooked that adaptation may demand independence as well as interaction (of parts). The learner-driver of a motor-car, for instance, who can only first keep the car in the center of the road, may find that any attempt at changing gear results in the car apparently trying to leave the road. Later, when he is more skilled, the act of changing gear will have no effect on the direction of the car's travel. Adaptation thus demands not only the integration of related activities but the independence of unrelated activities." (Ashby, 1952, p. 157)

(1957). Such a process of self-differentiation depends on active initiations and intentions, under conditions of equilibrium in the system, and on their relation to an ontogeny of *awareness* and *self-awareness* as goal achievement or failure is experienced. We have attempted to carry the model to this extent, covering some of the developments in the second 18 months of life, as a way of relating the aspects of basic regulation in the first 18 months to the changing picture of regulation in the second 18 months, determined by the increasing role at that point of active self-regulatory functions (Sander 1975).[8] It would appear reasonable to propose that ontogeny in language development of the second 18 months must be closely associated with these steps in ontogeny of personality organization, especially if language contributes particularly critically to the implementation of integration in both the system and the individual.

THE DATA

Let us turn briefly now to the kind of data which have emerged from the research of our group. Initial work first led to the above assumptions, and

[8] Interpersonal regulation and communication includes, in the second 18 months, the regulation of a group of more advanced interpersonal behaviors, namely, negativistic and aggressive behaviors, imitation, and imaginary games, as well as experiences of "recognition" or shared awareness, each of these carrying somewhat further in differentiation the regulations already manifested earlier. Within the second 18 months, the child becomes aware that another can know what he knows of himself; that is, his perceptions of himself, his intentions, and his state (i.e., his "internal" perceptions as well as his perceptions of his external world) can be validated or negated in his exchange with the partner. This is merely an advanced level of adapted coordination applied in the same model. One must assume the same progression of differentiation in the ontogeny of "internal" perception or "inner awareness." As the base of *validated "internal" perceptions*, now coming to exist as "internal representations," becomes included in the repertoire of adapted coordinations, an even richer complex of equilibria can be generated in the exchange system. From this base, the "disjoining" or disembedding of the integrative self-regulatory core can proceed, which begins to be labeled by 15 months as the "self" (Spitz, 1957). A continuity or "conservation" of the self is effected by directed and provocative aggressive behavior in a process of "reversal" (see Sander, 1975). The role of the use of words in this process of disembedding has been suggested by Dahl (1965) in his description of "an experiment in nature"—Helen Keller's experience of learning that each thing had a name. He suggests that the representation of the *thing* by the "word" frees the active organizing core to deploy the focus of "attention" from one *thing* to another, that is, to think. With words Helen Keller could "think" from one thing to another, unfettered by the complexity of the sensorimotor matrix in which each thing heretofore had been embedded. That Helen Keller may have had the word *water* before her illness at 19 months of age would seem not to invalidate the propositions Dahl makes, but even to substantiate the integrative role of the word in relation to reactivation of a previously consolidated self-core.

subsequent work was designed from them. Historically, our work began in 1958 with a monitoring bassinet which provided concurrent information in real clocktime on a set of infant variables related to crying and motility, and on a set of caretaker variables related to time of caretaker's approach to the crib removal of infant from the crib, and return of infant to the crib. The method has gradually become more sophisticated so that data can be reduced and analyzed by computer and include states of the infant in the crib along the sleep–awake continuum. The observations by the monitor during the in-crib time is extended by direct event-recorded observations of infant and caretaker over the full awake period from the transition to awake to the onset of the infant's transition to the next subsequent quiet-sleep period. We have been especially interested in regulation around the clock of infant states of sleep, awake, and crying and their relation to gross and microscopic aspects of the interaction of caretaker with infant, a set of variables related to the one being analyzed in their relation to the set of variables related to the other (see Sander, Chappell, & Snyder, 1975).

The bits and pieces of the body of empirical findings, which can be assembled from this work extending over a considerable number of years, contribute to a model of interactive regulation for the infant–caretaker system. Since most of our data can be found elsewhere (Sander, 1969, 1975; Sander & Julia, 1966; Sander et al., 1975; Sander, Stechler, Burns, & Julia, 1970; Sander, Julia, Stechler, & Burns, 1972; Condon, & Sander, 1974a 1974b; Cassell, & Sander, 1976; Burns, Sander, Stechler, & Julia, 1972), only a very brief listing of the main categories will be reviewed before discussing the model, although it is only in considering the details that the evidence can be adequately marshaled to document it.

1. The heirarchy of rhythmicities which organizes the behavior of the infant has been studied and reported on by a considerable number of investigators over the past decade or so. Our work has dealt mainly with the lower frequencies: the approximately 24 hour (circadian), the 4 to 6 hour and approximately 1 hour (ultradian), and currently the less than $\frac{1}{2}$ hour (infradian) in time series analysis of the monitor records. Although merely touched upon above, it is important to realize that this is but one end of a spectrum of rhythmicities which range down through movement, sucking, and breathing periodicities of the infant (some of which are in the time domain of social reciprocation and gaze regulation, reported by workers such as Brazelton, Tronick, Adamson, Als, & Wise, 1975, and Stern, 1971) to the domain of the rhythm hierarchy described by Condon which ranges from 1 second down to 0.04 to 0.2 second (Condon, 1974).[9]

---

[9] The role of basic rhythmicities in the organization of behavior, proposed by Lashley (1951), has been extensively investigated and discussed by Wolff (1967, 1968).

2. The first days after birth, regardless of caretaking environment, are characterized by a longer daily duration of awake and active states than is found again until the end of the first month of life (Sander et al., 1972). In these first days there is a disorganization and reorganization of sleep and awake periods which not only includes duration and occurrence within the 24-hour framework of naps and awake periods but also appears to include shifts in the finer structure of REM/NREM cycling and it characteristics. Relative disorganization of sleep and awake states is associated with increased crying of the infant, increased intervention time, and multiple interventions, all of which diminish again as reorganization emerges. Over the first postnatal week, when the infant is roomed-in with its own mother on a demand-feeding regimen, a coordination appears between infant state and caretaker activity, such as relation of infant state to intervention time, to mother's position of holding the infant, to her vocalizing to the infant, and so on (Sander et al., 1975).

3. There is an effect of caretaking environment on the rate of emergence and the extent of day–night differentiation of sleep and wakefulness in the infant over the first months of postnatal life (Sander et al., 1972). Moreover, there is a sex difference in this effect. In the demand-feeding regimen provided by a single caretaker rooming-in around the clock from the first day, a basic day–night organization appears between the 4th and 6th postnatal days (Sander & Julia, 1966). Among other things, this involves the settling of more than half of the longest sleep period (nap) of the 24 hours into the nightly 12 hours. For this particular sample, this was accomplished for all infants by the 10th postnatal day. However, it is the natural mother who, within the definition of a demand-feeding regimen, is free to "shape" the time of occurrence of naps and awake periods over the 24 hours so that they will coincide with the most convenient household schedule, whose record will show by the 7th day a beginning ordering of the entire 24-hour span in regard to time of occurrence of naps and awake periods (Sander et al., 1970). "Shaping" here can be viewed as an intuitive process, carried out by the mother, aimed at the phase shifting of ultradian rhythms (related to napping and awake spans), and involving, for example, keeping the baby awake longer in the evening so that he will sleep longer in the early morning, attempting to feed him more so he will take longer to become hungry, or waking him if he is napping too late in the afternoon and therefore will not be sleepy in the evening. There is an interactive effect of caretaker on sleep

---

Condon has discussed at length the communicational behavior of speaker and listener, the hierarchy of rhythmicities, and their relation to language acquisition and organization in a number of papers (e.g., Condon, 1974; Condon & Ogston, 1971). Regulation of mother–infant interaction via visual behavior has been investigated by Stechler and Carpenter (1967) and Stechler and Latz (1966).

and awake period length over the first 3 weeks of life (Pekarsky, Julia, & Sander, 1969).

4. There is an individual specificity by the end of the first week of life in the interactions with a caretaker who has been providing sole care of the infant from birth. This specificity can be thought of as a complex gestalt involving timing, sequence, cue, and so forth—a complex context in which the sequence of caretaking activities over the awake span is carried out.

In a cross-fostering design involving two foster caretakers evidence was obtained that by 10 days the individually fostered infant has formed a specific adaptation to the individual who is caring for him, so that a change of foster caretaker is associated with significant changes in crying and feeding behavior. Furthermore, in regard to specificity, a sample of natural mother–infant systems provides greater idiosyncrasy of regulatory interactions than appears in a sample of different infants individually cared for by the same foster mother. Regulation which is based on individual differences of both infant and caretaker is highly specific for them and leads to the unique and idiosyncratic characteristics of exchange in the natural mother system. Evidence of early specificity in perceptual processing was obtained by masking the natural mother's face on the 7th day of life over an entire awake period (the mother having roomed-in with her baby from the first day). A striking surprise reaction on the part of the infant occurs precisely at the time of initiation of feeding and is followed by effects on infant state and feeding variables. These evidences of individual specificity of adaptations in infant–caretaker exchanges can be considered to illustrate an initial bonding. They point as well to the role of specificity in regulatory processes (Cassel, & Sander, 1976).

5. Finally, there was a set of findings related to the course over the first 2 months of life which is followed by infants for whom specifically synchronized temporal organization is *not* established within the system over the first 10 days of life. These were infants who remained in the stressful, 4-hourly scheduled, noncontingent neonatal nursery caretaking with multiple caretakers for 10 days *before* beginning individual round-the-clock fostering. Effects were demonstrable in (1) the subsequent characteristics of sleep and awake state distributions in these infants, (2) their more frequent reaction to a visual stimulus by fussing and crying, (3) the course over the 2 months of the study of their looking behavior in response to visual stimuli, and (4) the greater week-to-week instability of the rank-order of infants within the sample in regard to a variety of variables (i.e., an instability of individual differences).

A MODEL OF INTERACTIVE REGULATION IN THE ADAPTED (STABILIZED) INFANT–CARETAKER SYSTEM

An illustrative (idealized) model can be drawn of the way the infant–caretaker exchange is regulated when the system reaches a level of relative adaptation by, let us say, the end of the third postnatal week. In the usual instance, by this time there is a basic structure to the 24-hour day, with the longest awake period occurring late in the day or early evening, and a number of earlier, briefer awakenings; the greater part of the longest sleep is occurring in the nightly 12 hours, with briefer naps during the day and perhaps some predictability as to their duration and occurrence in morning and afternoon. The duration, pace, amounts, and behavioral cueing of the infant related to the sucking and feeding interaction have become familiar, if not completely predictable, for the caretaker. A characteristic course or sequence of events over the entire awake period begins to "jell," as illustrated in Figure 1.

In this model of the full awake period we are taking the complete duration of the awake period as the basic unit of observation. There is an order and sequence to the course of events in the adapted system in which the time course of the awakening can be segmented into subunits of regulatory interactions, each with its own aims or goals and specific exchange patterns. In the diagram, 7 such segments are labeled: initial, preparation 1, feeding, social, open space, preparation 2, final. Dyads can be compared in regard to these segments—their boundaries, content, duration, and variability from observation to observation and from day to day. Although arrived at independently, this is the same general model that Stern (1974) has suggested for systematic study of the play interaction between mother and infant.

In Figure 1 the heavy line represents the course of the infant state as a vector of the direction of effects of the interaction of endogenous (infant) and exogenous (environmental) influences upon it. The arrows represent the direction of effect on state of the two sets of influences, coincidence of direction representing their matching or fittedness in regard to a given location in the awake period. As illustrated here, the direction of endogenous and exogenous influences coincide in regard to "initial," "preparation 1," "preparation 2," and "final" segments, the figure as a whole depicting an awake period in which the infant is not "ready" to return at once to sleep after the feeding. In an awake period such as this, although infant drowsiness may appear during the feeding, from which the mother stimulates the baby if she feels an inadequate intake has been obtained to that point, the infant recovers spontaneously from the drowsiness, and may, however, subsequently terminate the feeding. If the feeding has been comfortable, the succeeding span

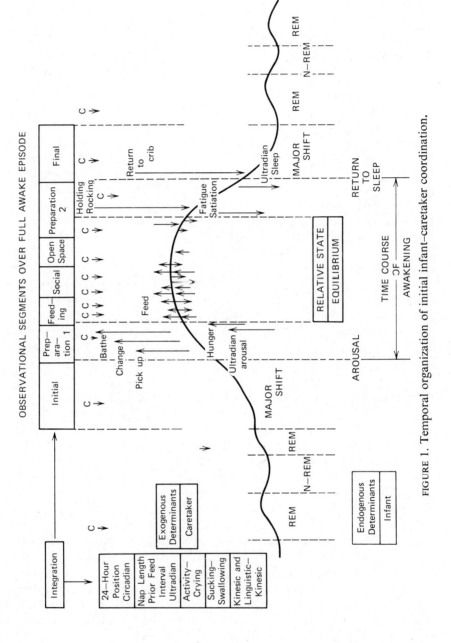

FIGURE 1. Temporal organization of initial infant-caretaker coordination.

is one of relative stability—an equilibrium of both endogenous and exogenous influences in which the behavior of neither mother nor infant is being preempted by regulatory necessity to restore stability and comfort. Two related but somewhat different segments can then be depicted: social exchange and a disengagement which has been labeled in the figure as "open space." In other than an idealized model, these will not usually occur as single separate spans, but will be broken up into smaller alternations.

The ontogenesis of social exchange and games between infant and caretaker and their clearly regulatory characteristics have been described by Call and Marschak (1966), Stern (1974), and others (e.g., Brazelton et al., 1975). These investigators have focused in the main on a somewhat later age (2 to 3 months), when social reciprocations have become well established. Obviously social exchange can occur during any of the segments, but in the model it is given a special place during the span of equilibrium, when the initiative to produce a contingent effect in the partner can begin to be traded back and forth by a variety of maneuvers, such as gaze direction or facial movement, in more extended sequences. Stern (1974) has pointed to the regulatory role of these exchanges in maintaining a level of excitement optimal for both partners. However, the relatively artificial sampling of reciprocal behaviors in the laboratory situation, or the effects of observation and recording procedures in the home, may obscure the occurrence of disengagements or "open spaces," as well as the basic differences in dyads in handling this part of the more extended awake period.

Major cultural differences in regard to early disengagement appear to exist as well, with the more "primitive" cultures eschewing such periods of separateness (rather than separation) until the infant is considerably older. In white middle-class America the "open space" finds the mother placing her infant in the feeding chair or infant seat, where he can view the room and entertain himself while she turns her attention to other tasks. The infant, still in a stable equilibrium in regard to state, can be presumed to be in a particular position in regard to self-regulation. In this state selectivity and deployment of attention presumably can be initiated apart from requirements of essential variables for basic regulation. In the maintenance of a level of arousal optimal for the infant, the exercise of movement, such as fist sucking or head turning, stimuli and discrepancies of relatively low intensity can be pursued, habituated, or manipulated in beginning the active organization of the operant schema. This provides a different perspective for the caregiver as well, in which the initiative of the infant to "entertain" himself is regarded as a sign of his progress in self-regulation, stability, and autonomy. Obviously the context provided for the infant here will represent an important longitudinal difference between dyads in terms of the changes it undergoes in furnishing appropriate complexity. In the light of Ashby's model of equilibrium in complex systems, one providing for temporary and partial independence of subsystems (i.e., here, the various sensorimotor functions), the conditions are present for optimal discrimination and schema stabilization relative to the infant's active role in the ontogenesis of cognitive functions.

Toward the end of the awake period, the duration of which is powerfully determined endogenously, instability of state reappears with a greater sensitivity to environmental interventions by a change of state (Sander et al., 1975). Here, again, infant and caregiver match "direction" in regard to the change of state in the infant and to the aim of the caregiver's intervention, respectively. In this coordination, the "meaning" of a given action has been established in relation to its place in the now-familiar sequential context, which is of course common to both. The relation of "meaning" to the stabilized context is depicted in Figure 1 by the locations of the letter C, each C indicating a different time of occurrence of the infant's cry. As one familiar with the background time course, the mother deduces the meaning of a cry to a large extent from the point in the sequence at which it occurs. The segments labeled "preparation 2" and "final" concern the subsequent aim of "putting the baby to sleep." Here specificity in the course of events seems particularly striking, as our experiments in perturbing the context indicate, such as by the masking of the mother (Cassel & Sander, 1976) or the substitution of a strange caretaker over an awake period.

There is an obvious difficulty in attempting to capture in a diagram an ongoing process which the ontogenesis of changing regulation in the infant–caretaker system represents. As the awake period is gradually extending in duration and stabilizing in location, its sequence of events—their order, duration, and complexity— is also gaining the stability of a familiar framework for both infant and caregiver. Although a foreground of day-to-day change and variety may be evident, an increasingly richer background context is shared between the partners as a familiar base from which new variations can be differentiated, these becoming stable in turn as they are incorporated into recurrent coordinations. Such a sequence of adapted interactional coordinations over the first 18 months of life was conceptualized (Sander, 1969) in relation to the appearance of new capabilities for selective initiation of activity on the part of the infant as he grows older. These new activities impose new demands for regulation in the system, new exchanges, and the necessity for new coordinations.

DISCUSSION

The aim of this chapter has been to bring together a viewpoint on regulation of infant states and interactions between infant and caregiving environment, synthesizing a set of assumptions and a range of empirical findings into a diagrammatic model. The question remains whether this picture of exchange in the establishment of initial adapted coordinations, and their subsequent ontogenetic changes and transformations, provides a framework of interactive "structures" based on regulation out of which later communicative processes or "structures" may arise. It seems evident that many basic elements which can be found in later communicational analyses are already part of the picture, when viewed from the standpoint of a biological systems model, its exchanges and regulatory mechanisms.

The diagram, itself a synthesis of a wide base of observations and empirical data, also depicts two concurrent integrations, a vertical and a horizontal. The vertical represents the broad range of rhythm frequencies which can be identified in recurrent fluctuations of values of variables. These are harmonized in relation to the integrated action of any present moment, a harmony that integrates as well the place of that moment in the sequential flow of events over time (i.e., a vertical plus a horizontal synthesis). Integration, as an actuality of the life process, must refer both to function (or mechanism) and to outcome, but from the perspective we have described it appears inherent in the way regulation is accomplished in the system. From this perspective paradoxical elements fall into place, which otherwise become harder and harder to harmonize conceptually as development proceeds into its more differentiated transformations. The tendency has been to resolve the matter by focusing upon one horn or the other of the dilemma, omitting the perspective of the open systems view of the life process itself, a dynamic in which each of the features is playing a part. Just as investigations of habituation and discrimination in early infancy have demonstrated preadapted functions ensuring bonding in the postnatal infant–caretaker system, a further avenue to the better understanding of "integration" may be opened by investigations of regulation from the viewpoint of the early infant–caretaker system and its longitudinally changing features, which accompany progressive behavioral differentiations and increasing complexity (Sander, 1975).[10]

A number of the apparent paradoxes and polarities which characterize exchanges between infant and surround have been described: (1) that between the *complexity* of a range of concurrent periodic events (phase synchronized in a present moment) and the precise individual *specificity* required for stable regulation of exchange; (2) that between a *context*, a simultaneity shared between the partners at the level of a background of both low-frequency fluctuations of states common to both and high-frequency rhythms

---

[10] A broadly based discussion of personality organization which is in harmony with the perspective we are presenting, although not dealing with ontogenesis specifically, is provided by Basch (1975).

(e.g., those of linguistic-kinesic synchrony), and a *content* of specifically initiated action with contingent effects, each upon the other; and (3) that related to the harmonizing of *synchrony* and *differentiation* within the system in the presence of the background context of equilibrium and the foreground content of self-initiated infant activity. Here we can only allude to another polarity—the unconscious–conscious relationship. The background framework of temporal organization, being largely unconscious, exists at one and the same immediate moment with the foreground of more differentiated, voluntary, goal-directed activity providing a *content* of awareness.

In the attention of the infant to contingent consequences of his activities, one sees in him a most sensitive operant contingency detector (Watson, 1967). Obviously there is a long ontogeny of active schema formation by which a "requisite variety" of coordinated behaviors become stabilized and function to ensure a mutually shared control of exchange in the system, as mother and infant both widen the active organization of their worlds. This we have tried to capture in the formulation of the negotiation of a sequence of issues of adaptation (Sander, 1969). The "reading" of intentions, or inference as to the aims of the behavior of the other, is but one step in this sequence and begins to provide a new basis of control and coordination in the ontogenesis of regulatory events. Here the caretaker's and toddler's projections provide also the possibility of misinterpretation of aims. The perception by one partner of the focus of attention of the other has been a central and powerful influence organizing regulatory behavior, almost from the outset of postnatal life, and bears a particular relation to inferences of intention. At the point when regulation at the level of inference as to intention emerges, words are also beginning to appear. Words can be seen as playing an important role as clues to the focus and configuration of attention of the toddler. The focus of attention, which from the outset is embedded in the context–content relationship, thus carries forward the function of the individual's integrative contribution to regulation in the system. Specification by words of the *relationships* which are being attended to is increasingly differentiated and now becomes the basis for new adaptive coordinations with the interpersonal surround. The concealing of attentive focus or intention by words is a later accomplishment as the toddler passes beyond the first 3 years and elaborates the construction of defenses.

We believe it useful to consider the infant and caretaking environment together as a biological system and to focus on the aspects of the regulation of exchange in the system as a way of approaching the problem of mutual adaptation, or as a context in which the ontogeny of communicational processes can be discussed. The inclusion of the final set of assumptions (related to the relevance of the model to psychic structure) follows from the conviction that human communication and language ontogeny must be understood in the light of human personality ontogenesis and that both must be congenial with a developmental model accounting for changing organization in an interactive regulative system of increasing differentiation and complexity. This view has been outlined in previous publications (Sander, 1975) and will be further developed elsewhere (Sander, 1976).

In the context of this volume perhaps the most important question is the need for the formulation of integrative mechanisms necessary for biological adaptation in the living organism. We take for granted the notion of the life process as an ongoing synthesis in an open-ended dynamic, one which is resolving basic polarities but leaving us with an "in-between" in the open endedness of the present moment—an open endedness that our living actively resolves in new organization. It may be that the rules or "structures" characterizing this integrative process will shed further light on common features relating regulation and communication.

References

Aschoff, J. Response curves in circadian periodicity in circadian clocks. In J. Aschoff (Ed.), *Proceedings of the Feldafing Summer School.* Amsterdam: Holland Publishing Co., 1965. Pp. 95–112.

Ashby, R. *Design for a brain.* London: Chapman and Hall, 1952.

Ashby, R. *An introduction to cybernetics.* London: Chapman & Hall, 1956.

Basch, M. F. Toward a theory that encompasses depression. In E. J. R. Anthony & T. Benedik (Eds.), *Depression and human existence.* Boston: Little Brown, 1975. Pp. 485–535.

Bertalanffy, L. v. *Problems of life: An evaluation of modern biological thought.* New York: Wiley, and London: Watts, 1952.

Bertalanffy, L. v. *General system theory: Foundations, development, applications.* New York: Braziller, 1968.

Brazelton, T. B., Tronick, E., Adamson, L., Als, H., & Wise, S. Early mother–infant reciprocity. In M. A. Hofer (Ed.), *The parent–infant relationship.* Summit, N.J.: Chemical Industries of Basil Associated Foundation, 1975.

Burns, P., Sander, L. W., Stechler, G., & Julia, H. Distress in feeding—short term effect of caretaker environment of the first 10 days. *Journal of the American Academy of Child Psychiatry*, July 1972, No. 3, **II,** 427–439.

Byers, P. Rhythms, information processing and human relations: toward a typology of communication. In P. Klopsfer & P. Bateson (Eds.), *Perspectives in ethology.* Vol. II. New York: Plenum Press, 1975.

Call, D. J., & Marschak, M. Styles and games in infancy. *Journal of the American Academy of Child Psychiatry*, April 1966, **5,** No. 2, 193–211.

Campbell, R., & Wales, R. The study of language acquisition. In J. Lyons (Ed.), *New horizons in linguistics.* London: Allen Lane, 1970.

Cassel, T. Z. K., & Sander, L. W. *Neonatal recognition processes and attachment: effects of masking mother's face at 7 days,* 1976 (in press).

Condon, W. S. Communication and order: The micro-"rhythm hierarchy" of speaker behavior. Paper presented at the School Psychologists Convention, New York City, 15 March 1973.

Condon, W. S. Multiple response to sound in dysfunctional children. *Journal of Autistic and Childhood Schizophrenia,* 1975, **5,** No. 1.

Condon, W. S., & Ogston, W. D. Speech and body motion synchrony of the speaker–hearer. In D. L. Harton & J. J. Jenkins (Eds.), *Perception of language.* Proceedings of a symposium at the Pittsburgh University Learning Research and Development Center, held 10–11 January 1968 (conference chairman, Paul M. Kjeldergaard). Columbus, Ohio: Merrill, 1971.

Condon, W. S., & Sander, L. W. Neonate movement is synchronized with adult speech: interactional participation and language acquisition. *Science,* 1974, **183,** 99–101. (a)

Condon, W. S., & Sander, L. W. Synchrony demonstrated between movements of the neonate and adult speech. *Child Development,* 1974, **43,** 456–462. (b)

Dahl, H. Observations on a "natural experiment": Helen Keller. *Journal of American Psychoanalytic Association,* July 1965, No. 3, **XIII,** 533–550.

De Saussure, F. *Course in general linguistics.* Part II. New York: The Philosophical Library, 1950.

Freedman, D. Behavioral assessment in infancy. In G. B. Stoelinga & J. Ten Bosch (Eds.), *Normal and abnormal development of brain and behavior.* Leyden, Netherlands: Leyden University Press, Boerhaave Series, 1971.

Gedo, J. *On a central organizing concept for psychoanalytic psychology.* Paper presented at panel on New Horizons in Metapsychology, Spring 1975, The American Psychoanalytic Association, Beverly Hills, 1975.

Habermas, J. Introductory remarks to a theory of communicative competence. Reprinted in H. P. Dreitzel (Ed.), *Recent sociology,* No. 2. London: Macmillan, 1970.

Halburg, F. Temporal coordination of physiologic functions. *Symposia on Quantitative Biology,* 1960, **25,** 289–310.

Hellbrügge, T., Lange, J. E., Rutenfranz, J., & Stehr, K. Circadian periodicity of physiological functions in different stages of infancy and childhood. *Annals of the New York Academy of Science,* 1964, **117,** 361–373.

Lashley, K. The problem of serial order in behavior. In F. A. Beach, K. O. Hebb, C. T. Morgan, & H. W. Nissen (Eds.), *The neuropsychology of Lashley.* New York: McGraw-Hill, 1954. Pp. 506–528.

Lettvin, J. Y., Maturana, H. R., McCulloch, W. S., & Pitts, W. H. What the frog's eye tells the frog's brain. *Proceedings of the Institute of Radio Engineers,* 1959, **47,** No. 11, 1940–1951.

Luce, G. G. *Biological rhythms in psychiatry and medicine.* National Clearinghouse for Mental Health Information, PH5 Publication No. 2088, 1970.

Marshal, J. C. Can humans talk? In J. Morton (Ed.), *Biological and sociological factors in psycholinguistics*. London: Rogos Press, 1971.

Moore, M. K., & Meltzoff, A. N. *Neonate imitation: A test of existence and mechanism*. Paper presented at the biennial meeting of the Society for Research in Child Development, Denver, Colo., April 1975.

Pekarsky, D., Julia, H., & Sander, L. W. *The influence of caretaker on the duration of the longest sleep and awake periods in infancy*. Unpublished manuscript, 1969.

Piaget, J. *The origins of intelligence in children*. New York: International Universities Press, 1952.

Pittendrigh, C. S. On temporal organization in living systems. In *Harvey Lecture Series, 1960–1961*. Vol. 56. New York: Academic Press, 1961. Pp. 93–125.

Prechtl, H. F. R. Polygraphic studies of the full term newborn. II. Computer analysis of the recorded data. In M. Bax & R. C. Mackeith (Eds.), *Studies in infancy: Clinic in developmental medicine 27*. Spastics International Medical Publication. London: Heinemann, 1968.

Richards, M. P. M. *The integration of a child into a social world*. London & New York: Cambridge University Press, 1974.

Ryan, J. Early language development: towards a communicational analysis. In M. P. M. Richards (Ed.), *The integration of a child into a social world*. London & New York: Cambridge University Press, 1974. Pp. 185–215.

Sander, L. W. Regulation and organization in the early infant–caretaker system. In R. Robinson (Ed.), *Brain and early behavior*. London: Academic Press, 1969.

Sander, L. W. Infant and caretaking environment: investigation and conceptualization of adaptive behavior in a system of increasing complexity. In E. J. Anthony (Ed.), *Explorations in child psychiatry*. New York: Plenum Press, 1975.

Sander, L. W. *Regulation of exchange in the infant–caretaker system: A viewpoint on the ontogeny of "structures."* Paper presented at State University of New York Downstate Medical Center Conference on Communicative Structures and Psychic Structures, 15–17 January 1976.

Sander, L., Chappell, P., & Snyder, P. *An investigation of change in the infant–caretaker system over the first week of life*. Paper presented at biennial meeting of the Society for Research in Child Development, April, 1975.

Sander, L. W., & Julia, H. Continuous interactional monitoring in the neonate. *Psychosomatic Medicine*, 1966, **28**, 822–835.

Sander, L. W., Julia, H., Stechler, G., & Burns, P. Continuous 24 hour interactional monitoring in infants reared in two caretaking environments. *Psychosomatic Medicine*, 1972, **34**, No. 3, 270–282.

Sander, L. W., Stechler, G., Burns, P., & Julia, H. Early mother–infant interaction and 240 patterns of activity and sleep. *Journal of the American Academy of Child Psychiatry*, 1970, **9**, No. 1, 103–123.

Spitz, R. A. *No and yes on the genesis of human communication.* New York: International Universities Press, 1957.

Stechler, G., & Carpenter, G. A viewpoint on early affective development. In J. Hellmuth (Ed.), *Exceptional infant.* Vol. I. New York: Brunner/Mazel, 1967. Pp. 163–189.

Stechler, G., & Latz, E. Some observations on attention and arousal in the human infant. *Journal of the American Academy of Child Psychiatry,* 1966, **5,** 517–525.

Stern, D. N. A micro-analysis of mother–infant interaction behavior regulating social contact between a mother and her $3\frac{1}{2}$ month old twins. *Journal of the American Academy of Child Psychiatry,* 1971, **10,** No. 3, 501–517.

Stern, D. The goal and structure of mother–infant play. *Journal of the American Academy of Child Psychiatry,* 1974, **13,** No. 3, 402–422.

Stern, D., Jaffe, J., Beebe, B., & Bennett, S. L. Communication within the mother–infant dyad. *Transactions of the New York Academy of Science,* 1976 (in press).

Watson, J. S. Memory and contingency analysis in infant learning. *Merrill-Palmer Quarterly,* 1967, **13,** No. 1, 55–77.

Weiss, P. $1+1 \neq 2$ (when one plus one does not equal two). In G. C. Quarton, T. Melnechuk, & F. O. Schmidt (Eds.), *The neurosciences study program.* New York: Rockefeller University Press, 1967. Pp. 801–821.

Weiss, P. Whither life science? *American Scientist,* March–April, 1970, **58,** No. 2, 156–163.

Wolff, P. H. The role of biological rhythms in early psychological development. *Bulletin of the Menninger Clinic,* 1967, **31,** 197–218.

Wolff, P. H. The serial organization of sucking in the young infant. *Pediatrics,* December 1968, **42,** No. 6.

Yamamoto, W. S., & Brobeck, J. R. *Physiological controls and regulations.* Philadelphia: W. B. Saunders, 1965.

CHAPTER 7

Prelinguistic Conversations[1]

ROY FREEDLE

and

MICHAEL LEWIS

Educational Testing Service

GENERAL OVERVIEW

Our main premise concerning language development is that formal language emerges from prelinguistic social–cognitive–perceptual interactions with adults and peers. We shall explore the phylogenetic and ontogenetic implications of this hypothesis, first, by relating it to such broad viewpoints as the evolutionary theory of encephalization and, second, by relating it to the impact of social structure and naturalistic function on formal language structure, this being the field of sociolinguistics. After a review of earlier results, we explore this premise with new data for 3-month-old infants and finally examine some longitudinal results relating the 3-month-old behaviors to linguistic behavior at age 2 years.

INTRODUCTION

One of the most complex of human behaviors is language, especially language in action as exemplified by the give and take of conversation. Although research into early language acquisition has traditionally focused on acquisition of the syntactic code, there is a growing awareness that to understand the growth of language one must look at language as it is actually used, in naturalistic interactive sequences of peer with peer or mother with child, for example. How does this complex behavior develop? Does it come about piece by piece, or is there a primitive matrix out of which the various specialized language aspects—all present in some protean form—gradually become

[1] We would like to thank Susan Lee-Painter and Laraine Schwartz for their extensive help with the data collection and data analyses phases, respectively. This research was supported in part by a National Institute of Child Health and Human Development Grant NO1–HD–42803.

157

differentiated? One way to answer this is to start at or near the beginning of human life.

Several hypotheses will be of concern to us here. After stating them, we shall review some background evidence for these premises.

HYPOTHESIS 1. Linguistic behavior has its origins in a general social communication system to which a formal lexicon and grammar are ultimately added.

HYPOTHESIS 2. The mother–infant interaction patterns, which consist of both vocal and sensorimotor components, constitute a social system designed to facilitate the growth of communication.

HYPOTHESIS 3. Of the various elements which compose the primitive communication system, the vocalization behaviors form a subsystem which is more important than the paravocal behaviors.

HYPOTHESIS 4. Prelinguistic behaviors are situationally bound, even at a very early age. It is from such constraints that semantics can potentially emerge.

RATIONALE FOR THE HYPOTHESES

HYPOTHESIS 1. Linguistic behavior has its origins in a general social communication system to which a formal lexicon and grammar are ultimately added.

The best way to illustrate what we mean by a general social communication matrix is to present a sample of naturalistic data representing a particular mother and her infant interacting over a short period of time. (The illustration is taken from Lewis & Freedle, 1973, p. 128.)

"F is sitting in her seat holding a rubber toy which is tied to the side of the chair. Mother has her back to F as she reaches for dish. F squeaks rubber toy making noise. As a 'consequence' F kicks her feet and squeals with apparent delight. Mother turns toward F smiling. F looks at mother and vocalizes. Mother walks toward F smiling and vocalizing. F quiets, eyes fixed on mother. Mother touches F's face. F vocalizes and moves her hands toward mother. Mother sits in front of F and vocalizes to her. (Talking about the toy which mother now holds.) F watches mother and listens. Mother pauses, F vocalizes. Mother touches F and vocalizes to her. F vocalizes."

In this example we see that each participant in the situation contributes many behaviors, with each behavior a potential channel for conveying information. The mother at various points vocalizes, touches, smiles, looks;

these behaviors, furthermore, occur in various simultaneous clusters or occur singly. The infant also contributes a variety of behaviors in alternation with the mother's behavior (or simultaneously with the mother's behavior) such as smiling, vocalizing, and reaching. The total pattern of this dyadic interaction consists of a complex web of behaviors which undergo continual change with the passage of time.

In our earlier paper (Lewis & Freedle, 1973) we maintained that the above network of dyadic interaction constitutes a communication network from which meaning can be conveyed (albeit ambiguous meaning) and out of which a more formal communication system consisting of formal language and gesture will eventuate for both partners.

The communication system does not typically allow every behavior to follow every other behavior (especially since one of the dyadic members, the mother, already possesses a formal language system which is structured and nonrandom). Hence one can say that the system is constrained; such constraint introduces the potentiality for meaning to emerge (see Garner, 1962). By "meaning" we meant the differentiation or partitioning of the infant's world—be it spatial, temporal, internal, or external.

Our earlier work presented several kinds of evidence regarding the general communication matrix. First we showed that the relationship of vocalization in contrast to the other nonvocal behaviors had a special significance in the early primitive communication matrix. In Table 1 we see that, when an infant vocalizes, the mother is most likely to respond with a vocalization of her own; her next most likely response is to either smile at, look at, or touch the infant. In like manner, given that the mother has just vocalized, the most likely behavior that the infant will engage in is also vocalization. To a much more reduced degree, infant vocalization is also likely to follow such maternally initiated behaviors as playing with, looking at, holding, or touching. The infant is least likely to spend time vocalizing when the mother changes his diaper, feeds him, rocks him, talks to another person, reads, or watches TV. In other words, there is something special in the general communication matrix regarding the vocalization–vocalization behaviors of both participants.

The second conclusion is that certain nonvocal behaviors are much more effective than others in tying into the vocalization behaviors: behaviors such as touching or holding (close physical proximity) and directive orientation of one person to another, as in the mother's looking or smiling at the infant, in contrast to engaging in other behaviors with functions which are not meant to be primarily social interactive. These situations are ones in which the infant is, rather, an "object" for which or upon which a special function is to be performed or fulfilled in playing out the role of primary caretaker. Thus different behaviors form different interaction potentials around the vocalization–vocalization interaction. The vocalization is the central behavior which maintains interaction, but other behaviors exist which also elicit this particular communicative interaction.

TABLE 1. A Portion of the General Communication Matrix of Infant and Maternal Behaviors as They Relate to the Vocalizations of Each

	Mean Number of 10-Second Intervals When Infant Initiates Vocalization; Mother Responds With:			Mean Number of 10-Second Intervals When Infant Vocalizes in Response to Mother-Initiated:		
	Total	Male	Female	Total	Male	Female
Touch	1.08	1.50	0.55	5.16	4.07	6.55
Hold	0.80	1.29	0.18	5.60	3.64	8.09
Vocalize	34.24	32.07	37.00	23.20	18.43	29.27
Look	2.36	2.86	1.73	6.40	4.79	8.45
Smile	2.76	2.86	2.64	5.88	4.64	7.45
Play with	0.48	0.57	0.36	7.88	5.71	10.64
Change	0.12	0.21	0.00	0.72	0.93	0.45
Feed	0.32	0.57	0.00	0.80	0.57	1.09
Rock	0.12	0.21	0.00	0.04	0.07	0.00
Vocalize to others	1.00	1.29	0.64	0.12	0.00	0.27
Read/TV	0.12	0.14	0.09	0.20	0.29	0.09

	Mean Number of 10-Second Intervals When Mother Initiates Vocalization; Infant Responds with:			Mean Number of 10-Second Intervals When Mother Vocalizes in Response to Infant-Initiated:		
	Total	Male	Female	Total	Male	Female
Vocalize	23.20	18.43	29.27	34.24	32.07	37.00
Movement	2.40	2.57	2.18	10.88	11.50	10.09
Fret/cry	2.16	1.93	2.45	18.68	16.86	21.00
Play	1.40	1.71	1.00	2.32	3.00	1.45
Smile	11.24	9.79	13.09	2.40	2.86	1.82

(Based on Table 1, Lewis and Freedle, 1973, p. 136.)

The general communication matrix has, to date, been little explored, partly because of the complexity of the number of different behaviors that can occur together or separately, and the number of different behavioral patterns that can precede or follow each other. Although regularities are quite evident among the vocal and nonvocal behaviors as presented in Table 1, our main focus has been and still is the vocalization states as forming a special subset of the general communication system.

We would like to emphasize, though, that a number of semantic distinctions can be deduced from the nonvocal behaviors as they change over time and as they change as a function of which of the two participants initiates or responds to the behavior. For example, we speculated that perceptual-cognitive schemata could be formed out of the nonvocal behaviors which might lead to or become the earliest forms of such semantic notions as "location of," "object or subject of," and "approach versus withdrawal." Thus some meaning may initially rely on the perceptual isolation and recognition of featural or relational differences in the external world, such as noticing direction or approach versus withdrawal, who does what to whom (a subject–object distinction), and so on. One can deduce further that the organism probably perceives such differences by noting a significant shift in the behavioral patterns which occur in situations that distinguish, for example, whether the infant is or is not the object of the mother's attention (because of her touching, looking at, or smiling at). Also, if behavioral patterns shift as a function of mere changes in location so that the particular location favors a different spontaneous emission of behaviors, one might claim that this forms a necessary, but perhaps not sufficient, basis for the development of the semantic notion of location, or for the more specific problem of mapping function to location. Similarly, a change in behavior when a stranger approaches an infant versus withdraws from the infant can be interpreted as a potential precursor of the semantic notion of direction (or the notion of present tense versus future tense, inasmuch as the approach of the stranger represents something going to happen). Thus it seemed more than reasonable to us to explore precursors of semantics in the general communication network of the very young infant. After all, we argued, it would be even more implausible to maintain that the infant magically leaps to semantic conceptions only after he begins to struggle with single-word utterances. No one can maintain that during the first year the infant is without any knowledge (e.g., see the work of Piaget, 1952; Vygotsky, 1962).

Interestingly enough, our early work provided statistical evidence that just vocalization behaviors alone contain primitive information regarding the infant's awareness of being the "object of" versus "not being the object of" the mother's vocalizations. What we wish to indicate at this point is that formal language patterns such as subject–object distinctions may inhere in these primitive communication matrices at many levels, including the vocalization level just mentioned.

HYPOTHESIS 2. The mother–infant interaction patterns, which consist of both vocal and sensorimotor components, constitute a social system designed to facilitate the growth of communication.

The evidence for this second hypothesis concerning the relationship between vocal, sensorimotor, and perceptual components and its developmental import for formal language acquisition will here go well beyond the usual biological evidence already familiar from the work of Lenneberg (1967). We wish to initiate a much broader foundation, using evolutionary evidence to provide a richer and deeper basis for discussions of how prelinguistic regularities of behavior lend themselves to mapping onto a formal language system.

An extensive evolutionary point of view has emerged from the work of Jerison (1973, 1976) which relates to our concern with language and prelinguistic systems. Jerison's interesting theory postulates that phylogenetically language first evolved out of an undifferentiated, noisy social interaction among protohumans to serve a perceptual mapping function. Only later, after its perceptual function had been fulfilled, did its flexible potential for general communication, such that its referential properties went well beyond the here-and-now function of perception, emerge. Hence we have, first, an undifferentiated matrix of vocal–paravocal interaction; second, a perceptual mapping function; and, third, a more formal language for communication. Jerison justifies this postulate as follows. If there were selection pressures toward the development of language just for communication, one could expect the evolutionary effect to be the development of a language system similar to the infrahuman language systems with a very limited and prewired set of sounds to represent a limited set of meanings (as in the cry of alarm among birds). But the flexibility of the language found among human beings suggests to him that their evolution was analogous to that of other *sensory integrative systems* which have the property of being unusually plastic and modifiable by early learning. Given this, the role of language in communication evolved as a side effect, its primary function being to map a spatial reality with a temporal code (i.e., a string of vocal symbols in time which represented spatial information, much as the sequential echoes received by a bat come to represent spatial information about whether or not an obstacle is in its course of flight, and how far that object is from the bat). This perceptual information associated with the evolved vocal system provided the organism with a much needed strengthening of sensory input about the external world.

Jerison's evidence on this point is complex, but the essence of it is as follows. Mammals developed from the therapsids. They occupied nocturnal niches which led to the development of rod vision, a rather crude visual system. This weak system also happened to be coupled with poor olfaction.

Selective pressure operated to force old systems, such as noisy social behavior, already present in the evolving mammals to serve new functions, and the new function most needed was improved sensory-perceptual information to supplement and integrate with the rather impoverished systems of rod vision and weak olfaction. Thus vocal–social behaviors which follow a temporal type patterning were adapted to serve a primary spatial–temporal perceptual function. To best utilize this information, greater encephalization gradually took place, especially among mammals, so as to develop association areas for integrating sensory information from these diverse sensory inputs.

Jerison (1976) argues that this view is theoretically elegant since it explains the evolution of an important novel adaptation in a species by relating it to the conservation of earlier patterns of adaptation.

"We can think of language as being merely an expression of another neural contribution to the construction of mental imagery, analogous to the contributions of the encephalized sensory systems and their association systems. We need language more to tell stories than to direct actions. In the telling we create mental images in our listeners that might normally be produced only by the memory of events as recorded and integrated by the sensory and perceptual systems of the brain" (p. 101).

A somewhat related point was made by Reitman (1965):

"Language is a recent acquisition. Physiologically, the localized speech center is uniquely human. Biological evidence suggests that when new organs arise, they operate through previously extant ones, modulating and moderating them rather than abolishing them. . . . Sperry reports evidence suggesting that the rule is true of speech as well. Human information processing in this view may be taken as basically perceptual, with words and language operating upon the basic perceptual system" (p. 250).

Integrating Jerison's hypothesis into our own consideration, we conclude that language evolution and ontogenetic acquisition of language come about through *social* interaction. Even the *perceptual* functions still served by language (as in the early language learning of the referential "here-and-now" aspects of the immediate environment) come about through social interaction; they do not evolve in a social vacuum (see Lewis & Cherry, Chapter 10 of this volume, pertaining to models which represent the interaction of linguistic–cognitive–social knowledge). What this observation suggests is that language and language development are intimately united with perceptual strategies (see Bever, 1970), social sensitivity, and general cognitive ability. This unity comes about through consideration of how language probably evolved over eons of time. Separate study of language in a vacuum may, in this view, lead to a very distorted idea of how to improve language learning, language instruction (once learned), and the development of special language skills, such as reading and writing, as well as the traditional skills of speaking and listening (see Smith and Miller, 1966, for further evolutionary perceptives).

We might follow Jerison's ideas into many directions to help rationalize our hypothesis that formal linguistic behavior has its origins in a general prelinguistic social communication system. The idea that language first serves a perceptual function and is integrated via association areas of the brain with the other senses helps to suggest the intimate relationship in the general communication matrix between vocalization and its elicitation by a mother's touching, looking at, smiling at, and vocalizing to. This was evident from Table 1. We could also utilize Jerison's concepts to speculate that there exists some weak (but nonlocalized) prewiring in the human brain that forms a necessary groundwork for language to evolve within the human neonate. This would help to account for the strong vocalization–vocalization binding that exists between the 3-month-old infant and his caretaker (again, see Table 1 for the evidence). Not only does the naturalistic evidence (Lewis & Freedle, 1973) show this relationship but it is also manifest in the experimental literature (Rheingold, Gewirtz, & Ross, 1959). Except for the deaf child (Furth, 1966), what this binding assures is a rather specific channel by which the social prelinguistic network can be activated so as to begin the process of acquisition of a first language. This process seems to begin as a representation of perceptual reality (again, the early literature emphasizes that the child comments extensively upon the immediately perceived "here-and-now" aspects of the environment). This evolves into a more mature propositional base from which imagined future perceptual events can be postulated (planned) as an abstract system which eventuates in formal deductions and inferences (Olson, 1972).

On the basis of Jerison's hypothesis, it would appear to be no accident that the caretaker first tries to shape the undifferentiated vocal but socially responsive infant into one who represents or maps the outer perceptual world onto an abstract sound system, that is, the sound system is made to act like another sensory system. The caretaker persists in this endeavour of mapping a set of names for objects (however, see Brown's, 1957, discussion of the many-many mapping of words and things) until the child comes to realize that "things" in the perceptual world have "names."

Of course, language, even early language, is not so simple. We do not go about naming everything that comes into view; we are capable of selective attention. Probably, this is due to the integrative association areas of the brain which merge perceptual information from the various sensory systems. The association areas allow us to select relevant properties for the given situation and to suppress other information from the several senses as irrelevant to the current circumstances.

HYPOTHESIS 3. Of the various elements which compose the primitive communication system, the vocalization behaviors form a subsystem which is more important than the paravocal behaviors.

In earlier papers (Freedle & Lewis, 1971; Lewis & Freedle, 1973) the authors presented naturalistic evidence that consistent nonrandom behavior is occurring between the vocalizations of mother and infant as a function of the sex of the infant, the socioeconomic background of the family, and the situation in which the vocalizations occurred. It was argued that this close relationship between the elicitation of vocalization in the infant, given that the mother has just vocalized (and, reciprocally, that the most likely behavior emitted by the mother is a vocalization, given that the infant has just vocalized), indicates the probable existence of an innate mechanism that operates selectively on the vocalization capabilities of mother and infant so as to prime this particular behavior for future developmental transformations which eventuate in a formal language system. Other data collected under experimentally controlled conditions (Rheingold et al., 1959) also support the viewpoint of an innate connection between vocalization–vocalization interaction among neonates and adult human beings. There also exists evidence indicating a special propensity of the infant to attend to various aspects of adult vocalizations. For example, Lieberman (1967) reported that infants of about 3 months appear to be able to respond differentially to friendly and to hostile voices. Other differentiations that infants appear capable of making are between exaggerated ("baby talk") and normal intonations. Also, Lieberman suggests that the cries of infants are primitive behaviors from which language may later evolve, inasmuch as he believes that the cries provide the basis for the linguistic function of intonation in adult speech. However, whereas Lieberman argues for an innately determined basis of crying behavior, the work of Bell and Ainsworth (1971) suggests that infant crying and caretaker response are subject to learning principles. Their work reveals that, contrary to simple response-learning theory, reinforcement of crying behavior in the first quarter-year (e.g., responding by holding the infant) produces, not more crying at 1 year, but more subsequent communicative behavior. The authors state that crying, even in the first quarter-year of life, is a communicative behavior, reinforcement of which leads subsequently to other, noncrying, communicative behaviors. Crying, then, is part of the general communicative network of the infant and his world.

Furthermore, regarding innateness, Lieberman indicates that speech frequency differences in infants will emerge as a function of who is talking to them; that is, infants will attempt to mimic the fundamental frequency of the person talking to them, whereas in a free-play situation the child's fundamental frequency is different, usually higher. Even at this very early age it is possible to identify regularities, such as the "innate breath group," which will later be adapted to serve a linguistic function—segmentation of the speech signal into sentences (Lieberman, 1967). Moreover, the work of several investigators suggests that phonemic contrasts in the language, for example /b/ and /p/, are differentially responded to at very early ages (Eimas, Siqueland, Jusczyk, & Vigorito, 1971).

In short, the evidence suggests that, at a very early age, infants respond selectively to aspects of the speech signal, and this is found not only for data collected in naturalistic ethnographic settings (Lewis & Freedle, 1973) but also for data collected under controlled laboratory conditions.

HYPOTHESIS 4. Prelinguistic behaviors are situationally bound, even at a very early age. It is from such constraints that semantics can potentially emerge.

We have mentioned that in the naturalistic setting of the home certain situations involving the 3-month-old and its caretaker occur with great regularity. Lewis and Freedle (1973) found that eight situations account for virtually all of the situations that the 3-month-old experiences; they are (from most to least frequent mother's lap, crib-bed, infant seat, table-tub, couch-sofa, playpen, floor, and jumper-swing (see Table 2). These naturalistically occurring situations have consequences for the frequency with which vocalization behaviors are engaged in by both the infant and its caretaker, and these differences are also seen in Table 2. For example, one can see that, even though mother's lap is the most frequent situation, it has the lowest percentage of infant vocalizations of all of the situations (17.1% out of the 288.4 10-second occasions in which a vocalization could have been realized). On the other hand, some of the least frequent situations, such as playpen and floor, account for the highest percentage of infant vocalizations (30.3 and 28.5%, respectively). In other words the frequency of a prelinguistic behavior —infant vocalization—is a function of the situational setting. The mother's relative frequency of vocalization also varies with the situational setting, but it does not seem to bear any simple functional relationship to the frequency with which the situation occurs.

Sociolinguists have emphasized the importance of studying formal languages (e.g., studying grammatical rules) as a function of ethnographic naturalistic situations. The reason for this emphasis is that one needs this

TABLE 2. (Adapted from Tables 4 and 5 of Lewis and Freedle, 1973, pp. 144–145)

a. Mean Number of 10-Second Intervals Spent in Each Situation

	Infant Seat	Playpen	Mother's Lap	Crib-Bed	Couch-Sofa	Floor	Table-Tub	Jumper-Swing	Other
Total	100.9	29.2	288.4	118.2	46.2	28.0	62.5	26.7	19.9
Male	80.2	33.0	329.5	91.6	42.0	35.1	52.9	29.7	24.0
Female	121.6	25.4	247.4	144.8	50.5	21.0	72.1	23.7	15.8

b. Relative Frequency of Occurrence of Infant and Maternal Vocalizations as a Function of Amount of Time Spent in Each Situation

	Infant Seat	Playpen	Mother's Lap	Crib-Bed	Couch-Sofa	Floor	Table-Tub	Jumper-Swing	Other
Infant vocalization									
Total	.233	.303	.171	.214	.200	.285	.216	.228	.211
Male	.308	.261	.183	.186	.170	.292	.225	.200	.228
Female	.179	.400	.150	.210	.227	.278	.207	.277	.137
Maternal vocalization									
Total	.338	.257	.404	.325	.474	.518	.475	.365	.337
Male	.332	.265	.313	.385	.481	.562	.447	.393	.298
Female	.350	.243	.441	.272	.468	.466	.503	.310	.387

naturalistic base in order to account for the *linguistic variation* that can be observed to occur at all levels of linguistic phenomena: be it phonological, morphological, grammatical, semantic, or pragmatic. A good part of the variation that occurs can be accounted for by sociolinguistic categories which are sensitive to the socioeconomic status of the language users, the listener–speaker status differences, the formality of the situational setting, the cultural group to which one owes allegiance, and so on. Indeed, the systematic uncovering of linguistic variation and the accounting for this variation in terms of naturalistic categories of social–cultural–cognitive behaviors constitute a major innovation in the study of language. The premises upon which it is based promise a revolution in our thinking about what linguistic science is, what its methods are to be, and how it is to develop (Bierwisch, 1976, has presented a more conservative interpretation of linguistic variation).

Our reason for discussing this new development in linguistics is that it offers a further rationale for our hypothesis that language develops out of a general social communication network of prelinguistic behaviors (on the part of the infant, at least), that these behaviors are, from an early age, situationally bound, and that these differential patternings of behavior as a function of situation and situational frequency form the nexus out of which formal language and semantics emerge. It is noteworthy that this hypothesis places the development of language in a social framework and thus is consistent not only with a sociolinguistic emphasis but also with our third hypothesis. Furthermore this hypothesis emphasizes *naturalistically occurring situations* as the basis for the development of formal language. This too is in keeping with sociolinguistic emphasis (with its naturalistic orientation) and is consistent with evolutionary emphasis on adaptation to ecological niches (this being represented by the stress on naturally occurring *situations* as the niche to which one must adapt).

The Role of Situation

Our difficulties are not over with respect to placing our enterprise into focus and proper context. We must also struggle with the vagueness of the concept of "situation." There are several choices open to us as to how we approach the concept of situation and how we define it for purposes of categorizing the setting with respect to early vocalization in the infant's naturalistic world.

One way is to take note of the locations which our culture says are significant (for the adult, at least) and to *assume* that these have significant consequences for the infant, even though his behavior might not yet reflect any real differences across all the situations so defined. Another approach is to try to define "situation" objectively, apart from cultural presuppositions about what is and is not important and salient in the environment. Since we do not know of any scoring system which has isolated objective features of any environment apart from any cultural value system, we have to abandon this second possibility. A third possibility is to conduct elaborate studies of how adults seem to partition their world of experience, to objectively isolate (through some method such as factor analysis) those dimensions of the experience which account for all the situations that these adults indicate they experience, and then to use these features or dimensions as basic concepts in defining the infant's situational experience, even though once again it must be taken on faith that such features will have the same perceptual impact on the young as they seem to have on the adult population. Interestingly enough, Pervin (1975a, 1975b) has actually studied adult situational setting from this last perspective. However, although the methods used are innovative and important, we doubt that the features found necessarily apply to the world of the infant and its primary caretaker.

As a first approximation we shall retain the "common-sense" categorization of the infant's situation by relying on the labels originally suggested in the Lewis and Freedle (1973) paper. In particular, we suggested that it was not so much the room (living room, dining room, etc.) that was important in categorizing the different environments as the particularized "location" or "location-with-respect-to-function." For example the situations we used were table-tub, floor, mother's lap, playpen, infant seat, jumper-swing, couch-sofa, and crib-bed. Many of these "situations" are distinguishable, not by the room they occur in, but by the special activity and function which they serve in the infant–caretaker interaction. Thus table-tub as a situation is for purposes of cleaning the infant, crib-bed is for purposes of letting the infant rest, and so on. We realize that we cannot claim objectivity in using these labels as necessarily of significant consequence to the infant's perceptual experience, but at the moment we see no viable alternative to defining "situation" other than by the "common-sense" notions, which are undoubtedly tainted with biases from Western industrial culture. Perhaps future theoretical work will free us from this momentary bind. With these disclaimers, let us now consider just what effect we can expect on vocalization behaviors as a function of such situational definitions as the eight mentioned above.

In earlier papers (Freedle & Lewis, 1971; Lewis & Freedle, 1973; Lewis & Lee-Painter, 1974) we explored a methodology for handling complex interactions of two individuals who not only vocalize to each other but can also point, smile, touch, and hold. We have hypothesized that such patterns, especially the vocalization patterns which occur with high frequency, may be differentially affected by the situational setting in which the infant interacts with its primary caretaker. We wish to study recurrent nonrandom patterns wherein particular behaviors become associated with particular situations. We speculate that these will form the basis for formal semantic knowledge. When randomness is punctuated with regularity, this forms the groundwork for potential meaning. Indeed, such regularity already possesses a kind of primitive meaning, but it is ambiguous. Only after formal language is finally ventured upon, does some of this ambiguity disappear.

Thus we speculate that through nonrandom *action* sequences (especially vocalization sequences) meaning is built up. Furthermore, the action sequences which become tied or associated differentially to different *situational* locations are a *necessary* precondition for formal meaning to emerge. Just the arbitrary production of strings of nonrandom vocalization events, apart from their situational context would not suffice to build up meaning. The above presumed facts are easy to lose sight of when we focus too much on the complexities of adult syntax. We must constantly remind ourselves that these groupings of symbols by themselves mean nothing unless they become associated with recurrent events in various situations of the real world; that is, meaning is a mapping from one set of entities (which here are the nonrandom vocalization patterns) to another set of entities (here the various situations in which the different vocalization patterns emerge with differential frequencies of occurrence).

As we explore the data we shall take two tacks:

1.   We shall attempt to deduce how the several naturalistically occurring situations (infant seat, crib-bed, playpen, floor, mother's lap, jump-swing, couch, and table-tub) differ in their physical stimulus properties (such as the presence of water or powders in the table-tub situation), their social properties (nearness of mother or ease of viewing her face; mother's lap as a situation involves close proximity and often allows for easy viewing of her face), their social functions (crib-bed serves a rest function), and so on. Table 3 presents some tentative features which help to reveal some reasons why the several situations may induce different vocalization patternings. In most of what follows we shall emphasize primarily the three most frequently occurring situations (mother's lap; infant seat; and crib-bed) because these give the most stable transitional probabilities in the vocalization–vocalization matrices.

2.   The second tack we shall take is to focus on special cells of the transitional probability matrices for the three most frequently occurring situations (ML, IS and CB) and for the total situational matrix. The special cells involve what we define to be prelinguistic conversational openings and closing. For adults, conversational openings and closings have been discussed by sociologists of language (Schegloff & Sachs, 1973). We shall describe the particulars of this approach in the next section.

TABLE 3. Some Potentially Important Aspects in Which Main Situations Differ

| Situation | New Sensory Stimulation? | Distance between Members of Dyad | | | Suggested Critical Features for Vocalization | | | |
| | | Large | Medium | Small | Function | | Free Movement for Infant? | Eye Contact and Gesture Freely Viewable? |
					Social?	Other?		
Tub-table	Yes (water, powder)			+	No	Clean	Not much	Yes
Jump-swing	Yes (proprioceptive feedback)		+		No	Mother busy	Semifree	Not necessarily
Couch	Maybe (texture)			+	Semisocial	Mother rest?	Semifree	Semiviewable
Floor	Yes (rug, no rug, smells) wide muscular movement	+			No	?	Yes	Not necessarily
Mother's lap	Maybe			+	Yes		Not much	Maybe
Crib-bed	Intended lack of new stimulation	+			No	Rest infant	Not intended	No
Infant seat	Maybe		+		No	Mother busy	Not much	Not necessarily
Playpen	Maybe (toy, textures,...)	+			No	Mother busy	Semifree	Not necessarily

PROCEDURE AND METHOD

Sample

Ninety-seven mother–infant dyads were observed in the naturalistic settings of their homes.[2] The infants were 3 months old (plus or minus 1 week). Although we shall focus only on the total sample as a function of situation, the actual sample represented equal numbers of male and female infants; also, infants were sampled as evenly as possible from the total range of socioeconomic background and from two racial groups, black and white.

Method

Each infant was seen in its home. Contact with the mothers was made in a variety of ways: through the mother's initiative, by looking through birth announcements in the newspapers, and through church groups in lower socioeconomic areas. Two observers were trained and used in this study, one for the black community and one for the white. The rho values for interobserver reliability for the vocal behaviors were typically in the .80's.

The mothers were instructed that the observer was interested in studying the infant's behavior. The observer sat next to, but out of sight of, the infant. It was stressed that the infant was to be observed, not the mother. Moreover, the mother was asked to try to forget the presence of the observer and not to engage her in conversation. When conversation was attempted, the observer reminded the mother to ignore her. Before observation, the observer spent time with the mother attempting to put her at ease.

A total of 720 10-second intervals was scored for the occurrence of vocalizations. If neither mother nor infant vocalized in a given 10-second period, that interval was called state 0 of the vocalization system. If the infant vocalized but the mother did not, this was defined as state 1 in the vocalization system. If just the mother vocalized, this was called state 2. If the mother vocalized to the observer or some other person, this was termed state 2i. If both mother and infant vocalized in the same 10-second period, this was defined as state 3 (it is this quick give and take in vocalizations of this state that most nearly approximate what we would regard as a "conversation"). Finally, if the mother vocalized to the observer or some other person, and the infant also happened to vocalize in the same 1-second period, this was called state 3i of the vocalization system.

A sensitive index of how these vocalization states (0, 1, 2, 2i, 3, 3i) change over successive 10-second time periods is provided by a transitional probability matrix. The details of how to model the data from the point of view of Markovian theory are given by Freedle and Lewis (1971). For our purposes here we need only the transitional matrix.

[2] Data on 44 of these subjects were presented in Lewis and Freedle (1973).

The transitional or conditional probabilities can be estimated as follows. Consider the following succession of vocalization states, obtained by coding the successive 10-second periods for a particular mother–infant pair: 3, 0, 1, 3, 1, 2, ... Set up a matrix with six rows and six columns labeled 0, 1, 2, 2i, 3, and 3i, reading from the top down for the rows, and similarly labeled reading from left to right across the columns. Using the above sequence, notice that the first pair of states is 3, 0. Enter a tally in the row labeled 3 and the column marked 0. The second and third states form the next pair, which is 0, 1. Enter another tally in the row labeled 0 and the column labeled 1. The next pair of states is 1, 3, so enter a tally in row 1 and column 3, and so on until all successive pairs of states have been tallied for this given mother–infant dyad. When this is done, sum up the tallies for each row and divide the frequency in each row cell by the sum for that row. The proportions that result in each row are then used as the estimates for the conditional probabilities of the transition matrix. For the date under consideration here, there were 719 tallied entries for each mother–infant pair studied.

The above procedure ignores the vocalization states that occur in different situations. To form a transitional matrix based on situational location, a very similar procedure is used. Suppose that a given infant is on the mother's lap for the first half of the observation session (time intervals 1 through 310). Then a transitional matrix for this mother–infant for the six vocalization states would have only 309 tallied entries in it for the mother's lap location. If mother and infant spent the remaining 310 10-second periods in the infant seat situation, another matrix involving the six vocalization states would be formed from the time intervals 311 through 720. It would have a total of 308 tallied entries. (Notice that the entry *across* situations gets lost in this situational analysis; that is, the pair of vocalization states from time interval 310 and from time interval 311 is ignored in forming the transition matrices as a function of situational location.)

RESULTS AND DISCUSSION

Table 4 presents the vocalization matrix for all 97 subjects (97 infants with mothers) summed over all situations. To convey an idea of the degree to which the three most frequently occurring situations (ML, IS, and CB) influence the pattern of these transitional probabilities, the vocalization–state transitions for these three situations are also presented in the table.[3]

We can note the following readily interpretable patterns. The probability that a state 3 will follow a state 3, that is, intense vocal interaction over

---

[3] A number of other behaviors were scored at the time the vocalization data were obtained; the reader is referred to Lewis and Freedle (1973) for details.

174

Roy Freedle and Michael Lewis

successive time intervals, is .491 for the infant on the mother's lap (situation ML), .631 when the infant is in the infant's seat (IS), and only .214 when the infant is in the crib or bed (CB). This intense vocal interaction is lowest when the infant is in the crib or bed and highest when he is in the infant seat. Since the function of placing an infant in the crib or bed is to allow him

TABLE 4.   Transition Probabilities Pooled over All Situations[a, b]

	State		Trial $n + 1$					
			0	1	2	2i	3	3i
Trial n	0	ML	58.3	3.7	23.3	6.7	7.4	0.7
		IS	57.3	8.7	20.7	5.3	7.3	0.7
		CB	54.5	9.0	27.5	4.8	3.6	0.6
		All	55.5	7.2	24.8	5.3	6.7	0.6
	1	ML	32.8	18.0	24.6	11.5	11.5	1.6
		IS	42.3	23.1	15.4	11.5	3.8	3.8
		CB	38.9	30.6	16.7	11.1	0.0	2.8
		All	35.1	34.2	14.2	9.5	5.2	1.7
	2	ML	29.0	6.7	47.0	8.3	7.8	1.1
		IS	25.2	4.6	48.1	7.6	13.7	0.8
		CB	27.1	1.6	56.6	7.0	6.2	1.6
		All	28.6	5.0	48.4	8.3	8.4	1.3
	2i	ML	19.0	6.3	22.2	43.7	6.3	2.4
		IS	16.3	7.0	46.5	23.3	7.0	0.0
		CB	28.6	0.0	32.1	25.0	14.3	0.0
		All	20.2	5.4	30.2	35.7	6.6	1.9
	3	ML	20.3	1.9	18.4	6.3	49.4	3.8
		IS	13.5	2.7	15.3	1.8	63.1	3.6
		CB	28.6	0.0	35.7	14.3	21.4	0.0
		All	19.8	3.5	20.1	4.7	48.7	3.2
	3i	ML	0.0	11.5	7.7	11.5	26.9	42.3
		IS	13.3	0.0	13.3	13.3	20.0	40.0
		CB	0.0	50.0	0.0	0.0	50.0	0.0
		All	15.1	7.5	13.2	11.3	20.8	32.1

[a] ML = mother's lap, IS = infant seat, CB = crib or bed, All = all situations, including ML, IS, CB, and six others.
[b] $N \geqslant 69,500$.

to rest (or hope that he will rest), the probability that the mother will allow for simultaneous vocalizations in this particular situation will be low. On the other hand, when the infant is supposed to be wide awake, as he is when in the infant seat, the mother will take the opportunity of strongly engaging him in "simultaneous conversation." In this case the large changes in the magnitude of entries in the transitional matrix across situations are easy to interpret.

Although there are differences across situations, one can also see that considerable stability exists in the relative magnitudes across situations; this is especially evident when comparing the entries for all situations versus particular situations. For example, the transition from state 0 to 0 is .583 for ML, 573 for IS, .545 for CB, and .555 for all situations. This entry is relatively stable regardless of situational setting.

Prelinguistic Conversational Openings and Closings

The best way to illustrate what we mean by prelinguistic conversational openings and closings, using vocalization states of a 3-month-old infant and its mother, is to present an example.

Suppose that we have the following string of vocalization states for a particular mother and infant:

00*1121*0000*1222*00000000*2223*000*3331111111111*00000000,

and so on. We have italicized the clusters of vocalization states wherein at least one person is vocalizing: either mother vocalizes (state 2), or infant vocalizes alone (state 1) or both vocalize in the same time interval (state 3). We ignore clusters that begin or end with states 2i and 3i because they are of little interest at this point. Notice that in the first group (1121) the infant *started* this cluster (because it begins with state 1) and also *ended* it (because it ends with state 1). In the second group (1222) the infant *started* the cluster but the mother *ended* it. Here is another way to define a start (a conversational opening). Any state (like 1, 2, or 3) which follows state 0 is an opening. Similarly, any state (like 1, 2, or 3) which is followed by state 0 is an ending (a conversational closing).

We wish to study the possibility that these starting and ending states for vocalization clusters have import for more formal linguistic development. We are also interested in whether differences in the magnitude of starting or ending states differ across socioeconomic status and sex of infant and as a function of situational setting. Thus we are interested in different vocalization patternings for all 3-month-olds as a function of social factors (SES and sex), as well as differences due to situational setting (ML, IS, and CB). The contribution of the mothers to differences is also of interest. Given such differences, we will then pursue the question of whether these measures of prelinguistic conversational openings and closings are significantly correlated with measures of linguistic development (e.g., in the 2-year-old child and his mother.

Sex Differences in Openings and Closings across All Situations

To provide a sensitive test of whether male and female infants differ in the degree to which they start or end vocalization clusters, we have used cumulative distributions for the following transitional probabilities: 1 to 0, 0 to 1. All male infants interacting with their mothers yield a particular transitional

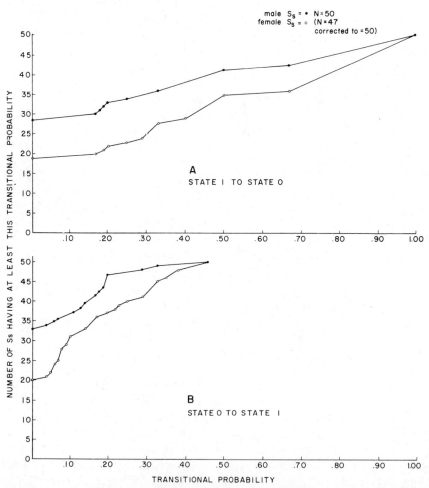

FIGURE 1. Conversational openings and closings for infants. A. Cumulative distributions over 50 males and 47 females (corrected to equal 50) for conversational closings. B. Similar results for conversational openings.

probability for moving from state 1 to state 0. This transition defines the end of vocalization clusters by the infant wherever they occur in the 2-hour interaction of mother with infant. Transitions from 0 to 1 define infant beginnings. This distribution (a frequency distribution) is then cumulated and compared with a similar distribution obtained from the female infants. The Kolmogorov–Smirnov (KS) test is then used to assess the significance of the difference between these two cumulative distributions.

Figure 1 presents the results. The KS two-sample test yields a significant sex difference; male infants *start* significantly more vocalization clusters than

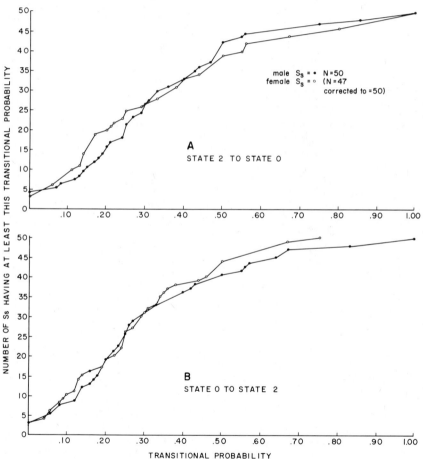

FIGURE 2. Conversational openings and closings for mothers. A. Cumulative distributions for conversational closings involving 50 mothers with male infants and 47 mothers with female infants (corrected to equal 50). B. Similar results for mother's conversational openings.

do female infants ($p < .05$, two tailed). Using the same figure, we also see that a significant sex difference is obtained for the relative frequency with which males *end* vocalization clusters ($p < .05$, two tailed). Males open and close significantly more vocalization clusters than do female infants.

A related question concerns a comparison of the cumulative distributions for the transitions from 2 to 0 (mother-terminated clusters) and from 0 to 2 (mother-initiated clusters) as a function of the sex of the infant. These results are presented in Figure 2. No differences in these curves are found.

The final comparison relevant to sex differences in openings and closings,

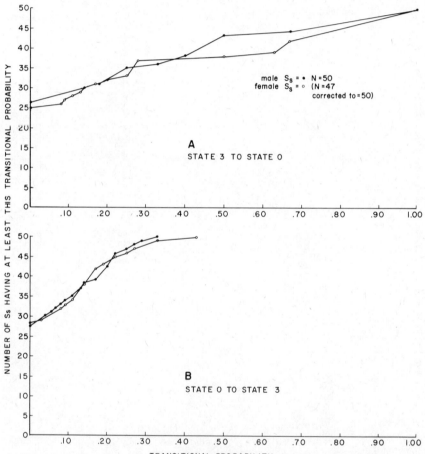

FIGURE 3. Conversational openings and closings for both mothers and infants vocalizing together. A. Cumulative distributions for joint conversational closings for 50 males and 47 females (corrected to equal 50). B. Similar results for joint conversational openings.

concerns the number of times both mother and infant open these vocalization clusters (0 followed by 3) and close them (3 followed by 0) as a function of the sex of the infant. Figure 3 presents the cumulative distributions. Again, no significant difference is found.

Comparisons involving just the infant's contribution (state 1) do yield sex differences in openings and closings of these clusters. The source of these differences is of course open to question, since the mothers of these infants may have shaped these significant differences. After all, with regard to the termination of clusters, it seems possible that the mothers could manage to let the male infant have the last "word," so to speak. In this sense it is quite possible that the mothers contribute to the observed sex differences at this early age. The mother's contribution to openings and closings of these clusters is not related to the sex of her infant, since the comparisons directly involving the mother's vocalizations (states 2 and 3) fail to yield a sex difference. As an additional check on the question of whether the mother's vocalization behavior significantly contributes to the fact that the male infant closes more vocalization clusters than the female, we also did the following analysis. This analysis uses vocalization states that depart from simple openings and closings. One can speculate that the transitions from state 1 (infant vocalizations alone) to state 2 (mother vocalizations alone) may contain important additional information about mothers' allowing their male infants to close more clusters. It seems reasonable, for example, that if mothers are simply allowing males to close more sequences, we should observe a lower transitional probability from 1 to 2 for male than for female infants. These comparisons across sex (and SES as well) failed to yield any significant differences. In other words, it appears that there may be an intrinsic sex difference for the observed difference in prelinguistic openings and closings. However, an additional factor is possible in that the mothers' nonvocal behaviors may be responsible for some of the observed infant vocalization differences. The data from Table 1, which showed a relationship between maternal nonvocal behaviors and infant vocal behaviors, strengthen this possibility.

Socioeconomic Factor in Openings and Closings across All Situations

A similar comparison was made to determine whether there is any difference between high and low socioeconomic status; male and female infants were combined for this analysis. Only infant openings produced a significant difference between high and low SES. The only maternal difference was that high-SES mothers produce more openings (02 transitions) than low-SES ones ($p < .05$). This suggests that the high-SES mothers' openings are precluding the high-SES infants' openings, which can account for why low-SES infants have more openings.

Individual Difference as a Function of Situation

The preceding discussion has examined sex and SES differences in openings and closings across all situations. We should like now to examine these differences as a function of the three most frequently occurring situations: mother's lap, infant seat, and crib-bed.

The general finding was that the mother showed significantly more openings and closings when her infant was on her lap than when it was either in the infant seat or crib-bed ($p < .05$ in each case). This finding supports our view that as a location-function the mother-lap is primarily intended to engage the infant in interaction. As such, the greater maternal openings and closings would be consistent with this finding.[4]

Longitudinal Results: Correlations of 3-Month-Old Data with 2-Year Data

Although the above results are interesting in their own right, the essential thrust of our argument—that language emerges from this prelinguistic behavior—requires that we demonstrate that the early prelinguistic acts of both mother and infant are related to the later linguistic behavior of each. Using twelve infants (6 males and 6 females) matched for social class and birth order, we undertook a longitudinal analysis.

Table 5 presents the Pearson product correlations between the vocalization data for prelinguistic openings and closings for the infants and for their mothers with three measures obtained when the child was 2 years of age. These measures are the child's mean length utterance (MLU), which is regarded as the single best indicator of language growth for the early years; the number of mother's questions; and the number of mother's directives expressed toward her 2-year-old child.

Prelinguistic Openings and Closings and MLU at Age 2

The infant's proportion of conversational closings at age 3 months is inversely and significantly correlated with the MLU at age 2 ($-.650$ for males alone and $-.585$ for both males and females). Infants who, so to speak, are given the last "word" (i.e., close a large number of conversational clusters)

---

[4] Previously we reported on whether infants "know" they are *the* objects of their mothers' vocalizations by comparing their vocal responses to state 2 and to state 2i (state 2 is mother vocalizes to infant; state 2i is mother vocalizes *not* to infant). Infants were found capable of this discrimination (Lewis & Freedle, 1973). How does this discrimination vary as a function of situation? The three situations which fail to show knowledge of being the "object of" are crib-bed, couch, and playpen. In all others, infants show a significant awareness that they are the objects of their mothers' vocalizations. The situation that most *strongly* shows this is the mother's lap. Thus situations can differentially prime primitive referential properties of communication: establishing whether or not one is engaged by another in conversation.

in their early vocal interactions tend to develop formal language more slowly than infants who contribute less to prelinguistic conversational closings. Perhaps the explanation here is that mothers who *allow* their infants to end vocalization sequences too often are somewhat less attentive and responsive to their children and leave them to their own devices for self-stimulation. The possibility is suggestive but requires further study. Interestingly, the infant's prelinguistic openings are unrelated to later infant and/or maternal variables. This finding strengthens our view that infant openings may be related more to activity levels than to conversational variables.

Mothers who begin many of the conversational clusters (02 transitions) have children with higher MLUs at age 2 (.670 for male and female combined). This finding seems to merge nicely with our speculations about the mother's role in controlling who opens and closes conversational sequences;

TABLE 5. Pearson Product Correlations Relating Prelinguistic Conversational Openings and Closings with Selected Language Measures Obtained for Both the Mother and Her 2-Year-Old Child

Selected Vocalizations When Infant is 3 Months Old	Mean Length Utterance of Child at Age 2 Years	Mother's Directives to Her 2-Year-Old Child	Mother's Questions to Her 2-Year-Old Child
Infant starts cluster			
0 to 1 (male) $N = 6$	.000	.000	.000
0 to 1 (female) $N = 6$	.000	.000	.000
0 to 1 (both) $N = 12$	.000	.000	.000
Mother starts cluster			
0 to 2 (to male) $N = 6$	.430	.678**	−.110
0 to 2 (to female) $N = 6$	.920**[a]	.003	.000
0 to 2 (both) $N = 12$	.670**	.126	.170
Infant ends cluster			
1 to 0 (male) $N = 6$	−.650*	−.347	.420
1 to 0 (female) $N = 6$	−.490	.620*[a]	−.620*
1 to 0 (both) $N = 12$	−.585*	.070	−.050
Mother ends cluster			
2 to 0 (with male) $N = 6$	−.450	−.580*	.380
2 to 0 (with female) $N = 6$	−.070	−.798**	.030
2 to 0 (both) $N = 12$	−.310	−.590*	.180

[a] *$p < .05$ level, **$p < .01$ level.

that is, mothers who initiate many sequences when their infants are young (i.e., mothers who are strongly motivated to interact and who demonstrate this by initiating vocal interactions) also produce children at age 2 who show greater language development as measured by MLU. This meshes with the finding that mothers who allow their infants to terminate vocal sequences have infants with lower MLUs at age 2. In other words, both correlations point to the mother as a significant shaper of the rate at which language can be acquired. The early prelinguistic conversations may, by this view, be indexed as a motivational measure (from the mother's perspective) which diagnoses and predicts the amount of attention and instruction the child will receive over the next 2 years, the outcome of which will be greater language development for children of attentive caretakers and lower language development for children of less attentive caretakers.

We also included two special language functions produced by the mother when her child is 2 years old: number of *directives* (e.g., "Watch out for the table") and number of *questions* (e.g., "Who is that?"). (See Lewis & Cherry, Chapter 10 of this volume, for definitions.) These two measures yield very different relationships with prelinguistic conversational openings and closings. In particular, directives yield five significant correlations, whereas questions provide only one. The most striking result for directives is the correlation between how often the mother closes the prelinguistic conversations and how often she uses directives when her child is 2 years old. The significant inverse relationships (for each sex and for the sexes combined) suggest that mothers who are more responsive (have more closings) with their infants later do not use directives with their children.

A related finding emerges from observation of infant closings at 3 months and their relationship to mother's directives and questions at 24 months. Assume that the 10 transition, which we have called infant closing, is negatively related to maternal responsivity, so that the less responsive the mother, the more infant closings. The data for females indicate that less responsive mothers at 3 months ask fewer questions at 24 months ($-.62$) and give more directives ($+.62$). The opposite finding is true for males. This consistency over age but opposite-sex pattern may reflect the differential socialization patterns of the mother as a function of the infant's sex. As such it is consistent with the related finding of Lewis and Cherry (Chapter 10, this volume).

We have suggested that the key to understanding the relationship between the 3-month prelinguistic conversations and the 2-year longitudinal data of both infant and mother is the notion of adult responsivity. The relationships among infant closings and maternal openings specifically reflect this variable. Thus a responsive mother at 3 months is a responsive mother at 2 years. The consequences for the child of a responsive caretaker appear to be an acceleration of the child's complexity of linguistic productions at age 2 years.

Finally, there appear to be sex patterns in our longitudinal data which reflect differential socialization rules in responsivity.

In demonstrating such ontogenetic patterns, we have found it useful to refer to the evolutionary theory of Jerison. In particular, we have suggested that the three-"stage" idea of Jerison—that out of a noisy social interaction emerges a perceptual function of language, which then evolves into a more abstract symbolic system for communication and future planning—may have its counterpart in the growth of language from the prelinguistic conversational interactions of caretaker and infant, through an intermediate phase of "simple" perceptual mapping, which in turn, by at least age 2 years, eventuates in a syntactic–semantic system for complex communication. Thus language development is here viewed as a complex interaction among cognitive, perceptual, and social bases over time.

Four hypotheses have been advanced to help guide our data analyses within the prelinguistic time segment and, longitudinally, across time segments. Briefly, these hypotheses are as follows: (a) linguistic behavior has its origins in a general social communication system to which a formal lexicon and grammar are ultimately added; (b) the mother–infant interaction patterns, which consist of both vocal and sensorimotor components, form a social system designed to facilitate the growth of communication; (c) of the various elements that compose the primitive communication system, the vocalization behaviors form a subsystem which is more important than the paravocal behaviors; and, (d) prelinguistic behaviors are situationally bound, even at a very early age; it is from such constraints that semantics can potentially emerge. In support of the hypotheses we have attempted to demonstrate the social nature of the primitive conversational system; we have suggested that sex differences may partly be tied to socialization concepts through contrastive uses of vocal versus nonvocal behaviors on the part of the mother; and we have examined how situational locations affect prelinguistic conversational openings and closings, as well as influencing semantic notions such as the infant's being the "object" of the mother's vocalizations.

Although many details remain obscure regarding the steps by which formal language competence emerges, the longitudinal findings and the internal regularities in the prelinguistic situationally based vocal interaction of the infant with his mother support our view that the origins of certain aspects of language and language pragmatics can be found in the earliest social interaction of the infant and his caretaker.

References

Bell, S., & Ainsworth, M. D. S. *Infant crying and maternal responsiveness: Reinforcement reassessed.* Unpublished manuscript, 1971.

Bever, T. G. The cognitive basis for linguistic structures. In J. R. Hayes (Ed.), *Cognition and the development of language.* New York: Wiley, 1970.

Bierwisch, M. Social differentiation of language structure. In T. Bever, J. Katz & T. Langendoen (Eds.), *An integrated theory of linguistic ability.* New York: Crowell Press, 1976.

Brown, R. *Words and things.* Glencoe, Ill.: Glencoe Press, 1957.

Eimas, P. D., Siqueland, E. R., Jusczyk, P., & Vigorito, J. Speech perception in infants. *Science*, 1971, **171**, 303–306.

Freedle, R. O., & Lewis, M. Application of Markov processes to the concept of state. *Research Bulletin 71–34.* Princeton, N.J.: Educational Testing Service, 1971.

Furth, H. G. *Thinking without language: Psychological implications of deafness.* New York: Free Press, 1966.

Garner, W. R. *Uncertainty and structure as psychological concepts.* New York: Wiley, 1962.

Jerison, H. J. *Evolution of the brain and intelligence.* New York: Academic Press, 1973.

Jerison, H. J. Paleoneurology and the evolution of mind. *Scientific American*, 1976, **234**, 64–79.

Lenneberg, E. *The biological basis of language.* New York: Wiley, 1967.

Lewis, M., & Freedle, R. O. Mother–infant dyad: The cradle of meaning. In P. Pilner, L. Krames & T. Alloway (Eds.), *Communication and affect: Language and thought.* New York: Academic Press, 1973.

Lewis, M., & Lee-Painter, S. An interactional approach to the mother–infant dyad. In M. Lewis & L. Rosenblum (Eds.), *The origins of behavior.* Vol. I: *The effect of the infant on its caregiver.* New York: Wiley, 1974.

Lieberman, P. *Intonation, perception, and language.* Cambridge, Mass.: M.I.T. Press, 1967.

Olson, D. R. Language use for communicating, instructing, and thinking. In R. Freedle & J. B. Carroll (Eds.), *Language comprehension and the acquisition of knowledge.* Washington, D.C.: Winston/Wiley, 1972.

Pervin, L. Definitions, measurements, and classifications of stimuli, situations, and environments. *Research Bulletin 75–23.* Princeton, N.J.: Educational Testing Service, 1975. (a)

Pervin, L. A free response description approach to the analysis of person–situation interaction. *Research Bulletin 75–22.* Princeton, N.J.: Educational Testing Service, 1975. (b)

Piaget, J. *The origins of behavior.* New York: Norton Simons, 1952.

Reitman, W. R. *Cognition and thought: An information processing approach.* New York: Wiley, 1965.

Rheingold, H. L., Gewirtz, J. L., & Ross, H. W. Social conditioning of vocalizations in the infant. *Journal of Comparative and Physiological Psychology*, 1959, **52**, 68–73.

Schegloff, E. A., & Sachs, H. Opening up closings. *Semiotica*, 1973, **8**, 289–327.

Smith, F., & Miller, G. A. *The genesis of language*. Cambridge, Mass.: M.I.T. Press, 1966.

Vygotsky, L. S. *Thought and language*. Cambridge, Mass.: M.I.T. Press, 1962.

CHAPTER 8

Interaction and the Concept of Development: The Biological and the Social Revisited

M. P. M. RICHARDS

Unit for Research on the Medical Applications of Psychology
Cambridge University

The confusion and barrenness of psychology is not to be explained by calling it a "young science"; its state is not comparable with that of physics, for instance, in its beginnings. For in psychology there are experimental methods and *conceptual confusion.*

The existence of the experimental method makes us think we have the means of solving the problems which trouble us, though problem and method pass one another by.

Ludwig Wittgenstein
Philosophical investigations, 1953

INTRODUCTION

For a long time more thoughtful psychologists have pointed out that development cannot be conceptualized as the product of either nature or nurture, and there is now a general consensus around some version of an "interactionist" position. This position might be summarized by stating that both biological and social factors are involved in all development and that these two kinds of factors "interact" to produce adult behavior. Such an approach seems to reduce the analysis of development to a two-step process; first, the identification of the factors that are involved in development and their classification into either the biological or social categories (or intraorganismic and environmental, etc.) and, secondly, the description of the interactive process.

Two difficulties are immediately apparent in this approach. The various factors often mentioned in discussions of development belong to quite distinct realms of description, so it is hard to see in what sense they can interact. For example, among the entities that have been supposed to interact are physiological and anatomical features of the neonate, styles of child rearing, social class of parents, the child's "genetic makeup" and children's conceptual categories. This confusion may have arisen partly because of the use of statistical techniques for the description of data that employ interaction terms. But, of course, a mathematical expression involving an interaction term is only a particular descriptive simplification derived from a set of data and may have no correspondence at all to what is going on in a developmental process. The confusion here is the same one as is involved when a statistical correlation is taken to imply a causal link. I will return to the problem of the conceptualizations of developmental processes that involve factors from different realms of description.

The second difficulty is a pragmatic one—the interactionist approach has been singularly unsuccessful in producing any theoretical advance. Certainly many studies have been carried out within the framework that have investigated the role of a wide range of factors in a variety of developmental processes (the majority of studies analyze a single factor while holding another small set constant by the selection of an appropriate sample), but this has not led to any detailed specification of the interaction process. Indeed, in many discussions of development it has become commonplace to avoid the issue altogether. This is often done by listing the factors thought to be involved in the particular developmental process and then stating that a "complex interaction" is involved. Authors tend to remain silent on the nature of the process of interaction and the methods that might be used to analyze it.

Given the large volume of research effort and the lack of theoretical advance, we should perhaps become more suspicious of the usual ways of formulating developmental problems. Progress may be retarded by misleading attempts at conceptualization. Indeed, as I shall now attempt to demonstrate, there are fundamental confusions in most, if not all, attempts to conceptualize developmental problems in interactionist terms. First, I will examine the two general categories that are opposed in interactionist formulations—the biological and the social. Then I shall discuss the process of interaction itself.

THE BIOLOGICAL

Several rather different kinds of criteria have been used to determine whether or not a particular developmental factor should be classified as biological. Perhaps the commonest criterion is that a factor should involve (or is) a physiological or anatomical characteristic of the organism. Hormonal mechanisms would serve as a good example here. Often aspects of behavior that are known to depend, at least in part, on such physiological and anatomical processes are classed as biological—as if by some mechanism of association or contagion. Thus we often find sexual behavior being described as biologically based. This argument may be carried a step further, so that differences in behavior between the sexes are described as biological. It is easy to demonstrate the confusion in these latter arguments, for there is no good reason to think that physiological processes are any more (or less) involved in the development of behavior that it is typical of one sex than in any other category of behavior. Chromosomal differences and variations in the levels of various hormones between the sexes are well known and in many arguments serve as the "biological basis" of the behavioral difference. However, this categorization implies the unlikely—indeed, impossible—conclusion, that such processes are not involved in behavior that is not classified as biological or biologically based. We may well know less about the physiological processes involved in, say, voting behavior, but physiological processes must be associated with *all* behavior.

Part of the problem here is that there is a conflation of arguments that attempt to categorize *behavior* in terms of its supposed origins in the biological or social sphere by labeling it as innate or learned (or along a continuance from environmentally stable to labile) and others that are concerned with the kinds of factors that may be involved in the process of development of a particular aspect of behavior or any other phenotypic feature of the organism (see Hinde, 1968, for further discussion of this point).

When a physiological difference is correlated with a behavioral difference, a causal process is often assumed. Hormone differences between the sexes have been held to be the *cause* of behavioral differences. Correlations do not necessarily imply a causal connection; but, more important still, there must be a process of *mediation* between the physiological and behavioral levels which will involve many other kinds of factors, including a consideration of the social context of the particular behavioral act. I will return to this point later.

The implication of much writing on the physiological basis of behavior is that such processes exist in a realm that is biological and separate from the social world. This can be shown to be false both phylogenically and ontogenically.

Natural selection is concerned with the numbers of offspring of particular genotypic characteristics left by parents. However, it operates on phenotypes, not genotypes. Phenotypes result from a process of development which is dependent on a social world as well as on a physical environment. Selection too is mediated by social processes. The social structure of a group may have a great deal to do with the reproductive potential (and therefore selection) of particular members, as will all other aspects of their social lives. Selection pressures will be more or less specific to particular sociological arrangements and will change during the process of cultural evolution. Thus it is false to think of a set of biological determinates which are immune to social arrangements.[1] In both evolutionary changes and individual development the social world completely interpenetrates the so-called biological world. This makes it quite illogical and confusing to label some aspects of development as biologically based. It is traditional in psychology to apply such labels to behavior that is associated with the "primary drives" of food and sex. But at every step our eating and sexual behaviors are molded and structured by our culture and social world. In view of these considerations it becomes plain that the labeling of particular aspects of the developmental process as biological becomes a purely arbitrary occupation—and indeed a very confusing one.

Two points of particular concern in developmental work can be conveniently dealt with at this point. First, there has been considerable discussion about whether the newborn infant is best viewed as a social or a biological organism. It has been argued that the infant is social because he/she produces social signals to which caretakers respond. I have argued against this view because it suggests that the infant's signals have meanings in themselves, rather than being a matter of social convention and individual negotiation between child and caretaker. Instead I suggested that the infant could be seen as being protosocial or presocial—a biological organism with a particular potentiality for becoming a member of a society (Richards, 1974). What the foregoing discussion makes clear, however, is that it is meaningless to argue in these terms. An infant is neither social nor, as Becker (1972) has suggested, "helpless, dependent animal matter." He/she has developed through an ontogenic process which is permeated by the social world (from the moment of conception and earlier), and this process itself has evolved in the context of earlier human societies.

The other point concerns historical and evolutionary change. Much psychological writing tends to assume a two-phase evolutionary process with man's origins being illustrated by the behavior of contemporary nonhuman primates and hunter-gatherer societies (man in a state of nature). Elements of behavioral development that are discernible in either or both of these

[1] Recently there has been renewed interest in selective pressures operating among and between parents and children and in the old problem of parental altruism (e.g., Trivers, 1972). It is as yet unclear what, if any, relevance this approach has for the discussion of human development. I suspect the relevance may be minimal because of the supreme importance of sociocultural changes in human evolution (Waddington, 1969). But in any case, though propositions about the selective advantages of altruism may suggest the existence of certain behavioral phenomena, these must be independently sought by behavioral investigation. There is no way in which postulated selective process can *explain* the development of behavior.

situations are often labeled as biological, and if they can be identified in contemporary industrial societies then are held to have a more "basic" character than processes than cannot be seen in these other situations. The ventral-ventral clinging of infant rhesus monkeys is a typical example. Some contemporary hunter-gatherers carry their infants on their bodies in slings (though others use cradle boards), whereas such arrangements are rare in industrial societies. Because clinging and close body contact are seen in these other situations, it is sometimes argued that such contact is a "basic need" of human infants. Such arguments suffer from the confusions I have already mentioned: that (a) one cannot isolate aspects of development as biological and therefore separate from the social sphere and (b) evolutionary change is partly a cultural matter. Physiologically and socially we are unlike hunter-gatherers, and we are rearing children for life in a very different society. Though extensive skin-to-skin contact for infants might modify their adult behavior, this cannot be regarded as something desirable in our society simply because of its supposed evolutionary history, any more than we should regard the high infant mortality of pre-agricultural societies as something we should strive to reproduce.

More fundamentally, this style of evolutionary argument confines all historical considerations to the biological sphere and so leaves us with a curiously ahistorical psychology. One can seek universal laws of the development of behavior only so long as one isolates behavior from social influence, and the quest for such law has a lot to do with contemporary confusions. This isolation is effectively achieved by consigning historical changes to the biological category. This, as I have argued elsewhere (Richards, 1975, a, b), means that we may be analyzing behavior in social contexts that did not exist a couple of generations ago. Patterns of interaction, for example, that may be held to be "essential" for the development of speech could depend on such recently created arrangements. Because of the ahistorical emphasis, the process of social change is relatively little explored, and almost no mention is made of the enormous changes in child-rearing patterns, mortality, population age structure, and so on that have occurred over the past 200 or 300 years. As Waddington (1960) has emphasized, sociocultural change has far outweighed gene pool alterations in human evolution.

THE SOCIAL

The categorization of particular factors as social in the interactionist equation is as arbitrary and misleading as the biological categorization. There are no purely social factors, as all behavior is developed through a process that involves the genotype and physiological and anatomical processes.

This is well illustrated by the work that demonstrates that infants respond selectively to speech sounds (e.g., Freidlander, 1970). Such a faculty presumably facilitates the development of speech and social communication but might be thought to be the function of physiological characteristics of the infant's ear and associated neural processes. Hence a social factor in development—the parents' speech—influences the infant through a physiological (biological) adaptation. Pitch is one of the sound characteristics that seem to distinguish human speech for the infant, but this depends on the anatomical features of the adult's vocal tract. So, wherever we turn, we find developmental processes that involve both physiological and social factors, *and* these interrelate in such a way that it is impossible to classify them in any way that provides a neat separation between the two. Attempts to do so mislead because they involve the implicit assumption that it is possible, at the behavioral level, to have elements that belong to one or other category and are isolated from any influence of the other. This assumption is then pushed a stage further, so that we have either biological or social determination—sex-typed behavior is determined by biological (hormonal) differences, or sex-typed behavior is determined by conditioning during childhood.

INTERACTION

The main point I have tried to make so far is that any classification of developmental factors into two opposed and interacting categories is an entirely arbitrary process. Given this confusion, it is hardly surprising that authors tend to be vague, to say the least, when describing the nature of the interactive process. Indeed, many who subscribe to various versions of interactionism make other statements in which they contradict themselves. Interactionism demands that a conceptual equality be accorded to the biological and social (or the organismic and environmental) sides of the equation, yet we frequently find interactionists making statements that imply a temporal or even spatial difference between the categories. Frequent mention is made of the biological *bases* of behavior, or—the converse—social life is seen as a crust of skin covering our biology (clothes for naked apes). The claims of a biological priority have the misleading effect of suggesting that infants are somehow more biological (or biologically determined) than adults or that genotypic differences stand outside the social world. For this reason some of the wilder claims of human ethologists or animal psychologists about human infants may go unchallenged, whereas the same arguments applied to human adults would be quickly recogized as absurd.

An analogues characterization is to refer to biological potentialities that may or may not become manifest in the social world. Or biology may be seen as setting limits to human development—as if the social world was never limiting. All these and other, similar statements illustrate the deep confusion and uncertainties that exist about the nature of the developmental process in contemporary psychology.

On top of these difficulties, there is also a tendency to infer the nature of the developmental processes from particular characterizations of adult behavior. Two examples can illustrate this. In ethology Lorenz, Eibl-Eibesfeldt, and others (e.g., Eibl-Eibesfeldt, 1970) have claimed that species-specific (or innate) behavior develops in such a way that environmental factors are unimportant (such a claim denies, of course, the existence of interaction, or at least suggests there may be special cases where one category is absent). A parallel argument has been used by Jensen (1971) in the IQ debate, where he has advanced an argument that rests on the assumption that a heritability calculation carries an implication about the nature of the developmental process (IQ is highly heritable; therefore environmental changes, like Headstart programs, are not likely to be effective). There are several falacies in this argument—the logical separation between a statement about a population and the development of an individual; the fact that phenotypes, not genotypes, are (or are not) influenced by a Headstart program, and so on—but the point I want to make here is that such statements are taken seriously, even by the developmental psychologists, and this is an indication of the widespread confusion about environmental matters.

The essential feature of the approach involving heritability calculations is to assign differences between individuals (in a population) to either genetic (i.e. biological) or environment causes (most importantly, social in the human case). A similar methodology has been advocated in animal research, where it is suggested that animals of the same genotype can be reared in varying environments or those of differing genotypes in the same environment. It is suggested that experiments of these kinds may allow phenotypic differences between individuals to be assigned to either a genetic or an environmental source. Because of practical difficulties it is unlikely that such an approach would be of much value in human research, but the main point I want to emphasize is that the search for sources of differences tells us nothing about the process of development (see Hinde, 1968). Also, of course, it involves the same dicotomy as I have been discussing above and the same confusions about spheres of knowledge—how can the genes interact with features of the social world?

WHAT IS BIOLOGY?

To begin disentangling some of the confusions I have mentioned, we need to ask the apparently simple question, what is biology? Dictionaries tend to be unhelpful and provide definitions of the kind "the study of living things" or "the study of animals." The first does not explain why sociology, for example, is not biology, and the second gives us no clues about the biological study of our own species. What is clear is that biology does not simply refer to the realm that is not social; the territories do not have a simple reciprocal relationship of this sort. In part, in the usage of psychologists "biological" is used to refer to another *level* of analysis than the behavioral—the physiological. In other contexts, however, it is used to refer to modes of analysis that have been employed on animal species when they are applied to our own. Here it may represent another way of analyzing the same phenomena, and there is no difference in levels. For example, human mating patterns and some of their consequences can be analyzed in terms of marriage arrangements and bastardy or in terms of inferred gene flow. These could simply represent different ways of approaching the same phenomena. But such apparently parallel descriptions may have different consequences. Viewing man's past in evolutionary terms will tend to emphasize morphological characters, whereas a social historian might well concentrate on changes in social structure.

From this I think it is clear that dividing the factors involved in developmental processes into two categories, the biological and the social, and opposing them will never provide a rational framework for analysis. Such approaches are dangerous politically because they easily slide into formulations which use notions of social and/or biological determinism. An alternative, and potentially much more fruitful, method is to concentrate on the *process* of development. In building up a network of the factors involved in a particular development process careful attention needs to be paid to various levels of analysis (or realms of knowledge). Depending on the purpose of the analysis, there may be more or less emphasis on physiological factors; but if these are included in the analysis, the kinds of processes that link them to the behavioral level will be different from those that may operate between factors at the behavioral level. Some processes of mediation must be inserted between the physiological and behavioral levels. To take a simple example, one may be able to show that there are physiological processes linking an infant's blood sugar level and the probability of crying. It would then be tempting to conclude that hunger causes crying. However, such an account would leave out processes of mediation. The link between blood sugar levels and crying may be produced in part because crying is taken by parents to be a sign of hunger. It may also depend on a particular tradition of looking after young babies that involves keeping them at some distance from their mothers, so that only sound can be used as a communicative signal. These are not simply theoretical possibilities because there are societies where the child is seldom off the mother's body, and there crying may have a very different meaning to both parent and child.

In our search for a theoretical basis for our work it is probably wise to give a clear definition of the universe that our theory is intended to cover. A general theory of behavioral development seems an unrealistic goal, and we need to specify clearly what aspects of development we are referring to. Usually such a goal will be a specific pattern of behavior shown at a specified phase in the life cycle and seen in defined situations. Again our theories need to be limited to particular cultures and historical times.

We also need to be clear about starting points. One of the reasons why "biological" factors may appear to preempt others in the developmental process is that the fertilized egg provides a convenient starting point for analysis. Usually the egg is described only in physiological terms, that is, in terms of the genes it carries. Thus a biological characterization is seen to be prior to any social considerations. The basic confusion here is the unnoticed change of level from the psychological sphere to the physiological. For most purposes in the analysis of behavioral development the newborn is a more convenient starting point that the zygote. The newborn has the added advantage that it is more obvious that he/she is an individual of social formation (but, of course, also having a physiology).

It is probably possible to provide satisfactory accounts of some processes of behavioral development without making reference to any factors that would be currently classified as biological. Such factors would be implicitly assumed. However, such an account would lack generality and might become very misleading if it was applied to situations where significant variation in the biological "constraints" occurred. A possible example here would be studies of neonatal behavior carried out on populations where male circumcision is very common (as in the United States). Circumcision apparently causes long-lasting changes of state regulation and possibly other aspects of behavior (Richard, Bernal, & Brackbill, 1975). These may well modify the activities of caretakers. An account of behavior which did not mention the presence or absence of circumcision (as is usual in American psychology) might well be inapplicable to populations where circumcision is very rare, as in Britain.

The extent to which an analysis is carried in various directions will vary with the nature of the particular problem and the researchers' location within disciplinary boundaries. In the research communities of Europe and America theory and practice have become widely divorced. "Interesting" or "important" questions tend to be defined in terms of very general and wide goals and the traditions of the particular discipline. Each discipline will have its own set of potential answers to a particular problem. A clinician faced with the problem of hyperactive children in the classroom may think in terms of neurological deficits and physiological abnormalities and would see answers in terms of drug treatments. To the developmental psychologist patterns of child rearing and mother–child relationships constitute a more likely focus, with some kind of therapy or counseling as the possible solution. An educationalist would be more likely to be interested in the curriculum and the organization of teaching and might press for segregation of certain children and the provision of special educational facilities. Each discipline has its own characteristic style of approach. However, we must remember that the division of knowledge into disciplines does not rest on any God-given classification but itself is a product of actions in a social world. The division between psychology and biology is in no sense a "natural" one; indeed, very misleading research is likely to result if the analysis of behavioral development proceeds within the demain that is traditionally the psychologist's without moving out into areas that have traditionally been assigned to the physiologist, sociologist, linguist, historian, and so on.

So far, I have mounted my argument in general terms. In the final section I shall discuss some aspects of the growth of communication in children, and in doing so I hope to illustrate in more detail what is involved in the analysis of developmental processes.

THE DEVELOPMENT OF COMMUNICATION

Contemporary work on language acquisition has stressed the continuties between preverbal behavior, particularly the relationships of the child and parents, and the emergence of language. Nelson (1973), for example, makes the "pretheoretical assumption" that "there is a basic continuity in developmental processes and structures. The same types of structure and processes are utilized throughout development, and changes in them are gradual and continuous ... For language development the implication of this assumption is that "preverbal" development is integrally related to later development" (p. 2). The key requirement therefore is to give substance to the phrase *integrally related*. So far, research has concentrated on the description of parent–child relationships in the preverbal period and on a search for correlations between individual differences noted in this period and those that may be found in speech measures collected later from the same children. It should be noted that this is an indirect approach to the basic question—the nature of the process of language acquisition—and unless certain precautions are observed it may provide very misleading answers. The approach is indirect because it searches for correlations of the *rate* of language acquisition assessed against chronological age. Most of the language measures used implicitly or explicitly employ a series of age-related steps, and individual variation is essentially measured in terms of the age at which each step is accomplished. So what is found in studies of this kind are factors that are associated with faster and slower rates of acquisition, and it is quite possible that factors related to variations in the rate of acquisition are relatively un-important in the acquisition process itself.

Studies in this tradition have, as yet, failed to find very impressive con-nections between the preverbal and verbal behavior in development, and more generally it has become fashionable to stress the lack of predictability in early development. But this seems to be a rather misleading view. Though we may not be very good at predicting the development of an individual child relative to his/her peers, the overall predictability of the develop-mental process is very high. For a population of infants, we can make a number of statements about the age at which they will achieve various mile-stones and the kinds of behavior they are likely to show at various ages which carry a high probability of being verified. This predictability is per-haps especially marked in aspects of language acquisition (Lenneberg, 1967), and this is a good example of what Waddington (1968) has described as a "chreod."

However, it must be noted that, as the analysis of child language proceeds and more complex measures are taken, a wider range of individual variation may be uncovered. And we are probably dealing with a situation where there are several routes to the same end point.

The extent of this predictability carries an important implication about the developmental processes involved, for it suggests that from the point of view of the child the wide variations in linguistic environments in which children live are of little importance to the acquisition process. Almost all children acquire language and become competent language users, so all their develop-mental environments must provide the necessary conditions for acquisi-tion. This implies that the necessary social conditions for acquisition are very wide and that the child must possess means of using common features in widely varying situations. Part of the relative invariance in children's per-formances, as compared with their environments, may be rather more ap-parent than real, as a number of studies (e.g., Snow, 1972; Phillips, 1973; Gelman & Shatz, chapter 2 of this volume) have shown systematic modifica-tions in adults' speech when it is addressed to children; however, even allow-ing for this, the variation in environments is still very wide. In theory, one can only directly infer the social conditions necessary for language acquisi-tion by comparing situations in which language never develops with those in which it does. Work so far done on these lines is rather unhelpful, however, because all it has shown is that adequate hearing is essential. In some ways work on blind children is more promising, as it may reveal more about the required interrelations of the speech environment, social behavior, and com-municative development (Urwin, 1975).

The classical answer to the paradox I have been discussing is to suggest that the process of acquisition is innate, but, as will be apparent in the light of the discussion above, such an assertion does not provide any answers. It tells nothing about the process and simply rephrases what we already know —that under the usual range of conditions in which children grow up, acquisition is predictable. The associated claims that the process is biologically based as is dependent on maturation are equally unrevealing in the face of these arguments.

In practice it follows from this discussion that any claim about the features of preverbal life that are necessary for acquisition may be easily dismissed if it describes conditions that are not more or less universal.

In contemporary research we have another problem that has been brought about by our own activities. We have become very self conscious about the processes of language acquisition. Coupled with this, early language competence has become the mark of successful child rearing among some social groups. As we tend to draw our research samples from the children of those who are familiar with developmental research, we may be creating self-verifying theories. Given the correlations between social class and language acquisition, there is likely to be an association between accelerated language development and knowledge of recent developmental research. Thus parents who have children who are likely anyway to be advanced on language measures are just those who are likely to adapt whatever interactional[2] strategies are currently in vogue among researchers.

Historical and cross-cultural research may be essential here for giving us some perspective from which to view our own culture. Of course we cannot assume that the present ages for developmental milestones will be the same for other societies and other times in history. We can draw an analogue here with age of puberty. Though this might appear to be a fixed point in development, dependent on maturation and so on, it has shown considerable change over the recent past. It is worth comparing this with language with respect to claims of innateness. Puberty would seem to display all the features that have been used to argue that language is innate.

Menarchy occurred at about $16\frac{1}{2}$-years a century ago in western Europe and has since been getting earlier at a rate of about 4 months per decade (Tanner, 1962; Laslett, 1971a). Though one must not underestimate the difficulties of the required research, it should be possible to obtain similar evidence about possible fluctuations in the age at which the first word was produced. Any changes found could be compared with the child-rearing practices of the time in question, and this might provide valuable clues about the role of the preverbal environment. A similar strategy could be employed in cross-cultural research.

Historical research is important too for understanding the origins of

[2] N.B. Here I am using "interaction" in another sense to describe the social interchange between two people.

present day practices in child rearing. For the point of view of studies of parent–child interaction in the preverbal period the important element is always the interpretation an adult places on the behavior of a child (Richards, 1974; Shotter, 1975). The issue is not that the child has cried, smiled, or pointed but that an adult has responded to the action in some way—or has ignored it. There is no necessary link between the infant's behavior and an adult's response to it; it depends on social convention. Animal research has been very misleading here because it has almost exclusively analyzed communicational system in behaviorist cause and effect terms. No space is allowed for social mediation. All too frequently those working at the human level have adopted the same strategy. This misleading tendency is reinforced by the search for evolutionary antecedents of human gestures in nonhuman primates. Homologies of the *form* of human gestures may well be found, as Darwin showed us, but such analyses tell us nothing about the conventions we may have about the meanings of actions and gestures. We can only search for these in our cultural past. The history of child-rearing practices is a rich field that is only beginning to be explored (e.g., Aries, 1962; Laslett, 1971b, 1972; De Mause, 1974; Rabb & Rotberg, 1971) and has yet to be systematically used in developmental psychology.

Antecedents of later performance

I pointed out earlier that studies have tended to find rather unimpressive correlations between individual differences during the preverbal and verbal periods. To illustrate some of the difficulties in this area I will summarize (fuller details are to be found in Dunn, 1975) some of the relevant data

TABLE 1.   Outline of Procedures Used in the First 14 Months

2–6 weeks before delivery	Interview of mother.
Delivery	Preceded collection of medical information by midwife. Observations of first mother–infant contact (when observer present).
Days 2, 3, 8, 9, 10	Observation of a feeding session on each day. Interview.
Days 0–10	Continuous diary kept by mother.
Day 8 or 9	Neurological examination and non-nutritive study test.
8 weeks (2 visits)	Observation of a feeding and 2 nonfeeding time awake periods. 48-hour diary kept by mother. Interview.
14 weeks, 20 weeks	Like 8 weeks, but no feeding observations.
30 weeks	Some infant assessment measures included at some visits.
60 weeks (2 visits)	Two observations of nonfeeding awake time, including tape recordings, of 1 hour each. Interview of mother. 48-hour diary.

from our longitudinal study in Cambridge. In this study a group of 77 medically "low risk" mothers and babies were visited at home during the children's first 5 years. Table 1 summarizes the schedule of visits. Further details of the sample selection, observational techniques, and so on may be found in Richards and Bernal (1972), Richards (1975b), Dunn and Richards (1975).

In the first 10-day period we found little evidence for the presence of a simple unitary dimension of maternal affectionate interest or warmth (Dunn & Richards, 1975; Dunn, 1974). Measures of maternal looking and smiling at the baby were related to the amount of "affectionate talking" to the baby, but these variables were not related to the amount of touching or caressing, or to measures of responsiveness to crying. the baby's rate of non nutritive sucking was positively correlated with the smiling, looking, and talking measures.

In the 8-, 14-, 20-, and 30-week observations, which did not include feeding, we found consistent individual differences in the amounts of touching, talking, and responsiveness to vocalizations and positive intercorrelations between the measures (see Table 2).

TABLE 2.   Spearman Rank Correlations[a] between Selected Maternal Measures at 8, 14, 20, and 30 weeks ($N = 60$–68)

	Touch at			Vocalization at				
	14	20	30	8	14	20	30	weeks
Touch								
at 8 weeks	.50			.53				
at 14 weeks		.58			.59			
at 20 weeks			.48			.56		
at 30 weeks							.63	

[a] All these correlations are significant at $p < .01$.

There were relationships between some maternal measures collected at these ages and data from the sucking test on day 8 (Table 3). However, responsiveness to crying measures collected during the 8- to 30-week period tended to be very unstable.

Comparison of the maternal measures over the 8- to 30-week period with those in the first 10 days showed rather few significant relationships. But for breast-feeding mothers, though not those that bottle fed, maternal touching in the first 10 days was correlated with measures of touching, vocalizing, and responsiveness to baby vocalization over the 8- to 30-week period. This differential relationship associated with feeding method suggests that the context of particular observation may be extremely important, a point to which I will return.

TABLE 3.   Spearman Rank Correlations between Tendency to Cry after Sucking Test (day 8) and Later Maternal Measures

Age (weeks)	Mother Vocalizes	Mother Touches	Mother Touches If Baby Vocalizes
14	$-.30$*[a]	$-.37$**[a]	.36**
20	.16	$-.22$†[a]	$-.29$*

[a] †$p < .05$, *$p < .01$, **$p < .001$.

At 14 months our observations were tape recorded, yielding usable transcripts for 36 of the mother–infant pairs. These observations gave high correlations between measures of the mother vocalizing to the baby and scores for the baby looking at, vocalizing to, and giving, showing, or pointing out objects to the mother (Table 4).

The infant measures which reflected the baby's "conversational" exchange of looks, vocalizations, and objects were, however, not related to measures of the mothers touching, handling, or carrying. From the tape recordings, the measure of the percentage of the baby's utterances that were responded to correlated with the amount of maternal vocalizing recorded in the observations ($r=.61$, $N=35$), and mother's vocalizations were especially likely to follow infant vocalizations that were (or assumed to be) requests for objects

TABLE 4.   Spearman Rank Correlations between Selected Measures at 14 Months ($N = 16$)

	2	3	4	5	6	7
1. Baby looks at mother	.86	.59	.63	.49	.40	$-$ [a]
2. Baby vocalizes to mother		.60	.43	.45	.40	$-$
3. Baby shows objects to mother			.44	.45		$-$
4. Mother vocalizes to baby				.83	.63	.45
5. % Baby vocalization followed by mother vocalization					.38	$-$
6. % Baby fuss followed by mother vocalization						$-$
7. Mother affectionate touch						

[a] $-$ = correlations below .20.

or help. The transcripts were also analyzed in terms of Nelson's (1973) categories of direction, acceptance, or rejection and the proportion of utterances
containing object words. Not surprisingly the latter measure showed a correlation with the baby's offering, showing, and pointing out objects to the
mother, but apart from this, there were no significant relationships between
the mother's verbal feedback indices and measures of responsiveness to the
baby's vocalization, fussing, or touching.

Thus the language feedback measures seem to relate to rather different
qualities of interaction from those derived from the observations, which
were very similar to the measures taken at earlier ages. Indeed, with the
latter measures we did find positive association with a range of the similar
measures taken in the 8- to 30-week period, though no such associations
were apparent for the 14-month maternal feedback indices. However, when
we went back to the first 10 days, correlations were found between a sucking
test measure and a factor made up from some of the maternal affectionate
measures and some of the 14-month mother vocalization measures (Table 5).

TABLE 5. Spearman Rank Correlations between First 10-day Measures and
Some from 14 months ($N = 30$)

	Mother Vocalizations	% Baby Utterances Responded to	% Baby Utterances as Demands	Maternal Acceptances
First 10-day maternal affection factor	.31*[a]	.55**[a]	.39*	.30*
Suck rate	—	.46**	.45**	—

[a] *$p < .05$, **$p < .01$.

The final correlation I will mention concerns the children's Stanford-Binet
IQ scores, measured at $4\frac{1}{2}$ years (Light, 1974). Though the IQ score did not
correlate with any of the measures of maternal responsiveness taken in the
first 14 months, it did relate positively to Nelson's acceptance measure at
14 months ($r=.52$, $N=28$, $p<.01$).

This very condensed account of a rather confusing pattern of correlations
may be summarized as follows:

1. Measures of some aspects of maternal affectionate behavior in the first
10 days correlated with measures of baby behavior at this period.

2. These measures did not show continuity with the consistent individual
differences in maternal behavior found between 8 and 30 weeks.

3. At 14 months, observational measures of the mother's vocalizations and her responses to the child's vocalizations and some characteristics of the interchange between child and mother were weakly related to the 30-week measures, and more strongly to the first 10-day measures.

4. Mothers who were active in responding to their babies' utterances at 14 months had babies who made many vocal requests for objects and help, and it was this interactive style that was related to the early measures of mother and baby behavior.

5. Stanford-Binet IQs collected at $4\frac{1}{2}$ years correlated with maternal acceptances at 14 months but not with other measures of interaction in the first 14 months.

What do these results tell us about the "integral relation" of development in the earlier and later phases? From results such as I have described it is tempting to conclude, contrary to some other claims (e.g., Ainsworth, Bell & Stayton, 1974), that the kinds of measures that are usually examined within the attachment rubric in the first year have little to do with subsequent cognitive and linguistic development. That, of course, would not rule out an integral relation but would suggest that it does not exist along this particular dimension. However, before reaching this conclusion, several weaknesses in the general methodology I have been describing should be mentioned. Already, I have noted that the strategy is an indirect one because it deals only with the relationships of individual differences, but even in these there are other difficulties. The most obvious of these involves the particular measures used; measures tend to be selected for traditional or pragmatic reasons rather than on the basis of any well-articulated theory, and one can always plausibly suggest that quite other patterns of correlation might be found if other measures were employed. Measures tend to be rather behavioristic; they concentrate on what may be easily recorded "objectively" and take little account of their meaning to either the actors or the situation. This is well illustrated by the different patterns of correlations we found for measures derived from breast and bottle feedings. These appear to be seen as rather different kinds of situations by the mothers. Breast feedings appear to be rather private occasions where the mother sees herself in a communicative and emotional exchange with her baby, whereas bottle feedings are much more instrumental from the baby's point of view. Here the mother's concern is mainly with getting the feed into the baby, and her social contact is often directed to the other adults present to a greater extent than to the baby (other adults are much more likely to be present during bottle feedings). Differences of this kind are not reflected in most of the measures used in mother–child interaction studies. Other evidence of this kind of effect comes from the lack of consistency of measures across contexts, which has been emphasized by Lewis and Freedle (1975). Somehow we have to evolve investigative methods that are much more reflective of the perceptions of the actors in whom we are interested.

At another level we perhaps should be much more critical of the methods of statistical analysis that we use with data of this kind. Correlating two sets of individual differences obtained at two points in development is in some ways an analogous technique to the methodology, mentioned above, of tracing origins of differences to either genetic or environmental factors. In the present case we searched for measures which we have taken that show similar patterns of variation across the individual children in the sample. If we obtained high correlations (or even low ones!), we tend to assume that the two measures are involved in the same developmental process. There is a danger here that we may build theories via our statistical techniques from relationships that may really be a product of the preconceptions that led us to employ certain measures. An arguable conclusion from this is that we should place much less emphasis on methods that concentrate on individual differences, at least until we have done a great deal more descriptive and theoretical work.

Looking at patterns of intercorrelation between measures of individual differences may be a much less powerful technique than trying to classify types of mothers and infants that show a typical range of behavior within and across situations. We are more likely to be able to get at *processes* of development by examining the characteristics of particular groups constructed by classification techniques than by patterns of intercorrelation of variables from heterogeneous groups. In our own study we have followed the development of a subgroup of our total sample which was defined by relatively poor status at birth and a pattern of regular night waking. This analysis has already demonstrated a wide range of other developmental features that seem typical of this subgroup (Barnes, 1974, 1975; Bernal, 1973). This is a strategy we plan to use much more widely in the future analysis of our results and one that seems to embody many of the desirable features of a descriptive approach.

The final point I want to make about observational studies such as our own is that they very seldom collect any data at the neurophysiological level and so, as I have mentioned above, are likely to give a misleading impression of the developmental processes. Obviously, there are considerable practical and ethical difficulties in physiological work, but some techniques that can be used are available. For example, one can take measures that reflect the degree of cortical lateralization in infants, which might be very illuminating if they were included in a study together with a range of psychological measures concerned with language acquisition.

References

Ainsworth, M. D. S., Bell, S. M., & Stayton, D. J. Infant–mother attachment and social development. In M. P. M. Richards (Ed.), *The integration of a child into a social world*. London: Cambridge University Press, 1974.

Aries, P. *Centuries of childhood*. London: Penguin, 1962.

Barnes, F. *On having a relatively poor status at birth: Some characteristics of the children and their mothers.* Paper presented at Ninth International Study Group on Developmental Neurology, Oxford, 1974.

Barnes, F. Accidents in the first 3 years of life. *Child Care, Health, and Development*, 1975, **1**, 435–447.

Becker, E. *The birth and death of meaning*. 2nd ed. London: Penguin, 1972.

Bernal, J. F. Night waking in infants during the first 14 months. *Developmental Medicine and Child Neurology*, 1973, **15**, 760–769.

De Mause, L. *The history of childhood*. New York: Psychohistory, 1974.

Dunn, J. F. Consistency and change in maternal style. In M. O'Connor (Ed.), *The parent–infant relationship*. London: Academic Press, 1974.

Dunn, J. *Patterns of early interaction: Continuities, and consequences?* Paper presented at the Loch Lomond Symposium, University of Strathclyde, September, 1975.

Dunn, J. F., & Richards, M. P. M. *Observations on the developing relationship between mother and baby in the neonatal period.* Paper presented at the Loch Lomond Symposium, University of Strathclyde, September 1975. To be published in H. R. Schaffer (Ed.), *The interactions of infants*. New York: Academic Press.

Eibl-Eibesfeldt, I. E. *Ethology: the biology of behavior*. New York: Holt, Rhinehart & Winston, 1970.

Freidlander, B. Z. Receptive language development in infancy: issues and problems. *Merrill-Palmer Quarterly*, 1970, **16**, 7–15.

Hinde, R. A. Dicotomies in the study of development. In J. M. Thoday & A. S. Parkes (Eds.), *Genetic and environmental influences on behaviour*. Edinburgh: Oliver & Boyd, 1968.

Jensen, A. R. In environment, heredity and intelligence. *Harvard Education Review* 1971. How much can we boost IQ and scholastic achievement? In *Environment heredity and intelligence*. Cambridge Mass.: Harvard Educational Review, 1971.

Laslett, P. Age at menarche in Europe since the eighteenth century. In J. K. Rabb & R. I. Rotberg (Eds.), *The family in history*. New York: Harper & Row, 1971. (a)

Laslett, P. *The world we have lost*. 2nd ed. London: Methuen, 1971 (b)

Laslett, P. (Ed.). *Household and family in past time*. London: Cambridge University Press, 1972.

Lenneberg, E. H. *Biological foundations of language*. New York: Wiley, 1967.

Lewis, M., & Freedle, R. *The mother and infant communication system: The effects of poverty.* Paper presented at the Biennial Conference of the International Society for the Study of Behavioural Development, Surrey, England, July, 1975.

Light, P. *The role-taking skills of four year old children.* Unpublished doctoral thesis, University of Cambridge, 1974.

Nelson, K. Structure and strategy in learning to talk. *Monographs of the Society for Research in Child Development,* 1973, **38,** No. 1–2.

Phillips, J. Syntax and vocabulary of mother's speech to young children: Age and sex comparisons. *Child Development,* 1973, **44,** 182–185.

Rabb, K. T., & Rotberg, R. I. (Eds.). *The family in history.* New York: Harper & Row, 1971.

Richards, M. P. M. First steps in becoming social. In M. P. M. Richards (Ed.), *The integration of a child into a social world.* London: Cambridge University Press, 1974.

Richards, M. P. M. History and the analysis of child development. Unpublished paper.

Richards, M. P. M. An ecological study of infant development in an urban setting in Britain. In P. H. Leiderman & S. R. Tulkin (Eds.), *Cultural and social influences in infancy and early childhood.* New York: Academic Press, 1975. (b)

Richards, M. P. M., & Bernal, J. R. An observational study of mother–infant interaction. In N. Blurton Jones (Ed.), *Ethological studies of child behaviour.* London: Cambridge University Press, 1972.

Richards, M. P. M., Bernal, J., & Brackbill, Y. Early behavioural differences: gender or circumcision? *Developmental Psychobiology,* 1976, **9,** 89–95.

Shotter, J. *Methodological issues in microanalytic study of mother–infant interaction.* Paper presented at Loch Lomond Symposium, University of Strathclyde, September, 1975. To be published in H. R. Schaffer (Ed.), *The interactions of infants.* New York: Academic Press.

Snow, C. Mother's speech to children learning language. *Child Development,* 1972, **43,** 549–565.

Tanner, J. M. *Growth at adolescence.* Oxford: Blackwell, 1962.

Trivers, R. L. Parental investment and sexual selection. In B. Campbell (Ed.), *Sexual selection and the descent of man, 1871–1971.* Chicago: Aldine, 1972.

Urwin, C. *The development of language and communication in blind children.* Doctoral thesis in preparation, University of Cambridge, 1975.

Waddington, C. H. *The ethical animal.* London: Allen and Unwin, 1960.

Waddington, C. H. (Ed.). *Towards a theoretical biology.* Vol. I: *Prolegomena.* Edinburgh: Edinburgh University Press, 1968.

Wittgenstein, L. *Philosophical investigations.* Oxford: Blackwell, 1953.

CHAPTER 9

Cognition and Communication: A Dialectic Paradigm for Development

IRVING E. SIGEL

and

RODNEY R. COCKING

Educational Testing Service

INTRODUCTION

The purpose of the chapter is to present a communication model for the study of representational thinking. The paradigm consists of three critical constructs, *distancing*, *discrepancy* and *dialectics*, which in their interconnectedness are presumed to facilitate the development of representational thought.

"Distancing" refers to a class of exogenous events (personal and non-personal), "discrepancy" defines the relationship between exogenous and endogenous factors, and "dialectics" is the process involved in stage transformation of representational thought.

The paradigm is grounded in Piagetian stage-dependent theory but extends and specifies the social-interactive components in particular. Although Piaget acknowledges the significance of social factors for cognitive development, he does not provide any details regarding the particularity of social factors. The distancing behaviors to be explicated in this chapter fill that gap.

Why Another Paradigm?

The model to be elaborated in this chapter extends current conceptualization of cognitive development in two ways: (1) it provides a specification of a class of exogenous events deemed necessary, although not sufficient, for the development of representational thinking, and (2) it provides definitions of the relationships among exogenous and endogenous factors.

Piaget argues that his theory rejects primacy of either exogenous or endogenous factors vis-à-vis cognitive development. He does, however, admit candidly that he emphasizes one or the other, depending on the audience. When speaking to psychologists, Piaget stresses endogenous factors since psychologists tend to overvalue the significance of external events; when addressing biologists, he reverses the emphasis, again because of biologists' emphasis on their own discipline. In spite of his plea for an even-handed approach, it is difficult to identify the particular class of exogenous events that is important (Piaget, 1971).

Piaget is not alone in the global use of the term *exogenous*. Except for some particular experimental strategies used in training studies and some crude enrichment in educational programs with disadvantaged children, very little specification of the necessary experiential events has been made. The distancing behaviors are purported to fill that gap. It is also necessary to define the relationship created by the distancing behaviors and the state of the organism. To that end the construct discrepancy is proposed. Finally, through the dialectic process, resolution of discrepancy occurs and subsequent change in the status of the individual evolves.

Dialectics provides a heuristic method for analysis of the organism–environment interaction. The rationale for this choice rests on its potential for (1) defining the relationship between distancing behaviors and the child's cognitive status, and (2) providing the typology by which the hierarchical nature of development can be examined.

STATEMENT OF THE PROBLEM

It must be kept in mind that these three constructs—distancing behaviors, discrepancy, and dialectics describe processes and conditions in which the primary actors are the child, significant others (parents, teachers, peers—any individual with whom the child interacts), and/or the physical environment. A developmental model must specify the effects of persons $\times$ events $\times$ time. In this discussion the persons–events interaction varies as a function of the changing maturity level of the participants. Our primary interest, of course, is to investigate the role of exogenous factors in the development of representational thinking. A related issue is how the child learns to comprehend representations of events, irrespective of the media of representation (pictures, verbalizations, gestures).

Basic Considerations

Cognitive growth must be conceptualized in biological and social contexts. From the biological perspective, we accept as given the intrinsic capability of the human organism to construct representations, to employ language, and to transform experiences into symbolic modes. Variations in performance of representational transformations are predicated on the assumption that social contexts play a dominant role in influencing the quality of representational thought, along with the capability of comprehending representational media (ikonic, verbal–symbolic, gestural, etc.).

Representations are adaptive modes eventuating in transformations and organization of experiences, resulting in mental representations that form guides for future behavior. The active organism engages the external environment and, through assimiliation and concurrent accommodation, constructs his reality.

The nature of the human organism further requires the establishment of a primary relationship with caretakers for survival. In this context, a communicative network begins which eventually is proliferated, engaging other social objects (peers, other adults) and exposing the child to varieties of communicative patterns. Although Piaget describes the development of sensorimotor intelligence in the first 2 years of life and the infant's outreach, the evolving competencies, such as understanding the permanence of objects, differentiation of the familiar from the unfamiliar, and nascent awareness of tracking to retain visual experience, he does not identify those social environmental features which influence the course and rate of such achievements (Piaget, 1952).

Our argument is that, although the biological nature of man ordains the capability and the processes for cognitive representations, the social (interpersonal and cultural) factors serve to activate, direct, and determine the quality and functions of representations.

THE DISTANCING HYPOTHESIS

Distancing behaviours can be characterized as to their form, function, and determinants. Each of these characteristics contributes to the development of representational competence, the capability to represent social, physical, and personal realities, and the concurrent development of an understanding of the media of representation (pictures, verbalizations, and gestures). Distancing behaviors are actually stimulus situations for the child in that they:

"create temporal and/or spatial and/or psychological distance between self and object. 'Distancing' is proposed as the concept to denote behaviors or events that separate the child cognitively from the immediate behavioral environment. The behaviors or events in question are those that require the child to attend to or react in terms of the nonpresent (future or past) or the nonpalpable." (Sigel, 1970, pp. 111–112)

Although distancing stimuli (behaviors of others and events) can emanate from social *and* physical events, the focus in this chapter will be on verbal or gestural distancing behaviors, in effect, communication from others to the child. The verbal/gestural distancing behaviors comprise one subset of the general class "distancing stimuli," and manipulation of the physical and/or social environment comprises another subset. The purpose of this presentation is to emphasize the direct, social communicative network as the social context. The hypothesis is as follows: There is a class of events which effect representational thinking comprised of distancing behaviors.

Forms of Distancing Behaviors

The distancing behaviors in this presentation are verbal and as verbal events contain characteristic features of verbal communication, for example, content (meaning) and a syntactical structure.

Each distancing behavior is defined in terms of the "mental demands" presented to the receiver of the message (see Table 1). For example, a distancing behavior is labeled *inferring cause–effect* because the message for the receiver is to engage in inferential thinking to determine causal relationships. Perusal of the table will show the range of messages which demand representational and inferential thinking.

TABLE 1.   Distancing Strategies[a]

To observe[b]	Asking the child to examine to observe, e.g., "Look at what I am doing."
To label	Naming a singular object or event, e.g., naming a place, person, alternate. No elaboration. "What color is the block?" "Where is Joel?"
To describe	Providing elaborated information of a single instance. Descriptions are static; provide no dynamic relationships among elements, no use and functional characteristics. "What did the car look like?"
To sequence	Temporal ordering of events, as in a story or carrying out a task. Steps articulated; *last, next, afterwards, start, begin* are possible key words. "First we will look at the pictures, then we will make up a story." Teacher telling, "Your turn is after Paul's." "Are you next?" (sometimes confused with structuring, as in "Paul, it's your turn.")
To reproduce	Reconstructing previous experiences, dynamic interaction of events, interdependence, functional. "How do you do that?"
To compare	Noting (describing or inferring) characteristics or properties.
(a) Describe similarities	Noting ostensive common characteristics (perceptual analysis). "Are those the same?"

(b) Describe differences	Noting ostensive differences among instances (perceptual analysis). "In what way are the truck and airplane different?"
(c) Infer similarities	Noting nonobservational commonalities (conceptual).
(d) Infer differences	Noting nonobservable differences (conceptual).
To propose alternatives	Offering different options, different ways of performing a task.
To combine	
(a) Symmetrical classifying	Recognizing the commonalities of a class of equivalent instances. "Why did you put those two together?"
(b) Asymmetrical classifying	Organizing instances in some sequential ordering—seeing the relationship as a continuum, seriation of any kind, comparative, where each instance is related to the previous one and the subsequent one, relative (big to small, more or less).
(1) Enumerating	Seriation: enumerating of number of things unalike; ordinal counting (1, 2, 3, 4, 5). "Count how many there are." "Is this tree bigger than that one?"
(c) Synthesizing	Reconstructing components into a unified whole; explicit pulling together; creating new form, sum of a number of discrete things.

---

[a] This is not an exhaustive list of strategies.

[b] Each strategy is a "demand" for the child to engage in particular operations which are inherent in the structure of the statement. The "demand" quality is implicit in the strategy. The form of the strategy may vary (see Table 2). The singular examples listed here are illustrative and not to be construed as exhaustive.

The form of the communicative strategy can be either declarative *or* interrogatory. In the declarative statement, the sender "tells" the receiver something, for example, "This is a pen (pointing to a pen)," or "The reason the rabbit went away is because the dog frightened him," a cause–effect statement.

Distancing strategies can also be interrogatories. A further distinction is made between questions which are for verification of messages already presented and questions which stimulate problem solving. The first type is the condition which could occur after a declarative statement has been made; for example, (a cause–effect statement), after reading a child a story the adult might say, "The reason the rabbit in the story ran away was that he was frightened." The child could then be asked, "Now why did the rabbit run away?" and the child could answer by reproducing part of the initial statement (e.g., "Because he was frightened").

On the other hand, question asking could take the form of an open-ended approach. Using the previous example, the adult might ask, "Why do you suppose the rabbit ran away?" The child reconstructs the encounter.

Another feature of a distancing strategy is the "temporal" aspect. The time form may be the contemporaneous present, the past, or the future. The time constraints reflect the *anticipatory schema* (future), *reconstructive schema* (past), or *contemporaneous constructions*. The various time constraints make different demands on the child. Anticipation requires organization of experience in the context of prediction or expectation, in contrast to the past, which requires an organization of previous experience with no projections into the future.

The temporal aspect of distancing is a crucial dimension since it is the coping with time that instigates representational thought. To reproduce or to reconstruct the past or to plan for the future requires mental representations.

Functions of Distancing Behaviors

Although distancing behaviors share the basic characteristic of a cognitive separation between the individual and the immediate present, they are presumed to vary in the degree and the way they activate this separation. The demand characteristics are contained in the message *and* the form. The function of the message is defined by the behavior as listed in Table 1; but the significance of the linguistic form is not to be overlooked, since structures of statements serve to affect mentations.

Declarative statements, which demand convergent responses, require passive listening, in contrast to inquiry, which demands active engagement; for example, "The dog's name is Gimcrack" versus "What is the dog's

TABLE 2.   Structural Characteristics of Distancing Behaviors

State-ment	Type	Declarative	Interrogatory			Imperative
			Direct	Indirect	Intonation	
Closed	convergent	The boy is upset because his dog ran away.	How did the boy feel when his dog ran away?	I wonder if the boy was sad when the dog ran away.	The dog ran away. The boy was sad.[a]	Tell me why the dog ran away.
Open	divergent[a]	There are other ways the boy could feel when his dog ray away.	What can you tell me about the boy and his dog?	The dog ran away. I wonder how the boy feels.	The dog ran away and you said he is sad about it; he might have some other feelings.[a]	Tell me about the boy and his dog.[b]

[a] The interrogatory is reflected in the intonation.
[b] The difference between declaratives and imperatives is intonation as well as syntactic structure

name?" or "Can you tell me anything about the dog?" A declarative distancing strategy does not require the child to employ the same mental operations as an inquiry. In the former, the child receives the message, may retain it, processes it, and may or may not have to demonstrate understanding of the message. The inquiry strategy makes specific requirements for the child to engage mentally to answer the question.

The demand characteristics of open-ended inquiry, in particular, function as *instigators, activators,* and *organizers* of mental operations. The only way the child can answer a question is to become *actively* engaged, producing those mental activities demanded by the inquiry.

Table 2 is a summary of the forms verbal distancing often takes when adults attempt to instigate thinking in children. The form, whether declarative, imperative, or one of the interrogatives, is effective to a greater or a lesser degree according to the open endedness, so that requests for convergent responses ("Tell me the name of the dog") are less demanding in their reliance on representational thinking than are more open-ended discussion initiators ("Tell me more about the story.").

Determinants of Distancing Behaviors

The kinds of distancing behaviors employed by adults and children are assumed to be due to at least three factors: (1) social–cultural characteristics, (2) idiosyncratic personal–social characteristics of participants, and (3) the setting in which the interaction occurs.

Social–Cultural Characteristics • The social–cultural factors define, in some measure, the type of interactions individuals have with each other. Conceivably in authoritative environments, children are told what and how to think about certain matters. This may vary with the conditions of the interaction. For example, social–cultural differences exist in how the child is encouraged to think and to represent authority, religion, and physical events. Whereas in some societies many givens are assumed and taken as valid, other societies have minimal restrictions of this sort (Cole & Scribner, 1974).

How ideas are represented also will vary along social–cultural lines. Some societies do not use graphic representations; others restrict their style and content. Perhaps more basic than these limitations are those that influence "how" and "what" thinking strategies are acceptable. Recent anthropological studies in cognitive development point to vast differences among cultures in the thought strategies used by adults and children which bear on developing representational competences (Cole & Scribner, 1974). Societies define many of the early child-rearing practices from feeding to handling. Among such contexts, different types of distancing behaviors are found.

Belief systems regarding infant capabilities also vary across cultures. Views of infants ranging from helpless "creatures" to active, outreaching organisms exist and influence the way in which adults interact with children and affect subsequent patterns of cognitive abilities in the child. Encouragement of passive acceptance of traditional ways should have different consequences for the child's approach to knowledge than encouragement of active engagement in problem-solving strategies. Societal patterns employing control and delay of actions in the service of planning would be presumed to have a different effect from an accepted pattern in which planning or control for children is not emphasized. Our own within-culture attitudes toward sex differences illustrate how societal expectations influence the patterns of cognitive competence (Maccoby & Jacklin, 1974). Social–cultural patterns of child-rearing therefore should have a marked effect on the pattern of distancing behaviors employed by significant others.

Idiosyncratic Personal–Social Characteristics of Participants • In spite of social–cultural patterns, individuals will vary in how they carry out social patterns; of course, individualization will vary in accord with the degree to which societies are relatively homogeneous or heterogeneous. In pluralistic societies such as ours, considerable variability exists in the belief systems adults have regarding chidren's competencies. There is some evidence to suggest that variations exist within and between social class groups in beliefs regarding children's comprehension and reasoning abilities (Sigel, Secrist, & Forman, 1973; Johnson & Sigel, 1975). There is reason to believe, then, that distancing behaviors will vary among parents as a result of their particular belief systems, which in turn may be related to educational and social status.

In addition to belief systems, two other factors should be identified: the role of the adults and the maturity level of the children. Parents and/or teachers may well define the type of distancing strategies. Teachers, for example, have children's learning as their responsibility. The teachers, furthermore, are usually highly sensitized to children's maturity levels and probably employ strategies that will take these into account. Their choice of strategies may well reflect their teaching philosophies. Thus the use of inquiry may vary as well as the type of questions posed.

Parents who perceive themselves in roles like teachers may use similar strategies. However, parents who define their relationships with their children differently may not engage in distancing strategies. In either case, the context of the home as different from the school probably leads to very different types of interactive situations.

The maturity level of the child is another critical feature which influences the types of distancing strategies to which the child is exposed. Adults vary their strategies, depending on their perceptions of the child's maturity level. Theoretically, children as young as 3 months, when receptive language is available, are targets of various distancing behavior (Lewis & Freedle, 1973). How sensitive the adult is to the child's ability to comprehend the particular behavior in question will be gauged by the adult's awareness of the child's response.

The social class status of the participants should be included under this rubric, since data show that the social class of the participants distinguishes patterns for distancing strategies. Working-class parents tend to focus on the contemporaneous present, for example, and employ directive statements, in contrast to middle-class parents, who are likely to use both anticipatory and reconstructive statements (Bernstein, 1961, 1962; Hess & Shipman, 1965; Sigel, 1960).

Situational Factors • The setting in which interactions occur is another source of influence. For example, observations of preschool teachers showed that they did more "structuring," telling in order to communicate the rules, during a game (e.g., "Go fish") than after reading a story, when the teachers employed open-ended questions.

The situations in the classroom have counterparts at home. The argument is that the social context in which an interaction occurs limits the degrees of freedom an adult will have in selecting particular distancing strategies. Situations may be planned (e.g., routines in schools and homes), and situations can arise fortuitously. In spite of the possibility of either, there is reason to believe that the variation in types of situations that will arise which will call for particular distancing strategies are determined in part by the individuals involved.

In sum, distancing strategies contain structural and functional properties which are hypothesized as having different effects on the development of representational thinking. Other factors were characterized as determinants. Three classes of characteristics were enumerated: Social–cultural, idosyncratic–personal–social, and situational.

Distancing strategies in open-ended forms function as activators of mental operations because they have the potential for creating a discrepancy between the child and the message of the distancing agent (the individual employing a distancing strategy). In every inquiry, there is minimally an implicit discrepancy between the quiescent state of the child and the activity demanded by the distancing strategy. A child listens to a story and is asked to anticipate an outcome or to represent a set of actions. This may be the minimal discrepancy between the child's state and the demand; but in the course of inquiry, discrepancies can be deliberately created.

DISCREPANCY MODEL AND ITS RELATIONSHIP TO DEVELOPMENT

Discrepancy, as we have indicated, is created by distancing strategies, particularly in the open-ended form. Discrepancy arises when there is a mismatch or a conflict between states. Three types of discrepancies can be identified: (1) *a mismatch between an internal event and an external event* (e.g., an infant reaches for a ball, and the ball moves every time he attempts to grasp it); (2) *a mismatch between two internal events*—an expectancy and an action are in conflict; and (3) *a mismatch between two external events* (e.g., a child is given a round, flat circle to roll and he rolls it; he is given a flat square and asked to roll it—it does not roll).

A mismatch, then, is a condition in which the organism comes into contact with particular environmental or exogenous events (objects, people) and in the course of this engagement experiences a discrepancy which can be resolved only by the organism's altering its approach.

Discrepancies propel the organism to change because of the inherent nature of the organism's inability to tolerate discrepancies. One of the biological givens is that living organisms require closure, order, and certainty; discrepancy results in disequilibrium which in turn incites the organism to action to resolve the uncertainty.

That the individual strives toward the resolution of discrepancies does not guarantee that such resolution is always forthcoming. There are discrepant events and experiences that are not resolvable.

It is not until middle to later childhood that the child learns to accept certain discrepancies as irresolvable. The infant and the preoperational child, we contend, have not developed the cognitive mechanisms to cope with these discrepancies. The tolerance of the discrepancy, short- or long-term, depends on the maturity level of the participants to accept and to understand the inevitability of such discrepancies. Thus, in our model, we have to encompass the striving for discrepancy resolution while simultaneously being and becoming aware of the inevitability of discrepancies.

The model should be construed, not as a tension reduction model, but rather as an action model in which certainty or a reduction of ambiguity is a key construct. That tension is reduced as a concomitant may be true, but our contention is that what propels the organism to action is the reduction of ambiguity and uncertainty, through self-regulatory mechanisms, properties integral to the biological nature of the individual (Dewey, 1929; Piaget, 1971).

Change occurs when a state of mismatch between the organism and the environment and the organism strives to resolve the mismatch (discrepancy).

The outcome of this change process is a new organization of behaviors. Therefore we may say that transformations occur as a function of discrepancies between the state of the organism and the environmental demands (or experiences).

Development is construed as a transformation process continuous and coherent with change, not only in quantity, but also in quality. The change that occurs is observable on three levels: first, there is a change in appearance (size, shape, volume); second, there is a change in competence, that is, the ability of the organism to behave differently (e.g., cognitively in terms of reasoning, motorically in terms of coordination of body parts); and third, there is a change in organization (differentiation–integration) of the various components into increasingly differentiated, yet coherent systems, as knowledge increases.

The developmental changes that occur in the cognitive domain, relative to representational thinking in competence and in organization, are products of encounters between the state of the organism and environmental demands (distancing behaviors). From a Piagetian perspective, encounters with the environment entail assimilation of new experiences and accompanying accommodations of cognitive organization. Since "no assimilation (occurs) without accommodation (whether previous or current), so in the same way there is no accommodation without assimilation, this is as much as to say that environment does not merely cause a series of prints or copies to be made which register themselves on the subject, but it also sets in motion active adjustments" (Piaget, 1971, p. 8n). Our argument is that the "active adjustments" are transformations of experiences and result in new representations.

Modes of Representation and the Role of Representation in Discrepancy Resolution

Mental resolutions of discrepancies, irrespective of type, require the use of representational thought and involve at least three strategies: assessment of alternatives (contemporaneous present), anticipation of the future, or reconstruction of the past. Each of these strategies requires the individual to create mental representations, since the total event is not in the physical, observable present. Problems ranging from Piagetian conservation tasks, where the child is to predict the height of water poured from a wide-mouthed beaker into a tall, narrow cylinder, to the planning of a birthday party by parent and child are examples in which the child has to anticipate an outcome—a cognitive activity involving representation (Piaget, 1951).

Modes of representation have been labeled by Bruner as motoric, ikonic, and verbal-symbolic (Bruner, 1966). Motoric representation corresponds to sensorimotor intelligence of Piaget, thereby being the initial mode. This is followed by the ikonic or utilization of imagery, which is characteristic of the preoperational period; the verbal-symbolic emerges with the advent of language. Very early in the life of the child, any one of these three is available. Even the verbal-symbolic is a representational modality available as soon as the child indicates some understanding of receptive language and shows recognitory memory. Thus we could argue that these three modalities are available to the child but are employed qualitatively and quantitatively differently. The course of their development is subject to particular types of experience—experiences which influence the relative emphasis individuals place on a particular modality, in spite of what we have already stated as the generic capability of human beings to employ these representational modes. It is our general thesis that these three modalities provide the vehicles by which thoughts are internally represented.

The media through which these modes can be represented symbolically can vary in dimensionality: unidimensional (e.g., time), two-dimensional (e.g., pictures), and three-dimensional (e.g., sculptures). There is no necessary correspondence between the child's use of the three representational modes and his competence to deal with representational media. In other words, children employing imagery may reconstruct previous experiences accurately but not be able to represent the image graphically, or to classify photographs of familiar objects equivalent to their three-dimensional counterparts (Sigel & McBane, 1967; Sigel & Olmsted, 1970). This type of discrepancy was found with very young children (under 4 years), among underprivileged children. *Representational competence* is the term applied to the capability of individuals to comprehend the equivalence of the various modes, even though one might show a preference to employ one mode over another.

The significance of this issue for our model resides in its implication for the development of representational thought. The development of motoric, ikonic, and verbal-symbolic modes of representation seem indigenous to the human condition, *but* the use of them in the service of understanding external representations emerges from personal experiences.

This discrepancy model can be systematized within a dialectic paradigm since the events in which the child is engaged can be encompassed within the laws of dialectics.

DISCREPANCY MODEL CONCEPTUALIZED IN A DIALECTIC PARADIGM

The discrepancies which we discussed in the introduction of this chapter can be conceptualized with a system of dialectics, whose laws cover most of the conditions relevant to thinking and logical reasoning. The three laws of dialectics that are relevant to us are as follow: Law I: unity and the struggle of opposites; Law II: transformation of quantitative into qualitative change; and Law III: the negation of the negation (Wozniak, 1975).

The law of unity and opposites holds that forces or categories which are mutually exclusive at the same time presuppose one another. There cannot be big without being small; there cannot be dark without there being light. In the Piagetian system there cannot be assimilation without there being accommodation.

The second law can best be stated in Wozniak's (1975) terms:

"With quality (that which makes up what an object is) quantity forms a unity, a representation of two aspects of the same object. The second law of dialectics addresses itself to the nature of this unity. When quantity is altered within certain limits, no transformation in the object is wrought; however, if quantitative change is sufficient magnitude, then such a change can pass into a change in quality; that is, the object may be effectively changed into another, into a new object. It acquires new characteristics and becomes subject to new laws to which it formerly did not conform. Such qualitative changes do not come about gradually but occur suddenly with a definite leap.'" (p. 33)

Transition from one stage of development to another is the cardinal type of illustration drawn from the Piagetian model.

The third law, the negation of the negation, is one in which the old is replaced by the new, and the new new subsequently is replaced by still another new. This type of conceptualization is most appropriate for development which is a spiral of continuing new forms replacing old ones. This is the principle most readily applicable to the construction that development never ceases. All forms have within themselves the seeds of their own destruction; they will be assimilated in the new, and the new will be the old. In a sense, this is the traditional notion of thesis, antithesis, synthesis, where the synthesis becomes the integration of the old and the new, with the new (synthesis) becoming the *new* thesis, setting the stage for the cycle, thesis–antithesis–synthesis—a life-long process. However, here is where the Piagetian conception of cognitive growth and the conception that the developmental transformations of cognitive structures are an ongoing system without end part ways. Piaget holds that the epitome of cognitive development is the period of formal operations, whereas for others there is a dialectic stage that characterizes the developmental period after formal operations (Riegel, 1973). Since our concern in this chapter is for the very young, we shall forego a discussion of this issue. However, it should be pointed out that in our model discrepancies of the type described are by no means restricted to the young child—they occur throughout life.

The Dialectic and the Concept of Development

The dialectical paradigm provides a model for conceptualizing development since its laws describe the transformational processes of development. Furthermore, dialectics seems descriptive of the natural world of object–person interactions. The initial contacts the child has with the environment of objects are active and dialectic by nature; utilization of the formal rules of dialectics provides a heuristic analytic tool by which to formulate developmental processes. The child engages in a dialectical process to evolve a system of constructs by which the social, personal, and physical realities are organized. He is engaged in a dialectical relationship between himself and the world, and he has to resolve contradictions of behavior of objects and of individuals. Thus the child has to engage objects and people in building his constructs. The outcome of this dialectic enagagement is the *personal* construct which serves as a guide—a mapping of the child's conception of reality. Constructs may be static or fixed, subject to change through engagements with objects, events, and persons. As the child engages the environment, he encounters discrepancies between the expected and the observed. Dialectics is the process interact–conflict–resolution-equilibration, which results in a temporary resolution until the next discrepancy occurs.

The Course of Development Change

The outcome of the dialectical interaction is a new representational construct or elaborated representation, different from the preceding, while conserving the previous experience. The result is a new structure which signifies a new developmental stage, and may be characterized by the five criteria proposed by Piaget for stages: *hierarchization, integration, consolidation, structuring,* and *equilibration* (Pinard & Laurendeau, 1969).

Hierarchization means simply that developmental change proceeds in a fixed order of successive levels, but "the invariance of this order, a requisite for every stage sequence, says nothing about chronological ages of accession and does not therefore exclude the possibility that the particulars of the physical, social, or cultural milieu might accelerate or retard the succession or even prevent a particular stage from appearing" (Pinard & Laurendeau, 1969, p. 125). The formulation is that:

"The décalages or developmental lags between very different cultural milieus will depend upon the nature of the tasks examined: these décalages would be maximum for tasks of a non-operational nature . . . a bit less for tasks of an operational nature but that call upon symbolic structures (number or language), even less in cases where perceptual configurations are in opposition to operational structuring (e.g., conservations) and least of all where the perceptual configurations and operational activities naturally support each other (e.g., seriations)." (Pinard & Laurendeau, 1969, p. 125)

Integration is a second characteristic attributed by Piaget to the notion of stage which is consistent with our discrepancy–dialectic model. The principle of integration asserts that acquisition of a given stage should integrate acquisitions of the preceding stage. This assertion has to be qualified to say that what is integrated is a transformation fo previous functions. After all, no one would hold that a lack of awareness of number correspondence is integrated into a subsequent understanding of number correspondence. The transformation is evident in the phenomenon of *vertical décalage*.

"The development of a given conceptual content (e.g., causality, space) is accomplished on several successive levels (sensorimotor, concrete-operational and formal operational) according to an analogical process in which this content already structured at a level established by earlier kinds of actions or operations is restructured at a higher level by a new kind of operation. These *vertical décalages* would be expressed . . . by a progressive differentiation of the various domains of application of the operations in the process of establishing themselves." (Pinard & Laurendeau, 1969, p. 127)

The vertical décalage is not additive, but rather transformed and enriched. The transformation is an outgrowth of a dialectical interaction, the new synthesis fulfilling the Piagetian concept of stage integration, since a synthesis is essentially an integration of the thesis/antithesis.

The third characteristic relevant for our model is *consolidation* which "must always involve at once an aspect of achievement of the recently acquired behavior and an aspect of preparation for the behavior of the following level" (Pinard & Laurendeau, 1969, p. 129). The period of consolidation is a period of synthesis, where the "recently acquired behavior" implies a plateau, however temporary, which serves as a stepping stone for subsequent behaviors.[1]

The fourth characteristic is structuring: acquisition of a given logical problem at a given stage suggests mastery of all problems that require a particular operation. This principle lies at the heart of the Piagetian theory of stages and is one which poses considerable difficulty for our model. Empirical evidence exists but is inconclusive regarding the assertion of stage

---

[1] The concept of a plateau is viewed as contradictory to a dialectical process, since it is argued that "stable plateaus of balance are the exception . . . as soon as a developmental task is completed and synchrony attained, new questions, doubts and contradictions arise within the individual and within society" (Riegel, 1975, pp. 51–52.) The series of theoretical and practical problems this assertion raises lies beyond the scope of our discussion.

synchrony. Development within stages is asynchronous with different operations appearing at different times (Inhelder & Piaget, 1964). The concept of horizontal decalage is used to cope with the apparent asynchrony. Most research testing Piaget's structuring hypothesis has ignored the significance of experience, along with particular task requirements. Thus, before the structuring hypothesis is rejected, it may be necessary to redefine asynchronous cognitive performance in terms of task and experiential factors. Asynchrony needs to be examined in terms of the dialectics.

Equilibration, the fifth attribute of stages, is, in a sense, redundant since it plays a role in cognitive organization similar to consolidative processes. Equilibration implies a balanced synchrony, which further suggests a developmental plateau. Since development is an ongoing dialectical process, the plateau is more of an hypothetical construct than an empirical reality. The individual is in a constant dynamic state, but does achieve stability, however temporary. Stability, as well as change, characterizes human growth and development. Without the former, we would have no consistency, no tradition—including scientific and developmental. In essence, stability and change coexist and are interdependent.

Thus the individual is never "staying" synchronously at a given level but proceeds from one level to another. Transitions between developmental levels have to be explained. This logical requirement brings us full circle to the argument that transitions are instigated by the interface between experiential discrepancies and the individual's intolerance of such a state of affairs.

If distancing behaviors vary in potential impact, it is conceivable that particular types will influence the course of development of certain mental operations. Is it not conceivable that the child whose encounters with significant adults focus on the here and now, with little encouragement to anticipate or plan, in contrast to the caregivers who make demands on the child from inferential reasoning, will evolve different thought strategies and representational competencies?

Differential patterns of distancing behaviors may account for horizontal décalage since they may provide the experiential differences that result in intraindividual variations in ontogenesis. Extrapolation from crosscultural studies which have demonstrated different rates of growth of conservation, for example, lend credence to our conjecture (Dasen, 1972). After all, one way parents vary across and within cultures is the way they interact with their children in terms of teaching strategies (Hess & Shipman, 1965). In sum, then, we propose that both discrepancies and subsequent dialectics may be instigated by distancing behaviors, which in turn influence the rate and the quality of representational thought.

DISCREPANCY MODEL AND ITS APPLICATION TO EARLY CHILDHOOD PRESCHOOL EDUCATION

In this chapter we have presented a description of a model of dialectic communication. The model emphasizes the interaction between the individual and exogenous factors which influence both the creation of cognitive conflicts through the presentation of discrepant information and the derivation of strategies for conflict resolution. Distancing behaviors on the part of adults were described as promoting cognitive growth in children because they instigate representational thought through the mismatches (conflicts) they highlight for the child. The strategies also provide organizational approaches toward conflict resolution by the child himself. The following is an example of the differences which eventuate between two nursery school groups when one is systematically exposed to conflict and conflict resolution through teachers' deployment of distancing behaviors, and the other group has no such program. The differences which we shall discuss were general across the data that we gathered on these children; we shall discuss only the domain of continuous liquid quantity conservation to illustrate the model.

CONSERVATION OF CONTINUOUS QUANTITY

We adopted the conservation of liquid task of Piaget, in part, to assess mental images and operations in preoperational children. Although we were interested in the conservation responses and justifications, our principal concern was for the anticipatory or prediction skills when children try to imagine physical transformations, and the ways in which they deal with discrepancies in the perceptual information. This task assesses the interaction between figurative and operational processes. In the task, the child is presented with the standard conservation of liquids problems and is asked (1) to anticipate the image of the liquid to be poured from one vessel into another; and (2) to observe the demonstration of pouring and then explain it. We employed two 250-ml beakers and a 50-ml cylinder as our vessels, and a glass carafe of the juice-of-the-day from the child's nursery school. Fifty milliliters of juice were poured into the standard, and the child himself established when the experimenter had put 50 ml to the standard mark into the second beaker. The cylinder had a space of about 5 ml between the 50-ml mark and the rim, and in our analyses we did not treat a prediction at the top of the cylinder differently from one at the top of the 50-ml mark.

If the child engaged in perceptually rigid thinking in predicting the level of the liquid in a new vessel which was both taller and smaller in diameter than the standard, the prediction would be a projection of the mental image of the standard onto the new vessel. This error is generally discussed as a "perceptually based error," which is to say that the mental image is superimposed in template fashion onto the new task. In contrast, we would consider a proportional transformation to be reflected in a response in which a 20%-full level in one vessel is predicted at a 20% level in any test vessel. In this prediction the child projects an image of higher liquid level but fails to employ a principle of compensation to account for both height and diameter differences between the two vessels. Craig, Love, and Olim (1973) discuss this as a "proportionality response." A correct prediction, of course, would be a 50-ml response or, in our study, a 50+.

The distancing program subjects, at Time 1, used the perceptual homologue at chance level, while 53% employed the proportion analogue and the remaining 35% gave a correct prediction. While 43% of the control group made a correct prediction at Time 1, the remaining control group children distributed their responses between proportion (analogic—21%) and perceptual (homologic—36%) predictions. A summary of percentages is presented in Table 3.

TABLE 3.   Conservation Predictions for Two Nursery School Groups. All values in percentages

		Response Type		
Group	Time	Perceptual	Proportional	Correct
Distancing	1	12	53	35
	2	0	22	78
Control	1	36	21	43
	2	14	36	50

At Time 2, 78% of the distancing group children were making correct predictions, whereas only one additional subject from the control group (50%) moved in the direction of imaging the correct liquid level. Thus, although groups did not differ significantly from one another at Time 1 ($p<.26$), the distancing group changed in the direction of correct anticipations over the two time periods ($p<.01$) and differed from the control group at Time 2 ($p<.02$), while the control group children themselves showed no significant changes over the two testings ($p<.57$). We might conclude that the discrepancy gap begins to close in a context where distancing behaviors are used systematically by instructing adults.

References

Bernstein, B. Social class and linguistic development: A theory of social learning. In A. H. Halsey, J. Floud & C. A. Anderson (Eds.), *Education, economy, and society.* New York: The Free Press, 1961.

Bernstein, B. Social class, linguistic codes and grammatical elements. *Language and Speech,* 1962, **5,** 221–240.

Bruner, J. S. *Studies in cognitive growth.* New York: Wiley, 1966.

Cole, M., & Scribner, S. *Culture and thought: A psychological introduction.* New York: Wiley, 1974.

Craig, G., Love, J. A., & Olim, E. G. Perceptual judgments in Piaget's conservation of liquid problem. *Child Development,* 1973, **44,** 372–375.

Dasen, P. R. Cross cultural Piagetian research: A summary. *Journal of Cross-Cultural Psychology,* 1972, **3,** 23–40.

Dewey, J. *The quest for certainty: A study of the relation of knowledge and action.* New York: Minton, Balch, 1929.

Hess, R. D., & Shipman, V. C. Early experience and the socialization of cognitive modes in children. *Child Development,* 1965, **36,** 869–886.

Inhelder, B., & Piaget, J. *The early growth of logic in the child.* New York: Harper & Row, 1964.

Johnson, J., & Sigel, I. E. *The relation between control and teaching in parental approaches to socialization: A new perspective.* Unpublished manuscript, 1975. (Available from Educational Testing Service, Princeton, N.J. 08540.)

Lewis, M., & Freedle, R. Mother–infant dyad: The cradle of meaning. In P. Pliner, L. Krames, & T. Alloway (Eds.), *Communication and affect: Language and thought.* New York: Academic Press, 1973.

Maccoby, E. E., & Jacklin, C. N. *The psychology of sex differences.* Stanford, Calif.: Stanford University Press, 1974.

Piaget, J. *Play, dreams, and imitation in childhood.* New York: Norton, 1951.

Piaget, J. *The origins of intelligence in children.* New York: International Universities Press, 1952.

Piaget, J. *Biology and knowledge.* Chicago: University of Chicago Press, 1971.

Pinard, A., & Laurendeau, M. "Stage" in Piaget's cognitive developmental theory: Exegesis of a concept. In D. Elkland & J. H. Flavell (Eds.), *Studies in cognitive development.* New York: Oxford University Press, 1969.

Riegel, K. Dialectic operations: The final period of cognitive development. *Human Development,* 1973, **16,** 346–370.

Riegel, K. Toward a dialectical theory of development. *Human Development,* 1975, **18,** 50–64.

Sigel, I. E. Influence techniques: A concept used to study parental behaviors. *Child Development,* 1960, **31,** 799–806.

Sigel, I. E. The distancing hypothesis: A causal hypothesis for the acquisition of representational thought. In M. R. Jones (Ed.), *Miami Symposium on the Prediction of Behavior, 1968: Effect of early experiences.* Coral Gables, Fla.: University of Miami Press, 1970.

Sigel, I. E., & McBane, B. Cognitive competence and level of symbolization among five-year-old children. In J. Hellmuth (Ed.), *The disadvantaged child.* Vol. I. Seattle, Wash.: Special Child Publications of the Seattle Sequin School, 1967.

Sigel, I. E., & Olmsted, P. Modification of cognitive skills among lower class Black children. In J. Hellmuth (Ed.), *The disadvantaged child.* Vol. 3: *Compensatory education: A national debate.* New York: Brunner/ Mazel, 1970.

Sigel, I. E., Secrist, A., & Forman, G. Psycho-educational intervention beginning at age two: Reflections and outcomes. In J. C. Stanley (Ed.), *Compensatory education for children, ages two to eight: Recent studies of educational intervention.* Baltimore, Md.: Johns Hopkins University Press, 1973.

Wozniak, R. H. Dialecticism and structuralism in Soviet philosophy and psychology. In K. F. Riegel & G. C. Rosewald (Eds.), *Structure and transformation: Developmental and historical aspects.* New York: Wiley, 1975.

CHAPTER 10

Social Behavior
and Language Acquisition[1]

MICHAEL LEWIS

and

LOUISE CHERRY

Educational Testing Service

The self has a character which is different from that of the physiological organism proper. The self is something which has development; it is not initially there, at birth, but arises in the process of social experience and activity, that is, develops in the given individual as a result of his relation to that process as a whole and to other individuals within that process.

G. H. Mead, *Mind, Self, and Society*, 1934

The development of language, social, and cognitive knowledge can be viewed in many different ways. These three domains of knowledge may exist independently of one another, and each may develop independently. Or these domains may be interrelated in unidimensional ways; for example, one may be derived from another in the course of development. Or all three domains of knowledge may be interrelated and interdependent, since all are ultimately aspects of the same unitary development of the individual, Mead's "self." Each model is generated from a different epistomology and serves different functions in the investigation of language knowledge. We would like to consider each of these positions separately, including an explication of the defining characteristics, the purposes and goals, and the research questions, as well as the implications of each of these positions.

[1] This research was supported by U.S. Public Health Service Postdoctoral Fellowship MH–08260 and National Institute of Child Health and Human Development Contract NO1–HD–42803. We would like to thank Jeannette Haviland for her helpful comments on this paper and Jane Leifer for helping with the data analysis.

227

THREE MODELS OF LANGUAGE KNOWLEDGE

Reductionist Model

The first model (Figure 1), which will be referred to as the Reductionist Model, is defined by the assumption that language, social, and cognitive knowledge exist independently of one another. Thus knowledge of language behavior, for example, is internal to the structure of language. Language is an innate capacity which is programmed genetically and unfolds during the course of development. The purpose of scientific inquiry is to explain satisfactorily observable language behavior, and one proceeds to do this by making a structural analysis of language per se. Social or cognitive behaviors are regarded as "noise" and are therefore excluded from consideration in the analysis. Specifically, those who operate within the Reductionist Model endeavor to explain both the developmental timing and the logical relationships of language behavior by formulating a model limited to linguistic constituents. Questions such as what is the sequence in which certain language behaviors develop, and what is the derivational complexity of speech at a particular time in development, can be asked using this model.

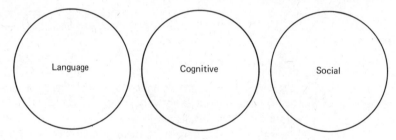

FIGURE 1. The Reductionist Model.

An example of a theory that falls within the Reductionist Model is the "language acquisition device" or LAD theory introduced by Chomsky (1957) and then elaborated by McNeill (1970). The LAD is likened to the innate human capacity which enables the child to construct a model of language, including rules for pronunciation and forming sentences, from the corpus of utterances that the child hears.

There are several implications of this model of scientific inquiry into language development. First of all, what is deemed to be social and/or cognitive behavior is either deemphasized or ignored. Thus the model limits the phenomena to be explained. Second, linguistic theory, per se, is strengthened, since the explanation for all language behavior can be found within a theory of language alone, and one does not have to consider other theories from sociology or psychology. A third implication of the Reductionist Model is that causality follows directly from one language behavior to another, and everything else is regarded as "noise." The fourth implication of this model is that, since disciplinary lines are strictly maintained, there is little communication among students of psychology, linguistics, and sociology. Thus the opportunities for the creation of programs designed to meet the broad and varied need of practitioners in education, health, and other fields are limited.

Interactionist Model

The second model (Figure 2), which will be referred to as the Interactionist Model, is defined by the assumption that language, social, and cognitive

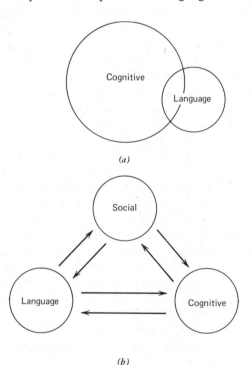

FIGURE 2. The Interactionist Model.

knowledge are interrelated in unidirectional ways. For example, language knowledge is derived from cognitive knowledge, or language and cognition develop separately but influence each other (Figures 2a and 2b, respectively). In this model, knowledge of language behavior is both internal and external to the structure of language. Language development interacts with social and cognitive development. For example, it is possible in one version of this model—in which language derives from cognition (Figure 2a)—to predict language behavior within the limits of cognitive behavior. Language, social, and cognitive knowledge are still discrete domains even though each affects the other. The purpose of scientific inquiry is, first of all, to define the relationship of the interaction of language, cognition, and social behavior, including the dynamics of this interaction. In addition, it is necessary to explain the parts of language, social, and cognitive behaviors which overlap. Finally, it is necessary to formulate a model of their interaction. Questions such as what is the sequence of development of language and cognitive behaviors, and what are the cognitive precursors or prerequisites of certain language behaviors, can be asked using this model.

Bever's (1970) position that language derives from cognitive development is an example of the Interactionalist Model. The child's learning of linguistic structure is possible only after he acquires many perceptual mechanisms. This position is illustrated by Figure 2a. The general proposition is that language knowledge is seen as deriving from the more central and primary cognitive knowledge. Vygotsky's (1965) position is different but also falls within the Interactionist Model. He claims that, although language and cognition each develops along its own course, each influences the other. Thus Vygotsky's position is illustrated by Figure 2b, where the three domains of knowledge are separate and can interrelate in simple ways.

There are four major implications of the Interactionist Model, which apply to both versions. The first is that the scientist ignores those parts of language, social, and cognitive behaviors where interaction does not take place. This model, like the Reductionist Model, limits the phenomena to be explained satisfactorily. Second, the Interactionist Model emphasizes the discrete nature of language, cognitive, and social knowledge. Third, this model implies direct causal relationships between discrete language, cognitive, and social knowledge. Thus language is seen as being the direct cause of cognition. Likewise, the language that the individual knows limits to a degree the conceptual organization that characterizes him at any given point (Whorphian position). Finally, both forms of this model encourage communication among disciplines, such as the opportunities for the creation of broad education programs.

Unified Model

The third model (Figure 3), which will be referred to as the Unified Model, is defined by the assumption that language, social, and cognitive knowledge are interrelated and interdependent since all are aspects of the same unified development of the individual. Individuals develop social, language, and cognitive knowledge in interaction with each other. Language, cognitive, and social knowledge are thus not discrete domains, but each is an aspect of the interaction of individuals.

One version of this model (*a*) defines the interrelationship of language, social, and cognitive knowledge as a dynamic flow in a state of constant change which exists within and without the individual. In a second version of this model (*b*) the relationship of language, social, and cognitive knowledge exists as the interaction of the three domains. Within this unified framework important developmental–linguistic phenomena can be observed.

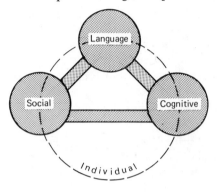

(*a*)

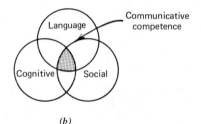

(*b*)

FIGURE 3. The Unified Model.

Development is conceptualized as a gradual differentiation among the various domains. The change from a unified, highly integrated system of knowledge to one which is differentiated and specialized occurs as a function of age. The knowledge system is like a tree, the trunk representing the unified and integrated system of knowledge, while the branches represent the separate areas of knowledge, some of which are interrelated whereas others are independent. This model allows for both the integration of knowledge from a developmental perspective and the functional independence of the end product.

The model also allows for a consideration of behaviors or skills which remain consistent over time, while undergoing transformations. For example, at first children understand the meaning of a linguistic act by its contextual meaning. Consider the situation of a mother requesting her 1-year-old child to eat an apple. For many months the high chair, in which the infant is sitting, has been associated with eating food, as has much of the adult's behavior toward the infant. At this point, it is easier for the infant to understand the command "Eat an apple" with the apple before him in the context of the kitchen than if this utterance were produced in some other context, such as the playroom, which is not commonly associated with eating. At some later point in development, linguistic acts independent of context are understood. Both Lewis and Freedle (1973) and Ervin-Tripp (in press) have made the point that comprehension of language is facilitated by the social context in which language is used. In addition, early language production, specifically utterances usually associated with the "here and now," demonstrates the importance of the interrelationship of the child's social–cognitive behavior with his linguistic competence. Only after this period of development can the child understand or produce language without its being embedded in a social context. Even adult understanding of language is often possible within the context of other social behaviors. Situational appropriateness, then, is part of the way in which language is both understood and learned. The derivation of language knowledge can be understood within a unified view of the individual's multiple knowledges.

The purpose of inquiry in the Unified Model is to investigate the language, social, and cognitive aspects of the individual's interaction so that observable human behavior can be explained satisfactorily. Thus the investigation is primarily oriented to uncovering the common basis for behavior that makes possible what some observers see as separate language, social, and cognitive behaviors. But these separate behaviors can be understood only as aspects of individual development. The scientist achieves these goals by formulating a model of individual development which includes language, social, and cognitive aspects, but sees them as a result of the interaction of individuals. Questions about the interrelationships among language, social, and cognitive development can be asked using this model. One can inquire, for example, what behaviors co-occur at a particular developmental period and whether the developmental sequences are related in specific ways.

An example of a theory that falls within the Unified Model is that of Lewis and Freedle (1973). They argue that there exists from birth a communication network between the infant and the mother and that the analogue of language is developed of and from aspects of this social–cognitive system. Their position is illustrated in Figure 3a, where the unitary knowledge primarily, and language in particular, develop from this function. Some theorists have referred to a "communicative competence" (Hymes, 1972) or "interactional competence" (Cicourel, 1974), which underlies our language, social, and cognitive behaviors in face-to-face interaction situations. Hymes (1972) has hypothesized that "communicative competence" is dependent on language knowledge as well as cognitive and social knowledge, which exist presumably as separate aspects. Hymes' position is illustrated in Figure 3b, where language, social, and cognitive knowledge exist, and the interaction of the three is "communicative competence."

The implications of the Unified Model include, in the first place, the understanding of language, social, and cognitive knowledge as aspects of individual development. Thus, unlike a Reductionist and an Interactionist Model, a Unified Model does not limit the phenomena to be explained to behavior that the scientist categorizes as language behavior or language–cognitive behavior. A second implication of the Unified Model is that, since this model emphasizes the wholistic nature of human behavior, one can but need not focus on the linguistic, social, or cognitive aspect. Third, this model implies that causal chains go from linguistic, social, or cognitive behavior back through an individual before resurfacing as new linguistic, social, or cognitive behavior, since these behaviors originate within the individual and not within any separate domain of knowledge. Finally, this model presupposes an interdisciplinary perspective including psychology, linguistics, sociology, and anthropology. The model thus necessitates intercommunication between disciplines, maximizing the flow of information. Of all the models, the Unified Model provides the broadest and most integrated basis for the creation of research applications. Since this model is concerned by definition with the unified development of the individual, the research that is generated by this model is relevant to the individual's development *in toto*. The opportunities for formulating programs to affect human development are limited only by the extent of the research generated.

In conclusion, our considerations of these three models of language development study bring to mind the well-known Indian fable of the blind men and the elephant. Several blind men, it will be recalled, wanted to know what an elephant is and each decided to investigate the phenomenon himself. Each of the men happened to touch a different part of the elephant, and thus each had a different perception and conception of the animal. Each thought he knew the true nature of the elephant; and although each was in part correct, all were wrong, because the elephant is more than these separate aspects. We can similarly consider the unified concept of individual development, of which there are linguistic, cognitive, and social aspects. None of these exists by itself, nor does each or all entirely explain individual development.

THE SOCIAL CONTEXT OF LANGUAGE ACQUISITION

Having argued for a unified view in the derivation and use of language, we must now determine how language behavior is to be studied. One approach is to investigate the origins of language by studying the child's sensorimotor competencies and relating these sensorimotor rules to language development. It is necessary to look at the young child's transactions with objects; the grammar of those transactions is believed to be the structure of subsequent linguistic behavior.

Although we also hold to the Unified Model, we have chosen the social world, as opposed to the sensorimotor world, of the young child as context. Our position that man is by nature a social animal and from birth enters into a social network has been argued elsewhere (Weinraub, Brooks, & Lewis, 1975). These two positions have support from a variety of sources.

Social Nature of Human Beings • We mean the statement that man is social by nature to refer to several human properties. First, *the infant is totally dependent on other social objects (usually but not exclusively his mother) for his very survival.* The infant would die if it were not for the care of others, and thus from an evolutionary perspective must have evolved competencies which facilitate these social relationships. One distinguishing species-specific behavior is that the adults have and use language, to each other and to the infant itself. From birth, hemispheric differentiation of speech and nonspeech sounds attests to the importance of this adult behavior for the infant (Molfese, 1972).

Second, as Lévi-Strauss has argued in *The savage mind* (1962), conceptualization, including language, *is a social contract*, a social agreement on the meaning of words. This social agreement between adults is passed to the child—in our terms this process is a social action. Finally, recent evidence points to the sociobiological connection between adult and infant wherein the *regulation of the infant's biological function is dependent on his social world* (Sander, 1975). The work of Condon and Sander (1974a, 1974b) pointing out the coordination between the mother's speech flow and the infant's movement is evidence of this sociobiological connection. Social behavior and the social nature of the infant both are an evolutionary pressure and seem obvious as an ontogenetic fact.

Social Network • The social network is made up of social objects, functions, and situations, and these are only partially related. Social objects refer to people and things (e.g., stuffed animals), while social functions are all the activities which take place within the social network. Situations refer to the context of a social network and as such have a relationship to function. For example, feeding behavior, a social function, takes place under specific situations. Although feeding function and situation have relatively little variance, we possibly could find functions and situations which are markedly variable. Social objects and social functions are often related. For example, "mothering" (a function) and mother (an object) usually are considered synonymous. The relationships between functions, objects, and situations impart meaning since they form discriminable units—units which the infant is capable of perceiving and responding to. As Lewis and Freedle (1973) have pointed out, these discriminable units must form the basis of meaning.

One final proposition is necessary for our position in regard to the social context of language acquisition. *Knowledge is acquired through direct and indirect interaction with the social world.* Although we do not understand the nature or manner of the acquisition of the knowledge, the young child's knowledge is acquired from his social interactions. Direct interaction always involves the child as one of the participants in each interaction—in the case of language, being spoken to or speaking to. Indirect interactions involve the child's being influenced by and learning from interactions among people which do not include the child. We suspect that this indirectly acquired knowledge, although rarely considered, is most important for the infant's language development. Since language is such an important and frequent action between people, the infant's observation of this behavior between significant others must be of importance for the child's own knowledge about language.

This theme of knowledge in general, or language in particular, as evolving from the interaction of the infant with his social world is too complex to be fully dealt with here. Rather we wish to offer this as a possibility and as a counter theme to the prevailing view of cognitive–linguistic connection. Thus, instead of looking for the origins of language in cognitive action, we wish to examine its origins within a social–cognitive[2] perspective. In the following sections we will describe two empirical studies, one in language and social cognition and one in language use and socialization, in order to illustrate the research questions which can be generated from our position.

Language Study and Social Cognition

One can study language development within a social framework, and a study of infant's labeling is an example of this approach. Brooks and Lewis (1975) studied the first labels used by infants aged 9 to 36 months in order to examine social differentiation on the basis of labeling behavior, and to explore the origins of the social labels "daddy" and "mommy." Nine different pictures (mother, father, adult male and female, self, male and female infant

[2] We recognize the importance of cognition in all human behavior, but wish to emphasize the social communicative bases of meaning.

same age as subject, male and female children about 10 years old) were shown, one at a time to each infant.

At 15 months, the age of first labeling, infants labeled pictures of their fathers correctly but not pictures of their mothers. By 18 months all labeled pictures of their fathers correctly, some using "daddy" incorrectly, that is overgeneralizing the label. By 18 months, they were using the label "mommy" for their mothers but with no overgeneralization. Mothers of the 15-month-olds confirmed, when asked, that "daddy" preceded "mommy" in their children's first speech. Jakobson (1962) also found this to be the case. Brooks and Lewis (1975) suggest two possible explanations for the data. Perhaps a distancing (either physical or cognitive) between the infant and the father facilitates labeling. Fathers may be more "abstract" to their infants because fathers are around them for relatively little time. An alternative explanation offered is that infants may hear their mothers labeling their fathers more often than the reverse, and this differential experience may account for the phenomenon. In a recent test of this possibility, Dunn (personal communication) checked the verbal transcripts of 38 different mother–14-month-old infant pairs seen in their homes for at least two hours. Dunn reports 103 "mommy" and 43 "daddy" references in over 5000 utterances. Thus the distancing hypothesis receives support. However, either explanation involves the use of the social behavior of social objects to account for the acquisition of early labeling behavior, that is, learning to apply a lexical unit to an object.

This particular study also provides evidence for the lag between acquisition of the lexicon and social cognition. Recall that at 18 months some infants were overgeneralizing the label "daddy." Examination of the errors reveals that only adult male pictures received this label, not adult females or children of either sex. Since infants of 15 months have no problem in discriminating their fathers from other adult males, it seems that this overgeneralization is not error but rather an attempt by the infant to apply a lexical unit (when asked to do so) to a social object in the absence of a lexical unit for that social object. In fact, such "errors" suggest that the child already possesses the concepts of gender and age. Other work from our laboratory would support this contention (Lewis & Brooks, 1975). Older children's labeling behavior also suggests this to be true since the labeling of adult men at 21–27 months changes from "daddy" to "a daddy" or "the daddy" label. Not until 30 months does the child have the label "man," which is then applied correctly to the social object. This type of investigation reveals that the infant's use of social labels reflect his perceptions of his social world, and thus provides us with information about both language acquisition and social–cognitive organization.

These data are also useful when considering the developmental processes underlying change, be they lexical, cognitive, or social. Piaget has talked about decalage, the process by which organisms move from one stage to another, as one aspect of disequilibrium. Disequilibrium produces the motivation for this movement, while decalage would appear to effect disequilibrium. Social and lexical behavior can be shown to be in disequilibrium. The child experiences two different kinds of discrepancy within this particular kind of developmental process. In one kind the child has a discrepancy between his own perception of an object and his lexical unit for the object, as, for example, when he has one word for two objects, as in the case of "daddy" just discussed. In the second kind the child may have a discrepancy between his own lexical unit for an object and other people's lexical unit.

Language and Socialization

Another example of language and social development can be found in the relationship between socialization rules themselves and language acquisition. This type of formulation, embedding language and socialization into a simple system, is closer in fact to the Unified Model proposed earlier and is similar to Cicourel's (1974) "interactional competence."

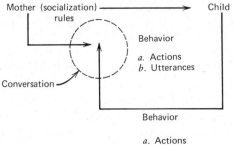

FIGURE 4. The use of language in the socialization process.

The young of the species become adult members of a particular group through the process of socialization. Thus the function of any socialization process is to produce an organism that is adapted to its specific surroundings. Language, meanings, and communication are all goals of socialization, as well as the means of promoting socialization. We have schematized this socialization process in Figure 4. Under rules of socialization the caregiver acts on the infant. These actions are both speech and nonspeech behaviors, which are controlled by socialization rules. In the case of speech actions, some mothers are more likely to emit speech than others. For example, Dutch mothers do not believe that children should be talked to (Lewis & Ban, 1973; Rebelsky & Abeles, 1969). Under the rule that "Children should be seen and not heard," the frequency of vocalization is lower than that of American mothers. The child also emits speech and nonspeech actions which can be responded to. In Figure 4 this example is schematized by the enclosed circle marked "Conversation." In this portion of the figure we see that the mother's linguistic behavior is used to reinforce her socialization rules by controlling the speech acts of the child through the nature of her responses to the child's behavior. For example, a prelinguistic speech action—a vocalization of an infant—is more likely to be responded to in a middle-class than in a lower-class home (Lewis & Wilson, 1972). Lewis and Freedle (1975) have argued that the specific socialization rule that children are "spoiled" by responsiveness may account for this differential behavior.

The model of socialization and speech actions we have presented suggests that language behavior is part of a larger interaction pattern between adult members of a group and the young child who is being socialized into that group. To explore this model, we have taken a specific socialization rule: sex role development in general, and proximity seeking in particular.

In our culture, there appears to be a general socialization rule governing children's proximity to their caregivers. With the increasing age of the child, parents move the child from proximal to distal forms of behavior. Concurrently with the decrease in proximal behaviors such as touching, distal behaviors such as eye contact become more important (Lewis & Ban, 1971). Another feature of our culture is that adult women are allowed more physical contact with other social objects than are men (Lewis, 1972a). The origins of this sex difference are found in infancy. Many studies have shown that young males are socialized faster in proximity seeking and maintaining than are females.[3] After the first few months of life, females receive more proximal behavior than males; and by the first year of life, females show more proximal behavior than males (Lewis, 1972a, 1972b), with this trend continuing for the first 4 years of life. Thus, although proximity decreases in general, for infants in the first 2 years of life, there are sex differences within this process.

Our model of socialization and language behavior suggests that there should be a relationship between sex differences in the language use and proximity behaviors of mothers and their children.

Sex Differences in Proximity and Speech Actions

Support for this position comes from a recent study of the play and speech behavior of a group of 2-year-olds and their mothers. Six males and six females matched for birth order and social class (all middle class—Groups 1 and 2 on the Hollingshead Scale) were observed for 15 minutes in a free-play

[3] Although it is a widely found phenomenon, it should be noted that this finding is still controversial since many studies fail to show this difference.

laboratory situation. Mothers were informed that their infants were being observed, and both child and parent were free to do as they pleased. The room was filled with an assortment of toys suitable for 2-year-olds while the mothers were provided with magazines to read. The spontaneous behaviors of the mothers and children were recorded on audiotape; the last 5 minutes was also recorded on videotape. In addition, two observers recorded the proximity of mother and child on an event recorder (interobserver reliability, estimated as number of agreements/number of agreements and disagreements, is quite high for proximity—.95).

The audiotape recordings were transcribed, including everything that was said by the mother and child during the play session. The transcripts were typed and coded "blind" with respect to the sex of the child. Quantitative measures coded included total number of utterances and total number of turns. Qualitative measures coded reflected verbal responsivity and included speakers repeating each other's utterances and mothers' use of directives (requests for action), questions (requests for information), and acknowledgments, as well as children's answering their mothers' questions.

The physical distance data indicated that females and their mothers were in greater proximity than were males and their mothers (517 seconds versus 425, $p < .07$). Likewise, in terms of distal behavior, in this case looking, mothers of males (and males) looked more at each other than mothers of females (and females): 534 seconds versus 431, $p < .04$. Thus there were sex differences in proximity over the 15 minutes of the play.

There is a relationship between this differential socialization and language usage. Question asking is by nature interactive, requiring a response by the person to whom the question is addressed. People often use questions as a means of producing and maintaining interactions, especially if they are relative strangers. In addition, the question answering often elicits a response by the one asking the question. Thus questions are "conversation-maintaining" devices. In contrast, a directive does not require a verbal response and often is not given one. In terms of the model in Figure 4, questions by the mother should be associated with the socialization rule of staying close, while directives should be associated with staying away. The data support this position. Girls, proximity seekers, are asked more questions by their mothers than boys (see Table 1 for a summary of the results), whereas boys receive more directives. Moreover, other conversation-maintaining devices, such as percentage of maternal other repetitions as well as percentage of mother acknowledgments of children's answers and mother turns, all show a greater amount for girls than boys. Finally, even maternal utterances and MLUs show greater amounts directed toward girls than boys. *This differential maternal behavior as a function of the child's sex is unrelated to the child's linguistic behavior, since in general there are no sex differences in*

*children's language performance, for example, the MLU for girls was 2.06
as compared to 1.92 for boys.*

Other data suggest that the maternal language behavior is mediated, not
by the child's language behavior, but by a more general sex role rule. To
explore this association still further, several correlational analyses were performed. The small sample size for this type of inquiry must temper our conclusions. When we correlate proximity with percentage of questions for all

TABLE 1. Mean Mother–Child Speech Scores ($N = 12$)

	Sex of Child		
	Mean for Girls	Mean for Boys	Mann–Whitney Test p Values
Total child utterances	111.3	97.8	.17
Total child turns	66.2	58.6	.08
MLU for child	2.06	1.92	.17
Percentage of child answers	.36	.34	.34
Percentage of child other repetition	.18	.14	.14
Total mother utterances	149.3	119.8	.03
Total mother turns	71.8	62.0	.11
MLU for mother	4.40	3.68	.01
Percentage of mother questions	.33	.25	.04
Percentage of mother acknowledgments	.71	.61	.11
Percentage of mother directives	.17	.20	.07
Percentage of mother other repetition	.65	.46	.05

twelve subjects, we find a zero relationship ($r = -.08$); however, the correlation by sex indicates that question asking and proximity are positively
related for girls ($r = .34$) but negatively related for boys ($r = -.52$). Distal
(child's looking) behavior is negatively correlated with questions for girls
($r = -.71$) and positively correlated with questions for boys ($r = .13$). Thus
there is a sex difference between proximity seeking and questions. For girls,
proximal behavior is positively assoicated, whereas distal behavior is
negatively associated, with maternal question asking. For boys, proximal
behavior is negatively associated, whereas distal behavior is slightly positively related, to maternal question asking.

Observation of the relationship between proximity seeking and percentage
of mother's directives shows a reverse pattern. For girls, proximal behavior
is negatively related to directive use ($r = -.67$), whereas distal behavior is
positively related ($r = .46$). For boys, distal behavior is negatively correlated
with directive use ($r = -.90$), whereas proximal behavior is unrelated to

directive use ($r = -.04$). To summarize, it appears that, for girls, maternal question asking or directive use is related to proximity. For boys, the most parsimonious conclusion is that the more contact between mother and child, either proximal or distal, the less speech (either question or directives) the mother produces. This is further supported by the relationship between total utterances of either mother or child and proximity, and total turns and proximity. For boys, the correlations were $-.64$, $-.45$, and $-.87$ (an average of $-.65$) for proximity and maternal utterances, proximity and child utterances, and proximity and total turns, respectively. The same correlations for girls were $-.39$, $.25$, and $.19$ (an average of $+.02$), respectively.

In sum, this set of data suggests that there is a relationship between maternal language use and the physical distance between the child and the mother. These findings may reflect a general socialization rule governing sex role appropriate behavior, in which boys are encouraged to move away and become independent of the mother whereas girls are allowed (or encouraged) to stay close. Mothers may use verbal and nonverbal behaviors for this purpose. The pattern of differential maternal behavior may eventually affect the child's language usage. Perhaps such patterns are responsible for female language becoming oriented toward its social usage, whereas male language use becomes centered on more distal or abstract features. There is already some evidence that adult language use can be characterized in this way (Barron, 1971; Soskin & John, 1963; Strodtbeck & Mann, 1956; Thorne & Henley, 1975).

Social Behavior as Grammar

Although much of our discussion has centered on the usage of language, the rules underlining the construction of language—its grammar—might also be considered from a social behavior perspective. The following examples are presented with the idea of showing the feasibility of such an approach.

It is consistent with our theoretical position that social action could be used to search for subsequent grammatical rules. For example, the approach of the mother, the presence of the mother, and finally her departure could be used as the prototype of tense. Approach could be characterized by something that is going to happen—anticipation as future tense. Ongoing interaction might be analogous to present tense; the end of interaction and departure, to past tense. Even the physical dimensions of persons approaching, being near, and departing should all be considered as prototypes of the meanings underlying our usage of tense. In this regard it is interesting to note that in studies on the approach of strangers the 8-month-old infant shows immediate distress by frowning, for example, as soon as the approaching stranger turns to leave. This turning (or the hiding of the face?) seems to act as some signal for the termination of the interaction even though the stranger is still present (Lewis & Haviland, 1975).

A second consideration of social behavior as grammar can be found in the behavior sequences or chains of behavior between infant and mother. These chains change over age (Lusk & Lewis, 1972) in terms of both length and composition. These chains of behavior have a set of rules governing their occurrence which involve how long a particular chain is, who initiates or terminates the chain, and what behaviors are likely to occur and in what sequence. These chains might be likened to sentences/words with the individual words/letters making up these sets. The rules governing these sets are now being explored (Lewis & Rosenblum, 1974). It may not be an overstatement to argue that the construction of these chains may be the prototype of subsequent linguistic rules. For example, the likelihood in English of an h following a t or of a noun following an article may be quite similar (in terms of the generation of rules, as is an infant vocalization) to maternal vocalization in the interaction of a 12-week-old and his caregiver (Lewis, 1972b).

In a recent exploration of this problem, we looked at three length actor changes in 12-week-old infants and their mothers: infant, mother, infant. The question we asked was what was the probability, given an initial infant vocalization, of another infant vocalization after some maternal behavior:

infant voc,   mother x,   infant voc

The results indicate that the likelihood of a second infant vocalization is dependent first on whether the mother behaves in response and then on the nature of her response. Maternal vocalization appears at least twice as likely as, for example, a maternal touch, smile, or look in maintaining or eliciting the infant–mother vocalization interaction. Thus it is not just responding (reinforcement), but rather the nature of the response, which determines the chaining features.

In conclusion, we believe that language development can best be studied and understood as part of the socialization processes that characterize the child's transactions with others. Patterns of early caregiver–child interaction provide the matrix for the child's development. The child's acquisition of knowledge (both meaning and grammatical constructions) are dependent on his early transactions with his social world. We have argued for an ethological basis of this social context in which language is both the means and the end of the socialization process. As George Herbert Mead (1934) stated in the quotation at the beginning of this chapter, it is the individual who develops as a result of the processes of social experiences, activities, and interactions with other individuals. To focus upon one aspect of the development of the individual, such as language development, is possible. To understand that aspect, however, one must study the development of the individual in his social context.

References

Barron, M. Sex-typed language: The production of grammatical cases. *Acta Sociologica*, 1971, **14**(1–2), 24–72.

Bever, T. The cognitive basis for linguistic structures. In J. Hayes (Ed.), *Cognition and the development of language*. New York: Wiley, 1970. Pp. 279–362.

Brooks, J., & Lewis, M. *Person perception and verbal labeling: The development of social labels*. A version of this paper was presented at both the Society for Research in Child Development meetings, Denver, April 1975, and the Eastern Psychological Association meetings, New York City, April 1975.

Chomsky, N. *Syntactic structures*. The Hague: Mouton, 1957.

Cicourel, A. *Cognitive sociology*. New York: Free Press, 1974.

Condon, W. S., & Sander, L. W. Neonate movement is synchronized with adult speech: Interactional participation and language acquisition. *Science*, 1974, **183**, 99–101. (a)

Condon, W. S., & Sander, L. W. Synchrony demonstrated between movements of the neonate and adult speech. *Child Development*, 1974, **45**, 456–462. (b)

Dunn, J. Personal communication, October 1975.

Ervin-Tripp, S. Wait for me, roller-skate: The structure of directives. In J. & J. Gumperz (Eds.), *Language socialization in context*. Cambridge, England: Cambridge University Press (in press).

Hymes, D. On communicative competence. In J. B. Pride & J. Holmes (Eds.), *Sociolinguistics*. Baltimore: Penguin Books, 1972.

Jakobson, R. Why "Mama" and "Papa"? In *Selected writings of Roman Jakobson*. The Hague: Mouton, 1962.

Lévi-Strauss, C. *The savage mind*. Chicago: University of Chicago Press, 1962.

Lewis, M. Parents and children: Sex-role development. *School Review*, 1972, **80**(2), 229–240. (a)

Lewis, M. State as an infant–environment interaction: An analysis of mother–infant interaction as a function of sex. *Merrill-Palmer Quarterly*, 1972, **18**, 95–121. (b)

Lewis, M., & Ban, P. *Stability of attachment behavior: A transformational analysis*. Paper presented at the Society for Research in Child Development meetings, Symposium on Attachment: Studies in Stability and Change, Minneapolis, April 1971.

Lewis, M., & Ban, P. *Variance and invariance in the mother–infant interaction: A cross-cultural study*. Paper presented at the Burg Wartenstein Symposium No. 57, Cultural and Social Influences in Infancy and Childhood, Burg Wartenstein, Austria, June 1973. Also, in P. H.

Leiderman & S. R. Tulkin (Eds.), *Cultural and social influences in infancy and early childhood*. Stanford, Calif.: Stanford University Press (in press).

Lewis, M., & Brooks, J. Infants' social perception: A constructivist view. In L. Cohen & P. Salapatek (Eds.), *Infant perception: From sensation to cognition*. New York: Academic Press, 1975.

Lewis, M., & Freedle, R. Mother–infant dyad: the cradle of meaning. In P. Pliner, L. Krames, & T. Alloway (Eds.), *Communication and affect: Language and thought*. New York: Academic Press, 1973.

Lewis, M., & Freedle, R. *The mother and infant communication system: The effects of poverty*. Paper presented at the Biennial Conference of the International Society for the Study of Behavioural Development, Symposium on Ecology and Social Class: Socialization, Cognitive, and Language Development, Surrey, England, July 1975.

Lewis, M., & Haviland, J. *Social responses to social objects: Infant fear or infant greeting?* Invited plenary address at the XIVth International Ethological Conference, Parma, Italy, August–September 1975.

Lewis, M., & Rosenblum, L. (Eds.), *The origins of behavior*. Vol. I. *The effect of the infant on its caregiver*. New York: Wiley, 1974.

Lewis, M., & Wilson, D. C. Infant development in lower class American families. *Human Development*, 1972, **15**(2), 112–127.

Lusk, D., & Lewis, M. Mother–infant interaction and infant development among the Wolof of Senegal. *Human Development*, 1972, **15**(1), 58–69.

McNeill, D. The development of language. In P. Mussen (Ed.), *Carmichael's manual of child psychology*. New York: Wiley, 1970.

Mead, G. H. *Mind, self, and society*. Chicago: University of Chicago Press, 1934.

Molfese, D. L. *Cerebral asymmetry in infants, children and adults: Auditory evoked responses to speech and noise stimuli*. Unpublished doctoral dissertation, Pennsylvania State University, 1972.

Piaget, J. *Play, dreams, and imitation in childhood*. Translated by C. Gattegno & F. M. Hodgson. New York: W. W. Norton, 1951.

Piaget, J. *The origins of intelligence in children*. Translated by M. Cook. New York: International Universities Press, 1952.

Piaget, J. *The language and thought of the child*. New York: Meridian, World, 1969.

Rebelsky, F., & Abeles, G. *Infancy in Holland and the United States*. Paper presented at the Society for Research in Child Development meeting, Santa Monica, March 1969.

Sander, L. Infant and caretaking environment: Investigation and conceptualization of adaptive behavior in a system of increasing complexity. In E. J. Anthony (Ed.), *The child psychiatrist as investigator*. New York: Plenum, 1975.

Soskin, W., & John, V. The study of spontaneous talk. In R. Barker (Ed.), *The stream of behavior*. New York: Appleton-Century-Crofts, 1963.

Strodtbeck, F., & Mann, R. Sex role differentiation in jury deliberations. *Sociometry*, 1956, **19**, 3–11.

Thorne, B., & Henley, N. *Language and sex: Difference and dominance.* Rowley, Mass.: Newbury House, 1975.

Vygotsky, L. *Thought and language.* Cambridge, Mass.: M.I.T. Press, 1965.

Weinraub, M., Brooks, J., & Lewis, M. *The social network: A reconsideration of the concept of attachment.* Unpublished manuscript, Educational Testing Service, 1975.

CHAPTER 11

From Gesture to the First Word: on Cognitive and Social Prerequisites[1]

ELIZABETH BATES

University of Colorado

LAURA BENIGNI

Consiglio Nazionale della Ricerche

INGE BRETHERTON

University of Colorado

LUIGIA CAMAIONI

Consiglio Nazionales della Ricerche

and

VIRGINIA VOLTERRA

University of Rome

This chapter represents a transitional moment in our thinking. We began studying infant cognition and communication with a theory that struck us as profound enough at the time. Still more happily, the first round of data seemed consonant with that theory. However, the more we thought about the relationship between cognitive and social-communicative events, the more complex the issue became. Before we plunged into the long process of film transcription and endless statistical analyses we had to stop and reconsider our goals. This chapter reflects our effort to define the notion of "prerequisite" much more carefully, and to make our predictions clear before we test them.

[1] We are deeply indebted to Vicki Carlsen, Dorothy Holloway, Jocelyn Javits, Dorothy Poulsen, Marcia Rosser and Glenn Wasek for their hard work in data collection (without pay!), their sensitivity and intelligence in dealing with young infants, and their support and interest in the project since that time. Particular thanks are due to Marcia Rosser and Glenn Wasek for their criticisms in the preparation of this manuscript. We are indebted also to the University of Colorado Council on Creative Research, the University of Colorado Bio-Medical Fund, and the Consiglio Nazionale delle Ricerche, Istituto di Psicologia, for their support of this research.

The chapter is divided into the following sections:

1. A brief summary of the original longitudinal study upon which our current research is based, and an examination of several related studies that other people were carrying out around the same time—no doubt in response to the same "missing pieces" in the puzzle.

2. A very long but unavoidable examination of possible models for the interdependence of language, cognition, and social development, leading to a redefinition of the term *prerequisite*.

3. A brief summary of the design of our follow-up study.

4. Some findings from our follow-up study in support of the particular interdependence model adopted here.

THE LONGITUDINAL STUDY AND RELATED RESEARCH

Psycholinguistics is a rapidly changing field, which takes many of its richest heuristic notions from another rapidly changing field, generative linguistics. As each problem is solved and/or abandoned, the next research question is generally obvious to many people. When we began our longitudinal study in 1972 (see Bates, Camaioni, & Volterra, 1975), we were responding to two converging questions which had begun to appear in the literature:

1. Can the performative analysis be extended back into the period before speech begins?

2. Can certain universal social-communicative events be traced to a cognitive base in sensorimotor development?

Since we had all been engaged in previous research on early semantic development and communicative interaction, we had been impressed by the apparently rich structures that could already be inferred at the beginning of one- and two-word speech. This suggested to us the possibility that many semantic–pragmatic events had a history before speech. As we shall see, the same questions had become apparent to a number of other researchers during this period.

Regarding the first question, it is probably no longer necessary to define the concept of "speech act" or "performative" for an audience of psychologists. Just as the Chomskian notions of deep structure and transformation are common fare, and need not be defined at the beginning of every article using those constructs, the performative analysis has also become increasingly familiar. Quite briefly, the term *performative* in both language philosophy (Austin, 1962) and recent linguistic theory (Ross, 1970; Gordon & Lakoff, 1971), refers to the act that the speaker intends to carry out with his sentence—declaring, promising, asking questions, and so on. (See Cole &

Morgan, 1975, for a detailed examination of speech act theory by a number of linguists and philosophers.) The performative or "speech act" analysis has been applied with some success to early childhood speech (Antinucci & Parisi, 1973; Antinucci & Volterra, 1973; Ingram, 1971; Greenfield & Smith, 1976; Bates, 1976). All these studies indicate that at least two performatives —commanding and declaring— are clearly distinguishable in the first one-word utterances of young children. In our longitudinal study, we sought to establish when these performative intentions are first manifested in gestural communication before speech, and to follow the development of these pre-verbal performatives through to the beginning of speech.

In particular, we were interested in cognitive and social prerequisites to these communicative developments. At the time that we began our study, the definition of the term *prerequisite* seemed quite obvious to us: a "pre-requisite" is a development that must occur before a second development, dependent in some way on the first, can take place. As we shall see later on, this definition has proved to be inadequate for meaningful research on the relationship between cognition and communication.

Our interest in cognitive prerequisites to preverbal communication was part of a general interest in the cognitive basis of syntactic–semantic development, as expressed by MacNamara (1972), Sinclair (1972), Schlesinger (1973), Brown (1973), Bowerman (1969), and Greenfield and Smith (1976). This interest was in turn a reaction against the nativist, language-specific approach to syntax that had characterized earlier research on child language (e.g., McNeill, 1970). In the same way, the growing interest in the pragmatics of language, including speech act analysis, could also be viewed as a reaction against a "mental objects" approach to linguistic structures. In its emphasis on language in use, pragmatic analysis provides an alternative view of language, as a social event carried out by human beings, in realistic communicative contexts. Hence research on pragmatics in child language permits a reintegration of the study of language development with research on cognitive and social development in children. Each of us involved in the pre-speech project had been engaged before 1972 in research on the pragmatics of early speech. We were, then, intrigued by the possibility of carrying pragmatic analysis as far back in development as we could take it, integrating communicative development with existing research on cognition and social interaction in the first year of life.

Finally, when we began our project, we had been particularly influenced by a brief presentation by A. Lock in 1972 at the Second International Child Language Symposium in Florence. In a paper entitled "From out of no-where . . .," Lock reported informal observations of one child from around 6 to 11 months, demonstrating a continuity from the child's actions on objects to his first tentative efforts to involve adults in those actions through eye contact, reaching, vocalization, and so on. Lock described the development of communicative intentions, not as a radical, qualitative shift, but rather as a smooth and continuous change with definable endpoints, but very unclear boundaries in between. On the basis of Lock's excellent paper, we became optimistic about the possibility of demonstrating transitions from sensorimotor action schemes to verbal communication. We thus began our project with three converging interests:

1. The continuity from precommunicative schemes, to preverbal communication, to verbal interaction.

2. Developments in other domains (e.g., cognition and social relations) which accompany and (perhaps) bring about this gradual shift.

3. The kinds of performative intentions (e.g., declaring, ordering, asking) that emerge from the above developments.

These same three emphases—continuity, prerequisite developments, and communicative taxonomies—also seem to characterize parallel research by other authors in the same period.

First, let us briefly describe our own project (Bates et al., 1975). The longitudinal study involved three infant girls, aged 2, 6, and 12 months, respectively, at the beginning of the study. We visited their homes at 2-week intervals, observing and videotaping spontaneous play and social interaction, and carrying out some rather unsystematic cognitive testing based on Piaget's theory of sensorimotor development (Piaget, 1954). The study covered an 8-month period; at the end of this period, the three infants overlapped one another in development. During the entire project, diary records were kept by the mothers. The videotapes, off-camera observations, and diary records were used to compile tables of social, cognitive, and communicative developments (the full set of data tables has been published, in Italian, in Camaioni, Volterra, & Bates, 1976).

In brief, the results indicated that the primary cognitive prerequisite for gestural performatives is Piaget's sensorimotor stage 5, defined as "the invention of new means to familiar ends." Particularly relevant are developments related to causality and means–end relations, sometimes referred to as *tool use*. In the 40 days in which the 10- to 11-month old subject used supports to pull objects, and tools or sticks to push other objects, she also began (1) to use objects as "tools" to obtain adult attention (showing, giving, communicative pointing), and (2) to invoke adult help in obtaining objects. The use of objects to obtain adult attention was termed the *protodeclarative*, and it was within these same kinds of communicative sequences that the first one-word labeling later appeared. The use of adults to obtain objects was referred to as the *protoimperative*. Like the protodeclaratives, these imperative schemes also led directly to the eventual use of words with imperative intent. However, words did not appear in either of these two communicative schemes until a later period, corresponding to Piaget's sensorimotor stage 6, the capacity for mental representation and the use of symbols. During this later period, the first referential uses of words co-occurred with nonverbal manifestations of stage 6, including the beginning of symbolic or "pretend" play, deferred imitation, memory for absent objects or people, and the ability to follow invisible displacements.

We concluded that the cognitive prerequisite for preverbal, intentional communication is sensorimotor stage 5, the invention of new means to familiar ends. In particular, causal developments involved in tool use seemed to be related to the ability to use objects to obtain adult attention, and adult help to obtain objects. Because these intentional communications did not necessarily involve speech, this stage was termed the *illocutionary phase* in communicative development after Austin (1962). The *locutionary phase*, involving the use of words in the same performative sequences, seemed to require a further cognitive development, characterized by Piaget as the stage 6 symbolic capacity.

The use of such terms as *phase* and *stage* implies sudden and qualitative shifts. We would like to emphasize instead the gradual transitions from one stage to another. For example, the first word or "locution" did not just spring forward fully formed at the end of the first year. Between the two stages, we witnessed a gradual transition from (*a*) wordlike sounds in the service of performative functions (e.g., the sound "na-na" or "Mmm!" used to accompany all requests for any type of object or action), to (*b*) semi-referential words, in which some minimal relation between sound and referent can be determined, but only within a ritualized, function-based range (e.g., the use of the Italian word "Da!" or "Give!" as an accompaniment to the act of exchanging objects), to (*c*) referential words, or sounds which appear to "stand for" their referents in a range of contexts (e.g., "woo-woo" to designate dogs).

Within the preverbal stage we also witnessed further "substages." The child began seeking adult laughter and comment without the use of intervening objects, by "showing off" or repeating behaviors that had successfully elicited adult attention on previous occasions. Then the child began to extend her arm forward and show or give objects that she had been playing with. In the case of Carlotta, our middle subject, this scheme first involved a sort of pseudo-giving, in which she touched an object to the adult hand but did not let go of it. Both giving and showing gradually became stable, ritual acts, so that the children would look around, or even cross the room to obtain objects to be shown or given. Finally, the last development among these preverbal "declaratives" involved communicative pointing at objects out of arm's reach. This event is particularly interesting, since Carlotta had been engaging in noncommunicative pointing for several weeks, both in examining objects close up and in staring at things at a distance that had surprised her (e.g., a dog barking). However, in these apparently noncommunicative sequences, she never turned to make eye contact or otherwise obtain confirmation from the adult. Later on, the same pointing act was much more clearly used while sharing attention to objects with an adult. In fact, Carlotta went through a rather curious transitional period in which she would point to the object, swing around and point to the adult, and then return to point to the object. These three components gradually smoothed into the single deictic act of pointing-at-object while turning the head to look at the adult. In interpreting this developmental sequence, we agreed with Werner and Kaplan (1963), who suggest that pointing first develops outside communicative contexts, as an act which aids in both singling out the object and pushing it away in an effort to distinguish "me" from "it." Later on, this same cognitive act is incorporated into prepared communicative schemes.

In other writings (Camaioni et al., 1976; Bates, 1976) we have gone into much more detail on the nature of performatives, and on aspects of both Piaget's theory of cognitive development and a number of theories of social development (e.g., Bowlby, 1969; Spitz, 1965) as they relate to the development of preverbal communication. We cannot repeat those arguments here. But it may be useful, at least, to confess some of our failures and inclarities in early versions of this work. In our longitudinal study, stages 5 and 6 were manifested in interactions with physical objects before they appeared in social-communicative sequences. In our first written account of the project, we implied that the physical-cognitive *behaviors* of a given stage must necessarily precede (i.e., were prerequisite to) social-communicative *behaviors* of the same stage. It is this misreading of Piaget that we are most anxious to correct here. This point should become clear later on, when we discuss models for the interdependence of thought and language.

When we began circulating a preliminary report of the above project, we came into contact with a number of similar articles by other authors. Since all of these influenced the design of our follow-up project, it would be useful to review them briefly here.

The approach most similar to ours is found in a thesis by Sugarman (1973). Sugarman stresses the notion of prerequisite cognitive and social schemes, which are gradually combined into complex communicative sequences as a function of stages in sensorimotor development. Her research involved two studies: a combination of longitudinal and cross-sectional observations of seven infants from 4 to 14 months, and a pilot study of six institutionalized infants observed cross sectionally. Sugarman used much more systematic cognitive testing than Bates, administering a version of the Uzgiris and

Hunt scales for sensorimotor development (Uzgiris & Hunt, 1975). In addition, she used a more systematic set of tasks for eliciting preverbal requests from children. Sugarman divides her results into three sensorimotor stages:

1. *Sensorimotor Stage 3.* Piaget defines this period as the stage of secondary circular reactions or schemes for making interesting events last. In general, stage 3 is marked by the ability to initiate and continue simple interactions with social and nonsocial objects. Sugarman notes that during this stage infants develop "simple object-oriented acts" (e.g., sucking, banging, and staring at a toy) and "simple person-oriented acts" (e.g., smiling and waving the arms to continue an interesting social exchange). However, the children do not yet combine a variety of person or object schemes into an integrated unit. Nor do they combine person schemes with object schemes.

2. *Sensorimotor Stage 4.* According to Piaget, this is the stage of complex coordinations of secondary circular reactions. During this period, Sugarman finds that the child can sustain either a social or a nonsocial goal for some time, interchanging and recombining his various schemes in the service of respective social or nonsocial goals. However, the child never interrupts a "complex object-oriented act" to insert person schemes, nor does he insert object schemes into "complex person-oriented acts." In short, the two repertoires are kept separate.

3. *Sensorimotor Stage 5.* Piaget defines this stage in terms of tertiary circular reactions, or the invention of new means to familiar ends. In this period, Sugarman notes that the child can interrupt a complex object- or person-oriented act to insert schemes from another repertoire. Hence the child begins to interrupt interactions with objects or efforts to obtain them and uses social signals in an attempt to obtain adult help with the enterprise.

This latter finding is completely consistent with our longitudinal study. Both studies emphasize (1) the continuity from precommunicative to communicative behaviors, and (2) the way in which social and nonsocial schemes are combined in novel means–end sequences. Sugarman does not stress performatives, or taxonomies of communicative intentions. Her findings are directed almost entirely toward what we have labeled the "protoimperative." However, her analysis is compatible with our position on protodeclaratives as well.

Dore, in a dissertation entitled *On the development of speech acts* (1973) and in a series of subsequent papers (1974, 1975), has been particularly interested in classes of performatives and their history before and during early speech. Dore provides a stage model for the transition from preverbal communication to the completion of language acquisition, pointing out both the continuity between stages and the qualitative changes that take place in both the pragmatic and the syntactic–semantic component of a communicative act:

1. *Stage 1—Prelinguistic Communication.* The content of communicative acts at this stage consists in "cognitive schemes," while the child's intention with regard to that content is described in terms of "orectic attitudes" (affective-conative states in the child, e.g., hunger or discomfort, which determine the strength, form, and direction of his preverbal communication).

2. *Stage II—Presyntactic Communication.* This stage is linguistic, in that the child uses words, but it is presyntactic insofar as the child uses only one word at a time. At this point the contents of communicative acts are expressed as "word forms" (in transition from the cognitive schemes of the earlier stage). The child's communicative intention with regard to those word forms is expressed primarily with prosodic patterns or intonation. Dore lays more emphasis on these vocal-intonational patterns than do the other studies being reported here, but is in turn somewhat less interested in visual–gestural phenomena.

3. *Stage III—Syntactic Communication.* At this stage, content and intention, cognitive schemes and orectic attitudes, interact in the child's acquisition of syntactic patterns for combining more than one word form. Intonation, word order, lexical selection, and so on are involved in the expression of both content and performative intent, so that the two are no longer as clearly separate as in the previous stages.

4. *Stage IV—Speech Acts.* At this stage, the child has mastered the most relevant aspects of the adult code. Hence the adult linguistic distinction between "propositions" (evolved from cognitive content) and "illocutionary force" (evolved from orectic attitudes) can be applied to child speech.

There are a number of notable differences between Dore's approach and the Sugarman and Bates et al. papers. For example, although his study emphasized results for only two children, Dore is very interested in the question of individual differences in strategy for acquiring language. He suggests that some infants may be "word babies," interested primarily in the referential or "ideational" functions of language. Others are "intonation babies," who begin with complex intonation contours (in some instances even before speech) and word combinations treated as one unit (including imitations of unanalyzed adult phrases). The intonation babies also tend to be more interested in practical, goal-oriented uses of language, as opposed to the word babies, who seem more interested in "expressing thoughts to themselves." This analysis bears some relation to work by Halliday (1975; see below), whom Dore cites in this regard. Hence an initial "specialization" by the infant in either cognitive content or orectic attitudes may influence his attention to and interest in the linguistic forms that these two components take across the four stages. In addition, Dore expresses interest in the question of cognitive prerequisites for language, although he places much more emphasis on sensorimotor stage 4 as the cognitive source for communicative intentions. However, since Dore's analysis of the of stage 4 is based on Piagetian age norms alone, rather than cognitive observations in his own sample, this presentation is somewhat less convincing than Sugarman's. Finally, Dore differs from Sugarman and Bates et al. in stressing language-specific and perhaps innate skills beyond those that can be derived from sensorimotor cognition.

Carter (1974, 1975) goes into much greater detail than any of the three studies cited above regarding the various functions or classes of preverbal communications. In contrast to our search for protoforms of adult categories like declaratives and imperatives, Carter's taxonomy of communicative intentions is empirically derived, based on observations of separate classes of gesture–sound combinations as they are used in a variety of contexts. For example, she derives categories like the following:

1. *Attention to object*: gesture=point, hold out, or hold up object; vocalization=basically *l*- or *d*-initial utterances (e.g., *la, daet*).

2. *Request object*: gesture=open-handed reach; vocalization=basically *m*-initial utterances.

3. *Request transfer of object*: gesture=holding out when giving someone an object, and open-handed reach when requesting an object from someone; vocalization=*h*-initial utterances.

The function of the utterance is defined by the child's behavior before and after the interchange and by the nonverbal context. Each function is given a separate classification if it is continually marked by the same gesture–vocalization pair.

Carter derives a list of approximately 10 such functions, suggesting that these sound–gesture markers are "sensorimotor morphemes" that will eventually develop into verbal expression of the same function. In the sensorimotor period, however, the gesture is more clearly a defining characteristic of the communicative function. Later on, the phonological markers will be refined into increasingly wordlike sounds, at which point they will become more important cues for defining the function. Hence, more than any of the above studies, Carter stresses the slow continuity in development within each communicative class from sensorimotor to symbolic expression. She also invokes Piagetian notions of cognitive development to explain this shift. However, Carter is less interested in cognitive stages than in the transition between stages.

To summarize so far, all four of these studies have stressed continuity to a greater or lesser degree. Sugarman is less interested in performative taxonomies than Bates et al., Carter, or Dore. Bates et al. and Dore tend to impose their performative classes from speech act theory, albeit defending their taxonomies with observations of the function served by the child's preverbal schemes. Carter, on the other hand, derives her taxonomy from the data. In doing so, she is less able to capture the transition into adult speech act categories. However, she can, by staying closer to the data, follow more carefully the transitions *within* the child's own communicative schemes. All four of these studies invoke, to different degrees, the notion of cognitive prerequisites, with special reference to Piaget's theory of sensorimotor development. In contrast to these four, two other studies, by Halliday (1975) and Bruner (1975a, 1975b), stress the social bases of language more than the notion of cognitive prerequisites.

Bruner suggests that both the semantic structure of language (e.g., case relations like "agent" and "benefactor," logical notions of predication, discourse structure of topic and comment) and the pragmatic or performative functions of language are ultimately derived from the structure of social interaction. Reference, for example, derives from "joint attention to objects" by mother and child. Case relations are developed through ritualized social exchanges and games in which the child learns the nature of a given semantic role by taking that role in reciprocal interactions. Bruner stresses continuity and gradual ritualization of schemes rather than qualitative reorganization into stages. Also, although he mentions a heterogeneous set of linguistic structures that might result from social exchange, he is not particularly interested in performative taxonomies.

Halliday, like Bruner, is primarily interested in the contribution of social development to language acquisition. Unlike Bruner, he provides a systematic list of social functions served by preverbal and early verbal communication. However, Halliday's taxonomy is based on his own, unique approach to adult grammar. He does not borrow the categories of performative or speech act analysis, as do Bates et al. and Dore. Nor does he, like Carter, derive his taxonomy empirically from the child's behavior. Instead, he imposes an a priori list of social functions on the data (derived from his sociolinguistic theory of adult language), and makes predictions about the order in which these functions should appear. Halliday's skill as a linguist and his painstaking observations of gestural and intonational phenomena yield a remarkable and unique set of observations. However, there is much less effort to integrate the child's communicative development with traditional (or nontraditional) work on cognitive and social development. This may be either a drawback or a virtue of the work, depending on the reader's point of view.

A number of other papers on early performatives and/or cognitive bases of communication have also appeared (e.g., Ingram, 1974, 1975; Kaye, 1975; Collis, 1975; Delack & Fowlow, 1975; Myers, 1975; Shields, 1975; Sylvester-Bradley & Trevarthen, 1975; Wells, 1975). Clearly the zeitgeist has led many of us directly into this set of questions. At a London conference on child language, Cromer (1975) was sufficiently dismayed by the preponderance of papers on pragmatics, semantics, cognitive bases of language, social bases of language, and the like that he made an eloquent plea for a return to syntax. Indeed, it is possible that the overemphasis on syntax in the 1960s, to the neglect of related functions, has led to an equivalent reaction in favor of nonsyntactic aspects of development. Nevertheless, as we shall see shortly, so many more questions remain to be answered regarding infant communication that we may be in this period for several years to come.

Let us turn to some theoretical questions concerning the nature of the relationship of language, cognition, and social development. In particular, we are interested in redefining the term *prerequisite*, so that we can make clearer statements about the meaning of our findings.

ON DEFINING "PREREQUISITE": MODELS FOR THE INTERDEPENDENCE OF LANGUAGE, COGNITION, AND SOCIAL DEVELOPMENT

So far we have used the terms *cognitive prerequisites* and *social prerequisites* as though their meanings were self-evident. Indeed, when we began our longitudinal study of infant communication, we thought we knew precisely what we were looking for. Upon closer examination, however, it became clear that there are a variety of models for the interdependence of language, cognition, and social development. In fact, the closer we looked at the problem, the more the number of possible relations multiplied. In some cases the conceptual distinctions between models are more obvious than their empirical consequences. In other cases the different epistemological models dictate very different predictions.

In the next section we will begin with an examination of the classical problem of language–thought relations, outlining at least six possible models for independence and/or interdependence between the two systems. Then we will extend the same analysis to the three-way interaction of language, thought, and social development.

Before beginning, we should clarify some of the terms we are using. Throughout this paper, we have used some rather general terms like *systems*, *domains*, and *structures*. Obviously we are assuming from the outset that there is something identifiable as *language*, which is conceptually and empirically separable from something else called *cognition* or *thought*, which is in turn distinct from another thing called *social development* or *social interaction*. What level are we talking about? We could be discussing language as an entity apart from the human beings who use it. Or we could be discussing some sort of physiological substrate, a "hardware" system that exists "inside" individuals. We could be using the term *system* to describe a set of observable behaviors, without making inferences about underlying structures. *In this paper, we will talk about linguistic, cognitive, and social "systems" or "domains" in yet another sense, to refer to some sort of software package, a "program" than an individual child or adult "has," which permits him to generate behaviors that are externally identifiable as "linguistic," "cognitive," or "social."* In discussing the interdependence of systems, we are trying to determine whether there are indeed three separate programs corresponding to the three behavioral domains, or whether the three apparently separate domains in some sense share the same underlying structural principles. Obviously such an enterprise involves extensive inference, from observable behaviors to hypothetical underlying programs. However, we do not share the behaviorist view that such inference is inherently "unscientific."

This brings us to another point that must be clarified before proceeding. Note that we are concentrating here on the notion of "dependence." This is not necessarily the same thing as "causality." We are not talking about language causing cognition in Aristotle's sense of efficient causality (i.e., the rock causes the window to break). *Rather, we are talking about a developmental dependence such that one system requires input from another in order to derive or build its structure.* It is patently obvious that language, thought, and social development must interact. But are they interdependent, and if so to what degree and in what way?

We ask the reader's patience with this exercise, and hope that our efforts are accepted with at the very least a sense of humor. As we shall see shortly, an initially simple problem grows rapidly out of hand when we begin to take it seriously. Nevertheless, this exercise has been a useful and necessary step in our own thinking as we approach analysis of our follow-up project. Perhaps that is a sign above all of our own naïveté at the outset. Still, since the recent literature abounds in promissory notes concerning cognitive and social bases of communicative development, we offer the following thoughts as a small contribution to fulfilling those promises.

Thought and Language

Let us begin with an obvious but necessary disclaimer: the classical problem of the relation between thought and language has been a major theme in philosophy and psychology for centuries. Hence any "review" of the area is presumptuous indeed. We will build our review on an earlier one by Jenkins (1969), who also apologizes for oversimplifying a complex problem. Jenkins puts forth three positions on the interdependence of thought and language:

1. Thought *is* language.
2. Thought depends on language.
3. Language depends on thought.

In the notation that we will be using here, these three positions can be re-written as follows:

1. L=C (language=cognition).
2. L←C (cognition depends on language).
3. L→C (language depends on cognition).

Here the directional arrow is a variant of the logical symbol for entailment.

Position 1: L=C • Jenkins suggests that the first position may well be a straw man. It is certainly difficult to find modern research from this point of view. However, Jenkins draws several citations from Watson (in McGuigan, 1966), suggesting that for the more radical early behaviorists thought is nothing more or less than internalized, subvocal speech (from "Talking and thinking," *Behaviorism*):

"What the psychologists have hitherto called thought is in short, nothing but talking to ourselves."
"We can say that 'thinking' is largely *subvocal talking . . .* provided we hasten to explain that it can occur without words."

From this rather extreme point of view, it would be useless to discuss distinctions and determinacies between thought and language, since thought is merely language to oneself. There is even a certain amount of support for this claim, insofar as thought (as reported by subjects) is often accompanied by measurable electromuscular readings (EMG) from the mouth and vocal tract area. Nevertheless, few researchers today would accept the strong version of Watson's hypothesis.

We can, however, accord Position 1 a goodsized crowd of supporters if we extend it to cover writers who find the entire enterprise of language–thought analysis a useless one. If one does not admit that thought and language are in any way separate, distinguishable domains—at least in any empirically meaningful way—then Position 1 (L=C) might be acceptable as a formal statement of that belief. As we approach several thousand plausible models of language–thought–social interactions, this position may become increasingly attractive to some readers.

Position 2: L←C • According to Jenkins, Position 2 characterizes several different lines of research in psychology. In particular, he attributes this position to much of Soviet psychology, based on Pavlov's (1927) notion of the "second signal system." Most Americans are familiar with Pavlov's work on the "primary signal system," the principles of conditioning and establishment of US–CS bonds that characterize learning in organisms up and down the phylogenetic scale. To explain the great differences in learning between human beings and lower organisms, however, Pavlov postulated another, qualitatively different mechanism: human language serves as a second signal system which can control and regulate the signals from the primary system. In a sense, language furnishes a sort of lightweight, efficient control mechanism which can be corrected more easily—and with less serious risk—than the complete motor reflex system. In a series of experiments, Luria (1961) demonstrated that motor responses in children gradually come to be controlled by the second signal system. As their language develops, their management of various responses changes from slow acquisition and extinction (typical of conditioning in infrahumans) to rapid change in accordance with explicit verbal rules. From that point on, language, which in turn receives its structure from social reality, is the master system that controls and regulates all other internal and external responses.

Jenkins also places the work of the American anthropologist Benjamin Whorf in this category. According to the so-called strong Whorfian hypothesis, the particular language of a given community determines both logical and perceptual processes in individual members of that community. In short, the individual will actually *see* reality according to the categories of his language. Hence, if his language has no color terms to distinguish blue and green, he will not experience the two as categorically different colors. A summary of Whorf's position can be found in Carroll (1956). Discussions of his work and reports on experiments on the strong Whorfian hypothesis are again in Lenneberg (1953), Brown (1958), Hymes (1964), and virtually any introductory text on linguistic anthropology. Research on the strong version of Whorf's hypothesis has generally been disappointing. It is indeed true that native speakers will classify objects and events along lines predictable from their grammar and lexicon. However, when asked to sort objects according to dimensions not coded in their language, they are almost invariably capable of doing so. For example, Greenfield and Childs (in press) report that Chiapas weavers tend not to distinguish between reds, oranges, and pinks in weaving their traditional red-and-white patterns. And yet, when asked to sort red, orange, and pink stimuli into separate piles, they can carry out the task with little difficulty, despite the fact that their language has only one color term for the three distinctions. Greenfield concludes that the color distinction is perceptible for Chiapas speakers, but is simply not considered important.

Hence the lexicon and/or grammar of a language do not directly affect perception. But they can affect the relative weights given to various perceptual distinctions, by calling attention to some and neglecting others. Furthermore, Brown and Lenneberg (1954) and Lenneberg and Roberts (1956) note that memory for categories that can be coded linguistically is superior to memory for categories that cannot be labeled. These results have been summarized with the "codability hypothesis," a weak version of Whorf's position suggesting that language (*a*) facilitates perception by calling attention to distinctions that are important to the community, and (*b*) facilitates memory by providing a code for storage and recall of a given experience.

Position 2 also characterizes a tradition in language philosophy (not treated in Jenkins' review), including work by Russell (1905) and Carnap (1942). The assumption by philosophers in this area is that logical processes depend on adequate and correct use of language. Furthermore, insofar as thought depends on language, the analysis of language should yield the less accessible categories of thought. As we shall see shortly, there is another tradition in structural anthropology which also assumes that the analysis of language will yield isomorphic cognitive–cultural categories. But within this second anthropological tradition, the isomorphism is assumed to result from Position 3, the dependence of language on thought (Levi-Strauss, 1963).

Position 3: L→C • If we restrict ourselves to the three approaches outlined by Jenkins, Position 3 will characterize most of the recent research on child language, including our own. Jenkins suggests that this position occupies the popular "middle ground" in psychology, uniting theories that are in other respects quite different from one another.

First of all, a number of researchers have recommended studying the most important products of the mind, in order to discover the principles of the mind itself. Wundt (1892) suggested that the psychology of a people, or "folk psychology," could be determined by examining their social products, particularly language. Jenkins cites Dunlap (1934) in this regard, as follows:

"In studying the structure of the language of a people, we are studying the forms and methods of their thinking. In studying their vocabulary, we are finding their types of discrimination. The description of a language as the crystallized thought of a people, is far from wrong."

This view is, in a sense, a reverse of Whorf's position. Within anthropology, as we mentioned above, the work of Levi-Strauss (1963) and a number of structural or "cognitive" anthropologists (e.g., Tyler, 1969) makes the same assumption that thought determines the structure of language, so that an analysis of language will yield categories of thought. On the one hand, anthropologists engaged in such enterprise were particularly interested in cultural cognitive patterns that were unique to a given people. Hence a study of the kinship language in a given community should yield the cognitive categories of kinship for that people, a study of local botanical terminology could result in an "ethnobotany," and so forth. However, Levi-Strauss is quite explicit in claiming that, regardless of the particular categories chosen by a given community, the ways in which those categories are combined are determined by the universal characteristics of human logic.

According to Jenkins, the work of Osgood (e.g., Osgood, Suci, & Tannenbaum, 1957) and a number of other verbal mediation theorists belongs in this camp. Osgood describes verbal labels as a class of responses that are "attached to" experiences acquired through nonverbal channels. Hence, for a given individual, language receives most of its organization through a sort of grafting onto previous learning. This does not mean, of course, that the acquisition of verbal responses has no effect on consequent learning and experience. However, for Osgood the dependency between language and nonlinguistic experience is primarily one in which nonverbal experience determines verbal learning. Other verbal mediationists, for example, the Kendlers (Kendler & Kendler, 1959), tend toward the opposite position, stressing instead the qualitative differences in learning in children who have acquired verbal labels. Unlike Osgood, the Kendlers are perhaps closer to the position outlined by Pavlov and Luria, in which language becomes the "master system" controlling lower-order behaviors.

Jenkins also includes the work of Jean Piaget and his associates in Position 3, noting in particular Piaget's contention that language is a subsystem within a broader symbolic capacity. That symbolic capacity in turn depends on the development of sensorimotor intelligence, before speech. Even after language is acquired, the course of cognitive development (at least through concrete operations) depends primarily on successive reorganizations of action schemes that are in no way derived from linguistic categories. It is indeed true that Piagetians have continually opposed the "Carnapian" view that thought is derived from language. Sinclair (1969) has demonstrated that training in the linguistic terms used in concrete operational tasks (e.g., "more" vs. "less") does not improve performance on those tasks. Furth (1966) has summarized a great deal of research on cognitive capacities in the deaf, concluding that individuals who are deprived of anything resembling normal language learning can still perform at high levels on a broad range of cognitive tasks, including Piaget's concrete operations tasks. As a result, Piaget has been interpreted by many researchers as concluding (a) language depends on cognitive development, and (b) performance on cognitive tasks should precede performance on linguistic tasks appropriate to the same cognitive level. As we analyze Piaget's stand a little more closely in this chapter, we will suggest another model that more accurately describes a Piagetian approach to language development. In particular, we shall see that prediction (b) does not hold. However, certainly if we are restricted to the three positions outlined above, Piaget does belong in Position 3.

On the basis of his three-way analysis, Jenkins concludes with the inevitable item on multiple-choice tests, "all of the above":

"Thought *does* depend on language to the extent that it uses that subsystem of its much more extensive and complex machinery."

"Thought *is* language to the extent that natural language is a universal meta-language that can in principle capture any nuance of thought in any domain whatsoever."

"Language *does* depend on thought to the extent that it is one manifestation of the general universal rule system that governs all thought and to the extent that it uses inputs and constructs from all other systems operating under the general guidance of the universal system."

It is almost always more correct to choose gray when one is presented with black versus white. This is particularly true insofar as the above three positions are extremely different from one another. However, we feel that the three models presented thus far do not exhaust the logically plausible models for language–thought relations. In fact, we are about to suggest three more:

4. Language and cognition are interacting but independently derived systems:

$$L \quad C$$
$$\downarrow \quad \downarrow$$

5. Language and cognition are both derived—logically and ontogenetically—from a third system (homologue model):

$$L \quad C$$
$$\searrow \quad \swarrow$$
$$O$$

6. Language and cognition develop along parallel lines, in an isomorphic sequence of complexity, not because of a shared source but because of constraints inherent in the nature of all such complex systems (analogue model):

$$L \quad C$$
$$\hookleftarrow \quad \hookleftarrow$$

Although these three positions tend to be implicit rather than explicit in a number of recent writings, we can identify each with a corresponding line of research. Furthermore, these positions yield very different predictions for developmental research. In certain cases, the empirical consequences involve qualitative rather than quantitative analysis. We are, then, willing to accept as data a clear demonstration that two systems have a qualitatively similar structure.

Position 4: L   C • Position 4 is essentially a claim that language and cog-
$$\downarrow \quad \downarrow$$
nition have independent sources and sequences in development. Obviously the two systems are designed for eventual interaction, insofar as language will be used to encode thoughts. This does not necessarily mean, however,

that one is *derived* from the other. It is difficult to find a linguist or psycholinguist who states categorically that language and cognition follow independent courses of development. Nevertheless, most of the early (i.e., 1960–1968) research on the acquisition of syntax implies such a position. As Bates (1973) has stated elsewhere, the acceptance of a Chomskian grammar as a psychologically real model of language inevitably resulted in the position that language and cognition could not be derived ontogenetically from one another. Chomsky's insistence on an autonomous syntactic component that contributes the primary structural relations among sentence parts resulted in an assumption that children could not possibly derive or invent grammar by using heuristics from their knowledge of cognitive–semantic relations. Again, Chomsky himself did not categorically state that this would be impossible. In *Language and mind* (1968), he specifies that linguistics should be viewed as a subfield of cognitive psychology. And yet the very nature of a transformational grammar made it difficult to conceive of a developmental course in which language derives from cognition.

The resulting view was a rationalist, nativist view of mental development, in which both linguistic structures and cognitive structures arise independently out of a species-specific genetic program. Chomsky implied that the formal and substantive universals of syntax (i.e., knowledge that language is made up of deep structures, surface structures, and transformations, plus knowledge of the primary syntactic categories) are the best candidates for innate linguistic universals. McNeill (1966, 1970) has made this position explicit in several articles. However, in McNeill (1971) a modified position is presented, in which some linguistic universals derive from cognition and some do not. McNeill introduces the concept of "strong" versus "weak" linguistic universals. A weak universal is one for which cognition is a necessary *and* sufficient condition for development. In other words, given certain general, nonlinguistic categories and problem-solving strategies, the application of those cognitive structures to language learning will inevitably result in the discovery of universal linguistic principles. A strong linguistic universal is one for which cognition is a necessary, but *not* a sufficient, condition. Semantic categories and problem-solving strategies alone will not yield certain linguistic categories. Instead, some sort of innate knowledge of the structure of language itself is necessary for the discovery of strong universals. This position could be viewed as a mixture of Position 3 and Position 4, such that language is partially dependent on cognition, but must also have inputs from an independent, language-specific source. This mixed position could be formalized as

$$L \rightarrow C$$
$$\downarrow \quad \downarrow$$

We can, then, combine the models outlined thus far to describe mixed positions (an exception would be Position 1, which refuses to recognize a distinction between language and cognition and hence is logically incompatible with Positions 2 to 4). This is a particularly useful trick for describing the positions of theorists who change directionality at different developmental stages. For example, Vygotsky (1962) has presented a unique mixed position, halfway between the Soviet model characterized by Position 2, and Position 4 on independent sources in development. For Vygotsky, language and what he refers to as "tool thought" initially follow separate developmental courses, in the sense that one is in no way derived from or in control of the other. Somewhere between 3 and 6 years, the child's speech to himself becomes increasingly indistinct and abbreviated until it is completely "internalized." This abbreviated and unexpressed "inner speech" then serves to regulate and guide thought throughout the rest of life, as the kind of lightweight "master system" described by Pavlov and Luria. Hence, for Vygotsky, the period from 0 to 6 years is perhaps best expressed by Position 4. From age 6 onward, however, the relationship between language and thought is better expressed by Position 2. We could formulate this mixed view as.

$$L \leftarrow C$$
$$\downarrow \quad \downarrow$$

It might even be possible to describe Piaget with a mixture of Positions 2 to 4 across developmental stages. At least through the stage of concrete operations, it is indeed the case that Piaget does not recognize particular dependence of thought on language. However, Piaget and Inhelder (1969) suggest that attainment of formal operations may depend crucially on an ability to express thoughts in linguistic propositions. Hence, with the models presented so far, we could characterize Piaget's position on development from 0 to 12 years with Position 3. However, after 12 years of age cognitive development depends on the attainment of language, and hence could be described with a bidirectional mixture of Positions 2 and 3, formalized as

$$L \leftrightarrow C$$

As we shall see shortly, however, Piaget's views are better described with a model closer to Position 5.

Finally, Lenneberg (1967) is often cited as a proponent of the view that language has its own independent genetic source in development. It is indeed true that Lennenberg has amassed impressive evidence for a biological foundation of some sort underlying the species-specific human capacity for language. However, it is less clear that he sees the biological basis of language as a source independent of species-specific, human cognition. In fact, a number of passages in his 1967 book suggest the view that language is derived from broader nonlinguistic cognitive capacities:

"Language is the manifestation of species-specific cognitive propensities. . . .

There is evidence that cognitive function is a more basic and primary process than language, and that the dependence-relationship of language upon cognition is incomparably stronger than vice-versa." (p. 374)

Also, Lenneberg places greater stress on the innate basis of primarily semantic structures in language, pointing out the continuity between the ability to categorize events in words and general perceptual processing in higher species:

"The cognitive function underlying language consists of an adaptation of a ubiquitous process (among vertebrates) of categorization and extraction of similarities. The perception and production of language may be reduced on all levels to categorization processes, including the subsuming of narrow categories under more comprehensive ones and the subdivision of comprehensive categories into more specific ones." (p. 374)

Even with regard to the nonsemantic, syntactic phenomena described by Chomsky as "formal linguistic universals," Lenneberg suggests that syntactic structures are also manifestations of broader cognitive–perceptual processes:

"The characteristics of phrase–structure (as described by phrase-markers) appear as the natural outcome of an application of the differentiation principle to the acoustic patterns. Also, the transformational principle in language appears to be virtually identical with the cognitive principles that underlie the ability to categorize both the patterns of the environment and the patterns produced by our own movements." (p. 325)

It may, then, be a distortion of Lenneberg's views to place him under Position 4. Indeed, the foregoing quotations indicate a view that could almost be described with Position 3, the complete dependence of language on cognitive development (albeit innate cognition). The last quotation, on the nature of phrase-markers and transformations, sounds very much like an argument for weak linguistic universals. A conservative approach might be to classify Lenneberg with a mixture of Positions 3 and 4, as we did above with McNeill's strong linguistic universals. However, a still better approach would be to proceed to the next two, somewhat more subtle models of language–thought relations. It may well prove to be the case that both Piaget and Lenneberg are best described with Position 5, in which both language and cognition derive from a third, more general source.

Position 5: (Homologous Structures): L   C • Position 5 will cover any

$$L \searrow \quad \swarrow C$$
$$O$$

view in which the two systems under discussion are derived from the same third, separate source. For example, a number of theorists (see Greene, 1973) have suggested that cognition, perception, language, and other higher functions are ultimately derived from and/or mapped onto the more basic and primitive system of motor coordinates. This is tantamount to a claim that all higher functions have evolved in the service of motor behaviors or actions-in-the-world, and hence can be described with logical structures isomorphic with action schemes or procedures (see Hewitt, 1973, on "actor" as the basic unit of complex systems). At the risk of gross oversimplification, we might formalize this view with regard to language and cognition as

$$
\begin{array}{cc}
L & C \\
\searrow & \swarrow \\
& M
\end{array}
$$

in which M stands for a structured motor system.

Lenneberg stresses the role of categorization and extraction of properties in the evolution of human cognition and language. In a sense, then, both these systems depend on and are in some way derivable from the nature of perceptual processing in higher vertebrates. We could formalize this position as

$$
\begin{array}{cc}
L & C \\
\searrow & \swarrow \\
& P
\end{array}
$$

in which P represents the perceptual system, considered in its broadest possible sense.

Another version of Position 5 can also be attributed to Pascual-Leone's neo-Piagetion approach (Pascual-Leone, 1970). Pascual-Leone suggests that the progressive, qualitative reorganizations that characterize Piaget's stages are based, at least in part, on a series of quantitative increases in information-processing capacity. This analysis recalls discussions in the adult literature of "chunking" (e.g., Miller, 1970), a peculiar characteristic of short-term memory by which only 7 ± 2 units of information can be handled at a given moment. The particular content or nature of these units is virtually unspecified in the theory. If the adult can find some way to "chunk" a series of units of information together—almost any way will do—he can handle the entire information array as one unit in the limit of seven during a given moment in processing. Olson (1973) has also discussed possible effects of chunking on the development of language and memory. Pascual-Leone has, however, offered the strongest case concerning the relationship between increases in "central computing space" and consequent resegmentations and reorganizations of knowledge as represented in Piaget's stage theory. Presumably this shift in information-processing capacity will affect both language and nonlinguistic processing. Hence we could formalize Pascual-Leone's proposal with the notation used here as

$$
\begin{array}{cc}
L & C \\
\searrow & \swarrow \\
& I
\end{array}
$$

in which I stands for general information-processing constraints.

As noted earlier, Piaget is often interpreted according to Position 3, in which language derives from cognition. In one sense, this is an accurate interpretation, depending on how one defines cognition. Unfortunately, many readers interpret "cognition" to include not only an underlying logical system, but also the set of behaviours in what are traditionally called *cognitive tasks*. Hence, when Brown (1973) suggests that object permanence is a cognitive prerequisite for language, he presumably means that a child who is ready for language should be able to perform on tasks in which an object is hidden behind a screen, and so forth.

Taking Position 3 quite literally, we are justified in predicting that a stage 5 or 6 "cognitive behavior" should appear before a stage 5 or 6 "communicative behavior." Such predictions are easily confirmed or disconfirmed with developmental data on order of acquisition. Hence this theory is attractive on empirical grounds. However, it is *not* an adequate characterization of Piaget's view of cognitive development, and hence should not be adopted by researchers professing an interest in "Piagetian psycholinguistics."

Piaget divides every knowing act into two conceptually distinct (though empirically inseparable) aspects: assimilation and accommodation. To the degree that a child can carry out a prepared action scheme successfully (e.g., grasping a cup or sucking a nipple), he has assimilated reality to that action scheme. To the degree to which he must change his scheme to conform to reality (e.g., reshaping his grasp or changing the shape of his mouth in sucking), he has accommodated his schemes to reality. Certain aspects of the child's movements and actions on the world are of a highly generalizable nature, that is, they will work on virtually any kind of content. Examples are displacement, reversals, and substitution. Other aspects are more content specific and cannot generalize across a wide class of contents. Piaget suggests that the more assimilative, generalizable schemes or portions of schemes, through their gradual equilibration and reorganization with one another, form the basis for the development of logic. He applies the term *operative knowing* to those features of schemes (e.g., reversibility, transitivity) that are generalizable across contents. The development of the various logical stages results primarily from successive reorganizations of operative knowledge. The other, more content-specific aspects of schemes—those that must accommodate from one knowing act to another—are referred to as *figurative knowing*. Our knowledge of physical (and social) objects, as opposed to physical relationships, consists primarily of stable clusters of figurative schemes. Hence the set of perceptual and motor interactions that one consistently carries out with bottles leads to a perceptual–motor "bottle schema."

Some figurative schemes are more generalizable than others, leading to the "extraction of attributes" uniting classes of objects. The latter kind of figurative experience can in turn feed back onto the operative system, aiding in the establishment of a content-free, concrete operational capacity for classification, seriation, and so forth. Hence there is a continual interplay between figurative and operative knowing, with the two exerting influence on one another. Indeed, it might be more accurate to speak of these "components" as opposite poles on a continuum, from content-specific to content-free knowing. Nevertheless, according to Piaget, the major stages in intellectual development are defined primarily in terms of operative knowledge. Figurative knowledge increases gradually across time, but does not go through the kind of qualitative reorganization typical of operative progression through stages.

In regard to the problem at hand in this chapter, every behavior, including behavior on so-called pure cognitive tasks, has both figurative and operative aspects. We cannot observe operative knowing without figurative content. And yet our hypothetical stages are based on the operative characteristics of the child's knowledge across a given period of time. *Performance on object permanence or conversation tasks does not yield "pure cognition" any more than does performance on linguistic tasks.* Language is one figurative domain to which operative knowing is applied. Interactions with physical objects form yet another domain in which we can observe and infer the presence of operative schemes. There may be a temporal "decalage" such that the operative schemes of one stage are worked out in one figurative domain before they are worked out in another. But there is no a priori reason why a given stage should be achieved in one domain before it is achieved in another. In some instances, the materials of one domain may be in some way inherently more "resistant," so that it is more difficult for the child to work through operative relations. Hence performance in this domain will follow performance in others. In other cases, however, the decalage may be a function of a given child's particular motivation and/or experience with a given class of events.

It should be possible to build positive predictions about decalage between figurative domains into a theory of cognitive, linguistic, and social development. We will say more about this shortly. Nevertheless, for present purposes we can conclude that cognitive development (in the sense of performance on cognitive tasks) is related to language development insofar as the two domains are dependent on operative principles common to the two. Using the notation adopted here, we can formalize this more precise Piagetian position on language and cognitive development as follows:

$$L \quad C_f$$
$$\searrow \swarrow$$
$$O$$

in which C_f stands for performance on cognitive tasks, including figurative content in interactions with physical objects, and O stands for operative principles at a given developmental stage. Since figurative experience can feed back onto the developing operative system, it might be more accurate to make the arrows bidirectional. However, in studies in which we are trying to characterize the developmental stage at which particular communicative events take place, we are interested primarily in the dependence of language and cognitive performance on the postulated operative structure.

We should note here that the figurative–operative distinction becomes an empty claim if the horizontal decalage between two manifestations of the same hypothetical structure becomes indefinitely wide. For example, if children demonstrate stage 5 tool use several months before supposed stage 5 communication begins, what right do we have to interpret these two developments as applications of the same operative structure? In the straightforward "cognitive prerequisite" model (Position 3), where "pure cognition" as measured in "pure" cognitive tasks is invariably supposed to precede the same level of linguistic or social cognition, all claims are subject to disconfirmation. In the more sophisticated cognitive model outlined in Position 5, the "prerequisite" for both social and nonsocial behaviors is an unobservable operative structure. Hence our claims are far more difficult to confirm or to disconfirm. We can only predict that the various manifestations of a purported underlying structure should appear in *roughly* the same age range. Furthermore, within each domain the sequence of developments should be parallel (e.g., "mother permanence" with one screen should precede "mother permanence" with two screens, just as "object permanence" with one screen precedes "object permanence" with two screens). The ordinal relations *within* domains are easy enough to establish. But who is to determine the range beyond which a claim of interdependence in two domains is no longer useful? We must make an arbitrary decision that 2 weeks or 2 months or 2 years of decalage is enough to weaken the explanatory power of our figurative–operative interpretation. In other words, we can "prove" (or at least disprove) ordinal relations within domains, but we cannot incontrovertibly establish a dependence between domains.

There are ways of demonstrating at least some statistical support for a claim of linguistic–cognitive interdependence. According to the figurative–operative model, operative schemes develop through procedures carried out on various figurative "objects." If a child can successfully understand a given relationship or operation on one set of materials, he should have greater success on the next set of materials, since his operative schemes will be more stable. There should, then, be transfer from one domain to another, as the operative schemes improve with each successful application. Hence a child who successfully completes a development in the social or linguistic realm should arrive at the nonsocial version earlier than a child who has not yet worked the relationship through at all. Similarly, success in the non-social realm should contribute to success in interactions with social objects. We can, then, predict that across a sample of children there should be correlations in age of onset and level of performance for social, linguistic, and cognitive content areas with regard to a given operative "stage."

There are problems with this suggestion as well, however. How do we know that such a correlation is the product of a structural dependence? Suppose it is simply the case that precocious babies do everything earlier than do nonprecocious babies. Insofar as this is true, about the only underlying structure we can talk about is an ephemeral Spearman's *g*, or general intelligence. One way out of this difficulty is to administer a battery of cognitive and social-communicative tasks. Presumably, by factoring out the contribution of "general precocity," we can derive a pattern of correlations in which some cognitive tasks are better predictors of social-communicative development than others. It is the pattern of relations, and not the overall level of the correlations, that can tell us the most about structural interdependencies in various domains. We will return to this point later.

We are not advocating a "shotgun correlational approach" to cognitive development in various domains. Presumably, our developmental theories tell us which tasks *should* be related to one another on structural grounds, and which tasks should not. The various tasks that we include in our battery should be determined by predictions about the nature of social, linguistic, and cognitive development, and the operative structures that should be shared by the various figurative realms.

To summarize thus far, empirical support for Position 5 on the relationship between language and cognition can be obtained through four kinds of correlation or coincidence:

1. Logical correlation, that is, structural analyses pointing out precisely why, on qualitative theoretical grounds, we should expect two behaviors to be related to a central structure (an example is our analysis of tool use in stage 5 communication, in which the use of an object to obtain another object is structurally related to the use of an adult to obtain an object or an object to obtain an adult).

2. The appearance of social, linguistic, and cognitive manifestations of a postulated structure in roughly the same age range, regardless of the order in which these manifestations appear.

3. Demonstration of transfer from one realm to another, through correlations between time of onset and level of performance in one domain with time of onset and level of performance in another, across a sample of children.

4. Patterns of intercorrelation in which, regardless of the general strength

or level of various correlations, some tasks are better predictors of one another than others.

In addition, a theory of physical versus social manifestations of an operation is strengthened if we can predict the order of acquisition of each in terms either of the inherent difficulty of the material or of the motivation and experience of particular children. In this way, the concept of decalage becomes a positive prediction, rather than a post hoc means of explaining away age differences in onset.

Position 5 does, then, have certain empirical consequences. It is not so easily disconfirmed as Positions 2 and 3, and the model can at least be supported with both quantitative and qualitative data. Suppose, however, that we can point out convincing, qualitative isomorphisms in development in the linguistic versus nonlinguistic realm. Suppose, furthermore, that the sequence of developments in one domain is identical to that in another, with regard to levels of operative complexity. And yet we find absolutely no quantitative support for interdependence between the two realms; that is, performance on linguistic tasks simply does not correlate across a sample of children with performance on nonlinguistic tasks. What do we conclude? Must we return to Position 4, wherein language and cognitive development derive from separate sources? This would indeed be one solution, if we are willing to trust our qualitative analysis alone. And yet it is difficult to ignore what we perceive to be strikingly parallel structures in two seemingly separate areas of function. This brings us to a problem that is critical in all sciences that try to reconstruct histories, sequences, and processes on the basis of similar end points, including behavioral biology or ethology, diachronic linguistics, and physical anthropology. This is the problem of "homologous" versus "analogous" derivation of structures.

Position 6 (Analogous Structures): $L \quad C$ • Position 6, which we will define

shortly as the "analogue" position, characterizes the research of a number of psychologists who are strongly influenced by the Piagetian approach but do not accept certain central notions concerning the nature of stages. In particular, many of these researchers (e.g., Carey, 1974; Bruner, Olver, & Greenfield, 1966; Fischer, 1975) reject Piaget's concepts of horizontal and vertical decalage. If two developments are separated in time by several years, and yet can be interpreted as manifestations of the same underlying structure, Piaget still in many instances insists that these developments form part of a given operative stage. As Flavell (1971) notes in a review of stage theories, the concept of stage was introduced to describe the essential unity and similarity of developmental events within a given time period. If structurally similar events are separated widely across development whereas structurally dissimilar events co-occur in time, the concept of stage—at least as it is used to characterize a single child—becomes meaningless. We could say that the child is at stage X with regard to one skill while at stage Y with regard to another. But there is no need to posit a single operative level to characterize the child's functioning across domains. These critics feel that the concept of decalage, as used by Piaget is a meaningless label applied to salvage a concept of stage which has lost its usefulness.

However, most of these critics do accept the notion of qualitative re-organizations and increases in complexity within domains. Hence the notion of stage is useful for the description of skill-specific developments. Within such an approach, the figurative–operative distinction outlined above would be abandoned in favor of a unified analysis of organization and changes in organization across time within a given area of functioning. Since there is no single, unifying operative component, there is no reason to predict correlations in performance and age of onset between areas.

This need not necessarily mean that the sequence and pattern of development within a domain like language bear no relation to the sequence and pattern of development within nonlinguistic domains. Because of certain structural principles inherent in all complex systems (see, e.g., Buckley, 1967, or Simon, 1969), the construction of such systems in time will follow an inevitable logical order. Hence we can have an isomorphism in structure and sequence within language and cognition, respectively, without any sort of transfer of skill between the two systems. The two could in principle develop at very different points in time. Simon illustrates this system-theoretical approach to development with the metaphor of the soap bubble. In virtually all natural circumstances, bubbles are round. And yet it is pointless to ask where the "roundness" came from. The spherical structure of bubbles is not inherent in either the water, the soap, or that air that make up the end product. Rather, it is the only possible situation to achieving maximum volume with minimum surface. Every time an effort is made to do that, something perceivable as a sphere will inevitably result. The structure is inherent in the nature of the interaction itself, and not in the inputs to that interaction. Hence, according to Position 6, language and cognition might go through logically similar sequences of development, *not* because of some shared input, but because of the nature of problem solving in complex systems.

The distinction between Positions 5 and 6 is related to a problem often encountered both in ethology and in cultural anthropology (Hess, 1970; Eibl-Eiblesfeldt, 1970). A homologue is a structural similarity between diverse species or cultures which is the result of a common origin. All birds have wings (in some cases even vestigial, useless wings) because they are descended from a common genetic line. In Indo-European languages, the words for "mother" (*mere, madre, mutter,* etc.) resemble one another because the languages derive from the same historic roots. An analogue, on the other hand, is a structural similarity between species or cultures which is the result of adaptation to similar problems, without necessitating a common historical origin. Each species or society or individual organism "reinvents" the solution because it is the most efficient adaptation to a common circumstance. Hence any species adapting to a water habitat will have to "invent" or evolve means of locomotion appropriate to water (e.g., fins, webbed feet). Eibl-Eiblesfeldt points out several cases in which what was previously thought to be a homologue turned out instead to be derivable by analogue. The manner of drinking used by pigeons, sand grouse, and pin-tailed sand grouse (i.e., immersing the beak and sucking up the water) was initially interpreted as a homologue, and hence contributed to the belief that sand grouse and pigeons are closely related phylogenetically. However, Wickler (1961) demonstrated that a similar mode of drinking was rapidly invented in analogous fashion by grassfinches and other distantly related birds adapting to arid regions. In the area of language and cognition, Position 5 involves an inference that the commonality in structure between the two systems is a homologue, the result of shared origins. Position 6 suggests instead that the similarity in structure may be an analogue, involving similar types of problem solving rather than development from a single, shared source.

Greenfield (1975) is perhaps the most noteworthy example of Position 6 on the relation between language and cognition. In the first of a series of studies on "the grammar of action," Greenfield, Nelson, and Saltzman (1972) demonstrated that between 11 and 36 months of age children go through stages in the ability to nest a set of cups. The strategies used range from a primitive approach in which the child touches one cup to the others without letting go, to an orderly nesting in sequence from smallest to largest or vice versa. Greenfield et al. then pointed out striking parallels between this sequence of developments and a sequence in language development from simple topic-comment utterances to complex embedded sentences. Although both developments are completed between 11 and 36 months, there is no effort by the authors to relate performance on nesting cups to level of linguistic development within individual children. A proponent of Position 5 might predict correlations between the two tasks. However, Greenfield feels that this issue is not central to the question of structural isomorphs in action and grammar. She stresses that a decalage could be indefinitely wide, casting serious doubts on an interpretation in terms of single, unifying stages. She is, then, interested primarily in establishing qualitative similarities between domains, and isomorphism in the sequence of development within various domains. This stand becomes still clearer in the next series of studies on action grammar (e.g., Goodson & Greenfield,

1975; Greenfield & Westerman, 1973; Greenfield & Schneider, 1975). In these studies, the authors demonstrate structural parallels between sentence embedding in language development and the sequence of strategies used by 7- to 11-year-old children in building a hierarchically arranged mobile. In both tasks, the problem of interrupting center-embedded structures determines the sequence of complexity among various strategies for solving the problem. And yet, in the case of language, children manage to solve the problem of center embedding by 5 years of age, whereas in the mobile-construction task only 9- to 11-year-old children arrive at the difficult strategy of interrupting nested structures. Obviously, then, the "structure" that permits center embedding is not necessarily a characteristic of the *child* at a given age, but rather is a solution constructed at radically different ages, depending on the nature of the task. It is, then, an analogue rather than a homologue.

Some critics have rejected Greenfield's approach, precisely because her data yield only ordinal relations within domains and structural parallels between domains, without any demonstration of correlation between systems in individual children. The approach is clearly not "quantitative" in any traditional sense. However, in view of the nature of Greenfield's theory, there is no reason why correlational data would be appropriate. When a particular child "discovers" or constructs a strategy for solving a given problem, there is a sense in which the capacity for that strategy is "in" the child. Otherwise, we would not be able to explain why 9-year-olds do better than 7-year-olds on exactly the same task. And yet, since some materials do not yield a given strategy or structured solution to 7-year-olds whereas other materials do, there is also a sense in which the various solutions and their sequence are "in" the materials. However, if asked to state just *where* these various structures and strategies are across children and across tasks, we would have to conclude that they are emergents that exist only when the organism is interacting with materials. Their discovery in a given logical sequence is inevitable, and yet it is not a characteristic of either the child or the environment. Hence there is no reason why we should predict that a given child will consistently discover the same kinds of structures at a given age.

The distinction between homologous and analogous developments (i.e., Positions 5 and 6) is problematic for several of the chapters included in this volume. For example, Sander (Chapter 6), and Lewis and Cherry (Chapter 10) have pointed out parallels between the "social grammar" of early mother–child interaction and later patterns in verbal interaction. Marler (Chapter 4), and Gill and Rumbaugh (Chapter 5) have noted similarities in communicative systems between human beings and nonhuman species. All of these imply that a similarity in structure between two systems (i.e. an analogy) is equivalent to an interdependence between those two systems (i.e. an homology). The two positions are, however, logically and empirically distinct. This is precisely the problem that we have faced in our research on cognition and communication in infancy. We are, at this point, still working from Position 5, predicting transfer between domains, within individual children, as a function of some general operative developments that characterize the child's functioning at a given stage. However, the skill-specific, analogue approach to structural development may be the best option open to us if our efforts to demonstrate correlations between domains fail.

Let us briefly summarize the 6 positions described above and the kinds of predictions that each one yields for our study. Then we will go on to a discussion of the three-way interrelations of cognition, social development, and language according to the same six models.

First, Position 1 ($L=C$) reduces to a claim that there is no difference between language and thought. The two are equivalent or, at the very least, empirically inseparable. Hence Position 1 offers no predictions for our cross-sectional study of relations between cognition and communicative development, except perhaps a general prediction that the whole effort will fail.

Position 2 ($L \leftarrow C$) is a statement of the dependence of thought on language. In general, Position 2 is refuted by evidence for adequate cognitive functioning in the absence of language, for example, Furth's study of cognition in deaf children and adults. For our study, Position 2 might predict that the capacity for mental representation (e.g., performance on the invisible displacements items on the object permanence task) will not develop until some minimal linguistic capacity is established. Position 2 would be refuted by evidence of mental representation in infants before the appearance of speech.

Position 3 ($L \rightarrow C$) is a statement of the dependence of language on cognitive development, including cognitive behaviors appropriate to a given stage. Hence we would predict for our study that the capacity for language should in all instances be preceded by manifestations of a more general symbolic capacity, including symbolic play and mental representation in invisible displacement tasks. Position 3 would be refuted by evidence that some children begin speaking before they show nonverbal manifestations of Piaget's stage 6.

Position 4 ($L \quad C$) holds that language and cognition derive from inde-
$\quad\quad\quad\quad\quad\downarrow \quad\downarrow$
pendent sources and follow independent courses of development, even though the two systems may interact. The strongest version of this position is implicit in the work of Chomsky, who has suggested that certain universal,

meaning-free syntactic categories and relations may have independent, species-specific genetic bases. In certain respects, the predictions from Position 4 relevant to our study are similar to the global predictions from Position 1—namely, that the enterprise of establishing interdependency between language and cognition is unlikely to be successful. For the mixed, strong linguistic universals position proposed by McNeill, cognition is a necessary but not sufficient condition for the development of language. Support for this mixed position would come from demonstrations of a failure in the development of language when the necessary cognitive prerequisites are clearly present. For example, it is possible that further research on language-delayed and language-defective children may indicate that language acquisition depends not only on cognition but also on universal, language-specific developments that are missing or defective in this population. In the normal population of infants in our study, there are no clear-cut ways that we could demonstrate the presence or absence of language-specific mechanisms.

Position 5 is the model that we have tentatively adopted in our study. This is essentially a Piagetian version of Position 5, in which performances on both linguistic tasks and so-called pure cognitive tasks are dependent on underlying operative schemes shared by the two domains. In this model, we make no a priori predictions about the order in which communicative and cognitive manifestations of a given stage should appear. We predict instead that, although the order of appearance between domains may be reversed in some children, stage 5 communicative events and stage 5 cognitive events should occur in roughly the same time period across children. Similarly, referential speech and the various nonlinguistic manifestations of stage 6 should also appear in more or less the same time period, following stage 5. Where possible, we will make predictions about the sequence between cognitive and communicative events on the basis of the individual child's social environment and motivation (as measured in a set of observations on the nature of the mother–child attachment relationship). However, the primary support for our position comes from logical or structural parallels between domains, similar sequences of development within domains, rough co-occurence in time, and correlations between cognitive and communicative events across a sample of children.

Position 6, the analogue model, involves a claim that developing systems may be similar in structure and sequence, not because they depend on a third, shared source but because of constraints inherent in all complex systems. The only kind of data relevant to this position is essentially qualitative and ordinal data. Hence, on the basis of Position 6, we would make no predictions concerning correlations in onset time and level of performance for cognitive versus communicative developments. Rather, the sequence of developments within domains should be similar, and the structural nature of various stages and strategies should be isomorphic between linguistic and nonlinguistic areas. If in our follow-up study we fail to demonstrate correlations within individual children for stage 5 and stage 6 events, Position 5 will reduce to Position 6, in which only qualitative similarities have been demonstrated.

Language, Cognition, and Social Development

All six of the positions outlined above concerning the relation between language and cognition could also be applied to relations between cognition and social development. Furthermore, we could also postulate six similar models for the interdependency of social development and language. Table 1 summarizes these six models, in three domains, yielding 18 positions.

TABLE 1.   Models for the Interdependence of Language, Cognition, and Social Development

Position	A Language and Cognition	B Cognition and Social Development	C Language and Social Development
1	$L = C$	$S = C$	$S = L$
2	$L \leftarrow C$	$S \leftarrow C$	$S \leftarrow L$
3	$L \rightarrow C$	$S \rightarrow C$	$S \rightarrow L$
4	$L \downarrow \quad C \downarrow$	$S \downarrow \quad C \downarrow$	$S \downarrow \quad L \downarrow$
5	$L \quad C$ ↘ ↙ O	$S \quad C$ ↘ ↙ O	$S \quad L$ ↘ ↙ O
6	$L \hookleftarrow \quad C \hookleftarrow$	$S \hookleftarrow \quad C \hookleftarrow$	$S \hookleftarrow \quad L \hookleftarrow$

We could construct three-way models for the interdependence of language, thought, and social development by choosing one position from each column, in the ancient tradition of ordering from Chinese menus. If all the positions were equally compatible, this process would yield 6^3 or 216 possible positions on this question. As it happens, however, not all three-way combinations are logically plausible. For example, if we adopted Position 3 in language and cognition:

$$L \rightarrow C$$

and Position 2 on social–cognitive relations:

$$S \leftarrow C$$

we would have a situation in which language depends on cognition and cognition is in turn determined by social development. The simple principle of transitivity dictates that we also adopt Position 3 on the relation between language and social development, such that language depends on the social domain:

$$L \rightarrow S$$

Therefore, in choosing Position 3 from Column A and Position 2 from Column B, we are precluded from asserting Position 4 in Column C, or

$$L \quad S$$
$$\downarrow \quad \downarrow$$

in which language and social development are independent of one another in both source and sequence.

Our Chinese menu has already become a bit burdensome. But we have only begun to exhaust the various combinations. Recall our discussion of the mixed positions held by McNeill and Vygotsky. We admitted to the possibility of partial independence and partial dependence between domains. For example, McNeill has postulated the existence of strong linguistic universals, for which which cognition is a necessary but insufficient condition, that is,

$$L \rightarrow C$$
$$\downarrow \quad \downarrow$$

This position can be obtained from Table 2 by combining Models 3 and 4 from Column A. In fact, the only model which cannot logically be combined with the others from the same column is Position 1, which recognizes no separation (and hence no interdependence) between language and cognition. We could, for example, have a situation in which much of the similarity in structure between two developing systems is due, not to a shared source, but to principles inherent in systems (Position 6). However, at certain points in the development of cognition, inputs from the language domain are absolutely essential (Position 2). This combination can be formalized as

$$L \leftarrow C$$
$$\hookleftarrow \quad \hookleftarrow$$

Suppose, furthermore, that the particular aspect of language which must develop in order for the correct inputs to cognition to occur is a species-specific and genetically based "language universal", derived from no non-linguistic source. This particular situation would require an addition from Position 4, yielding the combined form

$$L \leftarrow C$$
$$\downarrow\hookleftarrow \quad \hookleftarrow$$

If we begin to pull the same complex combinations out of the other two columns, we have a situation in which virtually any combination of positions from the three areas is, at least in principle, possible. For example, returning to the instance in which language depends on cognition and cognition is in turn determined by social inputs, we do indeed have a situation in which language necessarily depends on social development (at least as mediated through cognition). However, it is not necessarily true (if we are accepting mixed positions) that Position 4 on the independence of language and social development is precluded. For certain developmental features or certain developmental stages, language and socialization may require independent sources and sequences, yielding the combined position

$$
\begin{array}{c}
L \quad S \\
\downarrow \searrow \nearrow \downarrow \\
C
\end{array}
$$

If we exclude only Position 1 in all three columns from our exhaustive combinations, we find ourselves plugging the Chinese menu into a factorial equation, yielding something in the vicinity of 32,768 models for the interdependencies that hold among language, thought, and social development.

We could, of course, make our life's work out of Table 1, writing a computer program that would yield a fat matrix of notational combinations, and working out a way in which each combination could be meaningful. We could, for example, spend a sabbatical year staring at the model

and finding ways to test it out empirically. Hopefully, however, the point of this exercise is clear without resorting to computer printouts full of arrows and coiled springs. Many researchers (ourselves included) have been quite vague and imprecise in using the term *prerequisite*, as though the kind of interdependence it implies were straightforward and obvious. Instead, we find on more careful consideration that the number of possible models for the interdependence of these three systems is astronomically high. At the very least, we have now learned to be more specific in our future uses of the word *prerequisite*, pointing out precisely the kind of interdependence we are predicting and the kind of data that are relevant to that effort.

There are other conclusions that are also tempting. We could, among other things, conclude that the entire enterprise is ill fated, and that we shouldn't have postulated interdependence of systems in the first place. This becomes a particularly attractive solution when we also realize that there are other possible systems (e.g., perception) that may also impinge on the various relationships in Table 1. Consider the whole effort after Jenkins, as an enormous multiple-choice question, with 32,768 possible responses, to which the correct answer is "all of the above."

We have indeed considered that solution. However, in abandoning any effort at model building and attribution of causality, we would also have reduced our research to the kind of atheoretical description that, if only on aesthetic grounds, we do not find interesting. Although the number of models open to us is enormous, many (but not all) of them differ from one another in very interesting and meaningful ways. Indeed, many important and influential works in developmental theory have, at least implicitly, based their predictions on one of these models. To illustrate, let us return briefly to Table 1 and consider some of the more interesting permutations involving social development and cognition.

1. Position 1 ($S=C$) suggests that the two are inseparable realms, so that we can posit neither dependence nor independence. Since this position has been used to characterize all those who criticize making this effort in the first place, we should have no trouble filling this category with exponents. It might be more difficult, however, to find writers who would take a position parallel to Watson's position that thought *is* internalized language, so that thought is equated with internalized social interactions. However, something vaguely like an equation between the two can be found in the writing of symbolic interactionists (e.g., Mead, 1934), who suggest that the categories of thought and language are emergents from social exchange among human beings.

2. Position 2 ($S \leftarrow C$) includes all claims that cognition depends on and/ or derives from social-affective development and social-motivation. It seems quite fair to categorize the classical Freudian position on ego development here, insofar as the ego (equated by various writers with "consciousness," "rational processes," and "cognition") develops at the interface between id impulses and harsh environmental realities. Hence the course of cognitive development is viewed as the product of efforts to fulfill social and affective needs.

3. Position 3 ($S \rightarrow C$) is the model for social–cognitive development most often attributed to Piaget. This model predicts that "pure" cognition will first be established in interactions with nonsocial objects. When the particular cognitive scheme becomes relatively stable, it can then be applied to the social realm. This position is implicit in some of Kohlberg's (1969) writings on the development of moral reasoning, and the view of Flavell, Botkin, Fry, Wright, and Jarvis (1968) on the relation between social perspective taking and concrete operations. Selman (1971) has rendered this position explicit

with regard to substages in role taking and cognitive development. Recently, a number of authors (e.g., Bruner, 1975a,b) have criticized Piaget for stressing the importance of interactions with physical objects while deemphasizing the contribution of social motivation and experience to the development of intelligence. As we shall note shortly, however, this criticism is applicable only to the superficial "pure cognition" interpretation of Piaget.

4. Position 4 ($S \quad C$) involves claims that cognitive and social development
$$\downarrow \quad \downarrow$$
derive from independent sources and follow separate sequences. As in the case of Position 4 on language and cognition, this model tends to characterize a strong nativist approach to social development. Examples are ethological models of social interaction which attribute a major developmental role to the capacity to produce and receive species-specific social signals (e.g., Freedman, 1972; Hess, 1970).

Recall McNeill's mixed position regarding language and cognition. For weak linguistic universals, cognition is a necessary *and* sufficient condition for learning, formalizable as
$$L \rightarrow C$$
McNeill proposes, however, that language also involves strong linguistic universals for which cognition is a necessary but insufficient condition. This mixed proposal was formalized as
$$L \rightarrow C$$
$$\downarrow \quad \downarrow$$
A similar argument can be made for weak versus strong social universals. For example, Bowlby (1969) suggests that the development of mother–child attachment depends in part on the child's cognitive capacity to recognize Mother as a separate being. However, this cognitive input alone is not viewed as a sufficient condition for the development of an attachment bond. Additional mechanisms for the production and reception of specifically social signals are also required for a normal attachment relationship to develop. Hence mother–child attachment could be viewed as a strong social universal:
$$S \rightarrow C$$
$$\downarrow \quad \downarrow$$
Compare this position with Kohlberg's writings on the cognitive basis of moral reasoning, in which the attainment of a given cognitive stage is sufficient for the child to be able to work out the solution to certain moral dilemmas. Kohlberg's view seems closer to the concept of weak social universals, for which cognitive development is a necessary *and* sufficient condition:
$$S \rightarrow C$$

In the work of several neo-Freudian ego psychologists (e.g., White, 1963; Hartmann, 1958; Kris, 1954) we find a mixture of Position 2 and 4 on social–

cognitive interaction. In traditional psychoanalytic theory, the ego develops entirely out of the need to mediate between social–affective needs and an uncooperative environment. Hence the ego can be seen as a weak cognitive universal, developing from an entirely social–affective base:

$$S \leftarrow C$$

The ego psychologists have modified this position, suggesting various alterations in the theory to strengthen the autonomy of the ego in conflict-free spheres of activity, or to attribute to the ego some sort of access to energy sources of its own. Thus, White has talked about a "competence motive" for cognitive growth, Kris discusses "regression in the service of the ego," a process whereby the ego can rechannel affectively based, id energies into its own rational activities, and so forth. This approach can be viewed as an argument for strong cognitive universals, in which social motivation is a necessary but insufficient condition for ego development:

$$S \leftarrow C$$
$$\downarrow \quad \downarrow$$

5. According to Position 5 ($S \quad C$), social functioning is one of the figura-
$$\searrow \swarrow$$
$$O$$

tive domains to which operative principles can be applied. There is no a priori reason why interactions with physical objects should always precede interactions with social objects. The order in which a "decalage" between the two domains occurs can be a function of several factors. In certain instances, human beings may simply be unpredictable, difficult "material" for working out a given operative scheme. In other cases, the adult caretaker may be even more predictable and malleable than physical objects. One child may, for a variety of reasons, be more motivated in social than nonsocial interactions. Another child may simply have proportionally less experience with social beings than another. Other possibilities also exist. Pell (1970) has demonstrated that, for children with a stable, warm attachment relationship to the mother, "mother permanence" (i.e., the ability to follow mother behind a screen) develops before "object permanence." For children with an insecure attachment relationship, on the other hand, there is a tendency for object permanence to develop in advance of mother permanence (although both developments are later overall in children who are insecurely attached). This is an excellent illustration of a positive prediction of decalage made from Position 5 on social–cognitive relationships.

To establish interdependence between social and nonsocial domains, Position 5 requires the following types of data:

a. An isomorphism in structure and sequence between domains.

b. Approximately similar onset times for both the social and the nonsocial manifestations of a given stage.

   c. Across a sample of children, correlations between onset times and levels of performance in both domains, indicating some transfer of skill.

   d. Patterns of correlations in which certain social and cognitive tasks are more strongly related than others.

Finally, as noted with regard to language and cognition, Position 5 is strengthened if we can predict in advance the direction of decalage between social and nonsocial events, as a function of either the nature of the materials or the experience of individual children.

   6. Position 6 ($S \leftarrow C \rightarrow$) on cognition and social development would predict only qualitative isomorphisms between the two systems. These in turn would be a function, not of some shared developmental source or shared underlying structure (i.e., homology), but of constraints inherent in the nature of complex systems (i.e., analogy). For example, a child reasoning about the hierarchy of power relations or "popularity" among the children in his class (see Omark & Edelman, in press), will encounter problems in classification, nesting of categories, seriating from most to least popular. Because of the nature of the problem to be solved, certain more "primitive" solutions will be arrived at earlier than others. According to Position 5, the child should be capable of solving this problem of social hierarchies around the same developmental period that he can work with hierarchies of nonsocial objects. There may be some tolerable decalage between the two domains, but a child who has worked out the solution in one area should have that strategy as a content-free, operative scheme that can be applied to the next problem. The "solution" would be viewed as something "in the child." Position 6 would make no such prediction. Anyone solving the social hierarchy problem will have to go through a given series of steps to arrive at the most efficient strategy. He will also have to proceed through a similar sequence in solving problems in nonsocial hierarchies. However, the solution is not "in" the child, but in the interaction. Hence there is no reason why success in one realm should correlate with success in another realm across a sample of children.

   We could go through similar steps in outlining the six positions on the relationship between socialization and language. There are theorists who believe that socialization depends on or indeed consists in the master of language ($S \rightarrow L$). This view is, for example, also implicit in the Whorfian approach to linguistic anthropology. On the other hand, Halliday (1975) and Bruner (1975a, b) are among a number of psychologists who have suggested that the functions, categories, and relations of which language is comprised can be derived by the child from the structure of social interaction. Hence social development provides the frame for learning not just the purpose of communication, but its structure as well $(S \leftarrow L)$. Between these two extremes, we can find all the other positions outlined above, with partial dependence, partial independence, and isomorphisms based on the nature of systems rather than a shared source.

To summarize, of the 30,000 or so models for the possible interrelations of these three systems, probably the most accurate answer to the problem is the multiple-choice response "all of the above." However, this does not mean that we must throw up our hands and avoid research on the problem altogether. In the models adopted by economists, epigenetic ethologists, political scientists—in short, anyone dealing with enormously complex systems with "intelligent" subparts—the final product must account for partial causation, inputs and outputs that differ as a function of time and logical order of processing, simultaneous versus successive effects, and so forth. "All of the above" is no doubt true in some banal sense, but our task is to determine which types of interrelations are most important for certain developments, less integral to others, crucial for certain components of the system, optional and additive for other components, and so on. No one can do all these things in one grand research project. With each small problem that we select, we must determine the kinds of interrelations we expect to find, and design our research to yield whatever data can support or disconfirm our theory.

In addition to the types of qualitative, ordinal, and correlational research we have discussed here, other kinds of data are relevant to multidimensional, complex input–output models for interdependence within systems. What happens to the entire system when one component is removed? Obviously we cannot go around removing the Broca area from human subjects to see what happens to cognition and social relations in the absence of language (and, even if we could, very young children have an uncanny knack for growing new Broca areas in the other hemisphere). However, disabled or deviant samples of children do provide a sort of natural experiment on the interdependence of systems. For example, Furth's (1966) work on cognition in deaf subjects suggests that cognitive development is delayed in the absence of language, but that a very high level of functioning can eventually be reached. Urwin (1975) is currently engaged in some important research on the development of preverbal and verbal communication in blind infants. Preliminary results indicate that the inability to perceive visual cues (social and non-social) has unique effects on the form and content of early speech. Snyder (1975) has examined cognitive development in normal versus language-delayed children, using the Uzgiris and Hunt scales. She finds that the only sensorimotor scale to differentiate the two populations is the means–end scale, suggesting that these causal developments may be implicated in language development to a greater degree in than other cognitive skills. In some deviant populations, it is not at all clear which components are most responsible for a given syndrome. For example, autistic children are extremely slow in language development, although other aspects of cognitive functioning (e.g., manipulations of objects) may be intact. There is also some indication that autistic children are lacking in or resistant to social interactions—according to Freedman (1972), a characteristic that appears to be present at birth. Perhaps there is something in the autistic syndrome which independently affects both socialization and language. However, another possibility is that the lack of social motivation is created directly by the autistic syndrome, whereas the failure to produce language is an epiphenomenon of this social defect.

Other "natural experiments" on interdependence of systems are based on comparisons of development in two closely related species. We know for example, that gorillas and human beings go through remarkably similar sequences of cognitive development (Redshaw & Hughes, 1975). We also know that all the higher primates have strong social motivation and, in some ways, extremely similar courses of social development (Bowlby, 1969). And yet the human child finishes at a very different developmental end point from the gorilla young. One of the most notable differences involves the acquisition of language. If all the cognitive and social components between the two species were identical (which they are not), we would have strong support for a strong linguistic universals model, in which aspects of language depend on language-specific genetic inputs. However, if the two species differ not only with regard to language but also on several specific components of cognitive or social development, we may have some clue that these specific cognitive or social inputs are involved in the development of language. For example, in Redshaw and Hughes' study comparing gorilla infants with human infants in sensorimotor development, the authors report that almost all the various tasks are mastered earlier by the gorillas. However, two components in particular—the use of the stick as a tool (as opposed to the use of strings and other already existing supports), and the use of the adult experimenter as a means in problem solving (e.g., handing the experimenter the mechanical toy to make it walk again)—are apparently never mastered spontaneously by the gorilla infants. From our study on precursors of language, we have seen that creative tool use (e.g., the "invention" of the stick as means as opposed to the "discovery" of the cloth support as means), and the use of adults as tools in obtaining goals, both seem to precede and feed directly into the first uses of language. It may be that the failure to produce language-like systems in higher primates is due to the failure to produce certain kinds of means–end analyses that permit communication to develop. It is true, as Kohler noted in 1927, that under special conditions higher primates can be induced to invent tools. But, as the Gardners (1969) have discovered with the chimpanzee Washoe, and as Rumbaugh and Gill (Chapter 5 of this volume) have noted with chimpanzee Lana, under special conditions it is also possible to induce nonhuman primates to understand and produce symbolic communication.

There are, then, a variety of empirical approaches for entering into and understanding the workings of complex, interdependent systems. Since so many models are possible, at least in principle, we are well advised to determine in advance the kind of interdependence we expect, and to select a design that will yield such relationships if they do indeed exist. In the cross-sectional projects that we are currently analyzing, our working model for the relationships among cognition, social development, and communication in infancy is a combined version of Position 5:

$$S \quad C_f \quad L$$
$$\searrow \quad \downarrow \quad \swarrow$$
$$O$$

We are *not*, then, proposing that "pure cognitive" behaviors precede social-cognitive behaviors. Object permanence and object-to-object tool use are not in themselves prerequisites for comunicative development. Rather, performance on sensorimotor tasks and performance in social situations are both viewed as figurative manifestations of a common operative "stage" that is *in itself* biased toward neither social nor nonsocial interactions. Hence the "prerequisite" to social development, language development, and cognitive development (in the sense of performance on cognitive tasks) is the construction of operative schemes that characterize interactions with social and physical objects and events.

THE FOLLOW-UP STUDY: DESIGN

To test some of the hypotheses suggested by our longitudinal study and by related research, we undertook a study of 25 infants each of whom received four monthly home visits between the ages of $9\frac{1}{2}$ and $12\frac{1}{2}$ months. At least two observers were present during each of these 2-hour visits. To systematize our observations of cognitive development, we administered the complete set of Uzgiris and Hunt (1975) scales at each visit. During visits II, III and IV we administered as the starting item in each scale the last item unambiguously passed on the previous visit, in order to avoid fatiguing the infants. Our first study had taught us a great deal about the kinds of situations likely to elicit communicative behaviors. In addition to making observations of spontaneous play and social interaction with the mother and the observers, we therefore included, in sessions II and IV, a set of standard videotaped interactions. During sessions I and III we recorded spontaneous behaviors only, with the aid of checklists supplemented by notes. In addition, at each visit we carred out in-depth interviews with the mother concerning the child's communication and language, play, social development, and locomotor development. In these interviews, we did not merely ask whether Child A did Behavior X. Rather, we consistently probed for detailed anecdotes, giving examples of the kinds of activities in which we were interested in order to elicit anecdotal data. To help the mother remember to watch for these developments from one session to another, we left a checklist of behaviors on which she could make notes between sessions. Finally, around the child's first birthday, mother and child came to our laboratory to be filmed in the standardized "strange situation" (Ainsworth & Wittig, 1969), a situation designed to elicit play, exploration, and social behavior during very brief separations and reunions with mother and a stranger.

Thirteen of the infants were studied in Boulder by Bates and Bretherton. Twelve were followed in Rome by Benigni, Camaioni, and Volterra. There were slight differences in the makeup of the two samples, with more first-borns in the American sample.

Table 2 summarizes the design of the study and the nature of the subject population. Since this is only a preliminary report of our findings, we will not include here a list of all the variables within the interviews, observations, and videotapes (all of which will eventually be analyzed). In this chapter we will report primarily on the behaviors noted in the earlier study: showing off, giving, showing, communicative and noncommunicative referential and nonreferential speech, and symbolic play (see pp. 250–252 for definitions of these behaviors), as well as performance on some of the cognitive scales, particularly means–end, object permanence, space, schemes, and imitation (Uzgiris & Hunt, 1975).

We should add some words of caution, however. This study was carried out on two continents, with either expensive communications via transatlantic cable or utterly undependable communications via international postal service. We did design the study together in Rome in the summer of 1974, and carried out our design of coding categories and preliminary analyses together in the summer of 1975. In between, however, many small slips in standardization grew out of the multitude of minor, unforeseen decisions that must always be made in quasi-naturalistic infant research. If we had been predicting cultural differences, our findings would clearly be confounded by slight differences in method. Since we were more interested in developments common to the two cultures, we can at least congratulate ourselves that anything we find despite the differences in method must truly reflect robust developmental phenomena.

TABLE 2. Outline of Cross-Sectional Research
There were 25 subjects: 13 American, 12 Italian; 14 female, 11 male; 15 first born, 10 later born.

Session I	Session II	Session III	Strange Situation	Session IV
Mean age: 9; 14[a]	Mean age: 10; 16	Mean age: 11; 19	Mean age: 12; 09	Mean age: 12; 21
Upper limit: 9; 28	Upper limit: 11; 01	Upper limit: 12; 02	Upper limit: 13; 02	Upper limit: 13; 06
Lower limit: 8; 29	Lower limit: 10; 03	Lower limit: 11; 04	Lower limit: 11; 25	Lower limit: 12; 03
Median age: 9; 15	Median age: 10; 18	Median age: 11; 19	Median age: 12; 05	Median age: 12; 21
6 Piagetian scales	6 Piagetian scales	6 Piagetian scales		6 Piagetian scales
Maternal interview	Maternal interview	Maternal interview		Maternal interview
Home observation	Structured videosession	Home obsevation		Structured video-session
Checklist		Checklist		

[a] All ages in months.

THE FOLLOW-UP STUDY: PRELIMINARY RESULTS

Since we are beginning our analysis by positing Position 5, we will organize the report of preliminary results according to the criteria on p. 276 for establishing a model in which cognitive and communicative developments depend on shared, operative schemes.

Qualitative Similarities between Domains, and Isomorphisms in Developmental Sequence

The qualitative isomorphisms between cognition and communication in stages 5 and 6, respectively, were established to our satisfaction in the first longitudinal study (Bates, Camaioni, & Volterra, 1975). After Piaget (1954), we assumed that the operative schemes that should characterize sensori-motor stage 5 involve the invention of new means to familiar ends. On structural grounds, we can argue that this underlying capacity should charac-terize object-to-object tool use, as well as the ability to use signals from the social repertoire to obtain objects (Sugarman, 1973) and to use interactions with objects as a means to adult attention. Also, Piaget argues that stage 6 involves the capacity for mental representation and the use of symbols in such "internalized" action schemes. It follows by definition that referential speech (based on the symbolic relation between sign-vehicle and referent rather than the use of speechlike sounds to fulfill social functions) should appear around the same time as symbolic play and the ability to represent invisible displacements in object to permanence tasks. Whether these ana-logous structures actually do coincide in development is a separate question that will be examined below.

Regarding the criterion of isomorphism in *sequence* within domains, we have yet to carry out ordinal analyses (e.g., Guttman scaling) within the protocols of individual children. However, as indicated in Figures 1 to 5, across a sample of 25 children the sequence of developments observed within both cognition and communication paralleled the sequence found in the first study. For example, within the cognitive domain (Figure 1), success on stage 5 means–end and object permanence items preceded success on stage 6 means–end (not illustrated in the figures), stage 6 schemes (exploration and play with objects), and stage 6 object permanence. In the area of gestures and preverbal communication (Figure 2), "showing off" again preceded giving, showing, and noncommunicative pointing, as observed in the first study (see pp. 251–252). Communicative pointing was a late development in our sample of 25, as it was in the first longitudinal sample. In the area of language and sybolization (Figure 3), certain types of word comprehension appeared fairly early, in or even slightly before the period of preverbal com-munication. Also as was the case in our first study, nonreferential wordlike performatives appeared after word comprehension, and well before the onset of referential speech. To summarize, the predicted sequence between stages 5 and 6, in cognition and communication, respectively, was the same in the larger study as it was in the original longitudinal project.

We are fairly satisfied in having established analogies in both structure and sequence, within the respective areas of cognition and communication, in the first year of life. However, this criterion does not distinguish between Positions 5 and 6. To support the hypothesis that cognitive and communicative developments depend on some shared operative structure, we need further evidence.

Onset Times within a Similar Developmental Range for Cognitive and Communicative Events

Table 3 summarizes the percentages of children who were manifesting various communicative and noncommunicative behaviours at each session. These include variables on the maternal interviews for all four sessions, and observations for the first and third sessions only. Since much of the second and fourth sessions are on videotapes that are still being transcribed, we will not report observational data for those points. Finally, the cognitive entries in Table 3 represent children who either did or did not pass the specified items, rather than indicating their relative levels of performance. We do have interval data for both observations and cognitive testing, but we will not present those here. Hence Table 3 contains dichotomous results only arranged by session.

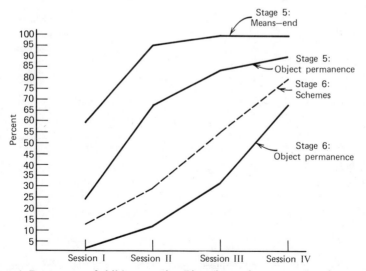

FIGURE 1. Percentage of children passing Piagetian tasks at stage 5 and stage 6 levels.

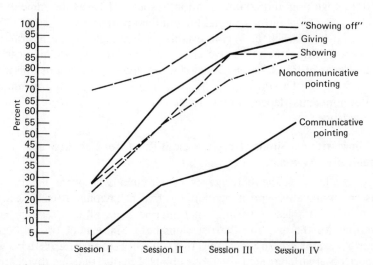

FIGURE 2. Percentage of children manifesting gestural behaviors, according to maternal interviews.

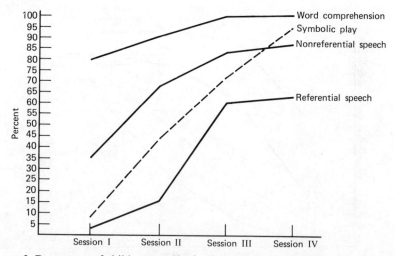

FIGURE 3. Percentage of children manifesting language and symbolic play, according to maternal interviews.

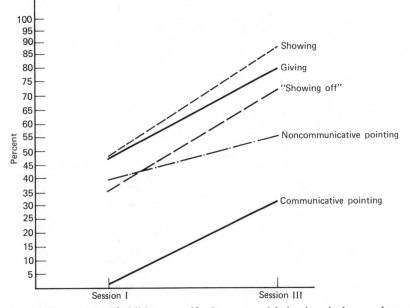

FIGURE 4. Percentage of children manifesting gestural behaviors in home observations.

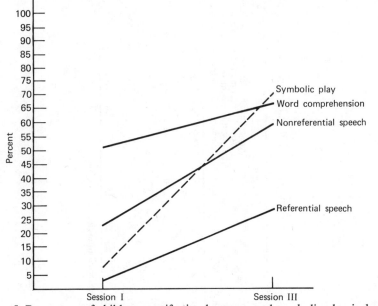

FIGURE 5. Percentage of children manifesting language and symbolic play in home observations.

TABLE 3.   Percentage of Children Manifesting Various Cognitive and Communicative Behaviors

	Gestures					Speech							
Session	"Showing off"	Giving	Showing	Non-comunicative Pointing	Comunicative Pointing	Word Comprehension	Non-referential Words	Referential Words	Symbolic Play	Stage 5 Causality	Stage 5 Object Permanence	Stage 6 Schemes	Stage 6 Object Permanence
I M[a]	72	28	28	24	0	80	36	4	8	60	24	12	0
O[a]	36	48	48	40	0	52	24	4	8				
II M	80	68	56	56	28	92	68	16	44	96	68	28	12
III M	100	88	88	76	36	100	84	60	72	100	84	56	32
O	72	80	88	56	32	68	60	28	72				
IV M	100	96	88	88	56	100	88	64	96	100	92	80	68

[a] M = Maternal interview, O = observation.

Figure illustrates the percentage of children passing stage 5 and stage 6 cognitive items in three areas. We have data for all six cognitive scales but selected only a couple of the better known and most representative items here. The stage 5 means–end item illustrated in Figure 1 is the use of a cloth or pillow support to pull an object near. The use of other support items (i.e., vertical and horizontal strings, and a stick to pull an object in) developed later than that of the item in Figure 1. If we were to graph performance on each of those items, the results would follow a curve similar to that for the cloth support, but at a somewhat lower level. Performance on using a stick as a support would fall at the end of stage 5, near the point where stage 6 items begin to be passed. Hence this item may represent a transition point from stage 5 to stage 6 means–end. The stage 5 object permanence curve represents performance in finding an object undergoing sequential displacements, and/or finding an object under two or more superimposed screens. Stage 5 object permanence is apparently more diffi-cult than the stage 5 means–end item for use of a cloth support. We can accept these two curves as the upper and lower boundaries of stage 5, for comparison with the graphs of communicative development. Similarly, the stage 6 object permanence curve reflects success on items involving invisible displacements (and hence some minimal demonstration of mental repre-sentation). This is clearly a much later development than stage 6 schemes, which involve recognition and execution of socially appropriate uses of objects (e.g., putting on a necklace, playing telephone with a telephone). We will say more about this kind of play shortly. At this point, however, let us accept the curve for stage 6 schemes as a lower boundary for symbolic functioning, with stage 6 object permanence illustrating an upper boundary for entrance into that stage.

To summarize, Figure 1 suggests that stage 5 does indeed form a separate period from stage 6. For present purposes, we are interested in comparing the cognitive developments in Figure 1 with the development of communi-cative behaviors, as a function of these two stages.

Figure 2 illustrates the maternal interview data for several aspects of pre-verbal communication and gesture. If we overlay Figure 2 on Figure 1, we can see that "showing off" is reported very early, perhaps even preceding stage 5. In our earlier study, we speculated (on the basis of similar findings) that "showing off" is actually a stage 4 manifestation of the "protodeclara-tive," insofar as the goal of adult attention and laughter is the same, but the means selected is a simple repetition of familiar schemes rather than use of an object-as-tool. This finding is supported by the comparison of maternal interview and cognitive data here. Next, giving, showing, and noncommuni-cative pointing cluster together, halfway between stage 5 means–end and stage 5 object permanence. This supports our suggestion that giving and showing are stage 5 communications. Noncommunicative pointing, which is involved in careful exploration of new objects, belongs in stage 5 as one of the schemes for discovering the nature of new objects. Finally, communicative pointing develops late and appears at the boundary between stage 5 and 6 behaviors (compare with Figure 1). This presents a number of interesting considerations concerning the role of pointing in the development of reference (Werner & Kaplan, 1963). We plan to follow this idea up more carefully in a series of qualitative analyses of early words and the contexts in which they are used.

Figure 3 illustrates the course of language and symbolic development in this sample. Word comprehension is clearly an early development, perhaps even in some minimal form before stage 5. After Huttenlocher (1974), we have collected more detailed data on the different kinds of word comprehension, particularly the distinction between comprehension in ritualized sequences like "Where is your belly-button?" and "Wave bye-bye" versus comprehension followed by goal-corrected search for the object names (e.g., "Go find the book"). The latter appeared much later in development, a developmental fact which may be related to the kinds of cognition involved in ritualized versus goal-corrected comprehension.

As predicted from our earlier study, nonreferential speech appeared together with other stage 5 communicative signals like giving and showing. This is consonant with our suggestion that nonreferential speech is not really a symbolic behavior, but rather a vocal performative signal equivalent in all functional respects to reaching, showing, and so forth. Referential speech, on the other hand, begins to appear much later. Overlaying Figure 1 and Figure 3, we can see that referential speech accompanies performance on invisible displacements (stage 6 object permanence), supporting our hypothesis that the two behaviors are manifestations of a stage 6 capacity for mental representation. The distinction between "functional" and "referential" speech has been noted by several other authors (e.g., Ingram, 1974; Piaget, 1962; Greenfield & Smith, 1976). We suggest that the developmental sequence is regularly found because it is based on differences in the operative level underlying the two types of word production.

Finally, the curve for symbolic play in Figure 3 lies halfway between stage 5 communication and stage 6 referential speech. We have more detailed data on the kind of symbolic or "pretend" play used by the children. Sinclair (1970) stresses the distinction between pretend play appropriate to the object (e.g., playing telephone with a telephone) and creative kinds of truly symbolic play in which rather different objects are made to serve a given function. An example of this latter kind of activity comes from our earlier observations on Carlotta (Bates et al., 1975), who at 12 months played telephone with a cigarette pack and with a spoon, respectively, on two occasions.

In Figure 3 we have collapsed these two types of play; hence the curve is primarily representative of the earlier, more primitive level of object-appropriate play. This sort of activity, as Sinclair suggests, is more accommodative and imitative than the later forms. *Just as word recognition precedes word production in development, early symbolic play may in fact involve recognition of the function of objects, whereas the later forms involve productive, assimilative use of objects as symbols.* Hence it is possible that the kind of symbolic play that predominates in this age range is a transitional activity between stage 5 schemes (i.e., exploration of the nature of objects) and stage 6 schemes (i.e., selecting an object to represent another in assimilative play).

Figures 4 and 5 present the observational data for preverbal communication and language-and-symbols, respectively, from sessions I and III. Overall, these figures tend to match the developmental curves for the maternal interview variables, but at a lower level. Clearly, the probability of our observing a given behavior is lower in our "itinerant research" than in the mother's own daily observations. However, a few variables, notably "showing off" and word comprehension, appear even less often than the various stage 5 communicative behaviors that they supposedly precede in development. This order reversal is probably due to the enormous difficulty of eliciting these two variables, as opposed to the ease of eliciting giving, showing, and the like, in our observation sessions. It was simply easier to motivate activities involving the exchange of objects and the examination of new toys and events.

To summarize thus far, the onset times for the predicted stage 5 and stage 6 behaviors do seem to match within a respectable range for the cognitive and communicative domains. We accept this as evidence in favor of a Position 5 "homologue" model for the interdependence of cognition and communication, as opposed to a Position 6 "analogue" model. On the basis of a Position 6 interpretation, the consistent co-occurrence of the two types of behavior can be explained only as fortuitous coincidence, perhaps due to the level of difficulty of the materials rather than to some set of schemes developing in the child, whereas Position 5 directly predicts the similar onset times.

Furthermore, we can effectively reject either a Position 2 or a Position 3 interpretation of the relationship between cognition and communication for these events. It is true that for the most part our subject manifested stage-appropriate cognitive behaviors slightly before parallel communicative behaviors. However, there were a substantial number of order reversals by some children, within certain categories (e.g., giving objects before using the support). Hence it is unlikely that cognition for physical objects "causes" communicative developments. It is more likely that the cognitive and communicative events observed here are based on some shared, underlying structure.

Patterns of Correlations in Onset Times and Level of Performance within Subjects

We have barely begun the long process of correlational analysis and can only report the most tentative trends in the data at this point. So far, we have looked primarily at correlations among dichotomous variables, which gave us relatively little variance to work with. Also, the subjects are all outrageously precocious, middle-class children, giving us even less variance on month-to-month testing. Finally, the slight differences in method between the Italian and American halves of the sample require carrying out partial correlations on nationality in the pooled data (in fact, the level of correlations is higher overall within the American and Italian samples taken individually). All of which is a prelude to saying that our correlational results so far are weak. Nevertheless, there are quite a few significant correlations, indicating some interesting and meaningful trends.

First, the between-session stability for the various *cognitive* tasks is averaging from .35 to .74. (Note that we are using a slightly different scoring system from that reported by Uzgiris and Hunt and may have to reanalyze the data with their system to obtain comparable results.) For infant research, which is notoriously unstable in terms of performance between sessions, this is within a respectable range. There is much less stability from one session to another within the *communicative* measures examined so far. This is in part due to the use of dichotomous, present–absent judgments, so that at one session virtually no one does Behavior X, while within two sessions almost everyone is doing it. We did perform one analysis collapsing the dichotomous ratings for four hypothesized stage 5 communications: giving, showing, communicative pointing, and nonreferential speech, for the maternal interview and for the home observations, respectively. (This analysis is justified insofar as the four variables do correlate individually with one another, see below.) Hence any child could score from 0 to 8 on the combined communicative measure. This combined variable was quite stable from one session to another, with session-to-session correlations of around .50 to .60. Hence children who begin communicating early (e.g., giving and/or showing) are likely to add to their repertoire (e.g., communicative pointing and nonreferential speech) faster and earlier than other children. Finally, we hope to obtain further results on session-to-session communicative development with the frequency data from the films and observations (as opposed to the dichotomous data reported here).

Secondly, the maternal interview variables generally correlate significantly with our own observations for the same behaviors, with correlations as high as .68. This supports our faith in the maternal judgments between sessions, and in our interview method of probing for anecdotes rather than absolute judgments from the mothers. The decision, for example, to classify a given word as "referential" or "nonreferential" was based on our interpretation of the details provided by the mother. We did not ask the mothers themselves to classify the variables. In fact, the major difference between maternal and observation variables in our study is probably a function of the relative frequency with which mothers versus itinerant researchers can observe the infants, and hence the probability that the two types of observers have noted a stable activity. Ingram (1975) has suggested that parents are "rich interpreters" of their children's behavior—another way of saying that they tend to see things that really are not there. In our sample, there was actually a tendency for the mothers to be quite conservative in making judgments about speech and symbolic play, so that we occasionally witnessed behaviors (generally those that we ourselves were particularly good at eliciting) that were quite surprising to the parents. Furthermore. there is a tendency for the maternal variables to correlate better with cognitive testing than do our own observations. This makes sense if we view the maternal reports as stable and consistent observations of the child, compared with our own random sampling.

The correlations among the various communicative behaviors (although low) tend to be higher than the correlations among the various cognitive scales. Uzgiris and Hunt contend that the six domains tapped by their scales reflect quite different underlying structures, albeit within a generally comparable range of difficulty from one stage to another. The low correlations of some cognitive scales with one another in our sample support their contention that these are rather separate skills.

Finally, the correlations between cognition and communication are quite low. Nevertheless, so far we have about twice as many significant correlations (at the $p < .05$ level) as we would expect by chance. Furthermore, the tentative patterns yielded by these correlations make good sense. We will have much more to say about these data in future reports, when we have completed more analyses involving frequency data, as well as item and factor analyses. There are, however, a few things that we can say at this point about the relation between cognition and communication at the end of the first year.

First, it appears that object permanence is not a particularly strong predictor, either within or between sessions, of communicative development. This is surprising on several grounds. Uzgiris and Hunt feel, for example, that the object permanence task is the strongest and most reliable measure among the six scales. Hence on purely psychometric grounds we would expect that scale to be a better predictor of almost anything. And yet object per-

manence rarely correlates with either preverbal communication or language
and symbolic behavior. Brown (1973), among others, has implicated object
permanence in language development, primarily on the theoretical grounds
concerning the question of mental representation for object-referents. And
yet Corrigan (1976), in a cross-sectional study of language and object permanence in 36 children, finds no significant correlation between the two behaviors.[2] On the other hand, Snyder (1975), as we mentioned earlier, reports
that, of the six scales from the Uzgiris and Hunt battery, only the means–end
scale discriminates fifteen language-delayed children from fifteen normal
children matched for MLU.

   These findings suggest that the dynamic, casual aspects of cognition (e.g.,
means–end) may provide more input to the development of communicative
intentions and the use of symbols than is derived from more "static," object-
oriented cognition. In our study, the collapsed measure for stage 5 communications (see above) correlated strongly (i.e., averaging in the .45 to .50
range), at all sessions and between sessions, with performance on the means–
end scale, and somewhat less strongly with performance on spatial relations
and schemes. Imitation did not begin to correlate significantly with communicative variables until around the last session. It is interesting to note that
both space and schemes correlate significantly with means–end, whereas they
do not correlate with each other. Yet all three scales, in varying degrees, are
good predictors of communicative development at the stage 5 level. It is
possible that space and schemes tap separate aspects of the means–end skills
that relate to communication. In this age range, schemes involve the child's
means for exploring and/or recognizing the function of objects. On the other
hand, the items in the space scale that provide most of the variance in this
age range involve putting objects inside one another, building towers, and
so forth. Hence the title *space* may be somewhat misleading, since most of
these items involve the same kinds of support relations and relations among
objects that characterize the means–ends scale. Factor analyses of cognitive
and communicative items may shed more light on the question being posed
here. At this point, however, we tentatively suggest that the cognitive understanding involved in the establishment and use of a communicative network
has more to do with dynamic, relational notions than with the permanence
and stability of objects.

   The analyses of symbolic behaviors and referential speech are less clear.
As was the case with the communicative variables, symbolic play seems to
be more closely related to space and means–end than to object permanence,
and also correlates weakly with referential speech. However, referential

---

[2] However, on the basis of more detailed analysis of two subjects followed longitudinally, Corrigan does think that certain *aspects* of language and object permanence
may be related.

speech in itself correlates only with symbolic play, and not with the other cognitive variables. Since the children had barely begun to use referential speech at the end of the study, we may have very little variance to work with. Alternatively, referential speech may bear a stronger relation to certain *items* in the cognitive scales than to others. Factor analyses and item analyses should shed more light on this possibility. Finally, it may indeed be the case that referential speech, unlike all the other communicative variables, involves some separate functions that are not tapped by our measures. At this point we cannot conclude anything.

With regard to the strange situation measure and the relationship of mother–child attachment to the above developments, we have virtually no data at this point. It may be the case that 25 children—just barely enough to make meaningful statistical statements for developmental variables—may be too few to yield conclusions about individual differences in social motivation as they relate to communication and cognition. For one thing, we have an abundance of securely attached infants with very little variation in the quality of the mother–child relationship. However, we feel confident that this approach, that is, predicting decalage on the basis of individual experience, is an important consideration for developmental research of this type.

Finally, we intend to devote a great deal of in-depth, qualitative analysis to the wealth of anecdotal data on symbolic play, language comprehension, and referential and nonreferential speech. This qualitative data should yield a more interesting view of the transitions between stages and the particular contexts in which the various behaviors examined here occur.

Even if all our fondest dreams and best predictions come true, we will not have come close to a complete model for communicative development in this age range. For one thing, we have not excluded all other possible models. Correlations are very weak evidence for interdependence, since the correlation could have been produced by some third, thoroughly capricious source. Nor can we conclude that two related developments do not *also* require independent language-specific or social-specific inputs in order to develop properly (i.e., Position 4). Above all, although our evidence provides some support for homologous rather than analogous developments between cognition and communication, the similarity in onset times and the correlations among variables are certainly not definitive data. *The strongest demonstration that one system depends on another in order to build its structure can be obtained only when the supposedly crucial input is withheld altogether.* As we noted earlier, data from defective populations, as well as comparisons between species, do yield an approximation of this "critical test." For example, Snyder's finding concerning the relationship between the means–end scale and language delay seems to implicate causal development in the language-delay syndrome. Similarly Redshaw and Hughes' (1975) observations about the "missing pieces" in gorilla cognition lend support to the interpretation that these cognitive inputs are required for the development of symbolic representation, communication, and language. In constructing an input–output model for the development of such a complex system, we will clearly need data from all these sources.

References

Ainsworth, M. D. S., & Wittig, B. A. Attachment and exploratory behavior of one-year-olds in a strange situation. In B. M. Foss (Ed.), *Determinants of infant behavior.* Vol. 4. London: Methuen, 1969. Pp. 111–136.

Antinucci, F., & Parisi, D. Early language acquisition: A model and some data. In C. Ferguson & D. Slobin (Eds.), *Studies in child language development.* New York: Holt, Rinehart and Winston, 1973.

Antinucci, F., & Volterra, V. Lo sviluppo della negazione nel linguaggio infantile: Uno studio pragmatico. In Studi per un modello del linguaggio. *Quaderni della Ricerca Scientifica.* Rome: Consiglio Nazionale delle Ricerche, Istituto di Psicologia, 1973.

Austin, J. L. *How to do things with words.* Cambridge: Oxford University Press, 1962.

Bates, E. Il paradigma linguistico e la psicologia evolutiva. *La critica sociologica,* Summer 1973. Pp. 1–22.

Bates, E. *Language and context: The acquisition of pragmatics.* New York: Academic Press, 1976.

Bates, E., Camaioni, L., & Volterra, V. *The acquisition of performatives prior to speech.* Rome: Consiglio Nazionale delle Ricerche, Istituto di Psicologia, 1973. (Revised version in *Merrill-Palmer Quarterly,* 1975, **21**(3), 205–226.)

Bell, S. The development of the concept of object as related to infant–mother attachment. *Child Development,* 1970, **41**, 291–313.

Bowerman, M. F. *Early syntactic development: A cross linguistic study with reference to Finnish.* Cambridge: Cambridge University Press, 1973. (Original citation 1969.)

Bowerman, M. F. Learning the structure of causative verbs: A study in the relationship of cognitive, semantic and syntactic development. *Papers and Reports on Child Language Development,* No. 8. Committee on Linguistics, Stanford University, Stanford, Calif., 1974.

Bowlby, J. *Attachment and loss.* Vol. I. London: Hogarth Press, 1969.

Brown, R. *Words and things.* Glencoe, Ill.: The Free Press, 1958.

Brown, R. *A first language.* Cambridge, Mass.: Harvard University Press, 1973.

Brown, R., & Lenneberg, E. A study in language and cognition. *Journal of Abnormal and Social Psychology,* 1954, **49**, 454–462.

Bruner, J. The ontogenesis of speech acts. *Journal of Child Language,* 1975, **2**(1). (a)

Bruner, J. *From communication to language: A psychological perspective.* Manuscript, Oxford University, 1975 (b)

Bruner, J., Olver, R., & Greenfield, P. M. *Studies in cognitive growth.* New York: Wiley, 1966.

Buckley, W. *Sociology and modern systems theory.* Englewood Cliffs, N.J.: Prentice-Hall, 1967.

Camaioni, L., Volterra, V., & Bates, E. *Communicazione nel primo anno di vita.* Turin: Boringhieri, 1976.

Carey, S. Cognitive competence. In K. Connolly & J. Brunn (Eds.), *The growth of competence.* New York: Academic Press. 1974. Pp. 169–193.

Carnap, R. *Introduction to semantics.* Cambridge, Mass.: Harvard University Press, 1942.

Carroll, J. B. (Ed.). *Language, thought and reality: Selected writings of Benjamin Lee Whorf.* Cambridge, Mass.: M.I.T. Press, 1956.

Carter, A. *Communication in the sensorimotor period.* Unpublished doctoral dissertation, University of California at Berkeley, 1974.

Carter, A. The transformation of sensorimotor morphemes into words: A case study of the development of "more" and "mine". *Journal of Child Language*, 1975, **2**(2).

Chomsky, N. *Language and mind.* New York: Harcourt, Brace & World, 1968.

Cole, P., & Morgan, J. L. (Eds.). *Syntax and semantics: Speech acts.* Vol. 3. New York: Academic Press, 1975.

Collis, G. *The integration of gaze and vocal behavior in the mother–infant dyad.* Paper presented to the Third International Child Language Symposium, London, September 1975.

Corrigan, R. *Patterns of individual communication and cognitive development.* Unpublished doctoral dissertation, University of Denver, 1976.

Cromer, R. Remarks addressed to the Third International Child Language Symposium, London, September 1975.

Delack, J., & Fowlow, P. *The ontogenesis of differential vocalization: Development of prosodic contrastivity during the first year of life.* Paper presented to the Third International Child Language Symposium, London, September 1975.

Dore, J. *On the development of speech acts.* Unpublished doctoral dissertation, City University of New York, 1973.

Dore, J. A pragmatic description of early language development. *Journal of Psycholinguistic Research*, 1974, **4**.

Dore, J. Holophrases, speech acts and language universals. *Journal of Child Language*, 1975, **2**, 1–20.

Dunlap, K. *Civilized life.* Baltimore: Williams & Williams, 1934.

Eibl-Eiblesfeldt, I. *Ethology: The biology of behavior.* New York: Holt, Rinehart and Winston, 1970.

Fischer, K. *A formal theory of cognitive development: Seven levels of understanding.* Manuscript, Denver University, 1975.

Flavell, J. Stage related properties of cognitive development. *Cognitive Psychology*, 1971, **2**, 421–453.

Flavell, J., Botkin, B. T., Fry, C. L., Wright, J. W., & Jarvis, P. E. *The development of role-taking and communication skills in children.* New York: Wiley, 1968.

Freedman, D. G. The origins of social behavior. In U. Bronfenbrenner (Ed.), *Influences on human development.* Illinois: Dryden Press, 1972.

Furth, H. *Thinking without language: Psychological implications of deafness.* New York: The Free Press, 1966.

Gardner, R. A., & Gardner, B. J. Teaching signs to a chimpanzee. *Science,* 1969, **165**, 664–672.

Goodson, B. D., & Greenfield, P. M. The search for structural principles in children's manipulative play: A parallel with linguistic development. *Child Development*, 1975, **46**(3), 734–746.

Gordon, D., & Lakoff, G. Conversational postulates. *Papers from the 7th Regional Meeting of the Chicago Linguistic Society*, 1971.

Greene, P. H. Problems of organization of motor systems. In R. Rosen and F. M. Snell (Eds.), *Progress in theoretical biology.* Vol. 2. New York: Academic Press, 1973. Pp. 303–338.

Greene, P. H. Proposed organization of heterarchical multivariable control systems. Parts 1 and 2. To appear in *The International Journal of Man–Machine Studies* (in press).

Greenfield, P. M. The grammar of action in cognitive development. In D. Walter (Ed.), *Human brain function.* Brain Information Service, Brain Research Institute, University of California, 1975.

Greenfield, P. M., & Childs, C. P. Weaving, color terms, and pattern representation: Cultural influences and cognitive development among the Zinacantecos of Southern Mexico. In J. M. Dawson (Ed.), *Proceedings of the First International Conference of the International Association for Cross-Cultural Psychology.* Hong Kong: Hong Kong University Press (in press).

Greenfield, P., Nelson, K., & Saltzman, E. The development of rulebound strategies for manipulating seriated cups: A parallel between action and grammar. *Cognitive Psychology*, 1972, **3**, 291–311.

Greenfield, P. M., & Schneider, L. *Building a tree structure: The development of hierarchical complexity and interrupted strategies in children's construction activity.* Manuscript, University of California at Los Angeles, 1975.

Greenfield, P., & Smith, J. *The structure of communication in early language development.* New York: Academic Press, 1976.

Greenfield, P. M., & Westerman, M. *Some psychological relations between action and language structures.* Unpublished manuscript, University of California at Los Angeles, 1973.

Halliday, M. A. K. *Learning how to mean: Explorations in the development of language.* London: Arnold, 1975.

Hartmann, H. *Ego psychology and the problem of adaptation.* New York: International Universities Press, 1958.

Hess, E. Ethology and developmental psychology. In P. Mussen (Ed.), *Carmichael's manual of child psychology*. New York: Wiley, 1970.

Hewes, G. W. Primate communication and the gestural origin of language. *Current Anthropology*, 1973, **14**(1–2), 5–24.

Hewitt, C. Actor. *Proceedings from the Third International Joint Conference on Artificial Intelligence*. Stanford, 1973.

Huttenlocher, J. Origins of language comprehension. In R. Solso (Ed.), *Theories in cognitive psychology*. New York: Erlbaum Associates, 1974.

Hymes, D. (Ed.) *Language in culture and society*. New York: Harper & Row, 1964.

Ingram, D. Transitivity in child language. *Language*, 1971, **47**, 888–910.

Ingram, D. *Stages in the development of one-word sentences*. Paper presented at the Stanford Child Language Forum, Stanford, 1974.

Ingram, D. *Language development and the sensorimotor period*. Paper presented to the Third International Child Language Symposium, London, September 1975.

Jenkins, J. J. Language and thought. In J. F. Voss (Ed.), *Approaches to thought*. Columbus, Ohio: Merrill, 1969. Pp. 211–237.

Kaye, K. *Toward the origin of dialogue*. Paper presented to the Loch Lomond Symposium. University of Stratclyde, September 1975.

Kendler, T., & Kendler, H. Reversal and nonreversal shifts in kindergarten children. *Journal of Experimental Psychology*, 1959, **58**, 56–60.

Kohlberg, L. Stage and sequence: The cognitive-developmental approach to socialization. In D. A. Goslin (Ed.), *Handbook of socialization theory and research*. New York: Rand McNally, 1969.

Kohler, W. *The mentality of apes*. New York: Harcourt, Brace, 1927.

Kris, E. Introduction to the origins of psychoanalysis. In *Letters of Wilhelm Fliess, drafts and notes: 1887–1902*, by Sigmund Freud, ed. by M. Bonaparte, A. Freud, & E. Kris. New York: Basic Books, 1954.

Lenneberg, E. Cognition and ethnolinguistics. *Language*, 1953, **23**, 463–471.

Lenneberg, E. H. *The biological foundations of language*. New York: Wiley, 1967.

Lenneberg, E., & Roberts, J. M. The language of experience. *Indiana University Publications in Anthropology and Linguistics, Memoir* 13, 1956.

Levi-Strauss, C. *Structural anthropology*. New York: Basic Books, 1963.

Lock, A. Acts, not sentences. Paper presented at the International Child Language Conference, Florence, 1972. In W. von Raffler-Engel & Y. Lebrun ,Eds.), *Baby talk and infant speech*. Holland: Swets and Zeitlinger B.V., 1976.

Luria, A. R. *The role of speech in the regulation of normal and abnormal behavior*. Oxford: Pergamon Press, 1961.

MacNamara, J. The cognitive basis of language learning in infants. *Psychological Review*, 1972, **79**, 1–13.

McGuigan, F. J. *Thinking: Studies of covert language processes*. New York: Appleton-Century-Crofts, 1966.

McNeill, D. The creation of language by children. In J. Lyons & R. J. Wales

(Eds.), *Psycholinguistic papers: Proceedings from the 1966 Edinburgh Conference*. Edinburgh: Edinburgh University Press, 1966.

McNeill, D. *The acquisition of language.* New York: Harper & Row, 1970.

McNeill, D. *Explaining linguistic universals.* Manuscript, University of Chicago, 1971.

Mead, G. H. Mind, self and society. Chicago: University of Chicago Press, 1934.

Miller, G. The magic number 7 ± 2. In G. Miller, *The psychology of communication*. New York: Penguin, 1970.

Myers, T. F. *The onset of dialogue.* Paper presented to the Third International Child Language Symposium, London, September 1975.

Olson, D. Developmental changes in memory and the acquisition of language. In T. Moore (Ed.), *Cognitive development and the acquisition of language*. New York: Academic Press, 1973.

Omark, D., & Edelman, M. Formation of dominance hierarchies in young children: Action and perception. In T. Williams (Ed.), *Psychological anthropology*. The Hague: Mouton (in press).

Osgood, C., Suci, G., & Hannenbaum, P. *The measurement of meaning.* Urbana: University of Illinois Press, 1957.

Pascual-Leone, J. A mathematical model for the transition rule in Piaget's developmental stages. *Acta Psychologica*, 1970, **32**, 301–345.

Pavlov, I. *Conditioned reflexes.* Oxford: Oxford University Press, 1927.

Piaget, J. *The construction of reality in the child.* New York: Ballantine, 1954.

Piaget, J. *Plays, dreams and imitation in childhood.* New York: Norton, 1962.

Piaget, J., & Inhelder, B. *The psychology of the child.* New York: Basic Books, 1969.

Redshaw, M., & Hughes, J. *Cognitive development in primate infancy.* Paper presented to the 137th annual meeting of the British Association for the Advancement of Science, University of Surrey at Guildford, 1975.

Ross, J. R. On declarative sentences. In R. A. Jakobs & P. S. Rosenbaum, (Eds.), *Readings in English transformational grammar*. Waltham, Mass.: Ginn, 1970.

Russell, B. On denoting. *Mind*, 1905, **14**, 479–493.

Schlesinger, I. M. *Relational concepts underlying language.* Paper presented at the National Institute of Child Health and Development Conference on Language Intervention with the Mentally Retarded, Wisconsin Dells, Wisconsin, 1973. Reprinted in R. Schiefelbusch & L. Lloyd (Eds.), *Language perspectives—Acquisition, retardation and intervention*. Baltimore: University Park Press, 1974.

Selman, R. Taking another's perspective: Role-taking development in early childhood. *Child Development*, 1971, **42**, 1721–1734.

Shields, M. *Cognition and communication in the acquisition of language.* Paper presented to the Third International Child Language Symposium, London, September 1975.

Simon, H. *The sciences of the artificial.* Cambridge, Mass.: M.I.T. Press, 1969.

Sinclair, H. Developmental psycholinguistics. In D. Elkind & J. Flavell (Eds.), *Studies in cognitive development.* New York: Oxford University Press, 1969.

Sinclair, H. The transition from sensorimotor behavior to symbolic activity. *Interchange,* 1970, **1,** 119–126.

Sinclair, H. Sensorimotor action patterns as a condition for the acquisition of syntax. In R. Huxley & E. Ingram (Eds.), *Language acquisition: Models and methods.* New York: Academic Press, 1972.

Snyder, L. *Pragmatics in language-deficient children: Prelinguistic and early verbal performatives and presuppositions.* Unpublished Ph.D. dissertation, University of Colorado, 1975.

Spitz, R. *The first year of life.* New York: International Universities Press, 1965.

Sugarman, S. *A description of communicative development in the prelanguage child.* Honors thesis, Hampshire College, 1973.

Sylvester-Bradley, B., & Trevarthen, C. *"Baby talk" as an adaptation to the infant's communication.* Paper presented to the Third International Child Language Symposium, London, September 1975.

Tyler, S. *Cognitive anthropology.* New York: Holt, Rinehart and Winston, 1969.

Urwin, C. *The development of a blind baby.* Unpublished manuscript, Cambridge University, 1975.

Uzgiris, I. C., & Hunt, J. McV. *Assessment in infancy: Ordinal scales of psychological development.* Champaign: University of Illinois Press, 1975.

Vygotsky, L. S. *Thought and language.* Cambridge, Mass.: M.I.T. Press, 1962.

Wells, G. *Interpersonal communication and the development of language.* Paper presented to the Third International Child Language Symposium, London, September 1975.

Werner, H., & Kaplan, B. *Symbol formation: An organismic-developmental to language and the expression of thought.* New York: Wiley, 1963.

White, R. W. Ego and reality in psychoanalytic theory. A proposal for independent ego energies. *Psychological Issues,* 1963, **3**(3).

Wickler, W. Uber die Stammesgeschichte und den okologischen Wert einiger Verhaltensweissen der *V. Tierpsychologie,* 1961, **18,** 242–320.

Wundt, W. *Lectures on human and animal psychology.* Translated from 2nd German edition (1892) by J. E. Creighton & E. B. Titchener. London: Sonnenschein.

CHAPTER 12

General Issues

THE QUESTION OF INTENT

COURTNEY B. CAZDEN

Harvard University

I know you believe you understand what you think I said, but I am not sure you realize that what you heard is not what I meant.

> *In ashtray on sale in Newark airport,*
> *on return from conference on communication and language, October 10 1975*

A conference focused on the ontogenetic origins of communication and language that includes both psychologists and ethologists is an ideal forum for raising methodological problems in decisions about communicative intent. By "communicative intent," I refer to the *why* of communcation, not the *what;* to illocutionary force, not locutionary content; to decisions about whether "Mommy give" is a comment or a request, not whether "Mommy sock" is agent-plus-object or possessor-possessed. As Dore (1975) points out, the term *intention* has been used in child language literature for both aspects of meaning. Judgments about both are problematic, but only the first is addressed here. My concern is wtih the grounds for labeling the developing child's intentions and for assigning particular utterances to particular categories. As both Bloom and Cazden say in their Commentary for Schacter et al. (1974), validity for such decisions is not guaranteed by even the most perfect interobserver reliability.

In discussion at the conference, Peter Marler spoke of parallel issues now current in ethology:

"For a long time intentionality seemed to be such a difficult concept to get a handle on that people were wary of it, and it assumed almost semimystical status. It went along with a lot of other things that were forbidden by a rigid behaviorist stance. You hear people now wondering about introducing it again. At the International Congress of Ethology a few months ago in Italy, speakers were asserting that there is a host of subtle phenomena in the behavior of animals which we prevent ourselves from exploring by taking this rigid stance. There is something to gain, it was argued, by loosening up and not worrying quite so much about imputing motives to animals. One half of me is sympathetic to that, and yet it also seems a potentially dangerous step. As a precaution one should at least try to specify in operational terms just what particular steps the notion of intention permits you to take which you could not have taken without it."

In research on child language, as in ethology, intentions were deliberately ignored, but for a different reason. Certainly one cannot label the developmental psycholinguistic tradition of the past 20 years as behaviorist. But the cognitive psychology with which linguistics have been combined has generally been concerned with the *what* of human behavior and the *how*, not the *why*. In research on child language, attention was given to the acquisition of structure only. With the advent of developmental sociolinguistics, however, the range of questions has been enlarged. Attention to the functions of language and to the complex relationship between function and form are themes of recent sociolinguistic research (Introduction to Mitchell-Kernan and Ervin-Tripp, in press). Many new questions about child language require the determination of communicative intent.

The first set of questions concerns the development of communicative intentions themselves. In what order do they develop? Halliday (1975) hypothesizes an order of development from earlier "instrumental" and regulatory" to later "informative," and has found that sequence in the development of one child. Bates et al. (Chapter 11 of this volume) find the same order in a larger sample and suggest an explanation in differences in the Piagetian operative level underlying each behavior. Schachter et al. (1974) hypothesized and found changes with age in the frequency of nine "functional-motivational categories" derived from Piagetian theory in preschool children from 2 to $4\frac{1}{2}$ years.

How do intentions develop? McNamara suggests that "it seems clear that there must be a set of universal signs, of face, physical gesture, and bodily movement, which the child interprets correctly and thus among other things comes to distinguish among speech acts" (1972, p. 8). Sander (Chapter 6 of this volume) and Richards (Chapter 8) describe the basic regulation of behavior between infant and caretaker that may contribute to the mutual recognition of intentions and thereby to the structure of intersubjectivity necessary for later dialogue. From a similar perspective, Bruner describes later stages in what he calls "the establishment of illocutionary effectiveness" (1975, p. 205). What is the relationship between the development of intentions and other aspects of the child's cognitive and social development? Bates et al. (Chapter 11) offer extensive discussion.

The second set of questions concerns developmental changes in the relationship between intentions and their realizations. Do communicative intents constitute an underlying continuity between prespeech and speech development (Bates et al., Chapter 11)? Does the differentiation of intent stimulate growth in the structural repertoire of children as it stimulates historical change from pidgins to creoles? Halliday takes function as primary in language acquisition and analyzes the development of form on that motivation. Is it generally true that there is initially a one-to-one relationship between a function and a particular form, as he suggests, or do children from the beginning use the same word to perform different speech acts (Dore, 1975), or is this a matter of individual differences in children's pattern of development? At the one-word stage, do children use prosodic patterns to differentiate among their intentions, as Dore (p. 32) asserts, or as Bloom (1973, p. 60) denies? At what age, and in what order, do children learn to produce and interpret alternative realizations of particular intentions (Ervin-Tripp and Miller, Chapter 1, and Garvey, Chapter 3, of this volume; Shatz, 1974)?

The third set of questions concerns differential influences on the child's development of utterances spoken with different intentions. Do utterances of the child herself, or her dialogue partner, spoken with some intentions have special saliency in influencing the acquisition of language structure because of the degree of child attention that they express or elicit? Mitchell-Kernan and Ervin-Tripp suggest, for example, that Keenan's (in press) analysis of the functions of imitations in child speech may take it possible to resolve the controversy over the value of such imitations for the acquisition of structure. "In particular, one might think that those repetitions which serve sequential integration by acknowledgement would be less important for formal learning than those with a 'heuristic' function, in Halliday's terms— when the child comments on something novel, to label or store it" (Mitchell-Kernan & Ervin-Tripp, Introduction, in press). Wells (1973, 1974) is the first to analyze both function and form in a sample of children large enough to make possible a new look at social class differences in language development. In his pilot sample of eight children, Wells did not find an expected relationship between frequency of interpersonal purposes and rates of development: "Interpreting Bernstein's claims that it is the differential use of language by different social groups that is chiefly responsible for inequalities in communicative skill, we had expected to find rate of development associated with proportion of utterances occurring in Representational and Tutorial sequences. This would have been explained in terms of the greater variety of meanings that are expressed in such sequences and of an anticipated greater demand for semantic and syntactic complexity—giving rise to an increase in MLU [mean length of utterance]—in realizing these meanings. But no relationship was found." (Wells, 1973, p. 123).

Finally, in analyses for which intentions are not focal, decisions about them will affect decisions about the hierarchical structure of a conversation, the boundaries and lengths of its units, and the labeling and categorization of those units for subsequent analyses.

The importance of these questions merits taking the step of including intentions in our analyses but does not solve the problem of criteria for valid attributions. As participants in conversation, we rely on our intuitions as speakers, on a transfer from what we would intend if we so spoke to what the speaker must be intending. But this transfer depends not only on a shared human intentional system but also on shared interpretations of the meaning of alternative realizations of particular intents. Analyzing the development of this full range of intentions in children, and of age and cultural differences in their realizations, is precisely the objective of our research. Reliance on our own intuitions must therefore always be validated by other evidence, a step not always taken in current research.

The most available interpretations of a child's intentions are the mother's. Developmentally, the very vagueness and underdifferentiation of the child's intentional system provide optimal conditions for maternal assistance to the child. "The context of rich interpretation provided by many mothers, combined with the considerable ambiguity of many one-word utterances, provides an extremely informative situation for the child as regards what she is taken to be meaning" (Ryan, 1974, p. 205). But how do we get independent validation of the "rich interpretation" the mother provides? Bates et al. (Chapter 11 of this volume) give encouraging evidence that their mothers' judgments not only correlated highly with observer judgments which, in turn, were warranted by other evidence, but also were more highly correlated than observer judgments with cognitive tests. But there may be differences in interpretive sensitivity among mothers, and we should not rely on them without the kind of check that Bates et al. have made.

What other information is available for determining the degree of differentiation of the child's intentional system at any point in time? And how do we decide on the metalinguistic terms with which to label our categories? Bates et al. (Chapter 11) contrast labels derived from speech act theory used by most researchers (e.g., Dore) with labels derived empirically by Carter (1975). See Bates et al. for further discussion of the advantages and disadvantages of these alternatives. Apart from labels, Dore's work and that of Carter are exemplary for the detail on which they ground their systems of intentional categories.

Carter's (1975) elegant analysis tracks the differentiation of an initial "object request schema" with a generalized illocutionary force into two more specific locutionary meanings during one child's second year of life. First, "he merely indicated his request for any type of object by means of two combined procedures: (1) reaching open-handed towards the desired object, and (2) emitting one or more monosyllabic utterances which were found to be free-varying in their vowel and intonation, yet to be consistently initiated by an [m] sound" (Carter, 1975, p. 234). Later, "mow" ("more") was uttered only in situations of second or later requests for a given object, while "moy" ("mine") was uttered only in situations where someone else was about to take the object reached for.

As everywhere in the study of language, the key ingredient here is contrast in co-occurring features of the child's linguistic and nonlinguistic behavior and of the speech situation. Such evidence is comparable to the temporal and situational analyses used in ethology for "motivational analysis" of the behavior of animals (Smith, 1974). Examples of contrasting features of the child's utterance are initial consonants (Carter) and lexical items (Bloom). Nonlinguistic behaviors may be gestures (pointing versus open-handed reach); focus of attention on listener or object; the child's awaiting or not awaiting a response; or the child's accepting or resisting subsequent adult action. Contrasting aspects of the speech situation may be aspects of objects or events, as for requests for recurrence, or of locations and sequences of behaviors, as for greetings. We should not attribute to the child more intentions than are warranted by mutually exclusive combinations of these behavior-situation features.

References

Bloom, L. *One word at a time.* The Hague: Mouton 1973.

Bruner, J. S. The ontogenesis of speech acts. *Journal of Child Language,* 1975, **2**, 1–19.

Carter, A. The transformation of sensorimotor morphemes into words: a case study of "more" and "mine." *Journal of Child Language,* 1975, **2**, 233–250.

Dore, J. Holophrases, speech acts and language universals. *Journal of Child Language,* 1975, **2**, 21–40.

Halliday, M. A. K. *Learning how to mean.* London: Arnold, 1975.

Keenan, E. The pragmatics of imitation in child language. In C. Mitchell-Kernan & S. Ervin-Tripp (Eds.), *Child discourse.* New York: Academic Press (in press).

McNamara, J. Cognitive basis of language learning in infants. *Psychological Review,* 1972, **79**, 1–13.

Mitchell-Kernan, C., & Ervin-Tripp, S. *Child discourse.* New York: Academic Press (in press).

Ryan, J. Early language development: towards a communicational analysis. In M. P. M. Richards (Ed.), *The integration of a child into a social world.* London: Cambridge University Press, 1974. Pp. 185–213.

Schacter, Frances Fuchs, et al. Everyday preschool interpersonal speech usage: methodological, developmental, and sociolinguistic studies.

Monographs of the Society for Research in Child Development, 1974, **39,** No. 3 (serial No. 156).

Shatz, M. *The comprehension of indirect directives: can two-year-olds shut the door?* Paper presented at summer meeting, Linguistic Society of America, Amherst, Mass., 1974.

Smith, P. K. Ethological methods. In B. Foss (Ed.), *New perspectives in child development*. Baltimore: Penguin, 1974. Pp. 85–136.

Wells, G. The context of children's early language experience. *Educational Review*, 1973, 114–125.

Wells, G. Learning to code experience through language. *Journal of Child Language*, 1974, **1,** 243–269.

MARKOVIAN COMMUNICATION RHYTHMS:
THEIR BIOLOGICAL SIGNIFICANCE

JOSEPH JAFFE

College of Physicians and Surgeons of Columbia University
and
The New York State Psychiatric Institute

My remarks are confined to the area I know best, the rhythms of human communicative behavior. The brain is an excellent metronome, especially when it is producing verse and song. Historians of science now suspect that Galileo's chronometer in his discovery of the law of falling bodies was his own singing (Drake, 1975). It should therefore come as no surprise that speech rate is a very stable aspect of behavior, being partly under the control of prosody. One regrets the paucity of real-time analysis in the developmental data presented in this volume, since the rates of many skilled behaviors increase with neural maturation. The articulation rate of singing, for example, is usually slower than that of speech. In what sense are sung sentences ontogenetically prior to spoken sentences? Evidence for dominance of the *right* cerebral hemisphere in the postnatal period has been reviewed (Brown & Jaffe, 1975). We suggested that the right brain is awaiting lullabyes, certainly a linguistic universal, as well as faces and the nonspeech sounds of the nursery. In this vein, Stern's study of the temporal patterns of caregivers' messages may illuminate the "wired-in expectancies" of the infant's nervous system (Stern, Jaffe, Beebe, & Bennett, 1975).

My second point, which concerns the title of my remarks, is closely related to the first. The stochastic models for this rhythmic hypothesis are summarized elsewhere (Jaffe & Feldstein, 1970). Our current goal is to see whether Markovian models can illuminate the incredible stability of communication rates mentioned previously. A few general definitions will help.

A rhythm is a sequence of two or more *events* (a temporal pattern) which recurs with detectable regularity, that is, more or less *periodically*. Restricting ourselves to two events for simplicity, we have the parameters of interest:

1. *The average rate of recurrence.* This is the reciprocal of the mean period duration, which in turn is the sum of the mean event durations.

2. *The degree of rhythmicity.* This is the variance of the period duration which in turn is less than, equal to, or greater than the sum of the event duration variances. Which of the three possibilities obtains is governed by the correlation of event durations within periods (Anderson, 1975).

In the general case, these parameters are independent; that is, sequences having identical rates can differ in rhythmicity and vice versa.

Rhythms produced by stochastic processes are subject to random variation. Two conditions are necessary and sufficient for the rhythm to be Markovian:

1. *A constant probability of prolonging the duration of each event.* This permits a short memory relative to the duration of the total sequence. It also says that the distribution of durations for each event must be a negative exponential.

2. *The durations of successive events are independent.* This defines a zero correlation between event durations within periods. In that case the degree of rhythmicity (period variance) is simply the sum of the event duration variances.

A major empirical finding of our 1970 monograph can now be restated. We analyzed each speaker's conversational behavior as a two-event sequence, vocalization and pause. Speakers in verbal interaction matched pause but not vocalization durations. The latter was a stable individual characteristic and relatively constant, whereas pause duration was exquisitely sensitive to interpersonal influence. Taken together, these findings indicate that *a rhythm was being matched*, though to a lesser extent than the matching of one of its component events.

Since that time, a variety of other communication rhythms have demonstrated Markovian characteristics. These include the rhythm of accent/stress within vocalizations as measured in our own laboratory (Anderson, 1975); the rhythm of mutual face gaze in mother–infant dyads and in adult conversations (Jaffe, Stern, & Peery, 1973; Natale, 1976). If Markovian rhythms are not unique to speech, could they represent a more general feature of communication?

Our research on families of stochastic processes yielded a lead. Empirical correlations between parameters of Markov chains can be uncovered by examining a large number of stationary processes. We repeatedly encountered negative correlations between the durations of events which comprise the rhythmic period, the net effect of which was to preserve the average rate of recurrence[1] (Jaffe & Breskin, 1970; Stern, 1974; Anderson, 1975). As noted previously, in the general case this empirical relation between the durations of the component events need have no necessary bearing on degree of rhythmicity. However, Markovian rhythms are subject to very special constraints! The underlying distributions of event durations are exponential, and in such single-parameter distributions the mean and variance are not independent; they vary in the same direction and can be derived mathematically from each other. These variances are, in turn, simply additive to determine the degree of rhythmicity (period variance). Thus the significance of our empirical finding: *Both rate of recurrence and degree of rhythmicity are simultaneously preserved in the face of a single underlying change in communicative impulse* (pressure of speech or visual attention).

Powerful mechanisms evolve to some purpose. What biologic advantage might attend a Markovian rhythm which also behaved in this fashion? Perhaps it is *efficiency of control* in the face of changing organismic states such that communication rhythm remains predictable to other organisms. We know that human bonding relies heavily on rhythmic entrainment. A very efficient mechanism, common to both verbal and nonverbal communication, is both parsimonious and esthetically satisfying. It has already proved to be of heuristic value in several laboratories in addition to our own (Henderson, 1974; Butterworth, 1975).

[1] An equivalent statement of this finding which gives more of a clue to underlying mechanisms is that of a *positive* correlation between the probability of initiating and the probability of maintaining an event.

References

Anderson, S. W. Ballistic control of rhythmic articulatory movements in natural speech. In D. R. Aaronson & R. W. Rieber (Eds.), Developmental psycholinguistics and communication disorders. *Annals of the New York Academy of Sciences*, 1975, **263**, 236–243.

Brown, J. W., & Jaffe, J. Hypothesis on cerebral dominance. *Neuropsychologia*, 1975, **13**, 107–110.

Butterworth, B. Hesitation and semantic planning in speech. *Journal of Psycholinguistic Research*, 1975, **4**, 75–87.

Drake, S. The role of music in Galileo's experiments. *Scientific American*, 1975, **232**, No. 6, 98–104.

Henderson, A. I. Time patterns in spontaneous speech: Cognitive stride or random walk? A reply to Jaffe et al. *Language and Speech*, 1974, **17**, 119–125.

Jaffe, J., & Breskin, S. Prediction of an individual speech pattern from dyadic interaction. *Perceptual and Motor Skills*, 1970, **30**, 363–368.

Jaffe, J., & Feldstein, S. *Rhythms of dialogue.* New York: Academic Press, 1970.

Jaffe, J., Stern, D. N., & Peery, J. C. "Conversational coupling" of gaze behavior in prelinguistic human development. *Journal of Psycholinguistic Research*, 1973, **2**, 321–329.

Natale, M. A Markovian model of adult gaze behavior. *Journal of Psycholinguistic Research*, 1976, **5**, 53–63.

Stern, D. N. Mother and infant at play: the dyadic interaction involving facial, vocal and gaze behaviors. In M. Lewis and L. Rosenblum (Eds.), *The effect of the infant on its caregiver.* New York: Wiley, 1974. Pp. 187–213.

Stern, D. N., Jaffe, J., Beebe, B., & Bennett, S. L. Vocalizing in unison and in alternation: two modes of communication within the mother–infant dyad. In D. R. Aaronson & R. W. Rieber (Eds.), Developmental psycholinguistics and communication disorders. *Annals of the New York Academy of Sciences*, 1975, **263**, 89–100.

Author Index

Subject Index